Foundations of
Language Development
A Multidisciplinary Approach
Volume 1

Eric Lenneberg: 1921–1975

Foundations of Language Development

A Multidisciplinary Approach

Volume 1

Edited by

Eric H. Lenneberg

Elizabeth Lenneberg

Department of Psychology
and Department of
Neurobiology and Behavior
Cornell University
Ithaca, New York

ACADEMIC PRESS   New York San Francisco London   1975
A Subsidiary of Harcourt Brace Jovanovich, Publishers

THE UNESCO PRESS   Paris

First published 1975 by THE UNESCO PRESS,
7 Place de Fontenoy, 75700 Paris, France and
ACADEMIC PRESS, INC. , 111 Fifth Avenue, New York, NY 10003

United Kingdom Edition published by
ACADEMIC PRESS, INC. (LONDON) LTD.
24/28 Oval Road, London NW1

Library of Congress Cataloging in Publication Data
Main entry under title:

Foundations of language development.

    (Unesco symposium)
    Result of the 1968 Symposium on Brain Research and
Human Behaviour, held in Paris.
    Includes bibliographies and index.
       1.   Children—Language—Addresses, essays, lectures.
2.   Languages—Psychology—Addresses, essays, lectures.
3.   Speech, Disorders of—Addresses, essays, lectures.
4.   Writing—Addresses, essays, lectures.
I.   Lenneberg, Eric H.   II.   Lenneberg, Elizabeth.
III.   Symposium on Brain Research and Human Behaviour,
Paris, 1968.   IV.   Title.   V.   Series: United Nations
Educational, Scientific and Cultural Organization.
Unesco symposium.   [DNLM: 1.   Language development—
Congresses.   2.   Language disorders—Congresses.   LB11
LB1139.L3 S989f 1968]
P118.F6   401'.9   74-27784
ISBN 0—12—443701—X (v. 1) (Academic Press, Inc.)
ISBN 92—3—101312—2 (v. 1) (The Unesco Press)

Eric H. Lenneberg

While these volumes were in the final stages of preparation, Eric Lenneberg died suddenly in White Plains, N.Y., on May 31, 1975. He was a man of boundless intellectual curiosity whose theoretical and integrative skills were without parallel in the study of language, brain, and behavior. Although he is most widely known for his pioneering work on the biological foundations of human language, his ultimate concern was the study of the mind and brain, the problem he was working on just prior to his death. He was the first to propose, in the late fifties, that the human capacity for language can be explained only on the basis of biological properties of man's brain and vocal tract, a point of view that has since been widely accepted and elaborated upon. His experiments and views were summarized in the groundbreaking book, *Biological Foundations of Language*, published in 1967.

Eric Lenneberg was born in Germany on September 19, 1921 and lived there for the first twelve years of his life. In 1933 he emigrated with his parents to Brazil. Seeking broader educational experience, he came to the United States in 1945. After one year's service in the United States Army he entered the University of Chicago in 1947, receiving a B.A. in 1949 and an M.A. degree in linguistics in 1951. He obtained his Ph.D. from Harvard University in 1955 in both psychology and linguistics, and subsequently accepted a post-doctoral fellowship in medical sciences at Harvard Medical School with further specialization in neurology and children's developmental disorders.

From 1959 to 1967 he held faculty positions at Harvard and Massachusetts

Institute of Technology while conducting basic research on language development in defective children at the Children's Hospital Medical Center in Boston. From 1967 to 1968 he was Professor of Psychology at the University of Michigan, and in 1968 he accepted an appointment as Professor of Psychology and Neurobiology at Cornell University, which he held to his death. He was the recipient of numerous scholarships, fellowships, and academic honors, including Russell Sage and Guggenheim fellowships and a National Institute of Health Career Award. He was married twice and had two children by his first wife.

Eric Lenneberg, because of his meticulous preparation in several disciplines, was able to bring to the study of language development a new perspective. He brought together the necessary developmental biological evidence in support of his hypothesis that language is a central, maturationally defined mental function which is relatively independent of learning, that "language is the manifestation of species-specific cognitive propensities." This has never been a particularly popular thesis for an empirical psychology, and the recent growth of interest in the language potential of other primates is a typical example of the conflict his theory was to encounter. Nonetheless, research in a wide range of areas related to language pathology, including speech defects, mental retardation, dyslexia, aphasia, and most importantly, deafness, demonstrates the indirect but lasting influence of his work. His application of the biological concept of critical or sensitive periods to the study of language remains a unique and powerful contribution to developmental psycholinguistics.

More fundamentally, Eric Lenneberg's conception of human behavior was different from that held by most research psychologists. Though sometimes called a "nativist," he believed the continuing debate over innate versus environmental factors in human behavior was irrelevant. Behavior for him was "but the outward manifestation of physiological and anatomical interactions under the impact of environmental stimulation." This is a point of view more congenial to biology than psychology, but one certainly destined to become increasingly important in the study of human behavior. His conception of the brain was that of a highly integrated organ constantly changing over time according to certain epigenetic trajectories. Therefore, information-processing or man-machine models of cognitive functioning were of limited value to him because they ignored the fourth dimension of time. He believed that man's functional activity cannot be separated from structural changes in the human brain.

For those of us who knew him, his unique preparation and the creative nature of his intellect made him an extraordinary colleague and teacher. We all gained immeasurably from contact with this courageous and profound thinker. It is to his memory that this volume is dedicated.

Eric R. Brown
New York University

Contents

3. Some Problems in Linguistic Theory 35

Giulio C. Lepschy

4. The Heuristic Principle in the Perception, Emergence, and Assimilation of Speech 43

A. A. Leontiev

II. Natural History 59

5. A Zoologist's View of Some Language Phenomena with Particular Emphasis on Vocal Learning 61

Fernando Nottebohm

6. Brain Development in Relation to Language 105

Marcus Jacobson

List of Contributors

Numbers in parentheses indicate the pages on which the authors' contributions begin.

J. de Ajuriaguerra (323), Psychiatric Clinic, University of Geneva, Geneva, Switzerland.

Francesco Antinucci (189), Institute of Psychology, National Council of Research, Rome, Italy

Melissa F. Bowerman (267), Bureau of Child Research Laboratories and Department of Linguistics, The University of Kansas, Lawrence, Kansas

Roger Brown (299), Department of Psychology and Social Relations, Harvard University, Cambridge, Massachusetts

Courtney B. Cazden (299), Graduate School of Education, Harvard University, Cambridge, Massachusetts

Macdonald Critchley (3), Institute of Neurology, London, England

Charles A. Ferguson (153), Committee on Linguistics, Stanford University, Stanford, California

Olga K. Garnica (153), Committee on Linguistics, Stanford University, Stanford, California

M. A. K. Halliday (239), Department of Linguistics, University of Illinois at Chicago Circle, Chicago, Illinois

Marcus Jacobson (105), Department of Physiology and Biophysics, University of Miami School of Medicine, Miami, Florida

André Roch Lecours (121), Faculty of Medicine of the University of Montreal, Montreal, Canada and Faculty of Medicine of the University of Paris, Paris, France

Eric H. Lenneberg (17), Department of Psychology and Department of Neurobiology and Behavior, Cornell University, Ithaca, New York

A. A. Leontiev (43), Pushkin Institute of Russian Language, Moscow, USSR

Giulio C. Lepschy (35), Department of Italian Studies, University of Reading, Reading, England

Sei Nakazima (181), Department of Psychology, Kyoto University, Kyoto, Japan

Fernando Nottebohm (61), Field Research Center for Ecology and Ethology, Rockefeller University, Millbrook, New York

Neil O'Connor (311), Medical Research Council Developmental Psychology Unit, London, England

Domenico Parisi (189), Institute of Psychology, National Council of Research, Rome, Italy

I. M. Schlesinger (203), Israel Institute of Applied Social Research and Hebrew University, Jerusalem, Israel

H. J. Sinclair (223), School of Psychology and Education Sciences, University of Geneva, Geneva, Switzerland

Dan I. Slobin (283), Department of Psychology, University of California, Berkeley, Berkeley, California

R. Tissot (323), Psychiatric Clinic, University of Geneva, Geneva, Switzerland

O. L. Zangwill (137), The Psychological Laboratory, University of Cambridge, Cambridge, England

Foreword

Foundations of Language Development is a specialized two-volume publication resulting from the 1968 Symposium on Brain Research and Human Behaviour convened by UNESCO in cooperation with the International Brain Research Organization (IBRO) in order to focus attention on the growing importance of brain research in modern society and to demonstrate the relationship between brain research and education, social sciences, and communication. Ambassador Carlos Chagas, the Brazilian Permanent Delegate to UNESCO, chaired the international organizing committee for the symposium, and his leadership extended to most of the ensuing activities, including the preparation of these two volumes. This work attempts to bring together the results of different kinds of studies relevant to the application of brain research to problems in education and more particularly to the problem of language learning in both normal children and handicapped and socioculturally deprived children.

The UNESCO Secretariat was fortunate in securing as editor the late Professor Eric H. Lenneberg of Cornell University, U.S.A., who, with the untiring cooperation of his wife, arranged for the contributions of many eminent specialists in the various research areas. Further, since the problems involved affect a great many people having no specialized background, a version for the layman is being prepared by Dr. Charles P. Bouton of Simon Fraser University, Canada. This will provide facts and advice that parents, medical practitioners, and educators should find of great practical value in attempting to solve problems concerning remedial training in language acquisition in individual cases.

Both publications represent a major contribution to the Anthropology and Language Science in Educational Development (ALSED) programs which UNESCO launched in 1973 with the publication of a collection of papers "Anthropology and language science in educational development" (*Educational Studies and Documents Series No. 11*, Paris, UNESCO, 1973).

UNESCO wishes to express its thanks to the editors, advisors, and contributors to these volumes on behalf of all those involved in the practical problems of remedial training in language acquisition.

The opinions expressed do not necessarily reflect the views of UNESCO.

Preface

The intention of these two volumes is to bring current viewpoints to the fore and to give an idea of the latest thinking in various areas; it is not an attempt to survey fields, and was not to be used by the contributing authors as a forum to argue any particular case. The book provides many a summary statement on the most recent, important discoveries and issues in the area of language development. Thus it is clear that these volumes will be useful particularly to those who are faced with practical decisions concerning language, including national language policy, language in the classroom, and language rehabilitation.

It is also important to point out that this book is a cooperative and international effort, in keeping with the UNESCO mandate. In these circumstances, the functions of the editors are different from those of an editor of an anthology or of conference proceedings. Particularly, the editors must insure proper representation rather than exercise selectivity according to their own convictions.

We should like to take this opportunity to express our thanks to Albert Legrand, who has helped us with many an editorial and translation problem, to Anton Burgers, whose frequent aid in administrative matters has been invaluable, to Adriano Buzzati-Traverso for his wise guidance and continuing interest in the project, to the advisory and editorial committees for help with the initial planning, and lastly, but most importantly, to Carlos Chagas, who conceived of the original plan for this book, who actively promoted the first stages of the drafting of its contents, and who has since then been our steadfast sponsor, adviser, and friend.

Eric and Elizabeth Lenneberg

Contents of Volume 2

I. Preliminaries

The most important recent development in the scientific study of language is Noam Chomsky's attempt to formalize syntax. The mathematical character of his writing has often engendered the idea that modern algebra and mathematical logic might soon play the role in linguistics that the calculus has played in mechanics and general technology. This popular feeling has been potentiated by the constant news of the latest intellectual feats of computers, such as the capacity to "translate" texts or to "comprehend sentences" and "talk back to" real people. Chomsky himself has always been highly skeptical of these enthusiastic reports and has viewed the occasional use of his system in computer programming as a trivial by-product of his general theories. His aims have been to elucidate the nature of language knowledge.

Since the vast majority of present-day publications in the field of language are applications, extensions, or explanations of Chomskyan ideas, the chapters in the following section try to place recent trends in linguistics in a wider context of scientific concepts. Critchley gives us a broad view of language and its problems. Lenneberg discusses those aspects of language development that seem to have greatest relevance to the biologist. Lepschy relates concepts of modern grammatical theory to earlier ideas in linguistics. Leontiev compares Anglo-American psycholinguistics to similar research in the Russian- and French-speaking world. Although most of these chapters touch only occasionally on language development in the child, they review critically the theoretical foundations upon which child language research is bound to be based.

1. Language

Macdonald Critchley

The art of language constitutes one of the most striking characteristics of *Homo sapiens*, therefore, an introductory chapter must logically refer to certain fundamental concepts. These might well be considered in retrospective or historical fashion. The topics under scrutiny would include (1) the relationship between animal communication and language proper; (2) the early metaphysical views as to the origin of speech; (3) the probable nature of the language employed by early man; (4) the dawn of our realization that cognitive processes are a function of the brain; (5) the growing conception that language is essentially a localizable cerebral function; (6) the birth of our knowledge concerning speech pathology; (7) the shortcomings of speech as a means of human communication; and finally (8) the attempts at predicting the future of language.

Nomenclature is an all-important starting point. Out of the numerous definitions of "language" that have been proffered, we may select one which is both comprehensive and crisp: "the expression and reception of ideas and feelings." Here is implied an alignment of language with the contemporary expression "communication," whereby information is passed from here to there. Note that the foregoing definition of language does not specify the means whereby ideas and feelings are expressed or understood, coded or decoded. Verbal symbols stand out conspicuously among these channels, but they certainly are not the sole means of communication. To define "speech" we can refer to "the expression and reception of ideas and feelings by way of verbal symbols" (i.e., words or any other verbal tools we may choose to regard as units of speech). Such a distinction between "language" and "speech" conforms with the usual practice in Great Britain, whereas in the United States of America "language" is often used as synonymous with "speech."

Closely related to definitions of speech (and language) is the question of its purposes, usages, or functions. According to Bréal, writing in 1897, "Speech was not made for the purposes of description, of narrative, or disinterested considerations. To express a desire, to intimate an order, to denote a taking possession of persons or of things—these were the first uses of a language. For many men they are still practically the only ones [Bréal, 1897]."

Of all accounts of the multitudinous functions of speech, the most comprehensive was drawn up by Holloway, who wrote:

Language is used to influence the actions or the feeling or the beliefs of other persons . . . it is used, more or less recited, to influence our own feelings . . . or our own beliefs . . . . It is used as in polite small talk to avoid awkward silences or to conform to certain norms of etiquette. It is used to pose questions, to make promises, requests, bids, surrenders, bets and the rest . . . and to count and calculate. It is used to deceive and to silence those who contradict us. It is used to enter pleas, to give testimony and make confessions . . . to take oath, to pray, to give thanks, and remit sins. It is used to act, to recite, to eulogize, to mourn, to curse, to compliment, to congratulate, to celebrate, to exercise magical powers upon subjects, to conjure and exorcise spirits. It is used to indicate the time at which something occurs, or the time at which someone is to act in a certain manner. For example, to start races or annouce their start or to drill a squad. It is used to remind us of what is already familiar. It is used to train and educate. It is used to construct verbal complexes like poems which conform to certain artistic requirements or canons. It is used to tell stories and to make jokes. It is used to promulgate laws including the rules of its own use and to provide illustrative examples of how they may be kept or broken, or of any other aspect of itself. Doubtless it is used in many other ways as well.

Finally, we should not forget the nine purposes of language, the last one of which was to give employment to philologists!

Communication in Animals and in Man

It would not be correct to refer to either the speech or the language of animals. Symbol manipulation is conventionally looked upon as all important in language. Except in certain rare and restricted circumstances, animals do not move in a climate of symbols. In discussing the distinction between animal cries and human speech, Bierens de Haan insisted that six conditions need to be fulfilled to justify the term language. The sounds emitted must be vocal, articulate, meaningful, indicative, intentional, and combinable. Animal noises fail to achieve these yardsticks. Those creatures that are vocal are rarely articulate. The sounds are devoid of meaning *sensu strictu*: they are not emitted in order to express an idea, even though they may unintentionally serve as communication. The creation of new words or new phrases out of the stock of ululations is not possible.

Hockett, who shrinks from the term "symbol," identified thirteen separate properties of language, which he called "design features." Although many of these hallmarks can be discerned in animal communicative systems, there are three which appear to be peculiar to man. These comprise (1) displacement, (2) productivity, and (3) duality. Hockett's "displacement" is what Pumphrey had earlier called "extensibility," and applies to the power to transcend the barriers of immediacy in time and place. This is more or less what Korzybski had in mind when he spoke of the "time-binding" property of language. Except perhaps for the dancing system of communication among bees, outside of human behavior this property is very rare. "Productivity" (Hockett) is the factor whereby new messages may be devised, and then intelligently coded and decoded, a principle that Chomsky later emphasized as "open-endedness." "Duality (of patterning)" refers to the basic structuring of language upon morphemes built upon phonemes.

It would not be amiss to look upon animal sounds as communication, although the communicative effect may not be really purposeful.

If this distinction between language and animal communication be accepted, then it becomes necessary to examine possible mechanisms whereby the more elaborate forms of primate communicaion merged into the simplest forms of human speech. Was it a case of a steady quantitative evolution that linked animal communication with human speech? Or was the change a qualitative one, which interrupted abruptly the progression from primate to *Homo sapiens*?

Hypotheses as to the Origins of Language

Simplest among the theories advanced to explain the distinctions are those that are theistic and entail a miraculous intervention. The Judaeico–Christian–Muslim systems of belief envisage an original pair of humans who were divinely endowed with the faculty of speech, which they duly transmitted to their progeny. Later, some cataclysmic event occurred, which fragmented the uniform primordial speech into a multiplicity of tongues. This is the myth of the shattered Tower of Babel.

The early theologians soon came into controversy. Was the original *lingua Adamica* a complex, mature linguistic system rich in its vocabulary, replete with abstractions, adorned with a syntax that permitted elaboration, definition, discrimination, and modifications of aspect? Or was it merely a handful of simple root forms? Most philosophers favored the former hypothesis. This led to a debate as to the nature of this primal language and whether it could be identified with any contemporary tongue. Much argument arose, but the favored notion was that the *lingua Adamica* was Hebrew, and some theologians went so far as to equate the *lingua Adamica* with the *lingua sacra* spoken in Paradise.

Alternative to the monogenetic hypothesis as to the miraculous birth of language was the theory of polygenesis. Language, it was said, arose *de novo* in different regions at different times and among different races. Although this notion rejected any *lingua Adamica*, it still did not altogether exclude a supernatural origin.

In the eighteenth and nineteenth centuries a number of theories emerged that were secular in kind. Even now the early philologists could not agree. Ideas of a continuous biological evolution were set off against the hypothesis of an abrupt though innate impulse toward self-expression. The monograph published in 1772 by the theologian–poet Johann Gottfried von Herder, entitled *Uber den Ursprung der Sprache*, forms an outstanding landmark in the origins of philology. These hypotheses deserve to be enumerated because of their intrinsic historical interest.

First came the theory of onomatopoeia, or sound imitation. It was suggested that man learned to speak as the result of mimicking sounds in nature. Another hypothesis was to the effect that speech began by an elaboration of interjections, which in turn took origin from animal calls and cries. Expletives can be regarded as audible gestures, and an inaudible pantomimic origin of language was also advocated by some writers, especially Noiré. A more recent idea looked upon speech in man as an elaboration of the sounds evoked by the glottal sphincter, which cuts off the mechanisms of swallowing and prevents food from entering the respiratory passages. More sophisticated were the arguments touched upon by Plato and in recent times strongly marshaled by Paget, stating that an intimate connection exists between the unconscious shaping of the buccal cavity, the phonemic properties of the sound emitted, and the meaning of the utterance. Less seductive, perhaps, was the idea that human speech took origin from song, especially in its relation to the dance. Finally, there was the "contact theory" put forward by Müller, that man's first speech was a reflection of the "ringing" property of his environment.

It is unnecessary to enumerate the evidence adduced by the adherents of the foregoing hypotheses. Nor to recall the recriminations, decrials, disparagements, censure, and even ridicule that circulated so readily between the respective protagonists. Their language of opprobrium is with us still, and we recall with amusement the facetious terminology of the rival advocates. These speculations are now best remembered as the bow-wow, pooh-pooh, yo-heave-ho, ta-ta, collywobble, click-click, tarara-boom-deay, and ding-dong hypotheses respectively.

The argument takes us back to the question whether one can descry between animal utterances and human speech differences of kind or merely of degree. M. Müller (1877) was in no doubt, for he proclaimed that "language is our Rubicon, and no brute will dare cross it ... Language is something more palpable than a fold of the brain or an angle of the skull. It admits of no caviling, and no process of natural selection will ever distill significant words out of the notes of birds or the cries of beasts."

Those words appeared in 1861, and ideas have since developed in lush profusion. One point must, however, be kept well to the fore when ruminating upon this topic of protolinguistics. From an anatomic, physiological angle, speech is a parasitic function, utilizing preformed buccolaryngeal structures, which were originally and still are designed to serve for the purposes of breathing and swallowing. Man did not develop out of the blue some entirely novel means for subserving the newly developed faculty of language, but utilized patterns of anatomy already in existence.

Some thinkers, including philologists like Sapir, have believed that linguistics alone will never solve the riddle of the origins of language in man. To them, the problem is a more fundamental one, which concerns the beginnings of symbolic behavior in man. According to Langer, this can be detected in some of the actions of the great apes, who may apparently attach peculiar significance to certain articles, utilizing them like toys.

The History of Ideas Underlying Thinking and Speech

It is sometimes overlooked that, in the history of medical thinking, the heart was for centuries and in many diverse civilizations regarded as the seat of thought as well as of the emotions. The first to proclaim dogmatically that processes of thinking took place in the head was Alcmaeon of Crotona. He was supported by Hippocrates and Galen, and also, with some reservations, by Plato. The matter was, however, never settled, and thereafter a considerable body of neo-Platonic theologians continued to equate the heart with intelligence. Eastern and Western Christian doctrines were at loggerheads over this subject. We witness the beginnings of the cult of the Sacred Heart, which dated from the mystical experience of St. Gertrude. The problem was further complicated by the intrusion of the concept of a soul or *psyche*. A number of metaphysicians sought to assign this intangible entity to some focal region or organ; the universalists, on the other hand, denied the soul any circumscribed habitation. We see elements of both casts of thought in the animistic beliefs of primitive peoples.

Independently, attention was being directed to the faculty of self-awareness, which almost insensibly became correlated with the brain rather than the whole body, the bloodstream, or any single viscus. This was the case despite the animadversions of such thinkers as van Helmont, Voltaire, and Diderot.

Language as a Function of the Brain

If philosophers were slow to correlate affective and cognitive processes with the functioning of the brain, medical men were even more tardy in realizing that language is essentially an aspect of cerebration. Early Egyptian surgeons, it is true, had observed speechlessness after skull wounds. Hippocrates all too briefly recorded the case of a woman who developed loss of speech together with a palsy of the right arm. Pliny was aware of the vulnerability of the faculty of memory for words. These early references were not pursued, however, and we need to turn the pages of medical history until we come to the seventeenth century before isolated reports of cases of speech defect occur (Chanet, Schmidt, Willis, Rommel). But well into the next century, physicians continued to ascribe diminution in the powers of expression to a hesitation, torpidity, or numbness of the tongue.

Alexander Crichton, in 1798, was one of the first to state categorically that loss of speech was a result neither of lingual paralysis nor yet of dementia, but was the consequence of a highly specific type of memory disturbance. Four years later appeared the posthumous work of Heberden, with similar observations on the pathology of speech loss.

However, it was F. J. Gall who first focused attention upon a correlation between the faculty of language and a delimited area of the brain. In his opinion, based upon a study of craniofacial conformations and clinical characteristics, there was an organ of language lying upon the posterior part of the superior orbital plate. Gall went further, tracing a connection between acquired loss of speech and disease of the foremost regions of the frontal lobes of the brain. This seat of language was but one of the 26 "organs of mind" he demarcated. These were later increased to 35 by his pupil Spurzheim, and to 43 by the Fowler brothers. Gall, for all the brilliance of his achievements, made two grave errors: He associated a structural overgrowth of a particular region of the brain with an excess of physiological activity, and he moreover believed that the conformation of the brain could be detected by a visual and manual study of the shape of the overlying skull.

Gall's researches gave an impetus to new thinking about the physiology of the brain, and, in turn, influenced contemporary philosophy. His ideas directed opinion away from the holism of Flourens and triggered off the nineteenth century ideas of cerebral localization. Gall modestly spoke of his studies as concerning merely the "functions of the brain." Early references in the literature spoke of zoonomy, cranioscopy, organology, or craniology. "Phrenology"—a term coined by the Fowler brothers—came later.

Gall should not be blamed because his disciples debased his teachings and spread a world-wide cult of divination, which has rightly passed into oblivion. His contributions to neuroanatomy and neurophysiology are unassailable. Contemporary assessments have thrown away the phrenological bathwater, but the baby, too, has unfortunately been lost.

When Gall first proclaimed his ideas on brain function, with particular reference to language, he sparked off an explosion of universal debate. His supporters and and his detractors locked horns in wordy combat. Chief among his protagonists was the influential Dean of the Faculty of Medicine in Paris, Professor Bouillaud. To him there was no question but that the supreme monitor of speech was to be found in the foremost lobes of the brain. In his confidence he offered to forfeit 500 francs to anyone who could produce the brain of a patient who during life had lost speech and which did not show any frontal lesion. Tentatively and with temerity, a certain Velpeau claimed the prize in 1843, submitting a specimen with bifrontal neoplasms. Before death the patient had been not only not bereft of speech but actually verbose.

We may turn now to Bouillaud's son-in-law, Ernest Auburtin. Perhaps the most important single date in the history of aphasiology is April 4, 1861, when he addressed the Anthropological Society of Paris upon the subject "the seat of the faculty of language." This was a well-reasoned plea for correlating the anterior lobes of the brain with the faculty of speech, based upon his own clinical experience as well as a formidable accumulation of data from the literature.

After this lecture Auburtin was approached by the secretary of the society, a brilliant young surgeon named Paul Broca, who invited him to visit the Bicêtre Hospital and see a long-standing hemiplegic and speechless mental defective who had contracted a septic infection of his leg. At autopsy a superficial lesion was found in the left frontal lobe. Broca demonstrated this specimen at the next meeting of the Anthropological Society, but no great interest was aroused. However, a month or two later another such case cropped up in Broca's service. Once again, post-mortem inspection of the brain revealed naked-eye changes in exactly the same place.

With the demonstration of this second specimen, the society became intrigued. An impressive series of comments and controversies was sparked off. Subsequent meetings became heated, even acrimonious. Much of the opposition stemmed from Gratiolet, who brought up the question of negative cases in which frank frontal lesions had not produced speechlessness. If a faculty of speech resides in the frontal lobes, how was it, he asked, that monkeys could not speak, though well endowed with these lobes? Loss of speech is not the same as loss of language, for speechless patients could still communicate by way of gesture.

Broca mildly protested that all he had done was to bring forward two pathological specimens to illustrate a rare and curious fact that chance had brought his way. He had no wish to take part in any debate upon the location of centers of speech. This sane and cautious attitude was regrettably not maintained, as his collection of case material grew, and other observers entered the fray along with their pieces of evidence and their prejudices.

In the place of the earlier term, "alalia," Broca coined the word "aphemia" to connote the type of speech loss he was observing. Thus there soon grew up a notion that aphemia was a focal symptom due to a local lesion of the brain, and that the normal faculty of speech was actually represented within the frontal lobes. At first Broca thought in terms of a bifrontal lesion and a bilateral speech centre.

Professor Bouillaud, the arrogant dean, at first looked askance at Broca, calling him "the St. Paul of the new doctrine" and "one of the organizers, subinventors, augmenters, revisers, and correctors" of Gall's pioneering and magnificent discoveries.

Almost against his will, Broca found himself a protagonist in the matter of cerebral localization and a pioneer in the philosophy of language and the problem of speech loss. At that time Broca was a busy and successful surgeon, who had contributed much to his profession. His principal interests outside of surgery were ethnological, his particular researches being craniometric, and he was steadily amassing a collection of skulls. His prestige and authority within the medical and scientific circles of Paris had become enormous quite apart from his contributions to neurology.

A few years later, Broca had stumbled on the fact that in the correlation between speechlessness and frontal lobe lesions there were two other features. In the first place, aphemia could follow a unilateral lesion of the brain. Second, it was usually the left hemisphere that was involved. He made these points clear in the *Bulletin of the Anthropological Society* in 1864, whereupon a Dr. Gustave Dax, a general practitioner in the small township of Sommières in the south of France, protested to the Academy of Medicine over the neglect of the discovery made by his father who, he said, had known for a long time that lesions that ablated the power of speech were always left-sided. He had indeed read a paper to that effect as long ago as 1836 at the Congrès Méridional. Broca was piqued, never having even heard of Dr. Marc Dax, the father, or of Gustave Dax, the son. He went to great pains to trace this alleged communication in the literature, but in vain. Dax junior, however, went so far as to produce the manuscript in question, which he had discovered in a bureau, and he reissued it in the *Gazette Hebdomadaire de Médecine et de Chirurgie* in 1865. In this paper his father, Dr. Marc Dax, had asserted that in 1800 he had seen a case of speechlessness in a cavalry officer, following a sabre wound of the left parietal region of the skull. Six other such cases came his way soon after. By 1836 he had observed more than 40 comparable examples, and he had collected a like number from the literature. From this evidence Dax *père* deduced that when verbal memory is impaired, one must look to the left hemisphere.

An attempt was thereupon made to designate a "Dax area" within the left hemisphere, but it misfired. It was Ferrier who first suggested that the foot of the third frontal convolution of the left side of the brain—the region under scrutiny—should be named "Broca's area." And so it was, and so it has continued, rightly or wrongly.

Early in 1864, we find Broca adopting the rôle of an etymological purist. In an open letter to Trousseau; who had recently advocated the term "aphasia," Broca made a strong plea for his own invention of "aphemia." Even though in modern Greek the term might suggest "infamy," as Trousseau had pointed out, Broca asserted that the root had gradually changed its meaning, and he invoked in his support the classical Greek. Aphemia had a slightly different connotation. Aphasia implied lack of speech from lack of ideas, whereas aphemia suggested that ideas were present but no words were available with which to clothe them. Aphasia could rightly be used to describe a polemist who, coming to the end of his argument, had nothing left to say. Moreover, aphasia implied a speechlessness through timidity or confusion. Broca also felt warmly toward the term "aphrasia," indicating an inability to form sentences. The Greek word *phraso* meant, he asserted, not merely "I speak" but furthermore "I speak clearly."

Broca's plea for the rejection of aphasia failed completely. Aphrasia did not survive, nor did aphemia despite the fact that Bastian and Pierre Marie maintained the term in a state of suspended animation for a few decades.

Throughout his career, Broca had shown himself to be not only a man of parts, but also the possessor of that rare quality of luck. In the history of aphasiology, Broca's life-long good fortune held. Auburtin became overshadowed by the chance which brought fame to Broca. Had the crazy Laborgne sought relief for his abscess at any hospital in Paris other than the Bicêtre, we should probably never have heard of Broca's area or Broca's aphasia, and the history of aphasiology would have been very different.

Linguistics and Semiology

Students of the behavioral sciences, including aphasiology, are well aware that speech is not the sole means of communication. A diversity of nonverbal instruments may be employed, and some of then are utilizable when articulate utterance is no longer available because of disease. As an offshoot of linguistics, the highly complex subject of semiotics or semiology has evolved. First conceived in 1916 by Saussure, the science of signs as constituting systems of signification has developed fast, incorporating material and ideas from general information theory and from the experiences of mass communication. Nowadays it constitutes an important aspect of the social sciences and has been described as a "second-order language." As in the case of other young disciplines characterized by a high level of abstraction in its thinking, taxonomies have multiplied, and terminology has grown unconscionably.

To those whose interest in language concerns particularly the pathology of speech, linguistics, information theory, and the science of signs are disciplines that are still somewhat unattainable. Yet aphasiologists are intimately concerned with the dissolution of language, and their clinical findings should, it might be thought, prove of interest and service to those who work with the mechanics underlying normal speech. So far linguistics has contributed but little to aphasiology, and vice versa, but this interdisciplinary aloofness is unlikely to continue. Aphasiologists are still at a loss when it comes to devising a satisfactory classification of their cases of acquired speech loss. It is possible that in time to come the most logical and acceptable grouping will be based upon the premises of linguistic theory, rather than an anatomy, physiology, or psychology. Physicians are also deeply interested in the ontogeny of speech, and attempts have tentatively been made to trace a parallel between the clinical patterns of the evolution of speech in the child and its dissolution through disease. This is an area in which medical observers might benefit considerably from collaboration with their colleagues in linguistics.

The Inadequacy of Verbal Symbols as Tools of Thought

Everyone interested in language—including aphasiologists—is well aware of the shortcomings of words as communicative coinage. All verbal symbols carry an "undertext" of meaning, which becomes more and more specific for the user. The undertext represents that part of a communication code that is unexpressed. Often the transmission of a piece of information goes astray; this is the phenomenon of *entropy*. No word really carries a significance that is universally identical. This renders exceedingly difficult the act of translation from one tongue to another. The fact that different systems of language are not straightforward interchangeable modes of expressing a common idea was neatly stated by Stuart Chase when he wrote "A few minutes in the glass palace of the United Nations in New York will quickly disabuse one of this quaint notion. When sufficient written or recorded material is available for linguistico-statistical analysis, it can be determined that no two persons utilize language in quite the same way; indeed, every writer and speaker may be said to possess his own personal idiolect, which he cannot readily disguise. We can predict that, with the aid of a computer, it may eventually be possible by a process of statistical analysis to recognize the authorship of any given text, just as we can identify an individual from his fingerprints. Whether *Hamlet* was written by Shakespeare or by Bacon or Marlowe is a question that is capable of solution along these lines.

A veritable cult of obscurity all too often obscures the transmission of ideas. But imprecision of language is often found to be the reflection of woolly thinking and careless writing, a fault to which linguistic philosophers, like metaphysicians and theologians, are vulnerable. Elsewhere I have quoted Blanshard's remark as to the alliance between clarity and precision.

> *To say that Major André was hanged is clear and definite; to say that he was killed is less definite, because you do not know in what way he was killed; to say that he died is still more indefinite because you do not even know whether his death was due to violence or to natural causes. If we were to use this statement as a varying symbol by which to rank writers for clearness, we might get something like the following: Swift, Macaulay and Shaw would say that André was hanged. Bradley would say that he was killed. Bosanquet would say that he died. Kant would say that his mortal existence achieved its termination. Hegel would say that a finite determination of infinity had been further determined by its own negation.*

Meaning can be enhanced by certain devices. One of these is redundancy, i.e. by lengthening the message; another is by resort to various forms of nonverbal communication, particularly gesture. Two features of language do not apply to animal communication. First of these is the employment of words not to inform but to misdirect. This is the phenomenon of the transmission of negative information. Herein lies the sinister weapon of propaganda, the armory of the advertiser. The second aspect of human speech is the deliberate use of silence as a modality of communication.

Despite the foregoing examples of the falsity and fickleness of words, it must be stated that psycholinguists are well aware that it is actually not possible wholly to conceal ideas either by the use of speech or by the deliberate employment of silence. Articulate speech is always accompanied by elaborate nonverbal phenomena, which can be perceived by the initiated and assessed. Indeed, these paraverbal concomitants are often far more faithful indices of the speaker's thoughts and feelings than the words selected. The techniques employed by these paralinguistic interpreters can be summed up quite briefly as the vocalizations (made up of characterizers, qualifiers, and segregates) and the various voice qualities (comprising pitch range and control; coordination of glottis and lip; articulation; and rhythm).

Aphasiologist can now utilize the foregoing techniques in order to record with extreme accuracy the communicative package that takes place during an interview with a patient with an impairment of speech. Although the repertoire of a severe aphasiac may be restricted to an astonishing degree—to a recurring "Yes" and "No," perhaps—the patient's meaning may be largely discerned by resort to such techniques of elaborate paralinguistic transcription.

The Future of Language

Because the pathology of language closely concerns the medical thinker, he may be pardoned for pondering briefly upon the possible future of verbal communication in man. In his professional capacity, he will certainly continue to witness its vagaries in language development brought about by brain disease.

Two trends can already be observed, and there is no reason to suspect that they will be arrested. First there is a tendency for the spoken and written forms of a language to diverge considerably; secondly, the increasing use of audiovisual means of instruction. Printed books may diminish in number; centuries hence the arts of reading and writing may once again be within the competency of only a specialist minority.

At the present time there are at least 3000 separate tongues in the world. In the Indian subcontinent there are about 225, and in Africa almost as many. The communication of ideas, especially those which are scientific, medical, humanistic, and political, will clamor louder and louder for some medium of expression that might be employed on a world-wide scale. Already attempts have been made to achieve international comprehensibility. The pace of these efforts will obviously increase, and the time may come when committees of language engineers will meet and evolve an acceptable "de-Babelization."

To date, over 200 artificial languages have been devised, some of them *a priori*, others *a posteriori*. None of them has achieved satisfactory acceptance nor is it probable that any one will succeed. A more likely endeavor will be a studied modification of some widely employed current language already in use. English has strong claims in this direction. It possesses many merits over most African and Asian tongues, being free from the grammatical shackles of concord and also from the semantic limitations of a tonal language. Furthermore, it fulfills the conditions laid down by Guérard (1922), namely (1) impersonality, being no one man's invention; (2) conservation—which does not rule out progressive improvement; (3) creativity; and (4) an impressive cultural background. English is the easiest second tongue now available to the largest number of persons, and it has the natural advantages of brevity, conciseness, and comparative freedom from the trammels of grammar. One can readily envisage a time when—by a process partly based on gradualness—English will have become the Latin of democracy. Nearly everyone will have at his command two media: first, his mother tongue, and then a simplified and painless form of English, which will constitute the auxiliary and universal *lingua Adamica restituta*.

But before that Utopian state of affairs comes about, many changes will be needed within the pattern and structure of the English language as it now exists. Much of this change would be the product of round-the-table committee work of language engineers, who would agree upon:

1. A consistent and logical form of spelling;
2. An even greater grammatical simplification (e.g., shedding of: the "to" of the infinitive; adjectival suffices that denote comparison; the inflective possessive case; irregular plurals; anomalous verb forms; and pronominal inconsistencies);
3. Pruning from the vocabulary of some of the luxuriant near-synonyms;
4. Necessary verbal coinage to correct ambiguities. For example, generic clarification will be needed of such terms as *uncle, aunt, cousin, child*. The pronouns *we* and *you* might be enriched by special inclusive and exclusive forms;
5. The sacrifice in written and printed texts of the typological diversities used currently, so that only one standardized form will be used in books, newspapers, and penmanship; and
6. In addition to this uniform typology, certain agreed paralinguistic processes of indexing, dating, or labeling (as suggested by Korzybski, and by Bell and Wheeler).

The composition of an obligatory bilingualism will be facilitated by improved techniques of teaching language. It will one day be better understood why it is that a very young child learns its mother tongue so quickly and so accurately, without resort to formal instruction. As Haugen has well said, bilingualism can be divided according to the age at which the second language system is acquired. If this be accepted, then it can be affirmed that infant and childhood bilingualisms are the optimal. Indeed, in many ways the latter is superior. Not only is the child still endowed with a brain of exquisite plasticity, but the second language will not be in constant competition with the first. Moreover, there is a valuable psychosocial factor. Ervin has referred to this as the child's "dependence on models," whereby he identifies himself with others in his entourage who satisfy his needs. This is a faculty that wanes at puberty, as an inhibiting consolidation of personality comes about. Pedagogues of the future will, it is hoped, be able to mimic or recapitulate these favorable factors and apply them to language instruction to pupils of an older age group.

All the foregoing remarks as to the probable nature of the *lingua Adamica restituta* apply to English solely in its role as a medium of international communication. This simplified English will serve to assist the symposiast, the politician, the trader, the courier, and the cosmopolite. It will rank as the linguistic currency of science and of medicine. But beside it, beyond it, and above it, there will—let us hope—remain inviolate the richness and the grandeur of our literary heritage, the English of poetry, fine writing, and belles lettres as elastic, dynamic, allusive, evocative, euphonious, and glorious as ever. In this, our private and rational use of English, we shall never relinguish the hallmarks of style. Let our prose continue to be appropriate, discerning, and persuasive, combining the virtues of harmony, order, sublimity, and beauty—in short, all the attributes of charm.

Should these predictions prove accurate, then centuries hence everyone—being an obligatory bilingual—will of necessity be at risk when he becomes the victim of disease or injury to his dominant cerebral hemisphere. In other words, every case of left brain damage will entail a bilingual—if not polyglot—aphasia. The complexity of the pattern of speech impairment in such circumstances is far greater than was ever imagined by such pioneers as Ribot or Pitrès. Today, the resulting picture of the speech remains of a dysphasic polyglot is so complicated that it can be unraveled only by probing into the patient's social, educational, and emotional background, the climate of the events surrounding the speech loss, and the role of the various available tongues.

The syndrome of bilingual (or multilingual) dysphasia entails another problem, namely an impairment of the faculty of "switching," that is to say, a ready transfer from one linguistic system to another. In normal polyglot subjects this is a skill that is associated with, but also independent of, the acquisition of more than one language. There is some evidence to suggest that this ability to transpose is mediated by a cerebral monitoring mechanism located close to, though not contiguous with, the so-called area of speech. When this region is involved along with the "speech-center," then the dysphasiac either adheres in a perseveratory fashion to one particular language, or he goes to the other extreme and involuntarily vacillates from one language to another.

Envoi

Disorders of language have been a source of debate ever since they formed part of the discipline of neurology a century ago. Within the rival camps of structuralists and dynamists there have been minor differences of opinion. No two aphasiacs are identical in their clinical pictures—as, indeed, one might expect from the knowledge that language is a built-in aspect of one's individual personality. In the same way, no two aphasiologists are entirely in agreement in their evaluations and opinions of their chosen problem. Today, aphasiology stands in a more promising position that ever before, for it is ready and eager to turn to other disciplines for guidance and consultation.

References

Critchley, M. *The divine banquet of the brain.* (Harveian Oration Longon: Royal College of Physicians, 1966.

Critchley, M. The falsity and fickleness of words.   (E. H. Young Lecture,   Bristol,   1965.)   In *Aphasiology.* London: Arnold, 1970. Ch. XIV.

Critchley, M. Lingua Adamica restituta. (Rickman Godlee Lecture, University College London, 1970). *Perspectives in Biology and Medicine, 14,* 1971, 507–521.

Guérard, A. L. *A short history of the international language movement.* London: T. Fisher Unwim, 1922.

2. The Concept of Language Differentiation

Eric H. Lenneberg

Language ability is seen as a process of (a) extracting relations from (or computing relations in) the physical environment, and (b) of relating these relationships. Although words are discrete entities, they represent or are the product of underlying continuous cognitive and physiological processes. These deeper continuities are reflected in the "fuzzy" nature of semantic, syntactic, and phonological categories, making sharp, formal distinctions and decisions difficult (the law of the excluded middle does not hold in many instances of linguistic analysis). Form classes are treated as syntactic relations, and these, in turn, are said to be due to neurophysiological processes and activity patterns. The patterns have a differentiation history in a biological sense. Child language development should be seen as a gradual unfolding of specialized relationships, each stage being dependent for its development on a characteristic preceding stage.

The Nature of Language

What should a neurophysiologist know about language before he attempts to search for its brain correlates? Definitions of language in terms of its social or ethological functions are quite irrelevant to his task; nor would we help him by giving an account of the various uses of language. What we must endeavor to do is to characterize language for him in its broadest aspects, yet concentrate on its intrinsic nature; we must try to convey to the physiologist what is happening when someone gives evidence of knowing a language.

The behavioral tests for knowledge of a given language are fairly simple. We show that an individual can follow verbal instructions, can answer yes/no questions, can paraphrase sentences, and so on. Such a test, however, begs the question: What kind of kettle of fish *is* language? The physiologist would wish to dispense with elaborate epistemological definitions; he would merely wish to know whether he might think of language as, for example, an extended system of conditioned reflexes or as a collection of associations. If either or both of these characterizations were adequate, then the neurophysiology of language would hardly differ, in principle, from even the simplest learning processes demonstrable in the most primitive of vertebrates. However, it can be shown that that which we recognize as knowledge of a language simply cannot be either a set of conditioned reflexes or a collection of associations between stimuli, even though one or the other aspect of language (usually the most marginal) may be affected by conditioning and associative processes. (This point has been made so often in the current psycholinguistic literature that it needs no elaboration here.)

The thesis of this article is that language knowledge is best represented as a family of processes or, in other words, as cerebral activity states—states that are labile and easily affected or modulated by environmental conditions. Their onto-genetic development depends on an interaction of factors: an initial history of differentiation of primitive physiological activity states (as a consequence of maturational events) brings the growing organism to a stage at which it becomes susceptible to specific influences from the environment; and the existence and availability of environmental conditions now help shape the direction of further transformations of the total repertoire of activity states. A brief look at the nature of language will illustrate the point.

Relations and Computations

Words and sentences concern relationships. In a verbal utterance an assertion is made or notice is given that a certain relationship holds in the world (and the addressee is invited to check or act on it), or an inquiry is issued as to whether a given relationship holds, or a command is given that demands of the addressee that he bring about certain relationships — physically, for instance, by asking him to put *a* on *b*, or mentally by asking him to relate the concepts *x* and *y* in such and such a way. We may think of the language acquisition process as a sequence of tasks in which the learner is constantly faced with problems such as "What does the word *w* stand for?" or "Is it true that here is an example of *w*?" Even when the child learns single words such as *table, chair, uncle, father, big, green, one, up*, and so on, he is required to ascertain whether or not certain relationships exist. The correctness of an answer to the question "Is this a table?" depends upon the particular relationships that must be verified — most important, whether the object might have a given relationship to people (real or imaginary) and their activities, such as *sitting at* or *working on*. Certain spatial relationships, such as shape, are also important, of course, as are a number of other, qualitative ones, such as stability or flatness.

The notion that words are simply labels of things has for some time now been discredited as a hopeless oversimplification. (The idea that words stand for categories is still acceptable, as long as it is made clear that each category can be defined only through the specification of a set of relationships—not by giving a range of absolute values of a finite number of fixed attributes.) Thus the subject who has learned to use a word correctly has learned to deal with the world in a prescribed way (to conceptualize the world). He has learned to perform certain cognitive operations upon potentially available data (various forms of physical energy), a procedure that might properly be called a *computation*. The important point here is that learning the meaning of even single words is not a passive process. Word learning requires intellectual activity, the operation of physiological processes.

The popular model for word acquisition as an "association between a visual and an auditory pattern" is misleading because the stimulus patterns that are frequently involved are, in the first place, so variable and their common denominator so abstract (e.g., *animal*, or *toy*) that the pattern recognition process itself can be regarded only as the end product of a set of formidable computations. Moreover, as is well known, at least half the vocabulary refers to conditions, situations, usages, and so on that are determinable only by acts of interpretation of not just one but a host of disparate stimulus patterns (e.g., the meaning of such words as *wanting, hitting,* or *big*). The role that the speech community plays during language learning is to make it clear to the subject that there are conditions in the world to which the words *animal, wanting, hitting,* or *big* refer; the community may indicate that "Here is a case where the word *w* applies." It is up to the learner to discover the particular computational processes that would result in the "correct solution" of the task given him ("Is this an example of *animal?*").

The effortless inculcation of word meanings (and more impressively of the methods for comprehending and producing sentences and discourse) in every normal child strongly suggests that the intellectual tasks required of the learning child—the computations he must select and perform—come rather naturally to him. Natural languages, despite their great diversity, seem to deal with the world in just such ways as are most appropriate to the human mind. It is this sort of thinking (along with the demonstration of various physiological, anatomical, and developmental peculiarities of *Homo sapiens*) that has led to the idea that there is a special biological propensity in man for the acquisition and use of natural languages (Lenneberg, 1967).[1]

Knowledge of word meanings entails, we have said, specific intellectual, computation-like activities. If we have evidence that someone knows a word, we must assume that there is a specific neurophysiological (or neurochemical) *process* that comes into play while the subject determines whether *x* is an example of the

---

[1] In the light of recent work with chimpanzees, it remains to be seen to what extent this biological propensity is species-specific; perhaps some aspects are merely family- or order-specific. Whatever the eventual taxonomy of language propensity may be, the fact remains that humans (both deaf and hearing) acquire a form of language that is quantitatively and qualitatively different from that of subhuman primates.

word *w*. One of the tasks facing the theorizing biologist is to define more precisely what the nature of such a process might be. For example, we might wish to review what evidence there is to postulate the processes to be intra- or intercellular; to propose locations in the brain where these processes might take place; to suggest connections between these processes and other brain processes, and so on. For the moment, it is sufficient to note that knowing the meaning of words is related to activity and process.

A word about the concept of activity states. We have called these states, metaphorically, *computational states*. A warning is in place here. Although the activities of a brain may be compared to the activities of a man-made computer, we must also keep in mind that there are some major differences between brains and at least those computers that are currently produced for practical purposes. The modern artifacts are essentially extensions of man's own mind. They perform a job for the user of the machine. But unless we are insensitive to the conjuring up of homunculi in the brain, we must assume that computational states of the brain are ends in themselves; they cannot be thought of as a set of operations with a "read-out." There is nothing that "makes use" of computations, such as is the case with computers. The computational or activity state itself is the final "purpose" here. One activity merely gives way to the next. A stoppage in the flow of changing activities spells out a state of stupor, coma, or death. Furthermore, computations performed by brains may run a somewhat haphazard course; they are easily affected by any one of a great number of activities that are simultaneously going on in the brain. This causes a certain degree of unpredictability, which, in fact, may be the basis for creativity in man, but which would be intolerable in the computing instruments built by man for practical purposes.

Continuities as Proper Psychological and Physiological Correlates

The analysis of language may give us certain ideas about the nature of the physiological processes responsible for verbal behavior, but it may also mislead us. For instance, the discrete nature of language (especially of the written word) must not be interpreted as a sign that the correlated physiological processes are likewise a collection of discrete, separate events or stable morphological structures. There are suggestions of underlying continuities on the semantic, syntactic, and phonological levels of analysis.

First let us take a look at semantics. There is a variety of indications that meanings are not discrete units. If we try to define the meaning of just about any word other than a proper name, we discover at once that there is never a single relationship that determines or exhaustively describes the full meaning of the word. Instead, we find a host of different relationships, some more central to the principal and most common meaning, others more marginal or accidental. All efforts to construct an "attribute space" into which any meaning could be mapped have been singularly unsuccessful. (Osgood's semantic space serves to characterize feelings toward word meanings, but certainly does not describe accurately the meaning and reference of any term.)

Recently, linguists have introduced the notion of *semantic features*, with the implication that there may be a finite class of stable and absolute semantic particles that combine to constitute all conceivable meanings. This would be tantamount to the old idea of elements or atoms of knowledge in general. So far there is little hope that this way of thinking could lead to any interesting results; it is quite likely, moreover, that a Gödel-type argument could be brought to bear on this approach, proving that it should be logically impossible to construct a sufficiently complete and yet consistent semantic system based on a finite number of fixed features.

We now know that even the reference (which is more restricted than the full meaning and should therefore be more easily described) of such apparently simple qualitative words as color terms is vague and fuzzy around the edges, and subject to surprising shifts of location in the physical color space. It is not certain whether there are absolutely fixed anchoring points for such words as *black*, *white*, or *red*; however, E. R. Heider (1971, 1972) cites evidence that the so-called focal colors of color categories (Lenneberg, 1956) have greater perceptual salience for children than the nonfocal ones. In view of this, it is the more remarkable that the semantic field of individual color words may be caused to shift around the color space to a considerable degree. It may be shown that the reference of a particular occurrence of a given color term depends on a number of factors; its meaning is relative to the meaning of the sentence or the context of that sentence (Lenneberg, 1961, 1967). Thus the semantic interpretations of words (and, indeed, of all but a few highly specialized sentences such as occur, for instance, in mathematical discourse) is variable, owing to the ubiquitous relational nature of meaning; further, the variations are of a continuous, not a discrete, nature. It is precisely this semantic property that is responsible for metaphorical and figurative usage. And the fact that there is nothing in the world (or in the mind) that might not be put into words emphasizes the nondiscrete nature of semantics; meanings can readily be extended to cover any of the points in the continuities that the physical world presents, our senses can perceive, and our minds can conceptualize. Thus the activity states that we attribute to the brain and that are hypothesized to constitute the physiological correlates of word knowledge must be thought of as being quite variable and as belonging to a continuum of possible states. From a neurophysiological point of view, words might best be regarded as the "decidua" or "frozen remains," the tokens of underlying dynamic and ever-changing processes, namely those that constitute language knowledge.

On the syntactic level, also, it is becoming clear that the discreteness of most units is basically a methodological abstraction. This has recently been emphasized especially by Ross 1972, 1974a, 1974b, unpublished), who points out that certain syntactic categories are not sharply demarcated, but grade into each other, thus forming a continuum rather than separate classes. He calls this kind of gradient a "category squish." For instance, the category Verb includes forms such as the present, perfect, and passive participles, each behaving syntactically less and less like a verb and more and more like an adjective; the word *burned* is barely less adjectival than the word *dry* in the sentences

(1)   *John dislikes* **burned** *toast.*
(2)   *John dislikes* **dry** *toast.*

On the other hand, in

(3)   *John dislikes* **raisin** *toast.*

the adjectival use of the noun *raisin* shows that adjectives and nouns also grade into each other. (At present, categorical phenomena of this sort are handled in generative grammar by constructing operations that transform, for example, a noun into an adjectival compound.) Ross argues persuasively that similar gradations also exist for other grammatical constructs (plurality, noun phrase, sentencehood, and so on), a position that is intuitively reasonable. Consider the problems in the use of grammatical number in connection with words such as *fish, people,* or *dissociation,* or in constructions such as *5 foot* (*feet*) *high.* The status of grammatical sentences has been debated since the dawn of linguistic science, and even the transformationalists admit varying degrees of grammaticality.

The lack of sharp distinction is also evident in the delimitation of syntax itself, which—as is well recognized now—interacts with semantics at most crucial points. Take Chomsky's early example:

(4)   *the shooting of the hunters*

which is ambiguous, whereas

(5)   *the raising of flowers*
(6)   *the growling of lions*

are not. Can this phenomenon be accounted for on purely syntactic, that is, wholly formal, grounds, as many linguists apparently thought at one time? The early explanations seemed to point in that direction: (4) might be construed as a transform derived from either of two different source sentences, namely *Hunters shoot* or NP + *shoot hunters*; whereas (5) could be derived transformationally only from NP + *raise flowers*; and (6) only from *Lions growl*; **Flowers raise* and **NP + growl lions* are clearly impossible. The fact that *raise* and *growl* are intransitive verbs was considered to be accidental to the argument. What mattered was that what was called the *kernel* in those days did not contain the starred sentences (or their respective schemata), and thus could not undergo the further operation, the transform to a phrase of the type *the* + V + *ing* + *of* + *the* + N. Linguistic concepts and terminology have changed since those days, but the basic problems have not. The grammar is now said to have a semantic component that interprets sentence schemata (phrase markers) and their associated words, the latter two having been generated by what is now called the *base.* Details aside, we are still left with the question of whether grammatical knowledge is separable from knowledge of the world. Linguists seem to be divided on this issue, although many sound as if they were confident that grammar as a whole (syntax and semantics) could be formalized and could be treated independently from what a speaker knows about the world. Personally, I have doubts about this, and believe that grammar in general, and syntax in particular, interact inextricably with general problems of knowing. Here are some of my reasons.

Take the phrases

(7)	*the jailing of the thieves*
(8)	*the bullying of the thieves*
(9)	*the stealing of the thieves*
(10)	*the stealing of the women*
(11)	*the stealing of the infants*

In this series, (8) and (10) are clearly ambiguous, whereas (7) and (11) are hardly ambiguous (both being more strongly related to NP + V + N than to N + V); conversely, (9) is not very ambiguous, because it is more closely related to N + V than to NP + V + N. In the old conceptual frame, we might have argued that speakers know that the kernel is not likely to contain the source sentences *Thieves jail*, *They steal thieves*, or *Infants steal*. Of course this is merely a statement on likelihood of occurrence, not on grammaticality, and yet it is this sense of likelihood, based on knowledge of the world, that influences the *structural* interpretation of sentences.

One might object that (7), (9), and (10) are *structurally* ambiguous even though they are *semantically* fairly unambiguous. The problem is far more complex. Take the sentences used to demonstrate the need for postulating deep structures:

| (12) | *John is eager to please.* |
| (13) | *John is easy to please.* |

It is clear that their grammatical structures are different because John is the subject of (12) but the object of (13). Since neither of these sentences is structurally ambiguous in the sense that (7), (9), or (11) might be said to be, we must assume that there is something in the words *eager* and *easy* that determines the structural interpretation here. One is tempted to say that the difference is that *eager* can refer only to a person, and *easy* only to a task. This, in turn, may look as if *easy* were structurally different from *eager* in terms of their "feature composition." Such a formulation merely conjures up new problems. First, it implies that the words belong to different form classes. If this is accepted, sentences (12) and (13) can no longer be said to have similar surface structure (making the surface—depth distinction less sharp). Second, it makes it awkward to account for sentences such as

| (14) | *John is wonderful to teach.* |

which is both semantically and structurally ambiguous (allowing a construction analogous to either (12) or (13)). Third, it introduces *feature* as a veritable *deus ex machina*: *any* kind of structural or semantic problem can be "explained" by having recourse to semantic entities whose own semantic status is left semantically undefined.

At any rate, the dividing line between syntax and semantics does not seem to be very sharp. It has not yet been proved that syntactic decisions (such as how to interpret the grammatical structure of a sentence) can, in most significant cases, be made without recourse to knowledge in general.

On the phonological level of analysis, it has been known now for over fifty years that the apparent discreteness of speech sounds is a perceptual illusion. A phoneme is but a category of physical sounds, and the sounds may be thought of as loci on a continuum. Since the categories overlap, a given sound may be interpreted as phoneme F_1 in one context and as F_2 in another. The phonemic analysis in terms of distinctive features does little to reinstate discreteness. The construct, *feature*, is introduced throughout modern linguistics as a single-valued function (phonological, semantic, grammatical features), and it has become customary to use a simple plus/minus ($+$, $-$) notation to indicate presence or absence of the feature— values one or zero. However, especially in phonology, it is clear that many features are actually names of continuous parameters frequently related to the articulatory freedoms of the vocal tract. It is not certain that features reflect physically discrete elements; in most instances, they seem to stand for continuities, just as words, syntactic categories, or phonemes do. At the very least, their limits (particularly their semantic limits) are never clearly demarcated.

In general, we see that whatever is discrete in language in fact refers to underlying continuities. Exceptions to this are more apparent than real. For example, proper names seem to refer to singularities; upon analysis, however, we are dealing merely with greater restrictions of the boundaries of a continuum. *Albert Einstein* is a specific person, but when names of this kind are introduced into language, they may quickly generalize to a whole family of Einsteinian aspects and usages. The notion of the underlying continuities is relevant to our attempts to tell the physiologist what language is like, because we are saying that the ultimate psychophysiological units in language are not discrete correlates but continuous processes and, furthermore, processes that allow of continuous deformations or transformations.

Linguistic Categories Are Relationships; They Are Definable Only Contextually

I think it is a mistake to look at categories such as *noun phrase, noun, verb, adjective*, and so on, as absolute constructs. Instead, these terms are the names of relations between concatenated words. A word such as *green* is no more an adjective, a verb, a noun, or a noun phrase when it appears in isolation than it is a subject or a predicate (cf. *The greening of America* or *Green is beautiful.*; John Updike has one of his characters in *Rabbit Redux* say: "Your mother stiff-armed Janice. . . ."). The fact that a given language such as English has certain words which, by common usage, are hardly ever allowed to behave toward other words in anything but a noun-like fashion should not obscure the fact that formally and structurally, words per se are neutral with respect to these categories. Take a string of words such as

(15)   *Scotch—police—sleep—like—fish.*

With a bit of imagination, it is possible to impute at least as many different phrase or sentence structures to this string as there are words in it. Notice how each word in the string may assume a verb function, and many of the words may also behave like adjectives, adjectival phrases, nouns, and noun phrases.

The syntactic relationship implied by designating a word as a verb or as a noun has in natural languages acquired an, alas, vague semantic significance. Nouns are more likely to imply steadiness or things, whereas verbs more often seem to be linked to action; and adjectives have something to do, in many instances, with quality. However, these semantic implications are incidental and, in fact, frequently inconsistent (*motion* is a noun; *calm* can be a verb); they are irrelevant to deciding whether a given word should behave like a noun or like some other syntactic category (that is, choosing the noun form or the verb form for a given meaning). Verbhood or nounhood does not seem to accrue from semantic considerations but from rather formal properties—from the manner in which the word relates to other words in a string; this relationship is formally marked either by affixes in inflecting languages or by position within the string, or by a combination of the two in analytic languages. When a child develops his language abilities, he develops a capacity to relate words to one another after a pattern; the various types of relationships, each roughly corresponding to a computation-like process, become gradually more and more differentiated. From an initial, coarse commutative relationship (where it is hard to tell in a two-word phrase which of the words is the topic and which the comment), more specialized categories emerge (more distinct topic and comment, i.e., predication). This differentiation history is obscured because the words the infant is using are interpreted by the adult as verbs, nouns, and so on, although they may, in fact, not yet be fully functioning as these relationships function in adult language.

Notice that in this discussion the fundamental premises are different from those of generative grammar, where grammatical categories take a position of primacy and are taken for granted. The student of language acquisition cannot simply describe his data in terms that assume as existing precisely those grammatical relationships whose very development the psychologist as well as the biologist must endeavor to discover.

Semantic and Syntactic Properties Have a Common Origin in Ontogeny

The syntactic relationships signaled in adult language by what we have called nounhood or verbhood are quite removed from semantics. As Chomsky pointed out in his earliest publications, certain strings of words may have a very definite syntactic structure and yet have a quite indefinite meaning. Nevertheless, there are enough affinities between the realms of syntax and semantics to suggest a common origin of these two aspects of language in the course of ontogenetic development.

When the child first begins to use single words, it is very obvious that the semantic field of each word is very large and coarse. Words such as *car, daddy,* and *cookie* seem to apply to a fairly undifferentiated class of objects, and the criteria for what might be called a *car* and what not are neither sharp nor rigorously applied by the beginning speaker. For a while, he adds to his vocabulary without, apparently, bothering to refine the semantic realms of the words acquired. Indeed, these realms are still so large and undefined that a rather small total vocabulary seems to suffice to make reference to the entire world of the child. I believe that the further increase of his vocabulary takes place at the expense, so to speak, of the overgeneralized extent of the semantic fields of his words. The number of words increases by letting the semantic fields of the already existing words shrink. The semantic classification system thus becomes more and more refined, and the function of each word becomes more specific and more specialized. This is analogous to differentiation of function in embryogenesis. And since I believe that words are the reflection of underlying computation-like, physiological processes, I think that the history of differentiation may be taken quite literally. (Differentiation is often dependent, in morphogenesis as in behavioral development, on certain environmental conditions and influences; there are certain functions, for example, that of visual perception, that do not unfold normally unless particular exogenous stimuli impinge on the developing organism. Thus a discussion of differentiation must not be confused with old-fashioned instinct theories or a naive nativism.)

Now, the increase of the vocabulary and the concomitant shrinkage of the respective semantic fields is not simply a crowding of classes into a physically constant continuum, such as would take place by refining the color vocabulary more and more. This sort of crowding probably plays quite a small role in the development of vocabularies. What become refined in the course of differentiation are the essential relations that must be computed in order to ascertain whether a certain configuration in the world conforms to the conditions summarized under the word *table, mother,* and so on. The relations and their respective computations become more and more exact and explicit. As a result, words emerge that seem to be more purely relational than the earlier words—*big, my, more,* and *up* are examples. (I do not wish to call this development a progression from the concrete to the abstract, because there is a sense in which the very first word is the most abstract of all. Since there can be no objective definition of the words *concrete* and *abstract,* little is gained by introducing these terms.)

I should like to propose that the differentiation in the field of semantics leads necessarily and organically to the first and most basic aspect of syntax, predication. Because of differentiation, a single word no longer refers coarsely to entire physical or social situations. No longer does the word *mommy* cover in a vague way every aspect of the familiar provider, nor the word *sock* the entire realm of sock topics. Two separate types of relations may be computed now from a single scene, one by the name of *mommy*, the other by the name of *sock*. If the child utters both words together now, it is at first difficult to decide whether the sequence is a syntactically independent concatenation or whether the sequential utterance implies a syntactic relationship such as predication. Perhaps at the first appearance of the joining of words, such a distinction seems unimportant. It is, however, important for the understanding of further development. Suppose the child simply uttered the words as thoughts flitted through his mind, so that the concatenating principle were either association of thoughts or the sequence in which objects are seen. This process would lead to the production of word strings with no internal structure; words within one utterance would not be related to one another functionally, and thus common syntax would not emerge. If, on the other hand, the joining of words is understood as the primitive beginning of syntactic relations—for instance in the sense that two sequentially uttered words must be interpreted as an interdependent pair, one word being the modifier of the other—then a principle has emerged that is capable of generating strings of the characteristic bracketing structure Chomsky has described. Students of child language are quite unanimous in assuming that the joining of words does represent from the beginning a syntactic interrelationship, even though there is some disagreement about the exact nature of this relationship. No one seems to believe that concatenation is ever random, and the subsequent stages of language development fully justify this position. Progress in semantic differentiation leads to syntactic development because the reduction of the semantic field of one word naturally entails the addition of specifiers, and thus leads to topic—comment constructions by means of modifying words—What about *mommy*? What about *sock*? The syntactic process of this primitive predication is actually preserved in a rather sophisticated, fully mature syntactic process, namely compounding. Gleitman and Gleitman (1970) cite an example of this process:

Volume Feeding Management Success Formula Award

(sign in a Philadelphia restaurant), which may be analyzed in terms of predicate pairs.[2]

There is, of course, much more to syntactic structuring than the simple predicate relationship and its iterated application. Eventually, there are many different types of relationships; how large the number is no one seems to know, and there are some reasons to believe that it is not a denumerable quantity. It seems to me that this proliferation of syntactic processes is also a consequence of semantic differentiation.

Once the primitive predication process is reasonably well established, the

---

[2]A more complex structure is found in the compound *Woman Mountain Rescue Team Leader*, which appeared in an article in a recent London newspaper.

operation may be applied iteratively, so that a pair is further modified by a third word. This would generate sentences such as *Kathryn bear tie*. At the same stage, one also finds *Lois make bridge, Kathryn fix tie, Daddy like coffee* (all examples taken from Bloom, 1970). As utterances are expanded in this fashion, it becomes clearer and clearer that form classes (primitive syntactic categories) are emerging, each one definable merely in terms of syntactic relations. The middle element seems to assume in some of the strings a more specialized or differentiated syntactic function than the general one of modification already present at an earlier stage. I would still be hesitant to say that the sentences consist of a sequence Noun—Verb—Noun, but would be inclined to say that the first and third word might belong to one form class, whereas the middle word has the function of specifying the relationship between the other two. Thus *Kathryn under bridge* would, by this interpretation, have the same structure—two words connected by an element that specifies the relationship between them. I like this interpretation because it accounts in a rather parsimonious way for the somewhat unpredictable sequences of words in three-word sentences at what Brown and his students call Stage II, without having to impute too much syntactic paraphernalia to the child who is just beginning to come into speech.

The identification of form classes at this stage is very difficult and always largely influenced by one's theoretical bias. Several psychologists like to interpret even the previous stage of two-word utterances as consisting of distinct form classes. Until someone proposes cogent and objective criteria by which to decide at this early stage whether there are distinct form classes, how many, and which they are, it is futile to weigh the issue in greater detail. That sooner or later in ontogeny form-classes make their appearance is beyond dispute, and the very fact that they are difficult to discern early substantiates my basic point, that form classes are the reflection of syntactic relations that gradually differentiate, concomitant with greater and greater semantic specification and thus longer strings of words.

Phrases and sentences of the type *X under Y, X is Y, X and Y* give the impression of consisting of two elements from a set (the vocabulary) united to one another by a fairly specific relationship, which is stipulated by the middle element. The latter is also an element of a set, namely the set of "relators." What is so characteristic of language, of this early as well as of any later stage, is that such sets are open, that they are poorly delimited, and that they intersect, that is, they are not mutually exclusive. Thus a word may be in the *XY* set as well as in the set of relators. This is merely another way of saying that words are not irrevocably born into fixed form classes, and that form classes can be defined only by the particular formal relationship that one word has to others in a sentence. Sentence structure is a relational affair; its ontogenetic development does not come about by stepwise accretion of ready-made types, rules, forms, features, and so on; it develops *pari passu*, one distinction being the consequence of others.

This point of view suggests that the increase in mean utterance length with advancing age is not a function of the child's increased memory span (which is frequently postulated, but for which there is no good evidence). It is, rather, a function of advancing differentiation in the realm of semantics, which does not lead to a splitting up of categories but to a diversification of types of syntactic relations. This, in turn, requires and brings with it the capacity to *relate relationships* (to have functors that relate the form classes that are in the process of emergence), and thus language operations begin to have a progressively more formal (abstract) aspect—further and further removed from the physical properties of the objects talked about.

I have no hesitation in speculating that the emergence of form classes, the increasing variety of special relations that words may have to one another, and the developing capacity for relating relations may well correspond to neurophysiological integrative activity in the process of differentiation, concomitant with maturation and differentiation of the structural constituents of the human brain.

Differentiation in the Growth of Vocabulary

There is no good empirical documentation of how the meanings of lexical items crystallize during language acquisition. We merely know that the meanings of some words are simply beyond the comprehension of children at certain ages; then the words begin to be used, but inaccurately; eventually the use is normalized and the customary meaning appears to be established. A look at the semantic fabric of the normal adult lexicon betrays, however, the conceptual interdependence of large families of words, suggesting that whole realms in the vocabulary have a common origin and may have developed their present, adult interrelated structure by a process of differentiation. The semantic structure under consideration here may be illustrated by the vocabulary for *quantity*; it will be discussed under six distinct headings.

OVERLAPS

By this I mean *partial synonymy*, which is ubiquitous in language and needs no comment. Examples in the vocabulary of quantity are

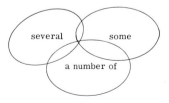

ORDERED OVERLAPS

The meanings of the three words above cannot be ordered with respect to each other. There are, however, other words denoting quantities that constitute a progression. Their semantic fields overlap; that is, they are not sharply delimited by each other, even though each word has a somewhat different meaning. An example of such a progression is

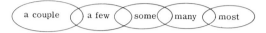

SHARP DISTINCTIONS BY EXTENSION

Although the semantic fields of a progression grade into one another, there are also words with sharply delimited fields that are related, nonetheless, to an ordered sequence of overlapping fields by an extension of the direction of the order. The sequence above may be extended in either direction, yielding to the left the word *one* and to the right the word *all*. Notice, however, that these two words suddenly introduce conceptual and logical properties that were simply absent from the other words (hence there is no overlap with them).[3]

OPPOSITES BY EXTENSION

If we extend the sequence even further to the left, beyond *one*, we come, logically, to the word *none*, which is antonymous to all the other words given.

OPPOSITES FROM BIFURCATIONS

The etymology of the word *none* is obvious: *no* + *one* (OE *ne* + *an*); and the distinction *one* versus *none* is synonymous with the distinction *something* versus *nothing*, i.e., *existence* versus *nonexistence*. But the concept of *existence* is neutral with respect to quantity; it applies to *one* as well as to *many*. Thus *existence* is a common denominator for *one* and *many*. Nevertheless,

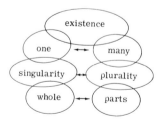

the latter two words each overlap with other words, giving rise to sequences that go into different directions, producing, in fact, pairs of antonyms.

---

[3]The special properties are best brought out in the context of syllogistic reasoning.

DISTINCTIONS THAT ARISE FROM THE SEMANTIC DIFFERENTIATION
BETWEEN DESCRIPTIONS OF STATES AND DESCRIPTIONS OF
ACTIONS THAT BRING ABOUT THESE STATES

The act of making *many* out of *few* or of reducing *few* to *one* gives rise to a rich vocabulary whose semantic fields are intimately related to the two semantic lines of the previous paragraph. For example, such verbs as *to add, join, increase,* and *to take from, divide, decrease,* as well as nouns like *addition* and *conjunction, subtraction* and *partition,* are all quite transparently related to singularity and plurality.

The vocabulary of quantity as a whole is not a semantic realm unto itself. It overlaps with or grades into other conceptual fields. For example, notions of equation, comparison, similarity are related to it; these, in turn, have an affinity with various conjunctions, adverbs, the copula, grammatical number, and so on, as shown by the meaning of words such as *and, same, like, is,* the grammatical plural, etc.

In short, meaning appears to be a tangled net of overlapping and interrelated concepts, at times reasonably well ordered, more often disconcertingly arbitrary, vague, and unruly. In the history of natural languages, the morphology of semantic fields changes more rapidly than any other aspect of language, many words acquiring new meaning within a matter of years. Meanings also change in ontogeny, and they are easily disturbed by pathological processes that interfere with normal mental life (such as schizophrenia or dementia). Thus one gathers that meaning reflects an extremely labile process or, to use our earlier terminology, very unstable activity states. Nevertheless, the various distinctions that constitute semantic structure as a whole, as it is congealed in a particular language at a particular period, are always dependent on so many other distinctions—are so multiply interrelated—that it seems likely that they come about by a process that is more analogous to the epigenesis of an organism (or the emergence of distinctiveness in a developing photograph) than to the accumulation of individual, autonomous achievements, or the learning of one autonomous trick after another. The vocabulary of quantity shows how vast realms of words are all interrelated in such a way that one can hardly define any one without presupposing definition of several other related ones. The concepts seem to hang together—to define one another; it is therefore hard to see how this sort of semantic knowledge could come about piecemeal. It seems more logical to assume that the distinctions gradually emerge from an initially undifferentiated whole, and that it is the *structure* that has a developmental history, rather than the *individual, isolated words.* Even if a particular word at a particular time has not been acquired by a child, the development of the structure will have created a readiness for learning the word in question, so that it is understood easily and learned without elaborate training when the opportunity arises.

It should be clear that the viewpoint advocated here makes a sharp distinction between language knowledge and general knowledge (of the world) impossible. The former appears as a part or consequence of the latter. Language cannot develop in the absence of semantic knowledge, and this is inseparable from a particular mode of knowing, namely the speaker's mode of knowing the world.

Conclusion

Language development in the child has been viewed in this article as a gradual increase in specializations and specificities, an ontogenetic development that I have called *differentiation*. The term is applied to postulated neurophysiological processes that presumably underlie semantic, syntactic, and phonological aspects of language. In order to underscore the importance of processes (that is, the dynamic nature of neurophysiological correlates of language), I have tried to show that discreteness of sounds, words, syntactic categories, and sentences is a secondary and physiologically nonessential feature of language (somewhat analogous to the discreteness of the broken pieces of a product that is produced by a continuous process). The relevant processes were referred to as activity states, which themselves are labile and easily (and continuously) deformable; the apparently infinite variability in shades of meaning, for instance, is thus thought to correspond to families of activity states, any one being a slight deformation of the other. The point was stressed that everything in language is of a relational nature and that what has to be learned in language acquisition is *how to relate*, or how to compute a relationship upon given physical data. The word *computation* was used metaphorically, however, since the brain's activity states must be considered as ends in themselves, not as means to convey a result to another agent.

This characterization of language and language development should be of interest to the neurosciences, because it helps to define the question of what the proper neurological correlates of language might be. If we want to understand the relationship between language and the brain, we must look for neurological processes, their nature and their function. On the other hand, the question of whether language is represented in this or that structure of the brain, whether there are specific language centers or not, is relatively inconsequential for our understanding of the brain mechanisms of language. It merely points to where the black box whose inner workings we are trying to understand might be located or what outside dimensions it might have. The controversy over the localization issue entirely circumvents the basic issues of language neurophysiology. This paper has tried to come closer to these issues by a new look at the nature of language.

References

Bloom, L. M. *Language development: Form and function in emerging grammars.* Cambridge, Mass.: MIT Press, 1970.
Gleitman, L. R., & Gleitman, H. *Phrase and paraphrase: Some innovative uses of language.* New York: Norton, 1970.

Heider, E. R. "Focal" color areas and the development of color names. *Developmental Psychology*, 1971, *4*, 447—455.

Heider, E. R. Universals in color naming and memory. *Journal of Experimental Psychology*, 1972, *93*; 10—20.

Lenneberg, E. H. The language of experience. Mem. 13, *International Journal of American Linguistics*, 1956, *22*, No. 2.

Lenneberg, E. H. Color naming, color recognition, color discrimination: a reappraisal. *Perceptual and Motor Skills*, 1961, *12*, 375—382.

Lenneberg, E. H. *Biological foundations of language.* New York: Wiley, 1967.

Ross, J. R. Act. In D. Davidson & G. Harman (Eds.), *Semantics of natural languages*, Dordrecht, Neth.: Reidel Publ., 1972.

Ross, J. R. The category squish: Endstation Hauptwort. In P. Peranteau *et al.* (Eds.), *Papers from the Eighth Regional Meeting of the Chicago Linguistic Society*, (offset) Chicago: Univ. of Chicago Linguistics Dep., 1974. (a).

Ross, J. R. Squishing. In E. Burtinsky (Ed.), *Festschrift for Martin Joos.* Toronto: Univ. of Toronto Press, 1974. (b).

3. Some Problems in Linguistic Theory

Giulio C. Lepschy

A discussion is offered of the position of modern linguistics in relation to other disciplines. The importance of Ferdinand de Saussure in establishing such a position is emphasized. Some questions are presented that Saussure has helped to place at the center of general linguistic interest; in particular, synchrony versus diachrony and *langue* versus *parole* are discussed in connection with the notions of competence versus performance, explanation, and rule, as they appear in generative theory. The conclusion touches on the relation between linguistics and semiotics.

Theory is never of any direct interest to the person who trains children or patients.

This motto is taken from a personal letter written by a great authority on the biological aspects of language. It should not suggest that I am about to discuss applied rather than theoretical linguistics. I am quoting it, rather, as a warning to the readers of this volume that this chapter has no direct practical application. This is not to say that linguistic theory has no use. On the contrary, I am convinced that some understanding and knowledge of the theoretical aspects of linguistics are useful to people dealing with practical problems involving language, although they cannot be directly applied to practical pursuits. We may look forward to a future when linguistics will be well integrated with the study of physics, physiology, and psychology, and when speech disorders will be understood and cured on the basis of our knowledge of language. But a remarkable feature of past and present linguistic studies is their independence from natural sciences such as physics and physiology, and even from a discipline like psychology (in so far as it is not defined to include linguistics), not to speak of medicine. There are, obviously, connections. But how tenuous they are is immediately apparent to anyone who consults the basic work by Lenneberg (1967). This independence works both ways: Linguistics has contributed little or nothing to the natural sciences and has been able to profit little or not at all from their advances. The few exceptions that come to mind turn out to be only apparent. The study of language has not been directly enriched by medical work on aphasia; only when a linguist like Jakobson (1941) has journeyed through the field and brought back his own insights to the domain of linguistic theory has the contact been fruitful. Acoustics has certainly provided information in a form suitable for use by phonologists (Pulgram, 1959); the development of computers has made it possible to process linguistic data on a scale and with a thoroughness previously undreamed of (Garvin, 1963; Hays, 1967). But of course we can have spectrograms of nonlinguistic noises, and computers can process nonlinguistic information; as soon as problems that are typical of language are faced, the lack of integration between modern science and technology, on the one hand, and linguistic theory, on the other, becomes plainly visible. Acoustics fails to pick out phonological units; computers cannot be programmed to translate successfully (in any way that is linguistically interesting). We can record and reproduce speech with the utmost precision, but have not managed to design devices such as the "automatic secretary" to write under dictation or to read from written texts. This is not surprising if one thinks that we have only the dimmest understanding of the skills involved in the corresponding human activities. The development of linguistics has, of course, been connected with the general development of the sciences, but only indirectly through the intellectual climate dominant in different periods— rationalist or empiricist philosophy, romanticism, idealism, positivism, behaviorism, and so on. There may have been cross-fertilization between linguistics and other disciplines, but it was due not so much to systematic integration as to scholars who were able to fly to and fro carrying some intellectual pollen. The real contacts of linguistics, in any case, have been mainly not with "hard" disciplines like physics or chemistry, but with "soft" ones like psychology, anthropology, sociology, or history. And even among the latter, it is remarkable of how little practical use linguistics has been. A notorious example is language teaching. In spite of the considerable amount of effort devoted to bringing linguistics to bear on language teaching, language learning has, as far as I can see, remained largely unaffected by the changes in teaching techniques, which one is tempted to see as dictated by fashion rather than by scientific progress. The fields in which contact with linguistics has been closest are the study of literary texts and comparative philology, both of which offer very little in the way of practical applications. The elaboration of linguistic theory is inextricably connected with the study of the kinship relationships among Indo-European languages.

The most important insights into the working of language were gained in the course of an "isolationist" effort, which aimed at studying language "in and for itself," to quote the words that Saussure's editors put at the conclusion of his *Cours* (Saussure, 1916). Linguists at that time tried to set up an autonomous method, an independent conceptual apparatus devised specifically for the study of language. This realization may come as a shock in these days, when the emphasis is on interdisciplinary integration and on trends like sociolinguistics or psycholinguistics, when some theoreticians even deny all autonomy to linguistics and present it as a branch of cognitive psychology. Whether these are positive developments, I would not care to discuss here. It is possible to feel that linguistics will become a real science the moment it disappears as an independent discipline because all problems arising from language will be satisfactorily answered by natural scientists using their own mode of discourse. Meanwhile I feel we are sufficiently far away from that moment for it to be worthwile to examine linguistics on its own terms. (For a good introduction, see the manual by Robins, 1964.)

Both the connection between philology and linguistics and the attempt to provide an autonomous foundation for linguistics are best exemplified by the work of Ferdinand de Saussure, who more rightfully than anyone else can be considered the father of modern linguistics; one may recall his pervading influence on the schools of Geneva, on French linguistics from Meillet down to contemporary structuralists, on the school of Copenhagen, on the school of Prague, and then, through Jakobson, on contemporary American trends (see the general survey by Lepschy, 1970). Even apart from specific trends, his ideas have permeated all modern linguistic thought. His insights and suggestions are still today astonishingly modern; some of them have never ceased to stimulate new theoretical developments. His work in the field of Indo-European phonology was as brilliant an application of structural linguistics as any produced after the much later conscious elaboration of structural linguistic methods, and some of his hypotheses in this field were proved true by subsequent discoveries made long after his death (Saussure, 1879). His reasearch on poetics, full of the most extraordinary flashes of intuition, was obviously far too modern for the time in which it was produced and even, one is tempted to say, for the stage reached by Saussure himself in his conscious reflections. It remained unfinished and unpublished; we can see today, when some fragments begin to be accessible in print, that it contains insights that present-day poetics is only slowly and laboriously approaching (Starobinski, 1971). But the field in which Saussure was most influential is general linguistics. This is also the field for which we have least material from his own hand, even in the shape of unpublished notes. The book that was to prove the most seminal work on linguistic theory in our century, the *Cours de linguistique générale*, was based mainly on notes taken by students during three courses given by Saussure between 1907 and 1911. It was published posthumously (1916). In recent years, philological work has been done (Godel, 1957) that has culminated in a critical edition of the *Cours* (Engler, 1967). The genesis and the precise value of many of Saussure's ideas remain obscure; a detailed discussion will be found in the annotated edition by De Mauro (1967). It is a witness to Saussure's greatness, however, that even today many of the central questions of linguistic theory are discussed within the conceptual framework and in the terms that Saussure used in discussing them in the *Cours*. I shall mention a few.

The synchronic point of view must be sharply separated from the diachronic one. This principle may appear to be one of the most obvious and undisputed achievements of modern linguistics. In fact, many linguists' attitude toward it is rather ambivalent. The school of Prague stressed from its beginning the impossibility and undesirability of an absolute separation of synchrony and diachrony (*Thèses*, 1929). In the United States, Sapir (1921) was always aware of the historical dimension, which added richness and complexity to linguistic synchrony. Bloomfield (1939), who was less sensitive to this aspect, noted in a curiously noncommittal way that he was setting up for Menomini certain theoretical basic forms bearing some resemblance to earlier, reconstructed Proto-Algonquian forms, and that the modifications required to obtain (within synchrony) the actual spoken forms, although stated in a purely descriptive order, approximated in content and order historical developments. This attitude is now becoming standard practice in generative phonology. We are given synchronic descriptions where formatives have a morphophonemic shape resembling earlier forms, and the rules of the phonological component appear to mirror diachronic developments. This, we are told, does not necessarily have to happen. It is possible for the synchronic statement to contradict the diachronic one (Chomsky & Halle, 1968; Halle, 1962). Usually, however, it does not, and this, we are made to understand, is not fortuitous; it is, in fact, significant. Unfortunately, there is, as far as I know, no satisfactory discussion of this significance. Language does work synchronically, and some elements of a diachronic character may be accounted for in terms of synchronic stylistic values; earlier forms, which are becoming obsolete, may appear synchronically as archaisms; diachrony appears as synchronic dynamism. It is as a synchronically working device that language is learned anew by every child. But there are some features that appear unredeemably awkward in a synchronic description and that seem to require a diachronic explanation (in at least one intuitively satisfactory sense of "explanation"). Obvious examples of this are normally offered by the morphology of languages. According to a well-established traditional view, synchronic description appears to be explanatory in the case of forms that result from analogic changes and have been made to fit into regular morphological patterns, at the price of irregularities in diachronic phonology; but a diachronic explanation is required for forms that, owing to regular diachronic phonological development, present a synchronic morphological irregularity. The problem has been exacerbated rather than clarified by the introduction of the notion of explanatory adequacy in generative grammar (Chomsky, 1962, 1965), connected with the discussion of evaluation procedures, linguistic universals, innate abilities, language acquisition, and the intuitions of the native speakers.

How does an explanatory theory work in other fields? What are the features of explanations in physics, physiology, anatomy? And in anthropology, sociology, history? This is, of course, a most unsophisticated question. But if it is not answered, I do not think that the problems relating to synchrony versus diachrony can be dealt with satisfactorily.

Another dichotomy that is central to Saussure's theory is that of *langue* versus *parole*. It refers to a question, or, rather, a group of questions, that have emerged in many different shapes in modern linguistics. Language is a social phenomenon that is manifested through individual acts of speech. Language can also be thought of as abstract, speech as concrete. Transformational generative linguistics has introduced a distinction between competence and performance (Chomsky, 1965). We certainly cannot identify this with Saussure's *langue* versus *parole* dichotomy. But it may be noted that *langue* has for Saussure a psychological character, and competence has for Chomsky a mental character. There is, of course, the problem of deciding what aspects of linguistic phenomena are present in *parole* and in performance, but do not belong to *langue* and competence, and vice versa.

In Saussure there is another important dichotomy, that between syntagmatic and associative relations; it is not identical with the *both—and* versus *either—or* dichotomy of glossematics (Hjelmslev, 1943); not all *both—and* relationships are syntagmatic, and not all *either—or* relationships are associative in the Saussurean sense. Hjelmslev (1938) did not help to clarify Saussure when he substituted "paradigmatic" for "associative." In any case, a *both—and* relationship is not necessarily identical with a concatenation of two successive units. Saussure made a conflation of different phenomena in that aspect of language that he called "linear." Some of these phenomena have been discussed, outside linguistics, in terms of the "serial order of behavior" (Lashley, 1951), and in relation to the general problem of teleology (Miller, Galanter, & Pribram, 1960), a principle explicitly defended by the school of Prague (Jakobson, Karcevsky, & Troubetzkoy, 1928; *Thèses*, 1929). Saussure was uncertain whether syntagms ought to belong to *langue*; in any case he excluded from *langue* the sentence, which results from individual creativity and is typical of *parole*. For Chomsky, individual creativity and the rules that generate the sentence are a central part of competence. Competence, in fact, accounts for infinite sentences that will never occur in performance because they are too long, too complicated, or simply not called for. Many, perhaps most, of the real sentences actually occurring in performance are not accounted for by competence because they are not well formed, being for various reasons ungrammatical. It seems to me that this question cannot fail to concern people who are interested in the practical side of language, that is, ultimately, in performance. How helpful is modern linguistics, with its emphasis on competence, in explaining facts of performance? And how necessary is the study of competence for understanding real life performance—the performance of patients who try to recover their speech, of children who are learning to speak their native language, of students who are learning a foreign language? How far is it possible and useful to distinguish whether competence or performance is impaired when a patient's speech is affected? And when a student knows the rules, say for Latin conditional sentences, at the conscious level (he is able to state them and to recognize them as they are applied in Latin texts) but makes mistakes in trying to apply them in his own Latin prose composition, is his competence or his performance defective? Linguistic competence, according to Chomsky, consists of what one knows about one's own language; it includes, besides conscious knowledge, "tacit" or "implicit" knowledge, part of which may never even be able to reach the level of consciousness. Competence is, at least in part, private knowledge. But, as Lashley (1949) stated, "Private knowledge is, on analysis, only private ignorance [p. 457]." What does one know *about* language when one knows how to speak? Could one equally ask: What does one know about physiology when one knows how to walk? Or should the question be: What does one know about walking when one knows how to walk? Hockett (1967, 1968) has explored these problems and has tried (none too successfully) to analyze the mechanisms of the conflicting unconscious pressures that are at the basis of slips of the tongue. The situation is even more involved if what we say is dictated by a partly unconscious competence, together with unconscious pressures that are excluded from competence and assigned to the domain of performance. Competence is abstract and idealized. An element of abstraction and idealization, however, seems to be necessarily involved in the setting up of a scientific theory, of a model, of an explanation. This also applies, presumably, to an explanation of performance. But the abstractions that are needed to explain performance, actual linguistic behavior, do not coincide with competence. Both in the *langue* versus *parole* and in the competence versus performance dichotomies, too much emphasis is placed on the opposition and too little on the interrelation of the two terms.

Generative grammar brings to the fore the notion of rule (Chomsky, 1961). It has been accused of reintroducing, through the notion of rule, the puristic ideals of traditional grammar. The accusation is not really justified; but the notion of rule is sufficiently involved and has a sufficiently complicated history, in linguistics and in other fields, to cause some perplexities. Do grammatical rules represent an ideal (competence), which performance tries to approximate despite the inevitable confusing disorder that appears in actual behavior? Or is actual behavior the real thing, the proper object of research, the phenomenon that ought to be explained as it is, and are rules abstract in the sense that they constitute approximate and incomplete models, which inevitably miss the richness and complexity of the reality that they try to represent and explain? A similar question may be asked with regard to other aspects of human activity; language belongs to a more general pattern-creating, structure-building ability, which structuralists try to identify in their analysis of culture and society. (I am here using "structuralism" to refer to a tradition that includes generative grammar; I am not using it in the polemically restricted sense that some transformationalists attribute to the label "structural linguistics," which they apply to points of view that are in many ways opposite to the principles and the ideals of the tradition that I have called structuralist.) In fact, analogous questions have been asked outside the humanities; they have been debated, without producing satisfactory answers, in the field of epistemology and in the philosophy of science.

Although the points I have touched on in this chapter have been presented exclusively from a linguistic point of view, in a deliberately provocative and isolationist manner, they can easily be transferred to fields of research outside language. There is another aspect, central to the discussion of language, which I have not previously mentioned because I do not know how it can be dealt with in the context of other disciplines. A central concern in linguistics is the question of meaning. Linguistic elements are considered to have two sides: an expression and a content, or, to use Saussure's terms again, a *signifiant* and a *signifié*. Besides, linguistic elements can be used not only literally but also figuratively, that is, with a metaphorical meaning. The use of figures of speech, which traditional rhetoric considered to be typical of poetry and literary composition, is in fact a constant and normal feature of ordinary language. One has only to glance at a printed page or listen to a few sentences of spontaneous conversation to realize that figurative speech is no less natural than literal speech. This emphasizes the closeness of the connection between poetics and linguistics, and the deficiency of any theory of language that does not recognize the central place that the rhetorical devices of figurative speech occupy in the working of language. Generative grammar fails to deal with this aspect in a natural way, in as far as it puts figurative usage at a lower degree of grammaticalness than literal usage and tries to account for it in terms of broken rules.

Once again, the semiotic character is central in language, but not limited to it. New insights concerning this point would be among the most useful contributions that students of other fields might make to the progress of linguistics (see, for a rich and rewarding discussion, Jakobson, 1970).

References

Bloomfield, L. Menomini morphophonemics. *Travaux du Cercle Linguistique de Prague*, 1939, *8*, 105—115.

Chomsky, N. On the notion "rule of grammar." *Proceedings of Symposia in Applied Mathematics*, 1961, *12*, 6—24.

Chomsky, N. Eplanatory models in linguistics. In E. Nagel, P. Suppes, & A. Tarski (Eds.), *Logic, methodology and philosophy of science, proceedings of the 1960 international congress*. Stanford, Calif.: Stanford Univ. Press, 1962. Pp. 528—550.

Chomsky, N. *Aspects of the theory of syntax*. Cambridge, Mass.: MIT Press, 1965.

Chomsky, N., & Halle, M. *The sound pattern of English*. New York: Harper, 1968.

De Mauro, T. *Ferdinand de Saussure. Corso di linguistica generale. Introduzione, traduzione e commento di Tullio de Mauro*. Bari: Laterza, 1967. [*Ferdinand de Saussure, Cours de linguistique générale*. Édition critique préparée par Tullio De Mauro. (French translation by L. J. Calvet.) Paris: Payot, 1972.]

Engler, R. *Ferdinand de Saussure. Cours de linguistique générale. Édition critique par Rudolf Engler*. Wiesbaden: Harrassowitz, 1967.

Garvin, P. (Ed.) *Natural language and the computer*. New York: McGraw-Hill, 1963.

Godel, R. *Les sources manuscrites du cours de linguistique générale de F. de Saussure*. Geneva: Droz & Paris: Minard, 1957.

Halle, M. Phonology in generative grammar. *Word*, 1962, *18*, 54—72.

Hays, D. G. *Introduction to computational linguistics*. New York: Amer. Elsevier, 1967.

Hjelmslev, L. Essai d'une théorie des morphèmes. *Actes, Congrès International de Linguistes, 4th, Copenhagen, 1936*, 1938, 140—150.

Hjelmsley, L. *Omkring Sprogteoriens Grundlaeggelse*. Copenhagen: Munksgaard, 1943. [*Prolegomena to a theory of language*. (Engl. transl. by F. J. Whitfield) Madison: Univ. of Wisconsin Press, 1961.]

Hockett, C. F. Where the tongue slips, there slip I. In *To honor Roman Jakobson*. The Hague: Mouton, 1967. Pp. 910–936.

Hockett, C. F. *The state of the art*. The Hague: Mouton, 1968.

Jakobson, R. *Kindersprache, Aphasie und allgemeine Lautgesetze*. Uppsala: Lundequistska Bokhandeln. 1941. (*Uppsala Universitets Årsskrift*, 1942, *9*, 1–83; *Språkvetenskapliga Sällskapets i Uppsala Förhandlingar*, 1940–1942). Also in *Selected writings*. Vol. I. The Hague: Mouton, 1962. Pp. 328–401. [*Child language, aphasia and phonological universals*. (Engl. transl. by A. R. Keiler) The Hague: Mouton, 1968.]

Jakobson, R. Linguistics. In R. Maheu (Ed.), *Main trends of research in the social and human sciences*. Part One: Social sciences. Paris & The Hague: Mouton (Unesco), 1970. Pp. 419–463. Also in *Selected writings*. Vol. II. The Hague: Mouton, 1971. Pp. 655–696. 711–722.

Jakobson, R., Karcevsky, S., Troubetzkoy, N. Quelles sont les méthodes les mieux appropriées à un exposé complet et pratique de la grammaire d'une langue quelconque? *Actes, Congrès International de Linguistes, 1st, the Hague*, 1928, 33–36. Also in *Selected writings*. Vol. I. The Hague: Mouton, 1962. Pp. 3–6.

Lashley, K. S. Persistent problems in the evolution of mind. 1949. In F. A. Beach, D. O. Hebb, C. T. Morgan, H. W. Nissen (Eds.), *The neuropsychology of Lashley. Selected papers of K. S. Lashley*. New York: McGraw-Hill, 1960. Pp. 455–477.

Lashley, K. S. The problem of serial order in behavior. 1951. In F. A. Beach, D. O. Hebb, C. T. Morgan, H. W. Nissen (Eds.), *The neuropsychology of Lashley. Selected papers of K. S. Lashley*. New York: McGraw-Hill, 1960. Pp. 506–528.

Lenneberg, E. H. *Biological foundations of language*. New York: Wiley, 1967.

Lepschy, G. C. *A survey of structural linguistics*. London: Faber & Faber, 1970.

Miller, G. A., Galanter, E., & Pribram, K. H. *Plans and the structure of behavior*. New York: Holt, 1960.

Pulgram, E. *Introduction to the spectrography of speech*. The Hague: Mouton, 1959.

Robins, R. H. *General linguistics. An introductory survey*. London: Longmans, Green, 1964.

Sapir, E. *Language. An introduction to the study of speech*. New York: Harcourt, 1921.

de Saussure, F. *Mémoire sur le système primitif des voyelles dans les langues Indo-Européennes*. Leipzig: Teubner, 1879. Also in *Recueil des publication scientifiques de Ferdinand de Saussure*. Geneva: Sonor, 1922. Pp. 1–268.

de Saussure, F. *Cours de linguistique générale*. Publié par Charles Bally et Albert Sechehaye avec la collaboration de Albert Riedlinger. Lausanne-Paris: Payot, 1916.

Starobinski, J. *Les mots sous les mots. Les anagrammes de Ferdinand de Saussure*. Paris: Gallimard, 1971.

Thèses. *Travaux du Cercle Linguistique de Prague*, 1929, *1*, 7–29.

4. The Heuristic Principle in the Perception, Emergence, and Assimilation of Speech

A. A. Leontiev

Modern trends in Anglo-American psycholinguistics are contrasted with French and Russian trends. The American predilection for formalization, computer modeling, and biological reductionism is discussed critically, and it is shown how the selection of strategies for language reception and expression calls for explanation by its own set of psychological principles.

Psycholinguistic Rules and Plans

If one attempts to make a very generalized psychological classification of existing research on psycholinguistics, one may see that such research falls into two categories. The first includes all the many experimental and theoretical investigations in which the process of spoken expression is treated as an isolated speech *reaction* (or chain of speech reactions) to a speech or nonspeech stimulus. Such reactions are governed by general laws. Habits of speech response are formed as a result of the statistically probable repetition of speech experience, projected onto the system of innate, general psychological mechanisms. It is only this general psychological organization that is innate and natural to man; the structuring of man's linguistic capacity, if indeed such structuring occurs (but compare, for instance, the work of B. F. Skinner), is a secondary phenomenon produced by the experience of speech. This research category includes the numerous investigations on verbal learning and also—as far as psycholinguistics is concerned—all those trends that are based to some extent on the psychological conception of neobehaviorism, in particular the Osgood school.

The second category is composed of work done along the lines of what is known as generative grammar, connected with the names of N. Chomsky and G. Miller (in France, the leader of this school is J. Mehler (1969), who published a well-known collection of translated works). The approach adopted by this school has been clearly defined in a book by Miller, Galanter, and Pribram (1960). Their definition of "plans" is as follows: "A Plan is any hierarchical process in the organism that can control the order in which a sequence of operations is to be performed [p. 16]." According to Miller *et al.* (1960), what is acquired is not a collection of specifically verbal skills (operations), which are then organized at a second stage, but a "plan," a schema, a program of speech behavior, implemented through a succession of verbal skills or verbal reactions of a more elementary type. "The pronounciation of a sentence in a normal manner is a skilled act.... Like any skill, it must be guided by a Plan.... Its structure is the hierarchy of grammatical rules of formation and transformation [p. 156]." The concept of *rules* is thus introduced. Let us try to discern the *psychological* reality behind this concept.

It is not for nothing that we have stressed the word "psychological." The point is that, in regard to rules, Miller and his school frequently confuse the rules of the organization of the linguistic *text* (rules for the generation of the text on the basis of an abstract model) with the rules of actual speech behavior, the rules that govern the process of the construction of human utterance, frequently asserting that even the abstract generative model constitutes the program of the corresponding utterance (cf. in this connection A. A. Leontiev, 1969).

The conception of the Miller school, as we know, is based largely on the TOTE concept (Test → Operate → Test → Exit), which expresses the basic hierarchical principle of the construction of behavior. The operational phase (O) may vary within wide limits and become in its turn an integrated act of TOTE; the test phase (T) remains unchanged, fixed. What does the test phase consist of in this case? As Miller himself points out, in a joint paper with Ojemann McKean (Miller & Ojemann McKean, 1964), "... in most general terms, linguistic rules are social conventions of the form 'when the same situation occurs again, do the same thing. Such statements would be meaningless, of course, if we could not recognize a new situation as similar to an old one, or if we did not know what it meant to do the same things. Each rule must be supported by a system of recognizable similarities and differences [p. 298]." In other words, the speaker must possess, in addition to the capacity to utilize the rules for operation (phase O) retained in his memory, the further capacity, a different one, to identify the words with the situation (phase T). The criterion for "testing" when identifying words is the generative model, that is, the linguistic knowledge of the speaker—grammatical and semantic rules. In addition, as Miller and Isard (1963) state, the speaker disposes of "pragmatic rules" enabling him to identify the context (situation) in which the sentence is used—this concept, however, is not explained. It is sufficient here to say that these pragmatic rules are as clearly fixed and strictly conditioned by the situation as are the grammatical and semantic rules by the linguistic structure.

Thus speech, in Miller's psycholinguistics, is the actualization of a preexisting scheme or plan. This plan is automatically selected in accordance with the situation constituting the stimulus and representing, in the words of John Dewey (1896, cited by Miller, 1960, "[T]hat phase of the forming coordination which represents the conditions which have to be met in bringing it to a successful issue [p. 30]." This automatic selection is achieved by pragmatic rules. The process of selection of the plan, corresponding to the test phase (T), is static; that of the actualization of the plan, corresponding to the operational phase (O), is dynamic and flexible, and it is in the course of this process that changes and adaptations occur. Rejection of the old plan and adoption of a new one may be caused either by the fact that the plan fails to give the desired results, or by the fact that it gives "undesirable" results, which becomes apparent in the course of the second test phase.

We have thus arrived at an unequivocally *algorithmic* view of speech behavior.[1] According to this view, the strategy of speech behavior is strictly governed by the analysis of the concrete situation; but the actual tactics vary, although only within the process of the realization of the plan, and only owing to the fact that the results obtained fail to meet requirements.[2] This theory is undoubtedly "stronger" (in the mathematical sense) than the "feedback" concept of speech, and its wide acceptance in current psycholinguistics is readily understandable. We may question, however, how far it is applicable to the description of the way in which speech processes actually take place.

Alternative Approaches

The psycholinguistic view just described is based on the idea that the decision regarding the plan is taken as a result of the application of various algorithmic rules for identifying the situation with the stimulus. This application occurs in Phase T_1 of the integrated TOTE operation, whereas the adoption of the actual grammatical plan constitutes Phase O of this operation—the phase which, according to Miller and his coauthors, itself constitutes the TOTE system. If the plan proves to be unsuitable in the conditions, we revert to Phase T_1 and make a correction in the pragmatic rules. We speak advisedly of a *correction*, since it is a case of "disagreement." According to Miller and others, the testing of different variations of the rules should correspond to the image of the desired result, and in its turn be integrated into the framework of the plan.

---

[1] *Algorithm*—"Specific directions for the execution of a series of operations in a specific order, such as to permit the solution of all the problems of a specific type. An algorithm leads from the initial data to the result required by a limited number of steps (actions); and the data vary within certain limits [Manturov, Solntsev, Sozkin, Fedin, 1965, p. 11]."

[2] We use the terms "strategy" and "tactics" in their ordinary meaning, not in the sense in which they are used in the book by Miller and others, quoted above. In other words, we take "tactics" to mean the predetermined selection and execution of a decision as to behavior, "strategy" to mean the predetermined selection of a set of decisions.

All this would be perfect if man, in fact, always acted according to this schema. But a great deal of experimental research has been done that shows that human behavior is far more complex and that the concept of plans in the variation described is unsatisfactory. Let us begin, at all events, by examining the *perception of speech*. It is essential to begin by considering this aspect, because experience shows that "nonstandard" strategies (such as, for instance, "rapid reading" or "scanning," which is certainly not algorithmic in the sense described above) play a particularly important part in the process of semantic speech perception, and especially in mass communication.

It is important to emphasize that we are dealing here specifically with strategies. In contemporary theories of speech perception, as we know, the idea of probability forecasting is very popular. This is defined as "the process of forestalling the whole, foreseeing the elements which will follow on a given element, on the basis of an estimate of the a priori probability of their appearing in the situation perceived as a whole. This process is based on advancing the most probable hypotheses, which are then confirmed or rejected [Zimnyaya, 1971, p. 42]." Even more widespread (though not universally accepted) is the more general idea of "analysis through synthesis," first proposed by Halle and Stevens (1964), the gist of which is that "the mechanism of understanding is essentially no different from the mechanism of planning a sentence for production [Lenneberg, 1967, p. 106]," and which includes active modeling of the structure of speech at various levels. But in both cases, it is a matter of the choice of one or another prognosis— a choice that is either fairly rigidly predetermined (in the theory of "analysis through synthesis") or else statistically predetermined (in works based on probability prognosis), that is, a choice concerning the *tactics* of perception. We are not concerned with private, individual decisions affecting individual speech, but with the most common *mode* of perception.

This common mode or strategy of perception is psychologically predetermined *before* we are directly confronted with any concrete stimulus. The key to the choice of this strategy is to be found in the *attitude* of the subject towards the objects perceived, an attitude that is imparted beforehand or takes shape in the course of his perceptual activity. A typical example of the effect of this attitude is the experimental situation described in the work of A. N. Leontiev and E. P. Krinchik (1964), when the intensification of the subjective significance, for the person tested, of some of the possible stimuli makes them have a "sensitizing" effect (A. A. Ukhtomsky) and considerably accelerates the processing of the information they convey. "Under the influence of the task set in the experiment, the subject, working on the basis of an estimate of the probable structure of the signals produced, optimizes the process of perceiving information so that, whilst his perception of frequent signals is somewhat slowed down, his perception of infrequent ones is considerably accelerated [A. N. Leontiev & Krinchik, 1964, p. 324]." This kind of subjective significance, or value, can be imparted to the objects perceived not in experimental conditions only, but also as a result of "predisposal" connected with the changing motives and emotions of the subject and, in the final analysis, with the change in the personal meaning of these objects. This notion is related to the concept of the "model of the desired future" in the works of N. A. Bernshtein (1966) and to I. T. Bzhalava's definition of *set* as a "heuristic program that facilitates the search for a means for solving a problem [Bzhalava, 1968, p. 14]."

Let us now apply the above to the actual perception of speech. In psycholinguistics, it is thought increasingly that in the search for words in long-term memory (in speech formation) or the identification of words (in speech perception), there are various operational aspects: one in the field of acoustical and articulational signals and another in that of semantic signs; in both these processes we rely on the statistically probable meaning of the signals employed (Anisfeld & Knapp, 1968; Frumkina & Vasilevich, 1967; A. A. Leontiev, 1969; Spreen, Borkowski, & Benton, 1967). In different situations of speech behavior, however, it is possible that a different type of process may predominate, as was pointed out—in relation to a more frequent case—by D. Norman (1966; cf. also Voronin, 1970). Thus, if the aim is to give a correct answer, one method of procedure will be used; if mistakes are allowed, but it is important to minimize the response latency, then another method will be selected. In particular, we are at liberty to select a specific strategy of identification in accordance with one type of subjective "logic" or another.

Extensive experimental investigations were recently carried out on the factors governing word perception when there is a high level of noise. It was found that the recipient *systematically* uses different strategies for the recognition of words according to the signal-to-noise ratio. In better conditions of perception, mainly phonetic signals are used. In the worst conditions (when the noise level is very high), frequency of occurrence becomes the predominant factor (Goldiamond & Hawkins, 1958). Lastly, in intermediate conditions, the effect of nonphonetic linguistic factors (polysemy, relation to various parts of speech) plays a role; in other words, semantic signals are intensively used (Zinder & Shtern, 1972). Another interesting point about this type of research is the fact that it clearly shows the importance of orientation in perception; stimuli that control this orientation are different in quality from those controlling the actual process of identification.

Similar results were obtained somewhat earlier by E. I. Issenina (1967) in her experimental research on the semantic perception of speech. She showed that

> According to the signals perceived when a word is identified, different subsystems are brought into action for the processing of linguistic information. The unit of decision in perception is not constant in size, but varies in accordance with the necessary and sufficient signals of the words that are perceived and the position of the determining and semidetermining words of the context [p. 21].

The unit of decision in the perception of an intelligible text may consist of separate words (when there is a minimum of obstruction), groups of words (when there is more obstruction and the context has to be taken into account) or, lastly, entire sentences. Preliminary decisions at the level of differential signals, phonemes, morphemes, and soon, may or may not be made, depending on the quality and quantity of the acoustic signals perceived.

Other similar experimental investigations along the same lines may also be cited. Thus L. V. Sakharny, when investigating the laws governing the comprehension of morphemes by means of association experiments, showed that subjects either continue to use a polyseme as a single lexeme or else rely, in their associations, on a word-building model, according to the meaning they attach to it (this, in turn, depends on their attitude and general turn of mind). Thus the word *diary* **dnevnik** was associated in the minds of secondary school children, through the "factor *L*" (lexeme), with words of the type of *lesson* **urok** and *exercise book* **tetrad**; students of an institute associated the word through the "factor *D*" (derivation) and often produced the word **vecernik** *night-school pupil* (*dnevnik* and *vecernik* being the colloquial terms used to denote students of the day and evening sections of the institute) (Sakharny, 1972). This experiment shows clearly that man in his perception of speech does not act merely as a filtering system, but goes about it in his own way, selecting his strategy and method of procedure in accordance with his set and the external signs he perceives.

In view of the above, it may be contended that the processes of the perception of speech, in certain situations, are not algorithmic, strictly determined by the specific situation and stimulus, but are governed by a *heuristic principle*.[3]

In other words, we do not necessarily select the optimum strategy (set of expectations) on the basis of the analysis and identification of the concrete stimulus or stimulating situation; selection may precede and determine the analysis, or it may be made on the basis of the evaluation of a manifestly incomplete collection of signals. Thus the problem of speech perception includes the concept of preliminary orientation or orientational activity, in the course of which we receive information about a set of situations and select a set of expectations (or set of possible solutions). The selection of the concrete solution, however—the concrete plan— occurs at the next stage of perception and is determined by the first step, though in a different way (even by what may be virtually a random search).

By accepting the theory of "analysis through synthesis" or any other active theory of speech perception, we are assuming that perception will be through

---

[3] *Heuristic* is taken to denote the "mechanisms which govern the degree to which the search for an answer from among a large number of different possibilities can be simplified [Tikhomirov & Terekhov, 1967, p. 26]." As we know, the heuristic theory is also widely accepted in the Cambridge (Mass.) school of thought headed by G. Miller; but the psychologists of this school regard the heuristic problem as merely a matter of selecting short cuts (cf. Fodor & Garrett, 1967). As to the conception of "heuristic plans" in the book by Miller *et al.* (1960) referred to above, this is similar to the heuristic programs of Newell, Simon, and others, which—in the authors' own words— constitute "metaplans," that is, represent the result of a generalized estimate of corrections at higher levels of organization.

a grammatical plan and, accordingly, that a choice of a set of such plans will be made. But the existing psycholinguistic models, based on generative grammars—more particularly, Miller's model—do not include any stages at which this choice can be made.[4] The absence of any such stage particularly affects the interpretation of the processes of the generation of speech, with which we now propose to deal.

Let us take as an example G. Miller's experiments on the psychological reality of grammatical rules, well known because they are mentioned in a number of American and European publications (Miller, 1962; Miller & Ojemann McKean, 1964). Miller's theory is based on the assumption that two completely different kinds of psychological approaches to sentences are possible, especially sentences of great complexity (in terms of transformational grammar). The first is to proceed "by images," each sentence being immediately grasped or perceived as a grammatical whole; the second is the transformation method, whereby the sentence is reduced to its basic structure (or, on the contrary, expanded from this structure). If we can show by experiment, Miller argued, that the subject proceeds by one or the other of these methods, this will either prove or disprove the psychological reality of transformational grammar. Miller took as a criterion the time taken for operating with sentences produced—according to the transformational theory—by two transformations. With the "transformation method" it was expected that the average response latency required for transforming a complex sentence into the kernel sentence would be close to the total time required for the analogous transformation of two simpler (single-step) constructions (thus the passive negative construction should require as much time as the passive plus the negative one). Those tested were given two lists of sentences and were given the task of finding in the right-hand list the analog of every sentence in the left-hand list.

As we know, the experiment (both in this case and in other series, based on oral speech) produced brilliant results, appearing to prove convincingly the additivity of the time for operating with test constructions. But how convincing does this experiment prove to be on closer examination?

It should be pointed out, first, that the fact that the operation is in two steps in the transformation method does not necessarily mean that the operation "by images" is a single-phase one. As Ilyasov (1968) states:

> It is assumed that, whatever the nature of the steps, a single-step transition is psychologically easier than a transition involving two or more steps, and should therefore take less time. This supposition is, of course, unfounded. It is justified only in the case of the transformational mechanism, where indeed the time required for one step must be less than for two. But in the case of independent generation, the time for transition from one structure to another structure having two categories may vary widely according to the type of generating structures,

---

[4] The model proposed by J. Morton (Cambridge, England) appears to be an exception (Morton, 1970). Compare also the experimental models constructed by other authors (for a survey of these, see A. A. Leontiev, 1969, pp. 109–115).

the individual methods of handling these structures, and a number of other factors. . . . Thus, even if the additivity expected by Miller is obtained, though Miller's experiment can indicate that speech generation and understanding by a transformational model is either possible or impossible, it cannot claim to prove that it is bound to take place [pp. 61–62].

But there is more to it than this. Miller (1962) tells us explicitly that the subjects in his experiments were first given some sample sentences and shown how one might transform these sentences grammatically. In other words, not only did Miller purposefully guide the persons he tested towards a certain strategy of behavior, he actually taught them this strategy. It is perfectly natural that, in these conditions, they should have acted as Miller expected them to! And it does not at all follow from his experiments that these syntactic operations are a normal and regular part of understanding and producing sentences.[5]

The conclusions that Miller himself drew from his experiment and that were accepted unquestioningly by his disciples are justified on one condition only, that is, if it is assumed that the mechanism of operating with the structure of spoken expression is of a rigid, algorithmic character, that the strategy thereof is innate in the users of the language or at any rate *given* them, and is not determined by the set or by the overall signals of a class of situations. This assumption is unlikely to be warranted; e.g., cf. the work of Carroll (1958), Tannenbaum and Williams (1968), and Rommetveit (1968)]. The "classical" psycholinguistic model, based on transformational grammar, leaves us no other choice.

This forces us to seek a psycholinguistic model that is heuristic in type, that is, one which (a) provides for a phase in which one *chooses the strategy* of speech behavior; (b) is in general flexible and permits of various different forms of operation with utterances at the various stages of the generation (perception) of speech; and (c) does not contradict the results obtained earlier when verifying the "psycholinguistic reality" of other models. In Soviet psychology, the foundations of this approach to the modeling of speech processes were laid by L. S. Vygotsky. The ideas of his school may be summed up as follows:

1. Speech should be regarded as *speech activity,* which is part of the productive, cognitive, or other activity of man and enables that activity to take place.

2. Activity as a whole (and speech activity as a part of this) is governed by a *motive* or hierarchy of motives; it has a preassigned *purpose* (determined, in the case of speech, by a nonvocal context) and a dynamic *structure,* ensuring the optimum attainment of the aim (see A. N. Leontiev, 1965).

---

[5]Both these defects in Miller's series of experiments were discussed in Soviet psycholinguistics as early as 1968 (see A. A. Leontiev, 1969, pp. 87–89, 103–104). At the same time, I. I. Ilyasov made a detailed analysis of Miller's methods and repeated his experiments, using Russian material. The results proved negative, that is, they failed to confirm Miller's hypotheses (Ilyasov, 1968). I. M. Lushchikhina reached similar conclusions in her experiment: "[T]o draw universally applicable conclusions about the part played by different transformations is, to say the least, premature [Lushchikhina, 1968, pp. 12–13]."

3. Speech activity must be taken in this connection as being similar to the solution of a cognitive problem, as an intellectual act (in the broad sense of the term). If we treat speech as a *process of solving a communication problem* (cf. Fraisse, 1963), we come naturally to the idea of the heuristic character of speech processes. Viewed from this angle, speech activity can be represented as a succession of phases, as follows: (a) orientation and planning, (b) execution, (c) verification (see A. A. Leontiev, 1972). Orientation, in turn, may be of two types: (a) orientation in the problem situation, leading to the revelation of the communicative intention; (b) orientation in the conditions of the communicative problem, culminating in programming (see the following item).

4. The orientation and planning phase (unlike the analogous phase in the TOTE scheme) may include the most complex *orientation activity*. Thus the process of understanding the text (in the conceptual system under consideration) is the orientation phase for the process of "recounting in your own words." The system of perceptive actions is the orientation phase for the verbal description of the results of perception. Orientation in the case of a dialogue includes other factors, such as forming an image of the other speaker, judging the distance between the speakers, the time setting of the conversation, and so on.[6] At this stage, too, the speaker considers the functional aspect of what is being said. The actual speech behavior is subordinated to the general organization of the process of solving the communication problem, and is determined in the course of the orientation activity.

5. This phase also includes the planning (programming) of vocal expression. However, this programming is carried out not in the linguistic code—not, that is to say, in the form of a "grammatical Plan"—but in an inner speech code, using as supports images and schemas, but not necessarily words or combinations of words (A. A. Leontiev, 1969, Zhinkin, 1967).

6. In this view, what Miller calls a "grammatical Plan" is part of the execution phase, and depends on the program adopted, which is embodied in the inner speech code (Ryabova, 1967; Ryabova & Shtern, 1968). Thus the choice of strategy in speech behavior is linked to orientation and inner programming, whereas the choice of tactics is linked to the execution phase.

Various attempts have been made to embody these theories (or part of them) in a specific psycholinguistic model (e.g., cf. A. A. Leontiev, 1969; Ryabova, 1967; Vereshchagin, 1968; Zimnyaya, 1969). In our model, in particular, which was devised in conjunction with T. V. Ryabova, the heuristic principle is applied consistently at all stages of the generative process (see A. A. Leontiev, 1969, pp. 213–215).

The actual mechanism of the operation of the heuristic principle can be effec-

---

[6] There is a parallel here with the views of the French psychologist S. Moscovici (1967) on the subject of the "psychosociology of language." (see also Ageev, 1972; this is an attempt to apply Moscovici's ideas to Russian linguistic material and to develop them further.)

tively demonstrated in the work of V. I. Batov (Batov and Kochinov, 1973). He investigated the heuristic principle in the speech behavior of a "false witness," that is, in the case of a deliberately false communication. One of the specific psycholinguistic characteristics of speech activity in this situation is the general raising of the level of motivation, which makes the structure of the communication "not ordinary;" the speaker endeavors to construct messages having few degrees of semantic liberty—that is, the least polysemous possible—so that all possible interpretations may be verified. This is reflected in the choice of less frequently used words, and the speaker is guided by a subjective awareness of the probability of a word.

It is extremely important to point out that the heuristic principle in speech generation and perception in fact forms the basis for the complete restoration of speech functions disturbed as a result of aphasia. Here, our psycholinguistic approach coincides with more general ideas about "functional systems" being the physiological basis of the formation and functioning of the higher psychic functions of man and with the principle of the localization of these functions in the cerebral cortex—the principle that is specific for man (A. N. Leontiev, 1965; Luria, 1963).

As we know, the theory of the forming of the child's linguistic faculty has also been worked out within the framework of generative grammar. It was put forward by N. Chomsky himself. He maintained that it was essential for the development of the child's "knowledge of language" to process language samples by a "language acquisition device." He proposed that the child gives evidence of an innate aptitude for mastery of language and inherent capacities for the execution of specific heuristic procedures.

These general ideas of Chomsky are embodied, for instance, by D. McNeill (1966, p. 38) in his principle of the "universal hierarchy of categories," which "guides the first steps of linguistic development." This hierarchy is, in fact, a collection of linguistic universals—or rather, a collection of hypotheses—and the development of children's speech, according to McNeill, proceeds by successively confirming, rejecting, or refining these inherent hypotheses in the process of communication. E. Lenneberg and, in particular, J. Morton are less categorical on the subject. They base their theories more consistently on the uniformity of the cognitive development of the child, and regard the universals of speech development as processes that reflect certain general psychological universals. At the same time, however, they consider that "language is the manifestation of species-specific cognitive propensities. It is the consequence of the biological peculiarities that make a human type of cognition possible [Lenneberg, 1967, p. 374; cf. Morton, 1971, p. 93]. In other words, general psychological principles are directly deduced from biological premises plus the process of the child's passive adaptation to the "social environment."

Since we have no room here to argue about this view (cf. A. A. Leontiev, 1972), we shall merely give a brief outline of our own position. The question is not whether there are any universal, inherent prerequisites determining the development of the psychic makeup and more particularly of the child's speech (and it is to this, precisely, that McNeill and similar authors of the Chomsky—Miller school reduce the problem of speech development). Speech is, of course, not hermetically sealed off from the other higher psychic functions of man; and speech, like the other higher psychic functions, is not simply the actualization of rigidly fixed mechanisms with which man is endowed once and for all and which are merely adapted, as it were, in the process of speech development. The ontogenesis of linguistic capacity is an extremely complex interaction between two processes: on the one hand, the process of communication of adults and the child,[7] a process which passes through a number of stages, developing and growing increasingly complicated and sophisticated; and, on the other, specialized functional systems, gradually forming and replacing one another in the child's psyche (Wallon, 1957). What really develops in the process of the development of children's speech is neither language (in the sense that linguists usually understand its development) nor the method of the realization of inherent mechanisms, but the nature of the interaction between the system of linguistic resources at the child's disposal and the way in which these resources function, that is, the *method of using language* for purposes of cognition and communication. Such, in fact, is the view taken by L. S. Vygotsky (1956) in his well-known monograph *Thinking and Speech*.

But if such is the case, we are not obliged to assume that all children will necessarily achieve the same result *by the same means*. The same functional mastery of speech may be achieved by various linguistic means, in which various methods are used, but in the last analysis, all of them equally satisfy the child's need for cognition and communication. This is in fact what happens.

The Russian psychologist I. Sikorsky, as early as the end of the 19th century, noted that children between one and two years of age may adopt various procedures when trying to imitate words difficult to pronounce; some follow the acrophonetic principle, taking the first syllable of the word (*ko* instead of **kóshka** *cat*), while others try to imitate the word as a whole (**tití** instead of **kirpičí** '*bricks*') (Sikorsky, 1899). Many similar observations have been made subsequently. It will suffice to refer to a phenomenon described by the present writer (A. A. Leontiev, 1965): the creation, by children (between the ages of 18 months and 2 years), of individual grammatical subsystems, whether paradigmatic or syntagmatic. Thus children whose mother tongue is Russian frequently use an "improvised" method of contrasting the form of the direct case with that of the oblique ones instead of the normal grammatical method (they have already understood the functional distinction between the two from the speech of adults). The speech of many children is marked by the independent appearance of a possessive construction, with reduplication of the final syllable of the word

---

[7] Or even of adults with the child. Here we are at the boundary between the idea of the "speech adaptation" of the child to its social milieu and the idea of society as an active *formative factor* in speech development. It is impossible not to agree with Peter Herriot (1970) when he writes ironically, in his extremely controversial book, "Adults often do a lot more than speak *in the presence of children*; for a start, they sometimes actually speak *to* them! [p. 104]"

indicating the possessor: *deda Alesha* but *deda Alesha-sha shapa*, instead of *shapka dedushki Aleshi* "the cap of grandpapa Alesha", and so on.

A more profound difference in the way in which children master their mother tongue is described by L. Bloom (1970), who analyzed the speech development of three children and demonstrated that they all followed somewhat different courses. She drew a distinction between two types of children's speech at the stage when they are first beginning to master syntax: "telegraphic speech" and "pivot speech." Children using the telegraphic strategy combine substantives with other meaningful words in different ways, modifying their grammatical function; both the little girls described by Bloom built up phrases, basically, in this manner. Typical utterances were, for instance, *read book,* **Gia** *book* (= *book of Gia*), *bear book, Mommy book* (where *book* fulfills the function of a predicate). Pivot strategy is characterized by the fact that substantives are used in a fixed grammatical function and in a constant syntactical context, so that only the collection of syntactical operators changes, and even so, only within narrow limits: *more book, no book,* and so on. It was thus that the third child (a boy) constructed his first utterances. The author's opinion, with which we can certainly concur, is that "the results of this study should cast some doubt on the view of language development as the same innately preprogrammed behavior for all children. . . . The differences . . . must reflect the importance of individual differences in the interaction between cognitive function and experience, which could not be assumed to be the same for any two children [Bloom, 1970, p. 277]." Special interest in this connection attaches to the fundamental research of Dingwall and Tuniks (1973), which showed a similar difference of strategy in a very wide range of empirical material.

The writer has been able to trace the mechanism of the influence of "individual experience" on the strategy of mastering language by observing his own children. The eldest child grew up alone; he had an unusual amount of contact with adults, but rarely heard books read aloud. This led him to adopt an intensive (telegraphic) strategy for mastering speech (cf. A. A. Leontiev, 1965). The younger children, twins, spent most of their time together and heard a great deal of reading. They learned to speak extensively, roughly by the method described by Braine (1963) as "contextual generalization," often reproducing a newly acquired word together with the context in which they learned it.

At all events, it is quite clear, at the present stage of research on children's speech, that speech development cannot be equated with the actualization of a rigid system of inherent "rules" when contact is made with the social environment. The mechanical device of the Chomsky type is a stage in contemporary genetical psychology that we have left behind. The assimilation of one's mother tongue undoubtedly presupposes the selection and differential utilization of various different strategies for the mastering of speech, and, in this sense, is subject to the heuristic principle expounded above.

Thus the facts demonstrate that the heuristic principle plays a much more significant role in the functioning and formation of language than is assigned to it by the psycholinguistic theory of Miller and the Cambridge school of psycholinguistics. That Miller and his school should underestimate the importance of the heuristic principle is fully comprehensible in view of their general psychological approach; but this principle, which they either reject or regard merely as a deviation from the general algorithmic organization of behavior, is (as is evident from the foregoing) an organic part of the psychological and psycholinguistic theories of French scientists (Wallon, Piaget, Fraisse) and Soviet scientists (Vygotsky and his school). The fact is that no psychological theory in which speech is regarded as a purposeful activity can fail to concur with the heuristic principle; the defect of the Miller school is that it regards speech behavior, as every other form of behavior, not as an activity directed towards an end, but as an extremely complex reaction to one kind of situation or another. Reading the book by Miller, Galanter, and Pribram gives a strange impression—that one knows all about *how* a person does things, but nothing, or almost nothing, about *why* he does them. And the whole of the psychological organization of behavior is one-sided in that it concentrates on the *conditions* of activity, but neglects the *purpose* of that activity. It is significant that the image of the desired result, according to these authors, should be merely the "conditions to be tried out." Thus the views of psycholinguists of the Miller school, despite their polemics against the advocates of the behaviorist approach to speech, do not, in fact, differ so widely from those of their opponents.

The main reason why the Miller school of psycholinguistics takes this line is undoubtedly the influence of cybernetics and, in particular, the desire to equate the language of psychological modeling as closely as possible with the language of cybernetic modeling, to assimilate the "plans" of human behavior to machine programs. This trend, which is fairly common in psychology, aims at inferring the characteristics of psychological models from abstract criteria, held to be equally applicable to man and machines—at measuring man by the yardstick applied to machines, in fact.

However, even if we aim consciously to impart the maximum objectivity and rigor to our analysis of psychological processes and the maximum degree of formalism to our models of activity, it is by no means evident, a priori, that such objectivity, rigor, and formalism can be attained by assimilating the models of one type to the models of another type, devised for different ends. The structure of human behavior is such that it has certain components, certain factors that cannot, at least immediately, be deduced from the "behavior" of the computer and that are specifically human. This applies first and foremost to that aspect of activity that relates to motivation and aims.

In the words of Albert Einstein (as quoted by Jean Piaget (1966) at the Psychological Congress in Moscow): *"Comme la psychologie est plus difficile que la physique!"*

References

Ageev, V. Situational variations of speech parameters. In A. A. Leontiev & T. V. Ryabova (Eds.), *Psycholinguistics and the teaching of the Russian language to foreigners.* Moscow: Moscow University Press, 1972. Pp. 180–199.

Anisfeld, M., & Knapp, M. Association synonymity and directionality in false recognition. *Journal of Experimental Psychology*, 1968, 77, 171–179.

Batov V. I. & Kochinov M. M. Effects of motive on word selection in alternative messages. In A. A. Bodalyov, A. V. Darinsky, E. S. Kuzmin, J. P. Volkov, A. A. Stepanov (Eds.), *Communication as object of theoretical and applied researches.* Leningrad: Leningrad Univ. Press, 1973. Pp. 9–10.

Bernshtein, N. A. *Essays on the physiology of movement and the physiology of activity.* Moscow: Medicina, 1966. [In Russian.]

Bloom, L. *Language development, form and function in emerging grammars.* Cambridge, Mass.: MIT Press, 1970.

Braine, M. D. S. On learning the grammatical order of words. *Psychological Review*, 1963, 70, 323–348.

Bzhalava, P. T. *Situation and behavior.* Moscow: Znanie, 1968. [In Russian.]

Carroll, J. B. Process and content in psychology. In R. Glazer *et al.* (Eds.), *Current trends in the description and analysis of behavior.* Pittsburgh: Univ. of Pittsburgh Press, 1958. Pp. 175–200.

Dewey, J. *The reflex arc concept in psychology.* 1896. Cited by Miller *et al.* (1960).

Dingwall, W. O., & Tuniks, G. Government and concord in Russian. A study in developmental psycholinguistics. In B. Kachru, R. B. Lees, T. Malkiel, A. Pietrangeli, & S. Saporta, Eds., *Papers in linguistics in honor of Henri and Renée Kahane.* Urbana: Univ. of Illinois Press, 1973. Pp. 126–184.

Fodor, J. A., & Garrett, M. Some syntactic determinants of sentential complexity. *Perception & Psychophysics* 1967, *2*, 281–296.

Fraisse, P. La psycholinguistique. In J. de Ajuriaguerra, F. Bresson, P. Fraisse, B. Inhelder, P. Oléron. J. Piaget, Eds., *Problèmes de psycholinguistique.* Paris: Presses Universitaires de France, 1963. Pp. 3–5.

Frumkina, R. M., & Vasilevich, A. P. Word frequency in the perception of speech. In A. A. Leontiev & T. V. Ryabova (Eds.), *Questions of speech generation and the teaching of language.* Moscow: Moscow Univ. Press, 1967. Pp. 17–38. [In Russian.]

Goldiamond, J., & Hawkins, W. F. Vexier versuch: the log relationship between word frequency and recognition obtained in the absence of stimulus words. *Journal of Experimental Psychology,* 1958, *56*, 457–463.

Halle, M., & Stevens, K. N. Speech recognition: a model and a program for research. In J. A. Fodor & J. J. Katz (Eds.), *The structure of language: Readings in the philosophy of language.* Englewood Cliffs, N.J.: Prentice-Hall, 1964, pp. 604–612.

Herriot, P. *An introduction to the psychology of language.* London: Methuen, 1970.

Ilyasov, I. I. G. Miller's experiment for testing the psychological significance of the transformational model. In A. A. Leontiev & T. V. Ryabova (Eds.), *Psychology of grammar.* Moscow: Moscow Univ. Press, 1968, pp. 50–66. [In Russian.]

Issenina, E. I. Distinguishing and recognition as a mechanism of phonemic hearing. Unpublished doctoral dissertation, Institute of Psychology, Academy of Pedagogical Sciences, Moscow, 1967. [In Russian.]

Lenneberg, E. H. *Biological foundations of language.* New York: Wiley, 1967.

Leontiev, A. A. *The word in speech activity.* Moscow: Nauka, 1965. [In Russian.]

Leontiev, A. A. *Psycholinguistic units in the generation of speech utterances.* Moscow: Nauka, 1969. [In Russian.]

Leontiev, A. A. Thinking in a foreign language: A psychological and methodological problem. *Inostrannye Jazyki v Shkole,* 1972, *1*, 24–30. [In Russian.]

Leontiev, A. N. *Problems of the development of the psyche.* (2nd ed.) Moscow: Mysl. 1965. [In Russian.]

Leontiev, A. N., & Krinchik, E. P. The processing of information by man in situations requiring a choice. In A. N. Leontiev, V. P. Zinchenko, D. Y. Panov Eds., *Inzhenernaja psihologija.* [*Human engineering.*] Moscow: Moscow Univ. Press, 1964, Pp. 19–64. [In Russian.]

Luria, A. N. *Man's mind and his psychic processes.* Vol. I. Moscow: A.P.N.—R.S.F.S.R., 1963. [In Russian.]

Lushchikhina, I. M. The role of various grammatical transformations in different conditions of speech communication. In A. A. Leontiev & R. M. Frumkina (Eds.), *Proceedings of the second symposium on psycholinguistics.* Moscow: Nauka, 1968. pp. 9–13. [In Russian.]

McNeill, D. Developmental psycholinguistics. In F. Smith & G. A. Miller (Eds.), *The genesis of language: A psycholinguistic approach.* Cambridge, Mass.: MIT Press, 1966. Pp. 15–84.

Manturov, O. V., Solntsev, Y. K., Sorzkin, Y. J., Fedin, N. G. In V. A. Ditkin Ed., *Glossary of Mathematical terms*. Moscow: Prosveshchenie, 1965. [In Russian.]

Mehler, J. (Ed.) *Psycholinguistique et grammaire générative*. Paris: Didier & Larousse, 1969.

Miller, G. A. Some psychological studies of grammar. *American Psychologist*, 1962, *17*, 748–762.

Miller, G. A., Galanter, E. & Pribram, K. H. *Plans and the structure of behavior*. New York: Holt, 1960.

Miller, G. A., & Isard, S. Some perceptual consequences of linguistic rules. *Journal of Verbal Learning and Verbal Behavior*, 1963, *2*, 217–228.

Miller, G. A., & Ojemann McKean, K. A chronometric study of some relations between sentences. *Quarterly Journal of Experimental Psychology*, 1964, *16*, 297–308.

Morton, J. A functional model for memory. In D. A. Norman (Ed.), *Models of human memory*. New York: Academic Press, 1970. Pp. 203–254.

Morton, J. What could possibly be innate? In J. Morton (Ed.), *Biological and social factors in psycholinguistics*. London: Logos Press, 1971. Pp. 82–97.

Moscovici, S. Communication processes and the properties of language. In L. Berkowitz (Ed.), *Advances in experimental social psychology*. Vol. 3. New York: Academic Press, 1967. Pp. 226–270.

Norman, D. A. Memory and decisions. *International Congress of Psychology, 18th, Moscow*, 1966, Symp. *22*, 41–54.

Piaget, J. La psychologie, les relations interdisciplinaires et le système des sciences. *International Congress of Psychology, 18th, Moscow*, 1966.

Rommetveit, R. *Words, meanings and messages*. New York: Academic Press, 1968.

Ryabova, T. V. Mechanism of speech generation on the basis of aphasiological data. In A. A. Leontiev & T. V. Ryabova (Eds.), *Questions of speech generation and language teaching*. Moscow: Moscow Univ. Press, 1967. Pp. 76–94. [In Russian.]

Ryabova, T. V., & Shtern, A. S. Study of grammatical structuralization (based on the results of the analysis of persons suffering from aphasia). In A. A. Leontiev & T. V. Ryabova (Eds.), *The psychology of grammar*. Moscow: Moscow Univ. Press, 1968, Pp. 78–105. [In Russian.]

Sakhamy, L. V. Structure of the significance of the word and the situation. In A. A. Leontiev, A. E. Ivanova, G. U. Andreyeva, E. A. Nozhkin, E. F. Tarasov, A. M. Shakhnarovich, Y. A. Sherkovin, (Eds.), *Proceedings of the fourth all-union symposium on psycholinguistics and the theory of communication*. Moscow: Nauka, 1972. Pp. 141–153. [In Russian.]

Sikorsky, I. A. The development of speech in children. *I. A. Sikorsky, collected works*. Vol. 2. Kiev: 1899. [In Russian.]

Spreen, O., Borkowski, I. G., & Benton, A. L. Auditory word recognition as a function of meaning, abstractness and phonetic structure. *Journal of Verbal Learning and Verbal Behavior*, 1967, *6*, 101–104.

Tannenbaum, P. H., & Williams, F. W. Generation of active and passive sentences as a function of subject and object focus. *Journal of Verbal Learning and Verbal Behavior*, 1968, 7, 246–250.

Tikhomirov, O. K., & Terekhov, V. A. The science of heuristic procedure applied to man. *Voprosy Psihologii*, 1967, *2*, 26–41. [In Russian.]

Vereshchagin, E. M. *The generation of speech, a latent process*. Moscow: Moscow Univ. Press, 1968. [In Russian.]

Voronin, B. F. Psychological model of the mechanism of the generation of mistakes in oral speech in a foreign language. In A. A. Leontiev, T. V. Ryabova Eds., *Problems of the psychology of speech and the psychology of language teaching encountered today*. Moscow: Moscow Univ. Press, 1970. Pp. 37–46. [In Russian.]

Vygotsky, L. S. Thinking and speech. In A. N. Leontiev, A. R. Luria (Eds.), *Selected psychological investigations*. Moscow: A.P.N.—R.S.F.S.R., 1956. Pp. 39–386. [In Russian.]

Wallon, H. *L'évolution psychologique de l'enfant*. Paris: Collin, 1957.

Zhinkin, N. I. Internal codes of language and external codes of speech. In *To honor Roman Jakobson*. The Hague: Mouton, 1967. Pp. 2355–2375. [In Russian.]

Zimnyaya, I. A. The probability factor in speech perception. In V. A. Vassilyev, O. A. Nork, L. P.

Blokhina, B. I. Jlyina, R. K. Potapova, V. S. Sokolova Eds., *Research on language and speech.* Moscow: Moscow State Pedogogical Institute of Foreign Languages, 1971. Pp. 142—145. [In Russian.]

Zinder, L. R. & Shtern, A. S. Factors influencing the recognition of words. In A. A. Leontiev, A. E. Ivanova, G. M. Andreyeva, E. A. Nozhin, E. F. Tarasov, A. M. Shakhnarovich, Y. A. Sherkovin Eds., Proceedings of the fourth all-union symposium on psycholinguistics and the theory of communication. Moscow: Nauka, 1972. Pp. 100—108. [In Russian.]

II. Natural History

The investigation of language from a biological point of view is not entirely new. The focus of attention has changed, however, and instead of looking at animals simply as less perfect creatures than man, whose means of communication are primitive forms of human language, biologists are now making more objective comparisons. In the following section, Nottebohm provides a magnificent review particularly of vocal learning, without committing the common mistake of treating animal communication as if it were a continuous and linear evolutionary series. Jacobson succeeds in bringing to bear some broad neuroembryological concepts to explain what is known about language development. Lecours presents important new data on the formation of myelin in the human nervous system and its possible causative relation to the growth of language learning capacities. Zangwill, finally, discusses the developmental process from the behavioral end, that is, the evidence for the emergence of cerebral dominance, which is so intimately related to the process of physiological differentiation.

5. A Zoologist's View of Some Language Phenomena with Particular Emphasis on Vocal Learning

Fernando Nottebohm

This chapter evaluates some developmental, evolutionary, and neural character-istics of vocal communication in mammals and birds and points to similarities to and differences from human language. The focus of comparison centers on one aspect of language, vocal learning, which then permits a taxonomically broad survey of relevant material. Vocal learning is defined as that type of vocal ontogeny that requires for its normal completion access to auditory information.

Introduction

Language occurs in only one species, man. Yet it is possible to make a case for the heuristic value of comparing vocal behavior in man and animals. My own interests are centered around the evolution of vocal communication and in par-ticular vocal learning, and thus many of the issues broached here revolve around this theme. Vocal learning is defined as that type of vocal ontogeny that requires for its normal completion access to auditory information.

Phenomena of vocal communication in animals are not likely to answer ques-tions about language phenomena in man. But comparisons between the two can prompt us to look at familiar facts in new ways, ask new questions, and gather new kinds of information. Cross-taxonomic comparisons render suspect some of the circular and fruitless "theories" woven around the uniqueness of man and his speech behavior.

The Comparative Analysis of Vocal Communication

Zoologists tend to approach a phenomenon by focusing on its evolutionary aspects. Related and unrelated taxa are compared, and anatomical, physiological, and behavioral characteristics are correlated with particular ways of life. To treat language in this manner presents an immediate problem. If we define language as the typically human set of sounds and rules governing vocal communication, then we can only note its absence in other animals and relate its occurrence to the human way of life. Nothing is predicted, nothing is tested, and of course nothing is learned. Alternatively, we may define the properties of human language so that we can explore their occurrence in other species. The latter approach was pioneered by Hockett (1960) and Marler (1961) and has led to what they call "the logical analysis of animal communication." The most noteworthy conclusion of this approach is that whereas human and animal signals can refer to internal and external events, only humans rearrange the signaling units so as to generate a potentially enormous array of messages. In man the ability to recombine signals so as to generate new meanings is accompanied by a mastery of syntax.

There are of course other differences between the communicatory systems of man and animals, and they also have been discussed by Hockett (1960). Man is able to refer to abstract ideas and to events remote in space and time, whereas most animals communicate about immediate events. Furthermore, human language is "open," so that new circumstances or things can be named, if necessary by creating new terms. Another difference is that all speaking humans can use all language elements. In animals, sex and age classes often have signals restricted to one class, or further restricted to just one class in reproductive condition. There are exceptions to these generalizations. So, for example, the waggle dance of bees is thought to communicate direction and distance to a food source that may be several miles away (von Frisch, 1967), and not all characteristics of human vocal signals are shared by all individuals. Young infants produce sounds characteristic of their age class and do not produce adult words. The physical properties of the vocal tract of newborn infants set a limit to the kinds of sounds it can generate, to the exclusion of many sounds typical of adult speech (Lieberman, Harris, Wolff, & Russell, 1971).

Comparisons between human language and animal communication must take into account vocal characteristics such as intonation, pitch, and amplitude, usually included under "paralanguage," as well as vocalizations such as laughter and crying. Paralanguage may be easy to homologize with animal communication; it conveys information about sex, age, and individual identity much as song is thought to do in many birds. Intonation and amplitude may convey information about the emotional state of the signaler, and this kind of information may be compared with animal sounds associated with play, escape, aggression, and so on.

The male courtship calls or courting songs of many songbirds have a strong resemblance to juvenile stages of song development known as subsong. An example of this can be found in the chaffinch, *Fingilla coelebs* (Marler, 1956a). A female soliciting for copulation produces sounds reminiscent of the food-begging calls of nestlings and fledglings. It is as if pair formation were facilitated by transposing relations to the mood and signals of a younger age, which then barred inter-individual attack and escape. In his classical work on phonological development in children, Roman Jakobson (1941) cites von der Gabelentz (1901) to the effect that "courting lovers quite frequently talk in child language," a lovers' language referred to in some cultures as "sweet talk." The communicatory potential of paralanguage is clearly independent from that of language, as is the age transposition of signals used in courting.

Another aspect of the logical analysis of animal communication is the search for correlations between signal role and signal structure. For example, sound propagation has characteristics likely to influence signal structure. High pitched sounds attenuate in air faster than low pitched ones, and high pitched sounds undergo greater dampening by foliage and other obstacles. It is well known to acousticians that sound sources are located by differences in phase, intensity, and time of arrival at both ears. The head of the listener casts a sound shadow for wavelengths smaller than its diameter, so that the ear on the side opposite to the sound source perceives the sound more faintly. Judgements of differences in time of arrival are facilitated by sounds with many discontinuities. Differences in phase aid in judging sound direction, provided that the wavelengths involved are no smaller than twice the distance between the ears (Stevens & Davis, 1938). Batteau (1967) has demonstrated mathematically that a sound is reflected from the ear pinna into the external auditoty meatus with a scatter of delays characteristic of its incoming angle; this permits monaural sound location without scanning of the head (review in Erulkar, 1972). Both monaural and binaural sound location would be expected to be more accurate with broad frequency spectra than with narrow band pure tones—intensity and time differences could then be determined for a series of simultaneous cues. Research on acoustic location of prey by barn owls (*Tyto alba*) confirms the importance of broad frequency spectra for sound location (Konishi, 1973).

From the preceding comments on the acoustics of sound it is clear that signals requiring easy location and long broadcast distances will have a different structure than signals meant to make location difficult, or used in short-range communication. Marler (1956b) has demonstrated this correlation between structure and function of vocalizations in the signaling systems of many birds. Alarm signals given upon detection of an aerial predator, such as a hawk, are high pitched pure tones that fade in and out; to the human ear such sounds have a truly ventriloquial character. Calls given to mob a perched or ground predator, such as an owl or cat, have an abrupt onset and a broad frequency spectrum and are frequently repeated.

Problems of sound absorption and reflection also prescribe different optimal signals for use in open spaces or forested areas. Morton (1970) has shown that grassland avian species tend to use higher frequencies and frequency modulated fundamentals. Birds living near the forest floor use sustained pure tones averaging some 2 kHz less in frequency than the previous group (see also Chappuis, 1971).

Marler (1967) notes that primates such as baboons, some macaque species, and chimpanzees, which live in open savannahs or on the forest floor, have vocalizations that are graded signals and cannot be categorized easily on the basis of acoustic qualities. In contrast, forest monkeys with predominantly arboreal habits, such as the squirrel and night monkeys, *Saimiri sciureus* (Winter, Ploog, & Latta, 1966) and *Aotus trivirgatus* (Moynihan, 1964), and many species of *Cercopithecus*, produce sounds that can be assigned to discrete spectrographic categories. Marler argues that graded vocal systems are used for short-range communication, between members of the same troop and under circumstances where visual cues are also available. The more arboreal species, with discontinuous vocal repertoires, use some of their calls for long-range communication, to broadcast territorial claims or under conditions where foliage obstructs use of complementary visual signals.

Winter (1969) notes that there probably are two subspecies of squirrel monkey. One, characterized as the "Gothic arch," does indeed have a stereotyped adult repertoire composed of discontinuous categories. The other one, known as the "Roman arch," shows greater group cohesiveness, a greater incidence of agonistic interactions, and a more variable vocal repertoire that includes graded transitions between signal types. Winter (1969) suggests that such signal gradation can best convey agonistic nuances used for intragroup communication. This agrees with Marler's (1967) suggestion that signals used at short range can be more variable. The correlation of signal gradedness and higher incidence of intragroup aggression shows the many variables that must be kept in mind when evaluating the significance of communicatory idiosyncrasies.

Gradedness in a communicatory system can be equated with variability void of communicatory significance, or it can stand for gradedness in the information conveyed. Reporting on the calls of rhesus monkeys, *Macaca mulatta*, Rowell and Hinde (1962) note that "many of their characters—length, pitch, harshness, loudness—are varied according to the exact circumstance in which they are made, and the degree of fear, urgency, etc., which they express. [p. 280]" The theoretical importance of distinguishing between gradedness and variability of vocal repertoires was further stressed by Green (1972). He was able to show that for the entire vocal repertoire of Japanese macaques, *Macaca fuscata*, gradedness in the signal is correlated with gradedness in the context or response elicited, and thus presumably has a communicatory significance.

Language phonemes are in the peculiar situation of constituting a graded system when considered by themselves, yet giving rise to discrete signals when combined into words. Since words, but not phonemes, have external referents, perhaps words ought to be considered as the natural units of communication, and language as a system of discreet signals. It is not known whether the vocalizations of other primates may be composed of subunits comparable to the phonemes of man.

Correlations between the audiospectrographic structure of language spoken by primitive societies and the social and environmental habits of such societies have not been attempted. However, we probably can assume that all existing languages have the potential to serve long- and short-range communicatory needs, a reflection of man's versatility and of the many uses to which language can be put.

Physically, human speech can be described as a low frequency (1–4 kHz) sound with a broad band spectrum and many temporal discontinuities. A search for correlations between signal role and signal structure has been rather unsuccessful in the case of language, though there are some exceptions. In some mountainous areas, vowel sounds prevail when voice is used to communicate over long distances, as in yodeling. Similar conditions are associated with the occurrence of whistled languages described for some pastoralist groups in Mexico, Gomera (Canary Islands), France, and Turkey (Busnel, Moles, & Gilbert, 1962; Busnel, Leroy, Lenneberg, & Moles, 1970; Classe, 1957; Cowan, 1948). In all these cases mountainous terrain with sparse vegetation aids in the amplification and conduction of sound. In other cultures, such as the South African bushmen, living in the open country and under conditions that might have fostered long distance communication, click languages have evolved, which would seem hardly suited for this purpose (Murdock, 1959). Presumably here, as in other savannah-dwelling primates, vocalizations are used predominantly for short-range communication. However, comparisons between culture and environment in humans must take into account historical factors such as invasions, migrations, and cultural exchange accompanying commerce. Furthermore, in many places man has drastically changed his environment. Present day correlations between sounds used and habitat may be accidental.

It is usually acknowledged that in most languages there is a rather arbitrary relationship between the semantic meaning of a word and the sound used to convey it. The words *danger* and *pleasure* bear no iconic relationship to the concepts they represent. Some animals are referred to by names of obvious onomatopoetic origin, such as the European chiffchaff and the North American wood peewee (two songbirds); in other cases there is no such obvious relation, as in *microorganism* and *whale* (Hockett, 1960).

It has been claimed that some language sounds convey phonetic symbolism. Sapir (1929) and S. S. Newman (1933) reported that English-speaking subjects associate high front vowels with smallness, low or back vowels with flatness or large size. Other tests (Holland & Wertheimer, 1964) show that sharp, pointed things are more likely to be associated with *t* or *k* sounds, while soft, smooth things tend to be associated with *l* or *m* sounds. The conventional test pair consists of the artificial words *takete* and *maluma*, to which people in widely different cultures and language groups are supposed to respond in a similar manner. If speakers of unrelated languages, with no prior exposure to English, show the same interpretative biases to meaningless language sounds, this would be an observation of great biological interest. However, careful testing of native speakers of Tamil, Korean, Japanese, and English failed to show consistent cross-cultural correlations between meaningless language sounds and the symbolism they suggest (Taylor & Taylor, 1962). The idea of universal phonetic symbolism remains unsupported by firm evidence.

Possibly the use of language sounds is so encrusted with cultural peculiarities that only very general cross-cultural universals will be found. Zipf (1949) noted that infrequent words are longer and often harder to pronounce, while Eisenberg (1971, p. 156) observes that words containing many consonants are harsh and may tend to be negatively associated. One might have guessed that the pattern of calls used in diverse contexts by the various age and sex groups of our ancestral form would have been accompanied by a sound symbolism still permeating, to some extent, vocal communication in modern man. If such a symbolism persists, it may be more in the way words are spoken than in their neutral phonetic form. Symbolic universals may have to be sought in paralanguage, not in language.

The Role of Learning in Vocal Ontogeny

NONHUMAN MAMMALS

There have been almost no longitudinal studies of vocal development in non-human mammals. An exception to this is an account of vocal development in two species of bat, *Myotis lucifugus* and *Eptesicus fuscus* (Gould, 1971). Individuals of these two species were kept in groups, with no attempt to evaluate the need for auditory models or the importance of auditory feedback.

With few exceptions, possible instances of vocal learning in nonhuman mammals must be inferred from very unsatisfactory evidence, as shown by the following examples. Elephant seals, *Mirounga occidentalis*, established on islands off the California coast, give threat vocalizations directed at other males. These vocalizations differ between colonies, constituting true dialects. The genetic or experiential contribution to these dialects remains unknown (Le Boeuf & Peterson, 1969).

The vocal talents of cetaceans present some intriguing possibilities. So, for example, the humpback whale, *Megaptera novaeangliae*, produces complex songs that last up to 30 min, and individuals repeat their song patterns with considerable accuracy (Payne & McVay, 1971). It is tempting to speculate that these complex performances are learned. However, it is difficult to see how much information might be gathered on the ontogeny of this elaborate behavior. On a less ambitious scale, common dolphins, *Delphinus delphis*, produce whistled patterns characteristic of each individual (Caldwell & Caldwell, 1968). This species has been bred in captivity (see references in Ridgway, 1972) and it should be possible to conduct experiments on its vocal ontogeny.

Among the anthropoid apes there is an intriguing report of vocal duetting in captive siamangs, *Symphalangus syndactilus*. Each pair of siamangs reportedly develops a pattern typical of that pair (Lamprecht, 1970). This skill may well involve auditorily guided vocal learning.

Japanese macaques, *Macaca fuscata*, give a loud call when finding food at sites where they are provisioned. This call differs in each of three different colonies studied in their natural habitat, though it forms part of a continuum shared by the three colonies sampled (Green, 1972). It is not clear whether this is an example of vocal learning or of social facilitation of a shared signal.

It will be obvious from the preceding reports that available suggestions of vocal learning in nonhuman mammals are at best indirect and circumstantial, and may disappear when rigorously tested. Attempts to teach chimpanzees, *Pan troglodytes*, to produce human words have usually failed. In the only successful attempt, the trainer's effort was tremendous and demanded direct manipulation of the pupil's buccal shape (Hayes & Hayes, 1952). This result may be attributed to the very different dimensions of the pharyngeal and buccal cavity in man and chimpanzees (Kelemen, 1958; Lieberman, Klatt, & Wilson, 1969). However, although the dimensions of these cavities need not have hindered chimpanzees from imitating conspecifics, there is no report of imitation or of vocal dialects in this species.

There has been a recent study of the vocalizations produced by rhesus monkeys, *Macaca mulatta*, reared in isolation from their mothers (J. D. Newman & Symmes, 1971). The experimental animals were separated from their mothers shortly after birth and reared without physical contact with other monkeys; however, they could hear the vocalizations of other conspecifics kept in the same colony room. Vocalizations of the social isolates were aberrant in several ways, including temporal organization, structure, and amplitude modulation. These abnormal vocal signals persisted until at least two years of age. Social isolation in this species is known to result in serious emotional disturbance (Harlow & Harlow, 1962). The possibility that the abnormal vocalizations of social isolates reflect such emotional unbalances, rather than a need for vocal learning, should be explored. The crucial experiment of charting vocal development in a deaf-born or early-deafened nonhuman mammal, hopefully circumventing emotional disturbance, still remains to be done. To this extent we are still ignorant about the role of auditory information of vocal development in mammals other than man.

MAN

Vocal development in humans, leading to language learning, requires availability of an auditory model and access to auditory feedback. Knowledge about many aspects of vocal development remains unsatisfactory. Thus, we may speculate about the function of crying, the most prevalent vocalization of early infancy. Crying is associated with many inconveniences experienced by the child. It is claimed that different patterns of crying correspond to different situations, such as hunger or pain (Wasz-Höckert, Lind, Vuorenkoski, Partanen, & Valanne, 1968). Evidence in favor of this view is unconvincing and would fit equally well the idea that the structure and intensity of crying are correlated with degree of stress. Although the adaptive significance of some instances of crying is clear—hunger and injury need prompt attention—it is questionable whether the sole function of this behavior is to secure parental attention. An enormous amount of crying seems triggered by air bubbles in the stomach, by intestinal pain (colic), by the discomfort of teething, by boredom, by impatience, by fatigue. It is hard to imagine that these problems could not have been circumvented, as in other primates, with less audible fuss. In fact, pediatricians acknowledge that a lot of infant crying cannot be ascribed to obvious discomfort (e.g., Spock, 1968). It is argued that the first months of an infant's life are a period of adjustment of his immature nervous and digestive systems to life in the outside world. According to this interpretation, the stresses of adjustment lead to crying (Spock, 1968, p. 183). This argument may correctly represent the immediate causes of crying; it does not address itself to the adaptive significance of the behavior itself.

Parents habituate little to the crying of their offspring and, as a result, spend many a miserable day and night during the infant's first months. We may wonder whether crying is not a device evolved by infants partly at least to discourage reproduction, and thus delay the arrival of the next sibling. A study of the cross-cultural incidence of crying in early infancy would be of interest. Deaf ring doves (*Streptopelia risoria*), unable to hear the food-begging calls of their squabs, soon stop feeding them and start a new clutch sooner than they otherwise would. Maintenance of the parental mood in this case relies at least partly on the auditory stimulation provided by the offspring (Nottebohm & Nottebohm, 1971). Might deaf mothers stop nursing prematurely and have an earlier recurrence of postpartum ovulation?

Conjointly, crying may also be a first and necessary step for the infant's normal vocal development, constituting an initial and generalized type of vocal practice. This idea has a parallel in the vocal development of birds. In chaffinches, as in many other songbirds, the first vocalizations are food-begging calls, the role of which may be likened to the crying of a hungry child. Food-begging calls gradually change into other calls and into rambling versions of song known as subsong, so that there is a developmental continuity leading to the acquisition of a vocal repertoire that is known to be learned by reference to auditory information (Nottebohm, 1972a). As infants develop, their crying patterns also give rise to the first, rudimentary cooing sounds. Crying may play an important role in initiating vocal development.

Lenneberg (1967) has emphasized that stages of vocal development in humans are biologically determined and correspond to maturational stages in the motor development of the organism. So, for example, during its first 6 months, the child produces predominantly vowel sounds known as cooing. This is followed by a period of more structured syllabic sounds known as babbling, which extends approximately to the twelfth month. The characteristics of successive cooing and babbling stages remain ill defined, so that variability between children is unclear. It seems likely that some of the sounds occurring during development are predictable, whereas others vary considerably between individuals.

Lenneberg (1967) reports that congenitally deaf children produce cooing and babbling sounds comparable to those of hearing age-mates. However, whereas hearing children tend to produce sequences including a variety of sounds, the babbling of deaf infants is more monotonous. In agreement with this observation is Webster's (1969) finding that 6-month-old infants stimulated with either vowel or consonant-vowel stimuli reduce their output of same-type sounds. If auditory feedback from their own vocalizations has a similar effect, it could be an important influence promoting varied babbling repertoires in hearing children.

The role of early vocal practice and of reinforcement remains controversial. Lenneberg (1967) argues that cooing and babbling contribute relatively little to vocal development. His strongest evidence seems to come from the case of a 14-month-old child who had been tracheotomized for 6 months, so that air flow bypassed the larynx. According to Lenneberg (1967) "A day after the tube had been removed and the opening closed the child produced the babbling sounds typical of the age. No practice or experience with hearing his own vocalizations was required [p. 140]." This observation seems inconclusive. Interindividual variability in vocal development makes it difficult to predict what would be "normal" vocalization in any one child at a particular age.

Age of onset of cultural vocal differences can be used to uncover the earliest effects of social reinforcement on some sound types. According to Nakazima (1962), after the period of repetitive babbling, children 9- to 12-months-old and not yet producing words frequently use intonations as if they were in a conversation. At this time sound spectrograms begin for the first time to allow differentiation of infants reared in Japanese and American milieux. J. Mehler (1971, p. 163) claims that as early as 6 months there are differences in the intonation of sounds produced by children of English families in the United States and Argentina. It is of interest that the sounds and intonation are abstracted from adult language even at a time when children do not yet imitate words.

Independently of what has been argued up to here, it seems possible that crying, cooing, and babbling play a role in the proprioceptive mapping of vocal output. Hemispheric representation of vocal skill may commence as a consequence of the sensory-motor experience of early vocal stages, so that experience of these stages may be a requisite for the normal development of a speech area.

Another aspect of language development has to do with the units that the young child perceives as meaningful language components. Several workers report that alphabetic units or phonemes may be abstractions unnatural to the language learning process (Liberman, Cooper, Shankweiler, & Studdert-Kennedy, 1967; Savin & Bever, 1970). Native American children who find it hard to master the English alphabet, with consequent reading difficulties, soon become proficient at reading English represented by Chinese characters (Rozin, Poritsky, & Sotsky, 1971). In Chinese there is a closer correspondence between the representation of the sound and of the semantic units, both corresponding to the word or morpheme. However, phonemic differences obviously do not go unnoticed to the ear, even when the listeners are very young infants. Eimas, Siqueland, Juszyk, and Vigorito (1971) have shown that month-old babies presented with a series of electronically generated sounds that are part of a continuum including the phonemes *p* and *d* treat these stimuli as a discontinuous set, much as adults do when recognizing the sounds accompanying the letters *p* and *d*. In this manner the young child shows himself predisposed to classify sounds according to distinctions basic to the phonologic structure of adult language (see also Liberman, 1957; Mattingly, Liberman, Syrdal, & Halwes, 1971).

At about 12 months of age children begin to master isolated words, and these words are predominantly used to name familiar objects or persons. Commencing at about age 2, the child experiments with combinations of words and a very rudimentary syntax. After 3-years-old with a growing vocabulary, syntactic usage gradually approximates that of adults (Lenneberg, 1967). Interestingly, children of age $2\frac{1}{2}$ use many syntactical and grammatical constructions that are incorrect by adult standards and that reveal a tendency to generalize beyond actual examples observed in adults. This evidence has been used to suggest that the child does not restrict himself to a gradual mastery of available models, but rather brings to the learning task predispositions that impose on the learning process rules that are comparable only in a general sense to those of adult language into which, via learning, they develop (Chomsky, 1967, 1968). Church (1971) points out that the semantic adequacy of the infant's evolving language may contribute to his temporary disregard of the more complex or correct syntax and grammar of adult language. According to this view, word combinations are determined by an understanding based on experience of their individual semantic roles, of what words can "do," an interpretation which, of course, is at variance with Chomsky's idea of a basic a priori language scheme.

BIRDS

This review of vocal development started with nonhuman mammals to emphasize how little we know about the vocal development of species other than man. It became clear, too, that few mammals are likely to acquire their vocal repertoire by reference to auditory models. Attention was then focused on humans to note some intriguing problem areas. Yet it is only when we come to birds that we find such great interspecific variability in vocal skills that we can explore some of the more elusive questions about the ontogeny and evolution of vocal learning. *Vocal learning* as used here refers to the influence of auditory information, including feedback, on vocal development.

The contribution of auditory feedback to vocal ontogeny can be tested by removal of both cochleas, which renders a bird chronically deaf. The occurrence of imitation as a normal component of vocal ontogeny can be tested by rearing hearing individuals in auditory isolation (see review in Konishi & Nottebohm, 1969). According to the importance of vocal imitation and auditory feedback, avian vocal ontogenies can be arranged in four groups.

1. *Conspecific auditory model and auditory feedback not necessary.* Domestic chicks (*Gallus domesticus*) hatched in an incubator and deafened on their first day after hatching develop a normal adult vocal repertoire (Konishi, 1963). Ring doves deafened at 5 days after hatching also develop normal vocalizations (Nottebohm & Nottebohm, 1971). When doves are foster-reared by parents of a different species, their vocalizations are not influenced by this misleading model (Lade & Thorpe, 1964; Whitman, 1919). Normal calls are also reported for turkeys, *Meleagris gallopavo*, deafened soon after hatching (Schleidt, 1964).

2. *Conspecific auditory model not necessary: Auditory feedback important but not indispensable for many normal traits of song.* Canaries, *Serinus canaria,* develop normal song when hand-reared from an early nestling stage (Metfessel, 1935; Poulsen, 1959). When canaries are hatched in chambers exposed to 100 dB of white noise, and then deafened at 1 month of age by removal of both cochleas, they are deprived of auditory feedback over the entire span of their vocal development. The song they produce as adults includes highly aberrant screeches and hisses, as well as the more typical trilled phrases. The song of these deaf birds resembles that of intact adults in that it includes a succession of distinct phrase types as well as many notes of normal structure and tonality. In this species, auditory feedback is necessary for the elimination of aberrant sounds and for the generation of large song repertoires (Marler, Konishi, Lutjen, & Waser, 1973; Marler, unpublished observations).

3. *Conspecific auditory model not indispensable, but auditory feedback necessary for normal song development.* Song sparrows, *Melospiza melodia,* hatched and reared by canary foster parents and prevented from hearing conspecifics, develop some songs of fairly normal wild-type quality and others that can be recognized as abnormal (Mulligan, 1966; D. E. Kroodsma, unpublished observations). Song sparrows deafened as juveniles develop a hoarse song totally lacking the structure of the wild-type pattern (Mulligan, 1966). Thus song sparrows are more dependent than canaries on auditory models and feedback for normal vocal development. However, both canaries and song sparrows are able to imitate the song of other conspecifics, and in this sense are facultative mimics (Poulsen, 1959; Mulligan, 1966).

4. *Conspecific auditory model and auditory feedback are indispensable.* In this group of birds, development of wild-type song is fully dependent on exposure to environmental sources. Chaffinches, eastern and western meadowlarks (*Sturnella magna* and *S. neglecta*), white-crowned sparrows (*Zonotrichia leucophrys*), cardinals (*Richmondena cardinalis*) and zebra finches (*Taeniopygia guttata*), hand-reared in auditory isolation from an early nestling age, produce abnormal song lacking the detailed patterns of wild conspecifics (Immelmann, 1969; Lanyon, 1957; Lemon & Scott, 1966; Marler & Tamura, 1964; Poulsen, 1951; Thorpe, 1954, 1958). The song of white-crowned sparrows, chaffinches, and cardinals deafened before onset of song is even more aberrant than that of their hand-reared counterparts (Dittus & Lemon, 1970; Konishi, 1965; Nottebohm, 1967, 1968). Whereas the entire vocal repertoire of chaffinches deafened at an early age is abnormal (Nottebohm, 1967, 1972a), the calls of adult cardinals also deafened as juveniles are no different from those of wild adults (Dittus & Lemon, 1970).

For the sake of simplicity it is tempting to attribute the effects of deafness on vocal development in birds to a loss of indispensable auditory information. If each stage of vocal development depends on an integration of motor, proprioceptive, and auditory information generated by preceding stages, then loss of hearing would disrupt this developmental interaction. But deafening may also bring about endocrine and motivational changes. Song development in chaffinches requires the presence of testosterone. Deaf chaffinches tend to be reluctant songsters, and their rate of singing will increase if they are implanted with exogenous testosterone. Thus one could argue that deafening influences song development by depressing testosterone levels. Other data do not support this interpretation. A male chaffinch castrated before it has ever sung, implanted with exogenous testosterone and exposed to normal song, develops normal wild-type song. Young male chaffinches deafened at the same age and also implanted with testosterone develop highly aberrant songs. Thus, given similar testosterone levels, chaffinches deafened before the onset of song develop abnormal song, whereas hearing birds develop normal song (Nottebohm, 1967, 1968, 1969a). In this case, then, interdiction of auditory feedback seems to have a direct effect on vocal development.

The effect of deafening on frequency of singing varies between species. According to Konishi (1964), loss of hearing has no appreciable effect upon frequency of singing in Oregon juncos, *Junco oreganus*, and the effect is small in ring doves (Nottebohm & Nottebohm, 1971). Surgically devocalized male budgerigars, *Melopsittacus undulatus*, undergo gonadal regression. Brockway (1967) attributes this effect to the loss of self-generated auditory stimulation; these birds could hear other sham-operated males, which retained their breeding gonadal condition and the corresponding vocal repertoire. Though the interpretation of this latter experiment is arguable, it seems likely that the relation between auditory stimulation and vocal behavior may in some cases be rather complex.

Access to an auditory model could have a direct effect on vocal output; alternatively, the auditory model could be acquired as a memory or template, then used to match the auditory feedback generated by the developing vocal patterns. Konishi (1965) has shown that the latter interpretation is the correct one. White-crowned sparrows exposed to a conspecific song model during their first two months of life, and then kept in auditory isolation, will reproduce the external model as they develop their song the following spring. If such birds are deafened before they have converted the *auditory* model into an output pattern, their song will be no different from that of conspecifics hand-reared in auditory isolation and deafened at the same age.

In contrast with the previous findings, predeafening *vocal* experience does affect the quality of adult song. The quality of songs developed by chaffinches deafened at various ages before they acquired stable adult song is correlated with the nature of their predeafening vocal experience, though not all of this experience is retained. Even at a time when a chaffinch has almost fully achieved the stable pattern of adult song, induced deafness will be followed by a partial loss of the vocal skill that had been acquired (Nottebohm, 1967, 1968). After the song of a white-crowned sparrow or chaffinch has reached the final adult pattern, a process known as "crystallization," loss of hearing does not hinder accurate reproduction of that same pattern in future years (review in Konishi & Nottebohm, 1969). Two broad stages may therefore be identified in the vocal ontogeny of chaffinches and white-crowned sparrows: In the developmental stage, singing is gradually shaped via the integration of vocal output and auditory feedback, until the details of an acquired auditory model are matched; following crystallization of this vocal development, a stable efferent pattern can continue to function independently of auditory feedback. In still another songbird, the cardinal, *Richmondena cardinalis*, loss of hearing after song crystallization leads to a drastic deterioration of song patterns (Dittus & Lemon, 1970). Eventually it is hoped that it will be possible to relate differences in the postdeafening retention of song to social peculiarities typical of each species.

Predispositions Brought to the Task of Vocal Learning

TIMING

Marler (in press) points out that when a developmental process relies heavily on learning from external sources, the *timing* and *nature* of what is learned are rarely left to chance.

Song learning in birds does not occur at all ages, nor is it a simple process. First a sound model must be acquired as an auditory memory. Then comes the process of altering vocal output until the auditory feedback it generates matches the acquired model. These two aspects of vocal learning may be completely separated in time, as in the white-crowned sparrow (Marler, 1970b; Marler & Tamura, 1964) or they may show considerable overlap, as in the chaffinch (Thorpe, 1958) and the zebra finch (Immelmann, 1969).

The onset of the critical period for model learning needs further study. Zebra finches develop their song from their fortieth to their eightieth post-hatching day. By the end of this period they produce a close replica of the song of their father or foster father. The model to be reproduced is not acquired all at once. Males isolated before their fortieth post-hatching day develop a song containing *some* of the song elements of the parental model as well as other novel sounds; otherwise their song differs from the model in length, rhythm, number, and sequence of elements. Males isolated between the fortieth and the sixty-sixth post-hatching day develop a song that consists solely of song elements of the parental model, but these elements are not delivered in the same order or in songs of the same length as the model. It is only when male zebra finches are separated from their father after the eightieth post-hatching day that they develop a song identical in all aspects to that of their father (Immelmann, 1969). These observations pose a problem. Are some characters of the model acquired at a particular developmental stage, or does the accuracy of model learning merely reflect the total period of exposure to it? Exact replication of the model may be possible only when tutoring and motor song development overlap in time. Tutoring after song has crystallized into the adult form has no further effect.

We may wonder whether the early abstraction of some traits of a vocal model is not of widespread occurrence among birds that learn their song by reference to external cues. This is an important methodological question. It has been theorized that birds taken from the nest during their first week and subsequently reared in auditory isolation produce an "isolate" type of song that owes little to external sources (e.g., Thorpe, 1958). Unfortunately, it is not known at what age young altricial birds start hearing the frequencies of adult song. The earliest effect of song tutoring on species such as the chaffinch and white-crowned sparrow remains undetermined.

Male chaffinches acquire their adult song during the first 10 months of a potential lifespan of 5 or more years (Thorpe, 1958). After song is established in its final stereotyped pattern, it will not change in subsequent years nor will new themes be added to the repertoire. We know that this is not strictly age dependent in the chaffinch. If onset of song, which depends on testosterone levels (Collard & Grevendal, 1946), is delayed by castration, the termination of the critical period for song learning is postponed. A 2-year-old bird that has had no singing experience, under the influence of testosterone, will develop a good imitation of a tutor model (Nottebohm, 1969a). It is not known whether the end of song learning in this species is determined by experiential or hormonal factors.

In the white-crowned sparrow the end of the critical period for model acquisition occurs approximately 50 days after hatching. Motor learning of song takes place between the eighth and tenth months of life. In this case vocal learning cannot be invoked as the immediate cause for the observed end of the critical period for model acquisition (Marler, 1970b).

A loss of the ability to acquire new vocalizations with increasing age is not an inescapable limitation of avian vocal systems. Oregon juncos, *Junco oreganus*, add new song themes to their repertoire in successive years (Marler, Kreith, & Tamura, 1962). A grey African parrot, *Psittacus erithacus*, will learn new imitations even after it is 20 years old (personal observation). Some cardueline birds modify their calls in successive years so as to match those of their mate or members of a flock (Mundinger, 1970).

Language learning in humans also has its critical periods. It is commonly acknowledged that second language learning is difficult after puberty (e.g., Lenneberg, 1967, Chapter 4). The words and grammar of the second language may be mastered, yet the "foreign" accent is difficult to overcome. It is as if the repertoire of sounds available were determined at an earlier age. Subsequent language learning has to make do with that repertoire. Interestingly enough, reduction of plasticity to acquire new language habits may be to some extent independent of the nature of preceding vocal experience. Onset of speech is delayed in mongoloids. Subsequent progress in language development is very slow and is recorded only in children younger than 14-years old (Lenneberg, Nichols, & Rosenberger, 1964). It seems possible that reduction of language plasticity in humans results from hormonal changes. It should be interesting to explore cases of hormonal disorders that extend the prepuberal condition. Would such individuals retain an ability to acquire new language sounds?

Other evidence in humans also points to a critical period for language learning.

In adults, aphasia results from lesioning the speech area of the dominant hemisphere (see review in Penfield & Roberts, 1959). A similar lesion in childhood does not have a permanent effect on language because the two hemispheres are not yet irreversibly specialized for function. A review of language recovery after brain lesion at different ages leads Lenneberg (1967, Chapter 4) to conclude that language behavior can be taken over by the subordinate hemisphere between the ages of 2—13, with an ever worsening prognosis thereafter.

The study of acquired deafness during childhood and in later life offers still another insight into the importance of age in language acquisition. Children lacking the auditory experience that accompanies language learning after age 2 find it difficult to benefit from language education in schools for the deaf. In contrast, children who become deaf after onset of speech habits, and who have had the accompanying auditory experience for a period as short as 1 year, respond much better to later language training. Thus, whereas "the prognosis for recovery from aphasia gets worse and worse with advancing age after ten, the prognosis for speech habilitation in the deaf improves directly with the advance of age at onset of the disorder [Lenneberg, 1967, p. 157]."

NATURE OF MODEL

Vocal imitation can be a very selective process. Chaffinches and white-crowned sparrows, which learn their song by imitating conspecific models, ignore the song of other species with which they may be tutored (Marler & Tamura, 1964; Thorpe, 1958). The developmental basis of such a preference remains unclear. In other cases, as in the zebra finch previously discussed, and in the bullfinch, *Pyrrhula pyrrhula* (Nicolai, 1956), imitation is restricted to parental models, which under normal circumstances also ensures conspecific adequacy. In still another group of birds, imitation includes the sounds of other species. The occurrence and significance of these auditory preferences are discussed in detail elsewhere (Marler, 1970b; Nottebohm, 1972b; Thorpe, 1958).

There are, of course, limitations to what we may be able to learn about language ontogeny. So, for example, it is not possible to rear infants under controlled auditory conditions so that they receive equal exposure to the sounds of humans and of another species, such as macaques or chimpanzees, without any intervening social cues. Would conspecific vocalizations be recognized and preferentially imitated?

The successive stages of vocal development are probably also part of the predispositions that each species brings to the learning task. Examples of this are the cooing and babbling of humans, and the various developmental stages of subsong that precede the onset of full song in birds. Subsong can be quite structured and typical of each species, as exemplified by the chaffinch (Nottebohm, 1972a). This suggests that learning of the end patterns, whether language in humans or song and calls in birds, is not an uncharted process of trial and error. Rather, it may consist of a series of preprogrammed learning excercises that facilitate the most economical acquisition of external models. This interpretation has not yet been tested. It is known, though, that chaffinches deafened before the onset of complex subsong produce more aberrant song patterns than chaffinches deafened after they have produced complex subsong (Nottebohm, 1968). From this we may extrapolate that subsong is an integral part of the song learning process.

The Origins of Vocal Learning

The emergence of vocal learning in humans, leading to language, has attracted much interest. A serious appraisal of this material is in order not only because of its intrinsic interest, but because views on language evolution are likely to bias the study of the physiological substrates of vocal learning in man.

VOCAL COMMUNICATION IN MAN'S ANCESTORS

It has been theorized that tool usage and language development were associated in the emergence of the human way of life. Yet, man and preman have not been unique in the use of tools. Chimpanzees, *Pan troglodytes*, have developed a rudimentary kind of tool usage that enables them to catch termites at termite mounds. Chimpanzees have also been observed introducing a chewed mass of leaves in water-filled cavities that are too narrow for direct drinking. After the manufactured "sponge" imbibes water, it is transferred to the mouth, thus quenching the animal's thirst (Goodall, 1964). Struhsaker and Hunkeler (1971) have evidence that chimpanzees use sticks and stones to crack open nuts placed for this purpose over another hard surface. Washburn (1969) acknowledges that for the more rudimentary kind of tool making, language may not be necessary, since the skill involved could be easily learned by copying. The same author suggests that the supreme adaptive value of human language lies in its ability to name something in the environment: "It appears that the origin of language is rooted in specific interest in environmental items that comes in after tool-use, and so it is the skill in tool-use that is also related ultimately to language [p. 179]." Marler (1967) also sees tool-use as affecting the development of language in an indirect manner. "Increase in the subdivision of labor in early human society, such that members of the same sex and age class might assume different roles, and the need for the signaler to select respondents among the array of possibilities, would create a need for dramatic increase in signal diversity [p. 774]." Etkin (1964) also emphasizes division of labor, so that differentiation of sexes in a hunting society led to their frequent temporal separation, stating: "A selection pressure is therefore present to permit the use of symbols in communication of experiences that had occurred in the absence of the partner. At the same time the development of such a mentality is likewise favored by the advantages of tool use in hunting [p. 85]."

Pfeiffer (1969) believes that the visual apparatus of primates led to a steady increase in the complexity of the perceived world. This perceived complexity was carried one step further by the manipulative adroitness of the hominid hand and by tool manufacture and use. These developments set the stage for the emergence of language. Pfeiffer speculates that the vocal innovators were children at play. "New symbolic activities which developed during play were probably accompanied by new symbolic vocalizations [p. 403]." Natural selection would then have favored detaching utterances from their connections with intense emotion and the present, though the reasons why this detachment would have survival value in children at play are not clear. Pfeiffer suggests that this change in vocal behavior was gradually retained by adults, by individuals living in a complex world and society in which communication about the past and the future and about things present and absent had selective advantage. In this sense, vocal evolution favored the emergence of a neotenous trait.

Another theory of tool-related emergence of language is offered by Diamond (1959). In this instance, gasping sounds "were uttered involuntarily in the course of a strenous effort of the arm. Being phonetically different from other human cries, and normally accompanying such effort, they were associated with it in the mind, and were uttered by a man seeking such assistance from his fellows, together with a gesture mimicking the desired action [p. 258]." Presumably in time, sound and gesture became independent. The crux of this argument lies in the need for new sounds to coordinate communal effort. Diamond acknowledges that many years earlier Alexander Murray (1823) had outlined a similar view with even greater detail.

According to the onomatopoeic theory of language, speech originated in the imitation of natural sounds, which then served to name animals and natural events. This theory struck Darwin (1871) as plausible: "May not some unusually wise ape-like animal have imitated the growl of a beast of prey, and thus told his fellow monkeys the nature of the expected danger? This would have been a first step in the formation of a language [p. 85]." Another idea rooted in Darwinian thought was advanced by Paget (1930), who posited that "gestures which were previously made by hand, were unconciously copied by movements or positions of the mouth, tongue, or lips [p. 132]." Then, "The great discovery was made that if, while making a gesture with the tongue and lips, air was blown through the oral or nasal cavities, the gesture became audible as a whispered speech sound [p. 133]." In time, out of this arose "A new system of conventional gesture of the organs of articulation from which all human speech took its origin [p. 134]."

The Danish linguist Jespersen (1922) imagined the first appearance of language in the form of song. "Language was born in the courting days of mankind; the first utterance of speech I fancy to myself like something between the nightly love lyrics of puss upon the tiles and melodious love songs of the nightingale [p. 434]." Speech then differentiated out of such a musical beginning. To this Diamond (1959) comments that "Every human being of normal mental powers can speak, but a vast number are incapable of song. As for courtship, if we are to judge from the habits of the bulk of mankind it has always been a singularly silent occupation [p. 272]." Jespersen's ideas probably reflected those of Darwin (1871) in the third chapter of the *Descent of Man.* Darwin suggested that man's progenitor "first used his voice in producing true musical cadences. . . . [p. 84]" an ability which was later used in an onomatopoeic manner.

Hockett and Ascher (1964) suggest a very specific series of events that they believe led to vocal learning. They see our early ancestors traversing a stage where bipedal locomotion freed the hand to carry food and tools. They go on to speculate: "What were the hominids to do with their mouths rendered thus relatively idle except when they were eating? The answer is: they chattered [p. 141]." According to Hockett and Ascher (1964), these chattering protohominids were hunters, and this way of life favored an increase in flexibility of vocal–auditory communication. A system of calls denoting discovery of food, detection of danger, and so on was overly restrictive. The protohominid met this problem by blending the old calls in various combinations so as to produce new signals. Hockett and Ascher conclude: "Indeed, we really have to believe that this was what happened, because the phenomenon of blending is the only logically possible way in which a closed system can develop towards an open one [p. 142]." Whereas formerly there was only a simple call category for a host of similar or related situations, and different calls for different categories of situation, now new calls resulting from the blending of old ones could meet each new situation. This, then, is how these authors envisage the transition between a genetically restricted system of vocal communication and an open, flexible, vocal repertoire.

These speculations on *why* and *how* language emerged are strictly *ad hoc* and applicable only to *Homo* or its immediate ancestors. It is impossible to evaluate them by comparison with phenomena observed in other species. None of these authors emphasizes the difficulties to be met as genetic control over the composition of the vocal repertoire is replaced by vocal learning. Yet, it is possible to separate in our thinking the emergence of vocal learning and the emergence of human language. As we shall see, relaxation of genetic control over vocal development can be achieved in the absence of a need to convey radically new messages. Once the development of vocal patterning shifted from a rigid ontogeny to one incorporating environmental models, then the stage may have been set for further elaboration of this signaling system into a plastic language such as we find in present-day man.

Individuals pioneering vocal learning must have left more offspring than individuals using the more constrained species-typical set of signals. Otherwise, vocal learning would not become established as a species characteristic. Since an innovation as drastic and complex as vocal learning could not have happened in one step, we must wonder about this trait's sufficient quantum of progression from one generation to the next.

It was pointed out earlier that the capacity to use a meaningful syntax is typical of man and does not occur in other natural communication systems. Whether syntactic use of vocal signals evolved before, after, or simultaneously with vocal learning we may never know.

CORRELATES OF VOCAL LEARNING IN BIRDS

Vocal learning is known to occur in songbirds, order Passeriformes, and in parrots, Psittaciformes. It probably also occurs in at least one hummingbird species, Apodiformes, and possibly in a toucanet, Piciformes (Snow, 1968; Wagner, 1944; Wiley, 1971). Vocal imitation is not known to occur in the remaining orders of birds. In those groups genetic factors dictating vocal ontogeny may predominate to the exclusion of auditory experience. Domestic fowl, order Galliformes, and ring doves, Columbiformes, are examples of this more rigid kind of vocal ontogeny.

Avian taxonomists consider Galliformes and Columbiformes closer in morphology, and possibly behavior, to the ancestral avian stock than groups such as Passeriformes, hummingbirds, parrots, and toucanets. Since the latter four groups are phylogenetically unrelated, vocal learning must have developed *de novo* in each of them. The alternative hypothesis, that vocal learning was discarded by the remaining 24 orders of birds, is highly improbable. Vocal development in birds thus shows a phylogenetic trend from auditory-independent strategies to more open and environmentally dependent vocal ontogenies.

Vocal learning is strongly correlated with occurrence of dialects and complex song repertoires. From this it will be argued that most instances of vocal learning in birds can probably be interpreted as subserving two basic purposes: (1) mating like with like, and (2) wooing, stimulating, and retaining a partner.

Mating like with like requires more than getting together two members of the same species and opposite sex. It probably also involves getting together members of a particular breeding population, born and reared under similar circumstances and thereby exposed to similar selective pressures. Vocal dialects can probably help achieve this, as first suggested by Marler and Tamura (1962). It is necessary to assume that female birds develop a preference for the song dialect of the area where they are born, and that this preference is revealed in their choice of partner. Males, in turn, must learn to sing the dialect of their birth area.

In *Zonotrichia leucophrys*, song preferences are acquired early in life (Marler, 1970b; Marler & Tamura, 1964). In *Z. capensis*, geographic discontinuities in dialect pattern correspond to life-zone interphases (Nottebohm, 1969b and in press; Nottebohm & Nottebohm, in press). Both kinds of evidence are in agreement with the proposed notion that vocal differences help to prevent panmixia between locally adapted populations. However, a role of song dialects in mating preferences must still be demonstrated. It is possible that dialects have evolved in different species in response to different selective pressures.

Selective factors favoring the emergence of vocal dialects would also favor vocal learning. Genetically determined vocal differences in neighboring populations of the same subspecies would be difficult to maintain. Any gene flow between such populations would tend to eliminate vocal differences. This would weaken the effectiveness of dialect roles, and certainly would make it impossible for them to serve as barriers to interbreeding between locally adapted populations. In contrast, dialects acquired as vocal traditions would persist even in the presence of genetic variability.

The second proposed role of vocal learning, that of maximally stimulating females, is derived from the following observations. Species that do not learn their song by reference to auditory models tend to have simple, monotonous songs and a paucity of song themes. In contrast to this, species that learn their song may have enormous repertoires, such as is the case of the Australian lyre bird, *Menura superba*, the European robin, *Erithacus rubecula*, the mistle thrush, *Turdus viscivorus*, the European blackbird, *Turdus merula*, and the New World mockingbird, *Mimus polyglottos*. Such complex repertoires exceed by far the needs for specific and individual recognition. In these species the apparently redundant complexity of song may serve a stimulatory role.

Bird song is credited with attracting females and repelling trespassing males (see review in Nottebohm, 1972b, 1975). A complex, varying signal may preclude habituation. Territorial claims may be thus more successfully stated, the bird with the more complex song succeeding in claiming a larger or better breeding territory. Female attraction also might be served by a more varied song, so that pairing occurs earlier, eggs are laid sooner, and possibly more clutches and offspring are reared per season. Complex song may also be an indicator of a male's fitness, so that females choosing that bird as a mate are likely to leave more offspring. Whether larger than average singing repertoires emerged because of their intrinsic stimulatory potency or because of their iconic value, selection for this trait would soon lead to its hypertrophy.

Genetically ruled vocal ontogenies leading to highly predictable vocal reper-toires as in Columbiformes and Galliformes probably cannot generate vocal complexity beyond a point. It is a matter of how much information relevant to complex species-specific motor patterning can be reliably coded into the genome. We can only guess what this limit of complexity might be. Once such a threshold is reached, pressures for further increase in vocal complexity would likely lead to a relaxation of rigid motor ontogenies, and to their replacement by more innova-tive strategies, such as could lead to improvisation of complex song repertoires. Improvisation, of course, must also follow genetic guidelines if its end product is to remain species-specific; however, such guidelines need not include motor pro-grams for each sound or song generated. A well-described example of song improvisation is that of the Oregon junco (Marler et al., 1962).

In species such as the bullfinch and zebra finch, vocal learning is expressed by male offspring imitating the song of their father (Immelmann, 1969; Nicolai, 1959). The advantages of such a system remain speculative. Individuals of opposite sex could use filial song learning to recognize familial bonds and inhibit dangerous levels of inbreeding. Among males, shared song would indicate close genetic affinity and could serve to foster agonistic tolerance.

In the shama bird, *Copsychus malabaricus*, bou bou shrike, *Laniarius aethiopicus*, and several cardueline finches, learned vocal repertoires common to members of a pair may facilitate mutual recognition at a distance (Gwinner & Kneutgen, 1962;

Mundinger, 1970; Thorpe, 1972; Thorpe & North, 1965). However, vocal recognition of parents or of mate is achieved by several seabird species that have simple calls, in the absence of any evidence of vocal learning (e.g., Tschanz, 1968; White, 1971).

Marler (1970b) and Nottebohm (1972b) have noted that vocal learning occurs in some groups that have undergone very prolific speciation. In these groups vocal learning may have been prompted by intense speciation, as a way for each species to gain rapid vocal identity. Alternatively, speciation may have been particularly intense in groups that had evolved vocal learning. In the first of these two alternatives, given several sympatric species lacking an easily recognizable vocal identity, with the attendant danger of hybridization, vocal learning by *some* species should have sufficed to eliminate ambiguities in species recognition among the remaining ones. Since vocal learning has very broad representation in those groups where it occurs, it seems more likely that it preceded intense speciation. Future research should help test this view.

Thus, an evaluation of the avian literature suggests that maximal female stimulation and breeding success and the advantages of vocal dialects have been primary causes favoring vocal learning in birds. Territorial defense, familial recognition, individual recognition, and intense speciation may also have influenced the evolutionary course of this phenomenon. With the exception of territorial defense and individual recognition, females would have been the sole agents of selection in that their choice of mate, based upon vocalizations, determined their breeding success and fitness of their progeny.

It also seems clear that a shift toward plastic vocal development in birds did occur even though the nature of the message conveyed by the vocalizations themselves was not radically new, namely, the presence of a particular male of a particular species, in possession of a territory and in breeding condition; in addition, dialects would also furnish information on the local affiliation of a bird.

STAGES LEADING TO VOCAL LEARNING

With the exception of oilbirds, *Steatornis caripensis*, and swiftlets, *Collocalia sp.* (Griffin, 1953; Medway, 1959), which produce sounds to echo-locate objects in the dark, vocalization in birds seems to have evolved for purposes of communication. Consequently, vocal learning must have evolved from a genetically prescribed motor ontogeny in such a way that all intervening stages served an adaptive communicatory function. This need not have been difficult. Even among species known or presumed not to learn their song and calls, such as domestic fowl and ducks, *Anas platyrrhynchos*, conspecific vocalizations are recognized by auditorily naive individuals (Gottlieb, 1971). In these cases selective responsiveness presupposes the occurrence of an internal auditory model or template (Marler, 1970a; Marler & Tamura, 1964). This very auditory template could then have provided a reference point for song learning, so that even as the variety of the song repertoire increased, it still reflected the species specific parameters of the template.

All birds that rely on vocal learning as a strategy for vocal development can also imitate at least other conspecifics. Thus we may wonder which came first: improvisation or vocal imitation. Birds that improvise their song repertoire may store it as an auditory memory that is "imitated" in future renderings, until crystallization of the song repertoire is achieved. To the extent that other conspecifics develop patterns acceptable to the species' template, the imitation of self-generated themes and of those produced by other conspecifics may be an almost inevitable result of vocal learning. Thus, the primacy of vocal improvisation or of vocal imitation need not be an arguable point; both may have arisen together. If this is so, then vocal ontogenies strictly dependent on imitation of other individuals, such as those leading to the acquisition of dialects, may be considered as specialized, secondary adaptations.

Why Did Not Other Primates Learn to Speak?

It has been argued that the absence of vocal imitation in nonhuman primates is attributable to their lack of an "arcuate bundle," which in the human brain connects the posterosuperior part of the temporal lobe with the lateral frontal region. Lesion of the arcuate bundle in humans supposedly impairs the ability to reproduce sounds heard (Konorski, 1963; also quoted in Thorpe, 1967). However, as pointed out by Geschwind (1967, pp. 17–18), a fiber tract comparable to the arcuate bundle of humans does in fact occur in other primates. Other authors have attributed the failure of chimpanzees to imitate human sounds to physical restrictions imposed by the vocal apparatus (Kelemen, 1958; Lieberman et al., 1969). However, the claim has not been made that the latter condition bars imitation of conspecific sounds.

Bronowski and Bellugi (1970) argue that "human language expresses a specifically human way of analyzing our experience of the external world [p. 673]." Thus, it is the human idiosyncrasy of analysis and synthesis that pervades language learning and makes it possible. The difficulty with such an interpretation is that it leaves much room for ambiguity. It does not set a clear limit to the speech talents that various nonhuman primates might have developed. So, for example, a female chimpanzee, Viki, was reared by humans and tested for concept-handling ability. For this purpose concept discrimination problems were presented employing generalized packs of picture cards, each of which illustrated some every day concept. Viki scored significantly better than chance, and quite similarly to preschool children of her own age, in discriminating animals from inanimate objects, male from female people, red from green, children from adults, circles from crosses, and complete drawings from incomplete ones (Hayes & Nissen, 1971).

At the time of her death, when almost 7-years-old, Viki had learned to produce four words, *mamma, papa, cup* (for a drink), and *up* (for a piggyback ride). These sounds were mastered with considerable help from her foster parents, which included manipulation of the buccal cavity. Viki also developed fragments of many language substitutes.

> *For example, she could ask for an automobile ride in several ways: gesturing toward the car outside, placing our hand on the right-hand knob of the drawer which contained the key to the front door, bringing the purse which must accompany us, showing us a picture of a car, or clicking her teeth together in her 'word' for this request. However, for unknown reasons, Viki's communication to us, vocal or otherwise, never went beyond her "wants" [Hayes and Nissen, 1971, p. 113].*

It has been argued that object naming is an ability that is unique to man and at the very center of the emergence of language (Lancaster, 1968). Viki's success with a few words and word-substitutes would seem sufficient to cast some doubt on the preceding assertion. Struhsaker (1967) has furnished evidence that some African arboreal monkeys use different alarm calls for aerial or ground predators, thus in a way naming these two categories. If these two sets of calls, intermediates of which have not been recorded (Struhsaker, personal communication), were learned by imitation, we would have here one of the rudiments of language. Naming ability is also well represented in two recent and successful attempts at teaching young chimpanzees a form of visual communication akin to language.

T. Gardner and Gardner (1971; R. A. Gardner & Gardner, 1969) reared a young female chimpanzee, Washoe, under conditions where all communication was mediated by hand signals extracted from the American Sign Language (ASL) used by the deaf. This method met with considerable success. By the end of her third year of training, Washoe had mastered 85 different signs representing objects, actions, and attributes and location signs such as *in*, *out*, *up*, and *down*. Washoe named objects with considerable accuracy even if the person presenting the stimulus and the person transcribing the sign were equally unaware of the nature of the objects presented. This is known as the "double blind" test, and insures that the signaling individual has no ancillary cues to guide its performance. Importantly also, Washoe had no difficulty in recognizing the same object through different modalities, so that an object was named correctly whether visually or auditorily perceived. Examples of this are provided by Washoe's use of the signs for *dog*, *cat*, and *bird* (B. T. Gardner & Gardner, 1971).

When addressing people, Washoe used signs singly or in combinations of two or more. Though no clear syntactic rules have emerged so far (R. Brown, 1970), this chimpanzee's use of symbols is neither random nor nonsensical, but semantically meaningful and closely related to context. From these observations B. T. Gardner and Gardner (1971) conclude: "At a minimum, these data indicate that Washoe's early use of ASL was sufficiently comparable to the early use of vocal language by very young children to justify further study of the communicative capacity of chimpanzees [p. 181]."

A comparable strategy of transposing language learning to the visual modality has been used by Premack (1971a, 1971b). In this case, plastic tokens of different shapes and colors, glued onto small magnets, were used to write statements on a magnetic board. Premack's goal was to show that a chimpanzee would not only learn to name things and actions, but also develop the conceptual expertise required to master some of the more syntactical aspects of language. In time, Sarah, Premack's young female chimpanzee, developed enough proficiency with her "language" of tokens that this in turn could be used to teach her new language relations.

Sarah's performance consists of fitting on to the blackboard and in a particular vertical order a series of tokens, each of which is the word for an object, action, relation, and so on. In this manner the chimpanzee generates meaningful statements. As an example, one of the trainers, Mary, may place an apple on a table where Sarah can see it. Before Sarah is allowed to take the apple, she has to "write" on the blackboard *Mary give apple Sarah*. In another type of test Sarah has to insert in a blank space the one word that will complete a correct statement or answer a question. This may be of the type, "What is A to B?" where the answer can be *same* or *different*. Depending on the nature of the test, the chimpanzee is given a choice of two to several possible "words" or tokens, which are placed on top of the table. On days when Sarah is cooperative her performance may be around 80 % correct. So far Sarah has mastered a repertoire of 100 different "words."

The work of the Gardners and of Premack has generated considerable controversy (e.g., Ploog & Melnechuck, 1971). Lenneberg and his students (personal communication) have repeated some of Premack's training schedules using similar tokens to stand for words. However, instead of working with chimpanzees, they tested young children and adults. Intriguingly, even after the subjects had achieved 100 % correct responses, they were quite unaware that the task on hand had anything to do with language, but rather took it to be some kind of puzzle. This is a serious criticism, and we may wonder to what extent language learning à la Gardner or à la Premack is intrinsically different from learning a complex series of responses, part of game programs rewarded according to context.

The equivalence of Premack's tokens with words would seem established by a feature analysis of tokens and of the objects they represent. Thus, as described by Premack (1971b):

> *After obtaining a features analysis of the apple, we repeated the test exactly except for replacing the object apple with the word for apple. Once again the subject was required to indicate whether the sample—now a piece of blue plastic—was for example red or green, round or square, etc. Although the sample was not longer a shiny red apple but a piece of blue plastic, the subject assigned to the plastic the same properties she earlier assigned to the apple* [p. 225].

This would not have been expected if the token had not been treated as an abstract representation of apple, indeed, as a word. The significance of tests of this nature is such that we may hope that Premack or future investigators will eventually publish detailed score sheets indicating number and order of all responses and schedules of reinforcement. One error in ten responses may yield a surprisingly high score of 90 %. Yet, if the error was in the first response, it may indicate only that the subject has learned the rules of problem solving, and this is different from its understanding what a token "means." Mastering the rules of problem solving should be particularly easy when, as Premack often does, only two alternative tokens are offered for each test of feature analysis. Premack has also claimed that his results show that a chimpanzee can learn to order "words" in sentences as if it had a grasp of syntax.

Premack's evaluation of the importance of his findings is best conveyed by quoting him.

> The mind appears to be a device for forming internal representations. If it were not, there could be neither words nor language. Because the mind is this kind of device, however, every response is a potential word. No special method is needed to produce words. The procedures that train animals will also produce words [p. 226].

And further on,

> There is as yet no indication of a ceiling on the animal's ability, nor is the training program itself, which is a first effort, optimal. If every complex rule can be broken into simpler components, the only ceiling on the chimp's accomplishments may be the astuteness of the training program. Man and chimpanzee may conceivably attain comparable limits, though in all likelihood by quite different steps [Premack, 1971b, p. 226].

To this he laconically adds: "Since man is required to teach the chimp language and not vice versa, we may continue to claim uniqueness [p. 228]."

Discussion of the significance of the Gardners' and Premack's findings will probably continue for many years. We may expect that the suspicion with which their results and claims have been received in some quarters and the uncritical enthusiasm that has greeted them in others will be tempered by independent and more detailed replications of their work. Perhaps the most that efforts of this kind can achieve is a confirmation of the belief that an absence of a humanoid vocal language in other primates is not attributable to their inferior abilities to abstract and generalize; nor does their lack of language result from an inability to name things or perceive relations. Indeed, we may have to conclude that though there is a huge intellectual gap between man and other living primates, the main barrier to the evolution of language in these other forms has been their lack of vocal learning.

The claim has been recently made that "One chimpanzee can convey to others, who have no other source of information, the presence, direction, quality, and relative quantity or preference value of distant hidden objects that he himself has not seen for several minutes [Menzel, 1971, p. 220]." However, the potential informant was temporarily removed from his companions and shown a hidden source of food or dummy predator, while the remainder of his group was held in a special enclosure. Such training and testing procedures may have created a specific expectation, namely that when the "isolate" was reintroduced to his group, his movements would lead to an interesting object. Despite this criticism, the fact remains that the isolate's manner of progression determines whether he is eagerly preceded by companions searching for food, or excitedly followed by individuals ready to confront and mob a "predator." Thus, some exchange of information about objects and events would seem to require no human training or language. However, the converse cannot be concluded; we cannot say that given access to vocal learning chimpanzees would not develop a style of language adapted to their particular mode of life. An ability for vocal learning *and* a context favoring complex communication may have been the two essential preconditions that led to the truly human breakthrough of language.

A review of vocal behavior in mammals and birds suggests that the emergence of vocal learning in the latter group may be related to the kinds of cues used by females in choosing a partner. Although some male mammals probably use song to advertise their sexual availability (see review in Nottebohm, 1972b), this phenomenon is rare in mammals as a group, while very common in birds. Should we conclude that language evolution in man was preceded by patterns of sexual advertisement and courtship not common to other primates? The only merit of such an indirect speculation is that it rests on a broad comparative biological inference. If our hominid ancestors used song in sexual advertisement and courtship, more recent selective forces have made such a habit much rarer.

The Neural Substrate of Vocal Behavior

There are in mammals and birds two basically different kinds of vocal ontogeny: one that depends on auditory experience, characterized here as vocal learning, and another one that is independent of auditory experience. It is of interest to review which neural traits underlie vocal behavior in general and which are typical of vocal learning.

MAN

The neurological conditions underlying language behavior in man are discussed elsewhere in this volume (Jacobson, Chap. 6; Lenneberg, Chap. 20; Bay, Chap. 21). Here I only wish to emphasize that based on available knowledge the neural substrates for vocal behavior in man differ from those in other mammals in at least two important aspects: (1) hemispheric dominance and (2) a greater involvement of the cerebral cortex.

OTHER MAMMALS

Our knowledge about the neural substrate of vocalizations in nonhuman primates and other mammals is modest. In the absence of speech and lacking the cooperation afforded by human patients, fewer methods and conditions can be used to map vocal areas. Furthermore, there has been an almost total separation between laboratories and scientists studying vocal communication in nonhuman primates, and other investigators trying to uncover the neurophysiological and neuroanatomical basis of such vocal behavior. It is as if investigators trying to plot speech areas in the human brain were unable to tell normal language apart from all its possible distortions and from nonspeech utterances. Interestingly too, there has been little integration between work on animals and clinical studies of aphasia in humans.

Magoun, Atlas, Ingersoll, and Ranson (1937) elicited complex, integrated, faciovocal responses in cats and rhesus monkeys by electrical stimulation of hypothalamic and midbrain regions. Lesions in these areas (Kelly, Beaten, & Magoun, 1946), particularly in the periaquaductal gray matter and adjacent tegmentum of the midbrain, greatly reduced faciovocal behavior in cats. Transection of the brain stem at the level of the midbrain-diencephalic junction preserved faciovocal activity. More recently Skultety (1961) has reported experiments in which the midbrain's periaqueductal grey was lesioned in dogs. He concluded that in order to produce mutism in dogs by periaqueductal lesions "a complete cross-sectional damage of the structure must be accomplished at a level beneath the superior colliculi [p. 246]."

W. R. Mehler (1969) notes that fiber tracts ascending from the spinal cord and thought to convey pain innervate profusely the mesencephalic periaqueductal grey and overlying layer of tectum. A prominent target of these fibers is the nucleus intercollicularis, which straddles the boundary between tectum and periaqueductal grey. Various authors (review in W. R. Mehler, 1962) have indicated that stimulation of this nucleus and its surrounding tissue in mammals elicits vocalizations and reactions suggestive of pain. A similarly positioned nucleus, also called intercollicularis, has been implicated in vocal behavior in birds (see next section). Not enough is known about the connectivity of the nucleus intercollicularis in birds to know if it is homologous to its mammalian homonym.

Despite an apparent relation in mammals between vocalization and areas innervated by pain fibers, it is not possible to conclude that experimentally induced mutism is a result of general desensitization. Skultety (1961) noted that one of his dogs muted by periaqueductal lesions, upon having its tail pinched, "Struggled, attempted to get at the source of noxious stimulation, but uttered no sound [p. 226]." The relation between vocalization and experimentally induced pain or arousal needs further study.

The limbic system of mammals, also involved in vocalization, is a phylogenetically old structure that has been graphically described as the hilus or neck of the cerebral hemispheres (Ruch 1960, p. 486). It includes the hippocampus, uncus, amygdala, septum, and cingulate and subcallosal gyri. Smith (1945) was the first to report vocalization in response to electrical stimulation of the anterior cingulate gyrus and of the uncus and adjacent part of the hippocampal gyrus in rhesus monkeys. Clark, Chow, Gillaspy, and Klotz (1949) produced vocal responses in one out of eight dogs when stimulating the anterior cingulate gyrus through implanted electrodes.

Kaada (1951) elicited a constant vocal response from an area in the forward upper portion of the cingulate gyrus, from the banks of the cingulate sulcus, and from the anterior end of the hippocampal gyrus in lightly anesthetized rhesus monkeys. The sounds elicited under those conditions were characterized as follows: "They resembled those which a monkey daily emits in its cage, varying from low cooing sounds to high pitched sounds and cries [p. 165]." Bilateral ablation of the cortical areas for motor representation of the vocal tract, that is of the lower pre-Rolandic region on the lateral surface of the frontal lobes, together with the rest of the motor areas, was without any effect on the vocal response from the cingulate or from the anterior hippocampal gyrus, indicating separate pathways from the latter areas to the subcortical mechanisms concerned with vocalization. This conclusion is not backed by a satisfactory pre- and postoperative analysis of the sounds emitted.

Friedman (1934) reported barking in dogs as a result of "stimulation of the cortex low down in the motor zone [p. 50]"; the context of Friedman's statement suggests that the area stimulated lay in the pre-Rolandic gyrus. He offered no details on the circumstances or methods of stimulation. His results should be reproduced.

The role of neocortical, limbic, and midbrain networks in determining the structure of vocalizations in mammals other than man remains poorly defined. It was noted earlier that transection of the brain stem at the level of the midbrain-diencephalic junction preserves faciovocal activity in cats (Kelly et al., 1946). These workers offered no adequate description of sounds before and after the operation. It is not yet possible to tell to what extent the *motor program* of natural vocalizations is represented at the various levels of the brain.

Working with lightly anesthetized rhesus monkeys, Showers and Crosby (1958) noted that head, neck, and facial movements possessing overtones of arousal and attack were present whenever the cingulate gyrus was stimulated. Two to 3 weeks after destruction of the cingulate gyrus, monkeys were more vocal and noisier than others in the colony; they were also more aggressive and less fearful than prior to the experiment. The same authors report that stimulation of the subcallosal gyrus resulted in forced expiration with vocalization. It seems probable that vocal responses triggered from the cingulate gyrus are part of an agonistic or emotional system capable of eliciting well-integrated behavior, including vocalizations.

Brickner (1940) obtained speech perseveration, and Penfield and Welch (1951) elicited vowel cries by electrical stimulation of the mesial frontal cortex (supplementary motor area) of humans. The area of the cingulate gyrus and bank of the cingulate sulcus from which Kaada (1951) and Showers and Crosby (1958) elicited vocalization in rhesus monkeys is adjacent to the supplementary motor area in man. The possibility that in man and other primates these two areas are part of an integrated network should be considered.

An involvement of the limbic system in vocalization has been confirmed in a very thorough study by Robinson (1967). He undertook electrical stimulation in the forebrain of unanesthetized rhesus monkeys, and paid special attention to the different types of utterances produced. Perhaps his most interesting finding is that different types of vocalizations were not randomly distributed in the limbic system, but specific vocalizations often occurred in definite loci. So, for example, "Vocalizations elicited from the anterior cingulate were primarily clear, resembling most closely the separation kōō [p. 352]." Robinson (1967) also indicates that when care was taken to avoid hippocampal seizures and afterdischarges, vocalization from the hippocampus was not obtained, though it was possible to elicit vocalization from the amygdala. For a complete description of the many points in the limbic system from which Robinson triggered vocalization the reader is referred to the original text, which also includes a valuable review of earlier literature. No laterality of response was apparent in Robinson's data.

Robinson's (1967) findings lead him to conclude:

> *Primate vocalization is principally embedded in the limbic system since the evoked vocalization closely resembled corresponding sounds given under field conditions. Although negative data must be interpreted cautiously, there is no evidence that neocortex participates in the production or organization of such sounds. . . . Primate vocalization is used pricipally in situations bearing some emotional valence such as threat, aggression, fear, pain, pleausre, feeding, and separation. The limbic system, which appears to mediate this type of emotional response, is an appropriate matrix for vocalization. . . . Thus, . . . it appears that human speech and primate vocalization depend on two different neural systems. The one is neocortical: the other limbic. This suggests that human speech did not develop "out of" primate vocalization, but arose from new tissue which permitted it the necessary detachment from immediate, emotional situations. The neurological evidence suggests that human language arose in parallel with primate vocalization, surpassed it, and relegated it to a subordinate role. We may suspect that limbic vocalization is still present in man and is manifested during emotional stress as cries, exclamations, etc. There is clinical evidence, in fact, that some vocalization is often preserved in dominant hemisphere lesions (Monrad-Krohn, 1958). This vocalization is crude and is characteristically uttered during periods of excitement. It bears a striking functional resemblance to the limbic vocalization of primates and may arise from the same structures [p. 353].*

These are interesting ideas, though they should be considered with some reservations. Vocalizations cannot be triggered in humans by stimulating electrically Broca's and Wernicke's areas. However, stimulation of these same areas interferes with ongoing speech behavior (Penfield & Roberts, 1959). It would seem as if the crucial experiments to test cortical involvement in the vocal behavior of nonhuman primates and other mammals should consist of stimulating via radio telemetry cortical areas of individuals vocalizing in a natural context, with particular focus on all those cortical areas known to influence vocal behavior in man. Such experiments could then be supplemented by studying the effects of lesioning those areas, noticing the effects of this on *natural* behavior.

The vocal repertoire of the squirrel monkey, *Saimiri sciurius*, was described by Winter et al. (1966). Other investigators in the same laboratory then proceeded to map brain areas from which natural vocalizations could be elicited by electrical stimulation of unanesthetized individuals restrained in a chair (Jürgens, 1969; Jürgens, Maurus, Ploog, & Winter, 1967). Of the 26 known call types of this species, eleven could be elicited by electrical stimulation. Most of the experimentally elicited calls were indistinguishable from spontaneously occurring ones. A concentration of vocalization points was found in the septal region, as well as in sections of the lateral and dorsal hypothalamus, with an emphasis on the periventricular region, a distribution comparable to that reported by Robinson (1967) in the rhesus monkey. Different calls did not have a homogeneous representation in the responsive areas. Contact and food calls were elicited, with only partial overlap, from the cingulate gyrus, septal region, and adjacent structures of the caudate nucleus, whereas calls expressing aggression and intense excitation were predominantly elicited, also with only partial overlap, from the cingulate gyrus, amygdala, hypothalamus, and the caudally adjoining periventricular grey. Contact and aggressive calls were on occasion accompanied by genital erection, which in this species is a social display. Jürgens (1969) comments on his findings in squirrel monkeys as follows:

> First, the just described brain structures do not represent a pure vocalization system; almost all of those structures mentioned are known to yield a lot of supplementary stimulus responses; the lateral hypothalamus may serve as an example, for it is known to produce not only vocalization, when stimulated, but also penile erection, excessive drinking, excessive eating, self-stimulation, head movements and several autonomic manifestations. Secondly, electrical brain stimulation is such an unphysiological method that one cannot expect that all structures participating in the elaboration of vocalization will be discovered by this technique. For example, ... Broca's area in man was reported by Penfield and co-workers to yield vocalization in human beings;[1] the correspond-

---

[1] Jürgens errs here. According to Penfield and Roberts (1959), a sustained or interrupted vowel cry, which at times may have a consonant component, is produced in human patients by stimulation of the Rolandic and supplementary motor areas of either hemisphere. Vocalization in man has not been elicited from other cortical areas. However, since Broca's area is thought to be important for the motor organization of speech in man, it is interesting that stimulation of a comparable area in the squirrel monkey should result in movement of the larynx, tongue, lips, and jaw.

ing region in the monkey produces movements of the larynx, tongue, lips and jaws, but no vocalization [p. 32].

Apfelbach (1972) reports that electrodes implanted in various parts of the gibbon's (*Hylobates lar*) brain elicit different calls, as follows: barking and contact calls from the midbrain's periaqueductal grey; hoots from medial lemniscus; play calls from nuclei pontis; alarm calls from ventral hypothalamus; "calls to synchronize the behavior of mated pairs" from ventral hippocampus. The electrically induced vocalizations demonstrated in his article matched closely the natural calls. Both members of a pair of gibbons engage in duetting series of calls. Apfelbach (1972) was unable to elicit electrically the male's or female's contribution to the duetting tirade. These observations are difficult to interpret. Apfelbach does not provide anatomical diagrams showing the position of the electrodes, nor does he provide a description of the circumstances under which calls were elicited. It would have been interesting to know whether electrodes were placed in the cingulum, septum, and amygdala. His article includes no comments on negative stimulation points.

From all that has been said in this section, it would seem that a relation between vocal behavior and the limbic system is clearly established in nonhuman mammals. There also seems to be a relation between hypothalamic and midbrain areas and vocal behavior. There is no evidence of functional lateralization in any of these systems. The role of the neocortex in vocalization in this group remains poorly defined, partly as a result of inadequate testing. Comparison of the neural substrates of vocal behavior in man and other mammals suggests that neural lateralization and extensive neocortical involvement may be correlates of vocal learning. For the reasons given earlier, this view must be considered preliminary and subject to further testing.

BIRDS

Kalischer (1905) searched for brain sites related to vocal behavior in parrots (*Amazona*) and cockatoos (*Kakatöe*) and reported that alarm calls could be evoked by stimulating the neostriatal area overlying the anterolateral archistriatum. He also was able to remove parts of the right and left hemispheres in these birds, an operation that was followed by only temporary losses of vocal skill.

More recently J. Brown (1965b, 1971) has undertaken a detailed search of brain loci from which vocalizations can be elicited by electrical stimulation. These studies were conducted with red-winged blackbirds (*Agelaius phoeniceus*) tested under local anesthesia or with chronically implanted electrodes. Responsive areas were found (1) in and near the nucleus intercollicularis of the midbrain, (2) in the septum and anteroventral area of the diencephalon, (3) in the archistriatum, and (4) in and near the occipitomesencephalic tract; a few high threshold points were also found in the hyperstriatum and neostriatum. Thresholds for evoked vocalizations were lowest in the midbrain, a finding of unclear significance. Whereas some of the vocalizations elicited by electrical stimulation were indistinguishable from calls given by wild birds, others were clearly abnormal. The most frequently evoked calls belonged to the various categories of general alarm calls; song was never elicited in this manner.

Work by other authors on brain sites responsible for vocal behavior tends to agree with Brown's findings, though there might be species and methodological differences. Electrical stimulation of the midbrain has been shown to elicit vocalizations in pigeons (Delius, 1971; Popa & Popa, 1933), in domestic fowl (Murphey and Phillips, 1967; Putkonen, 1967, p. 52), in the mallard, *Anas platyrhynchos* (Maley, 1969), in Japanese quail, *Coturnix c. japonica* (Potash, 1970a, 1970b), and in gulls, *Larus argentatus* and *L. fuscus* (Delius, 1971). Interestingly, Potash (1970b) reports that "The exact physical structure of the vocalizations elicited from a given electrode depended upon the intensity-frequency parameters used. In some instances brain-stimulation-elicited vocalizations resembled natural calls only when elicited by a relatively narrow range of intensity—frequency combinations [p. 166]." Potash also notes that electrodes implanted in close neuroanatomical proximity tend to produce similar sequences of vocalizations.

In addition to these sites, Åckerman (1966) has elicited bow cooing in pigeons by stimulating electrically preoptic and anterior hypothalamic areas. Peek and Phillips (1971) have elicited pulsed vocalizations reminiscent of those denoting mild arousal from the brain of anesthetized chickens. Peek and Phillips describe an apparently continuous system, active for vocalization, extending from the preoptic region to the most caudal portion of the medulla; in no case were vocalizations elicited from the striatum or spinal cord. Thresholds were lowest and calling was the most natural sounding and was elicited in the absence of other behavior in the area ventromedial to the inferior colliculus. The latter area includes the nucleus intercollicularis. In portions of the midbrain, pons and medulla vocalization substrates corresponded to areas also reported to yield respiratory responses in this and other species.

Delius (1971) reports evoked vocalization following electrical stimulation of the following nuclei in the brains of gulls and pigeons: ovoidalis of the diencephalon, intercollicularis and lateralis dorsalis of the midbrain, and posteromedialis of the hypothalamus.

Some of the brain areas reportedly involved in vocal control are part of the main auditory pathway. This is the case with the nucleus mesencephalicus lateralis dorsalis, and the nucleus ovoidalis of the diencephalon (Karten, 1968). However, J. D. Newman (1970) and Potash (1970a), working with red-winged blackbirds and Japanese quail respectively, have found that the threshold for eliciting vocalizations is lower in the nucleus intercollicularis of the midbrain than in the adjacent nucleus mesencephalicus lateralis dorsalis. This suggests a more direct vocal involvement for the former nucleus, less so for the latter one. J. Brown (1971) also emphasizes that in general stimulation of known sensory areas in the brain of red-winged blackbirds does not evoke vocalization, and thus the idea that vocalizations are evoked mainly by activation of sensory pathways to produce "hallucinations" is not confirmed by available data.

Data presented up to here strongly suggest that the nucleus intercollicularis of the avian midbrain plays a role in vocal behavior. Recently it has been shown that in the chaffinch, a songbird, the nucleus intercollicularis accumulates testosterone at much higher levels than most other brain areas (Zigmond, Nottebohm, & Pfaff, 1972). The significance of this finding remains unclear, though it is known that several vocalizations in this species, including song, are influenced by circulating testosterone levels.

Delius (1971) has proposed an efferent vocal system in the bird brain composed of the archistriatum, occipitomesencephalic tract, periventricular nuclei of the diencephalon, and nucleus intercolliculares of the midbrain, which could be tentatively extended to medullary levels. In support of such a hierarchical organization J. Brown (1971) notes that vocalizations evoked from midbrain sites are relatively simple and invariant when compared to those evoked from septal and diencephalic sites. Calls evoked by forebrain stimulation may be rather complex in abnormal ways, and sometimes contain elements of more complex vocalizations which are not elicited in complete form. Bilateral lesions in the area of the midbrain from which vocalizations are evoked by electrical stimulation cause long-lasting loss of alarm calls; such birds also show a loss of locomotor excitability and escape reactions. In the red-winged blackbirds operated on in this manner, recovery of the alarm call response takes from 10 to 84 days (J. Brown, 1965a).

Most of the vocalizations evoked by electrical stimulation of the avian brain correspond to calls usually given in an agonistic context, by frightened or aggressive animals. When chronically implanted electrodes are used with awake and unrestrained birds, the vocalizations elicited may (Åckerman, 1966; Delius, 1971; Potash, 1970b; Putkonen, 1967) or may not (Maley, 1969) be accompanied by other behavior with which they normally occur. In one case described by Potash (1970b) a posture typical of a call was elicited at a lower threshold than that triggering the simultaneous display of call plus posture. It seems possible that some of the vocal behavior elicited may be secondary to the evocation of a particular mood. One may wonder to what extent individual vocalizations have a neural substrate independent of the mood eliciting them.

Avian vocalizations are frequency modulated by the syrinx, placed at the junction of trachea and bronchi. In songbirds such as the chaffinch and canary, there is an internal tympaniform membrane in each bronchus, which oscillates as air goes by, producing sound. Each of these membranes is controlled by a complex set of muscles innervated by a branch of the hypoglossus nerve. In this way, the left hypoglossus exerts control over the left syringeal sound source, and the right hypoglossus over the right one. These two sound sources can modulate sounds independently of each other. Despite this anatomical symmetry, experiments on 12 chaffinches, 24 canaries, and 2 white-crowned sparrows, sectioning the right or left hypoglossus, have shown that in all cases the left hypoglossus controls two-thirds to all of the sounds which go to form song and other calls. Thus, it is justified to say that there is left hypoglossal dominance (Nottebohm, 1970, 1971, 1972a and unpublished observations). The effects of this operation are irreversible in adult chaffinches, but hypoglossal dominance is reversed when the left sound source is denervated before the onset of song learning.

THE NEURAL CORRELATES OF VOCAL LEARNING

A cross taxonomical comparison of nerual substrates involved in vocal behavior suggests that lateralization of function, as described in man (hemispheric) and some songbirds (hypoglossal), may be correlated with vocal learning. No lateralization of either type has been described in other mammals, though it should be sought in some of the species (e.g. cetacea) suspected of engaging in vocal learning. It will be interesting to see if birds that develop song independently of auditory information or feedback show hypoglossal lateralization of function.

It also seems likely that vocal control in most species is an inextricable part of broad motivational systems having to do with immediate needs such as feeding, agonistic interaction, and copulation, or with the broadcasting of pain and fear. It is interesting that speech is relatively independent of such an emotional substrate, though characteristics of its manifestation, earlier subsumed under paralanguage, are obviously less so.

It is more difficult to decide to what extent avian vocalizations are controlled by the basic emotions listed above. Territorial song is often delivered in the absence of auditory or visual stimulation from conspecifics, and under those circumstances may have a motivation all of its own. However, the same song may be given even more frequently during territorial disputes or courtship, contexts that subjectively would seem highly "emotional." Species such as the chaffinch also learn by reference to auditory input the calls they produce when mobbing a predator or courting a female (Marler, 1956b; Nottebohm, 1967, 1972a). Thus, it is not possible to say that learned vocal signals must be independent of the emotional substrate. The degree of emotional independence achieved by speech may be a secondary reflection of its propositional nature.

Vocal learning in man and birds, as described earlier is preceded by juvenile states of vocal practice known as babbling and subsong. These stages do not serve a communicatory function. Also, there is no reason to believe that babbling and subsong are triggered by basic emotions such as hunger, alarm, submission, agression, sexual intentions, or desire for company. It is tempting to conclude that vocal practice has to be freed of alien drives and of communicatory constraints before it allows for the open-ended experience that leads to vocal learning of consequence.

It is unclear whether electrically elicited vocalizations are a good way to map brain vocal areas. We may well wonder at the manner of action of something as unphysiological as the electrical fields generated by rather gross electrodes. Such interference with the normal business of the brain is unlikely to trigger directly the exquisitely timed patterns contributed by several complex networks of neurons. The success of electrical brain stimulation in triggering well-integrated behavior in vertebrates may commonly reside in its ability to influence motivational or emotional systems. It is the mood-dependent vocalization that is triggered by electrical stimulation. Normal speech and territorial birdsong, with their partial independence of neural substrates controlling pain, fear, agonism, ingestion, and copulation, are more difficult to elicit by electrical intrusion.

Speech-like utterances can be triggered electrically from the ventro-oral thalamus of humans, in apparent exception to the preceding argument. The description by Schaltenbrand, Spuler, Wahren, and Rümler (1971) of this ventro-oral nucleus speech is reminiscent of the garbled utterances often produced during dreams. Dreams, of course, tend to have a vivid emotional content. It is not yet possible to decide whether thalamic elicitation of speech implies the existence there of access to emotional, motor, or sensory networks governing speech.

It is still to early to propose a unified theory of neural correlates of vocal learning. Such a unified theory might not even be desirable. We need more and better information on all aspects of vocal behavior in a variety of species. In particular, there is an urgency to explore further the role of the neocortex in vocal control in nonhuman mammals and the role of thalamic and midbrain areas in speech control in man. Ironically, some of the more novel and richer insights on the interplay of neural substrates important for vocal behavior may come from a study of avian examples. The time is ripe for replacing ad hoc theories tailored after single species by a broad comparative study of the neural correlates of vocal learning in vertebrates.

Summary

1. Studies of vocal communication in man and animals are interesting in their own right. Their comparative interpretation has given rise to the logical analysis of animal communication. Insights derived from comparative studies question the significance of correlations or "explanations" based on single species.

2. The ability to recombine phonemes to produce an endless variety of words and the use of syntax to generate sentences is characteristic of humans; comparable phenomena have not been described in animals.

3. The structure of vocal signals in animals can be predicted to some extent from the nature of the message, the social structure of the species, and the environment through which the signal is broadcast. The first of these correlations is very tenuous or absent in language; the applicability of the other two to the human case is partial or dubious.

4. Comparisons between the vocal signals of animals and those of man might focus fruitfully on paralanguage, less so on language.

5. Attempts at showing a universal phonetic symbolism have failed. If such a symbolism exists it may be more in the way words are spoken than in their neutral

phonetic form. Symbolic universals may have to be sought in paralanguage, not in language.

6. Of all mammals, man is the only one known to engage in vocal learning. The crucial experiment of charting vocal development in a deaf-born or early deafened nonhuman mammal remains to be done. Circumstantial evidence raises the possibility that a few other mammalian species may imitate sounds, though much more information is needed to establish this point.

7. Early stages of vocal development in humans are still of uncertain significance. Crying, babbling, and cooing are cases in point. Parallels are drawn between these stages and vocal ontogeny in birds. The nature of predispositions brought to the task of vocal learning remains controversial; this is a fertile area for research.

8. Birds have evolved a variety of vocal ontogenies, characterized by various degrees of dependence on environmental information and auditory feedback. Some species develop a normal repertoire even when deafened soon after hatching.

9. In birds, as in humans, vocal learning seems to occur most readily within the age span defined as the critical period. Hormonal, experiential, and age factors contributing to this critical period are evaluated.

10. Most extant theories link the evolution of vocal learning in man to tool making and the need to convey new kinds of information. Yet, it is possible to separate in our thinking the emergence of vocal learning and the emergence of human language. The evolution of vocal learning in birds shows that relaxation of genetic control over vocal development can be achieved in the absence of a need to convey radically new messages. Once the development of vocal patterning shifted from a rigid ontogeny to one incorporating environmental models, then the stage may have been set for futher elaboration of this signalling system into a plastic language such as we find in present-day man.

11. It is argued that most instances of vocal learning in birds can probably be interpreted as subserving two basic purposes: (1) mating like with like (dialects) and (2) wooing, stimulating, and retaining a partner (complex song). In either case females would have been the main agents of selection in that their choice of mate, based upon vocalizations, determined their breeding success and fitness of their progeny.

12. All birds that rely on vocal learning as a strategy of vocal development can also imitate at least other conspecifics. Vocal improvisation and vocal imitation may have arisen together, as related manifestations of a developmental process that relies on vocal reproduction to match auditory memories.

13. The success of the Gardners and of Premack in teaching a visual language to young chimpanzees suggests that absence of a humanoid vocal language in other primates is not attributable to their inferior abilities to abstract and generalize; nor does their lack of language result from an inability to name things and perceive relations. Though there is a huge intellectual gap between man and other living primates, the main barrier to language in these other forms may have been their lack of vocal learning. An ability for vocal learnings *and* a context

favoring complex communication may have been the two essential preconditions that led to the truly human breakthrough of language.

14. In some songbirds known to learn their vocal repertoire by reference to auditory information, the left hypoglossus is dominant over its right counterpart in vocal control. However, electrical stimulation of the avian brain, with consequent vocalization, has yielded no suggestion of hemispheric dominance.

15. In nonhuman mammals there is a clear relation between the limbic system and vocal behavior. The limbic system is also involved in controlling a variety of emotions, of which vocalization may be just one manifestation. There is no evidence of functional lateralization in this system. No tests with nonhuman mammals have been conducted comparable to the mapping of cortical speech areas in humans, using electrically induced distortion or arrest of ongoing vocal behavior as the clue for establishing the role of a cortical area. To this extend our knowledge about cortical control of vocal behavior in species other than man remains unsatisfactory.

16. Speech is relatively independent of broad motivational systems such as those controlling aggression, fear, pain, hunger, and sexual interaction. The emotional independence of speech may be a secondary reflection of its propositional nature. Avian vocalizations closely tied to the emotional substrate are often learned.

17. It is suggested that vocal practice in the developing bird or mammal has to be freed of emotional control and communicatory constraints before it allows for the open-ended experience that leads to vocal learning.

18. It is still too early to propose a unified theory of neural correlates of vocal learning in vertebrates. An emerging correlation between vocal learning and neural dominance, as described in man and some birds, should be tested in a variety of vertebrates. The time is ripe for replacing ad hoc theories tailored after single species with a broad comparative approach.

References

Ackerman, B. Behavioural effects of electrical stimulation in the forebrain of the pigeon. I. Reproductive behaviour. *Behaviour*, 1966, *26*, 323—338.

Apfelbach, R. Electrically elicited vocalizations in the gibbon, *Hylobates lar* (Hylobatidae), and their behavioral significance. *Zeitschrift für Tierpsychologie*, 1972, *30*, 420—430.

Batteau, D. W. The role of the pinna in human localization. *Proceedings of the Royal Society, Series B* 1967, *168*, 158—180.

Brickner, R. M. A human cortical area producing repetitive phenomena when stimulated. *Journal of Neurophysiology*, 1940, *3*, 128—130.

Brockway, B. F. The influence of vocal behavior on the performer's testicular activity in budgerigars (*Melopsittacus undulatus*). *Wilson Bulletin*, 1967, *79*, 328—334.

Bronowski, J., & Bellugi, U. Language, name, and concept. *Science*, 1970, *168*, 669—673.

Brown, J. Loss of vocalizations caused by lesions in the nucleus mesencephalicus lateralis of the Redwinged Blackbird. *American Zoologist*, 1965, *5*, 693. (a)

Brown, J. Vocalization evoked from the optic lobe of a songbird. *Science*, 1965, *149*, 1002—1003. (b)

Brown, J. An exploratory study of vocalization areas in the brain of the Redwinged Blackbird (*Agelaius phoeniceus*). *Behaviour*, 1971, *39*, 91—127.

Brown, R. The first sentences of child and chimpanzee. In R. Brown (Ed.), *Psycholinguistics; selected papers by Roger Brown.* New York: Free Press, 1970, Pp. 208—231.

Busnel, R. G., Moles, A., & Gilbert, M. Un cas de langue sifflée utilisée dans les Pyrénées françaises. *Logos,* 1962, *5,* 76—91.

Busnel, R. G., Leroy, C., Lenneberg, E. H., & Moles A. Etudes de la langue sifflée de Kuskoy en Turquie. *Revue de Phonétique Appliquée,* 1970, *14/15,* 166 pp.

Caldwell, M. C., & Caldwell, D. K. Vocalizations of naive captive dolphins in small groups. *Science,* 1968, *159,* 1121—1123.

Chappuis, C. Un exemple de l'influence du milieu sur les emissions vocales des oiseaux: l'evolution des chants en forêt é quatoriale. *La Terre et la Vie,* 1971, *2,* 183—202.

Chomsky, N. The formal nature of language. Appendix to E. H. Lenneberg. *Biological foundations of language.* New York: Wiley, 1967.

Chomsky, N. *Language and mind.* New York: Harcourt, 1968.

Church, J. The ontogeny of language. In H. Moltz (Ed.), *The ontogeny of vertebrate behavior.* New York: Academic Press, 1971. Pp. 451—479.

Clark, G., Chow, K. L., Gillaspy, C. C., & Klotz, D. A. Stimulation of anterior cingulate region in dogs. *Journal of Neurophysiology,* 1949, *12,* 459—463.

Classe, A. Phonetics of the Silbo Gomero. *Archives Linguisticum,* 1957, *9,* 44—61.

Collard, J., & Grevendal, L. Etudes sur les charactères sexuels des Pinsons, *Fringilla coelebs* et *F. montifringilla. Gerfaut,* 1946, *2,* 89—107.

Cowan, G. M. Mazateco whistled speech. *Language,* 1948, *28,* 280—286.

Darwin, C. *The descent of man.* New York: Merril & Baker, 1874.

Delius, J. D. Neural substrates of vocalizations in gulls and pigeons. *Experimental Brain Research (Berlin),* 1971, *12,* 64—80.

Diamond, A. S. *The history and origin of language.* London: Methuen, 1959.

Dittus, W. P. J., & Lemon, R. E. Auditory feedback in the singing of cardinals. *Ibis,* 1970, *112,* 544—548.

Eimas, P. D., Siqueland, E. R., Jusezyk, P., & Vigorito, J. Speech perception in infants. *Science,* 1971, *171,* 303—306.

Eisenberg, J. F. In J. F. Eisenberg, W. S. Dillon, & S. D. Ripley (Eds.), *Man and beast: Comparative social behavior.* Washington, D.C.: Smithsonian Institution Press, 1971.

Erulkar, S. D. Comparative aspects of spatial localization of sound. *Physiological Review,* 1972, *52,* 237—360.

Etkin, W. Social behavioral factors in the emergence of man. In S. M. Garn (Ed.), *Culture and the direction of human evolution.* Detroit: Wayne State Univ. Press, 1964, Pp. 81—92.

Friedman, E. D. Neurological aspects of hoarseness. *New York State Journal of Medicine,* 1934, *34,* 48—50.

Gardner, B. T., & Gardner, R. A. Two-way communication with an infant chimpanzee. In A. M. Schrier & F. Stollnitz (Eds), *Behavior of nonhuman primates.* Vol. 4. New York: Academic Press, 1971. Pp. 117—184.

Gardner, R. A., & Gardner, B. T. Teaching sign language to a chimpanzee. *Science,* 1969, *165,* 664—672.

Geschwind, N. In C. H. Millikan & F. L. Darley (Eds.), *Brain mechanisms underlying speech and language,* New York: Grune & Stratton, 1967.

Goodall, J. Tool-using and aimed throwing in a community of free-living chimpanzees. *Nature (London),* 1964, *201,* 1264—1266.

Gottlieb, G. *Development of species identification in birds.* Chicago: Univ. of Chicago Press, 1971.

Gould, E. Studies of maternal-infant communication and development of vocalizations in the bats *Myotis* and *Eptesicus. Communications in Behavioral Biology,* 1971, *5,* 263—313.

Green, S. Communication by a graded vocal system in the Japanese monkey *Macaca fuscata.* Unpublished doctoral dissertation, Rockefeller University, 1972.

Griffin, D. R. Acoustic orientation in the oil bird, *Steatornis. Proceedings of the National Academy of Sciences, U.S.,* 1953, *39,* 884—893.

Gwinner, E., & Kneutgen, J. Über die biologische Bedeutung der "zweckdienlichen" Anwendung erlernter Laute bei Vögeln. *Zeitschrift für Tierpsychologie*, 1962, *19*, 692—696.

Harlow, H. F., & Harlow, M. K. Social deprivation in monkeys. *Scientific American*, 1962, *207*, 136—146.

Hayes, K. J., & Hayes, C. Imitation in a home raised chimpanzee. *Journal of Comparative and Physiological Psychology*, 1952, *45*, 450—459.

Hayes, K. J., & Nissen, C. H. Higher mental functions of a home-raised chimpanzee. In A. M. Schrier & F. Stollnitz (Eds.), *Behavior of nonhuman primates*. Vol. 4. New York: Academic Press, 1971, Pp. 59—115.

Hockett, C. F. Logical considerations in the study of animal communication. In W. E. Lanyon & W. N. Tavolga (Eds.), *Animal sounds and communication*. Washington, D.C.: Amer. Inst. Biol. Sci., 1960. 392—430.

Hockett, C. F., & Ascher, R. The human revolution. *Current Anthropology*, 1964, *3*, 135—147.

Holland, M. K., & Wertheimer, M. Some physiognomic aspects of naming, or, maluma and takete revisited. *Perceptual and Motor Skills*, 1964, *19*, 111—117.

Immelmann, K. Song development in the Zebra Finch and other estrildid finches. In R. A. Hinde (Ed.), *Bird vocalizations*. London & New York: Cambridge Univ. Press, 1969. Pp. 61—74.

Jakobson, R. *Kindersprache, Aphasie, und allgemeine Lautgesetze*. Uppsala: Upsala Universitets Aarsskrift, 1941. (English transl.), *Child language, aphasia, and phonological universals*. The Hague: Mouton, 1968.

Jespersen, O. *Language, its nature, development and origin*. London: Allen & Unwin, 1922.

Jürgens, U. Correlation between brain structure and vocalization type elicited in the squirrel monkey. *Proceedings, International Congress of Primatology, 2nd, Atlanta, Ga., 1968*, 1969, *3*, 28—33.

Jürgens, U., Maurus, M., Ploog, D., & Winter, P. Vocalization in the squirrel monkey (*Saimiri sciureus*) elicited by brain stimulation. *Experimental Brain Research (Berlin)*, 1967, *4*, 114—117.

Kaada, B. R. Somato-motor, autonomic, and electrocorticographic responses to electrical stimulation of "rhinencephalic" and other structures in primates, cat, and dog. *Acta Physiologica Scandinavica*, 1951, *24*, (Suppl. No. 83), 285 pp.

Kalischer, O. Das Grosshirn der Papagaien in anatomischer und physiologischer Beziehung. *Abhandlungen der Preussischen Akademie der Wissenschaften*, 1905, *4*, 1—105.

Karten, H. J. The ascending auditory pathway in the pigeon (*Columba livia*). II. Telencephalic projections of the nucleus ovoidalis thalami. *Brain Research*, 1968, *11*, 134—153.

Kelemen, G. Physiology of phonation in primates. *Logos*, 1958, *1*, 32—35.

Kelly, A. H., Beaton, L. E. & Magoun, H. W. A midbrain mechanism for facio-vocal activity. *Journal of Neurophysiology*, 1946, *9*, 181—189.

Konishi, M. The role of auditory feedback in the vocal behavior of the domestic fowl. *Zeitschrift für Tierpsychologie*, 1963, *20*, 349—367.

Konishi, M. Effects of deafening on song development in two species of juncos. *Condor*, 1964, *66*, 85—102.

Konishi, M. The role of auditory feedback in the control of vocalizations in the White-crowned Sparrow. *Zeitschrift für Tierpsychologie*, 1965, *22*, 770—783.

Konishi, M. Locatable and non-locatable acoustic signals for barn owls. *American Naturalist*, 1973, *107*, 775—785.

Konishi, M., & Nottebohm, F. Experimental studies in the ontogeny of avian vocalizations. In R. A. Hinde (Ed.), *Bird vocalizations*. London & New York: Cambridge Univ. Press, 1969. Pp. 29—48.

Konorski, J. Analiza patofizjologiczna Róznich Rudzajów Zaburzén Mowy I Próba ich Klasyficacji. *Polska Akademia Nauk, Rozprawy Wydziatre Nauk Medycznych*, 1963, *2*, 11—32.

Lade, B. I., & Thorpe, W. H. Dove songs as innately coded patterns of specific behavior. *Nature (London)*, 1964, *212*, 366—368.

Lamprecht, J. Duettgesang beim Siamang, *Symphalangus syndactylus* (Hominoidea, Hylobatinae). *Zeitschrift für Tierpsychologie*, 1970, *27*, 186—204.

Lancaster, J. B. Primate communication systems and the emergence of human language. In P. Jay (Ed.), *Primates: Studies in adaptation and variability*. New York: Holt, 1968. Pp. 439—457.

Lanyon, W. E. The comparative biology of the meadowlark (*Sturnella*) in Wisconsin. *Nuttall Ornithological Club (Cambridge. Mass.)* Publ. 1., 1957.

Le Boeuf, B. J., & Peterson, R. S. Dialects in elephant seals. *Science*, 1969, *166*, 1654–1656.

Lemon, R. E., & Scott, D. M. On the development of song in young cardinals. *Canadian Journal of Zoology*, 1966, *44*, 191–197.

Lenneberg, E. H. *Biological foundations of language*. New York: Wiley, 1967.

Lenneberg, E. H., Nichols, I. A., & Rosenberger, E. F. Primitive stages of language development in mongolism. In *Disorders of Communication*. Vol. 42. Research Publications, Association for Research in Nervous and Mental Disease. Baltimore: Williams & Wilkins, 1964. Pp. 119–137.

Liberman, A. M. Some results of research on speech perception. *Journal of the Acoustical Society of America*, 1957, *29*, 117–123.

Liberman, A. M., Cooper, F. S., Shankweiler, D. P. & Studdert-Kennedy, M. Perception of the speech code. *Psychological Review*, 1967, *74*, 431–461.

Lieberman, P. H., Harris, K. S., Wolff, P., & Russell, L. H. Newborn infant cry and nonhuman primate vocalization. *Journal of Speech and Hearing Research*, 1971, *14*, 718–727.

Lieberman, P. H., Klatt, D. H., & Wilson, W. H. Vocal tract limitations on the vowel repertoires of rhesus monkeys and other nonhuman primates. *Science*, 1969, *164*, 1185–1187.

Magoun, H. W., Atlas, D., Ingersoll, E. H., & Ranson, S. W. Associated facial, vocal and respiratory components of emotional expression: an experimental study. *Journal of Neurology Psychopathology*, 1937, *17*, 241–255.

Maley, M. J. Electrical stimulation of agonistic behaviour in the mallard. *Behaviour*, 1969, *34*, 138–160.

Marler, P. Behavior of the chaffinch, *Fringilla coelebs*. *Behaviour*, 1956, Suppl. 5, 1–184. (a)

Marler, P. The voice of the chaffinch and its function as a language. *Ibis*, 1956, *98*, 231–261. (b)

Marler, P. The logical analysis of animal communication. *Journal of Theoretical Biology*, 1961, *1*, 295–317.

Marler, P. Animal communication signals. *Science*, 1967, *157*, 769–774.

Marler, P. Birdsong and speech development: could there be parallels? *Amer. Scientist*, 1970, *58*, 669–673. (a)

Marler, P. A comparative approach to vocal learning: song development in white-crowned sparrows. *Journal of Comparative and Physiological Psychology*, 1970, *71* (Monogr.), 25 pp. (b)

Marler, P. On strategies of behavioral development. In G. Baerends, C. Beer, & A. Manning (Eds). *Evolution in behaviour*. Oxford: Clarendon Press. In press.

Marler, P., Konishi, M., Lutjen, A., & Waser, M. S. Effects of continuous noise on avian hearing and vocal development. *Proceedings of the National Academy of Sciences, U.S.*, 1973, *70*, 1393–1396.

Marler, P. Kreith, M., & Tamura M. Song development in hand-raised Oregon juncos. *Auk*, 1962, *79*, 12–30.

Marler, P., & Tamura M. Song dialects in three populations of white-crowned sparrow. *Condor*, 1962, *64*, 368–377.

Marler, P., & Tamura, M. Culturally transmitted patterns of vocal behavior in sparrows. *Science*, 1964, *146*, 1483–1486.

Mattingly, I. G., Liberman, A. M., Syrdal, A. K., & Halwes, T. Discrimination in speech and non-speech modes. *Cognitive Psychology*, 1971, *2*, 131–157.

Medway, L. Echo-location among *Collocalia*. *Nature (London)*, 1959, *184*, 1352–1353.

Mehler, J. In R. Huxley & E. Ingram (Eds.), *Language acquisition: Models and methods*. New York: Academic Press, 1971.

Mehler, W. R. The anatomy of the so-called "pain tract" in man: an analysis of the course and distribution of the ascending fibers of the fasciculus anterolateralis. In J. D. French & R. W. Porter (Eds.), *Basic research in paraplegia*. Springfield, Ill.: Thomas, 1962. Pp. 26–55.

Mehler, W. R. Some neurological species differences—a posteriori. *Annals of the New York Academy of Sciences*, 1969, *167*, 424–468.

Menzel, E. W., Jr. Communication about the environment in a group of young chimpanzees. *Folia Primatologica*, 1971, *15*, 220–232.

Metfessel, M. Roller canary song produced without learning from external source. *Science*, 1935, *81*, 470.

Monrad-Krohn, G. H. *The clinical examination of the nervous system*. New York: Paul B. Hoeber, 1958.

Morton, E. S. Ecological sources of selection on avian sounds. Unpublished doctoral dissertation, Yale University, 1970.

Moynihan, M. Some behavior patterns of platyrrhine monkeys. I. The night monkey (*Aotus trivirgatus*). *Smithsonian Miscellaneous Collections*, 1964, *146*, 84 pp.

Mulligan, J. A. Singing behavior and its development in the Song Sparrow, *Melospiza melodia*. *University of California, Berkeley, Publications in Zoology*, 1966, *81*, 1—76.

Mundinger, P. C. Vocal imitation and individual recognition of finch calls. *Science*, 1970, *168*, 480—482.

Murdock, G. P. *Africa: Its peoples and their culture history*. New York: McGraw-Hill, 1959.

Murphey, R. K., & Phillips, R. E. Central patterning of a vocalization in fowl. *Nature (London)*, 1967, *216*, 1125—1126.

Murray, A. *History of the European languages; or, researches into the affinities of the Teutonic, Greek, Celtic, Slavonic and Indian nations*. (2nd ed.) Edinburgh: Constable, 1823.

Nakazima, S. A comparative study of the speech developments of Japanese and American English in childhood. *Studia Phonologica*, 1962, *2*, 27—46.

Newman, J. D. Midbrain regions relevant to auditory communication in songbirds. *Brain Research*, 1970, *22*, 259—261.

Newman, J. D., Symmes, D. Abnormal vocalizations in isolation reared monkeys. *Proceedings, 79th Annual Convention, American Psychological Association*, 1971, *6*, 789. (Abstract)

Newman, S. S. Further experiments in phonetic symbolism. *American Journal of Psychology*, 1933, *45*, 53—75.

Nicolai, J. Zur Biologie und Ethologie des Gimpels (*Pyrrhula pyrrhula* L.) *Zeitschrift für Tierpsychologie*, 1956, *13*, 93—132.

Nicolai, J. Familientradition in der Gesagsentwicklung des Gimpels (*Pyrrhula pyrrhula* L.). *Journal für Ornithologie* 1959, *100*, 39—46.

Nottebohm, F. The role of sensory feedback in the development of avian vocalizations. In D. W. Snow (Ed.), *Proceedings of the 14th International Ornithological Congress*. Oxford: Blackwell, 1967. Pp. 265—280.

Nottebohm, F. Auditory experience and song development in the chaffinch. *Fringilla coelebs. Ibis*, 1968, *110*, 549—568.

Nottebohm, F. The "critical period" for song learning. *Ibis*, 1969, *111*, 386—387. (a)

Nottebohm, F. The song of the chingolo, *Zonotrichia capensis*, in Argentina: description and evaluation of a system of dialects. *Condor*, 1969, *71*, 299—315. (b)

Nottebohm, F. Ontogeny of bird song. *Science*, 1970, *167*, 950—956.

Nottebohm, F. Neural lateralization of vocal control in a passerine bird. I. Song. *Journal of Experimental Zoology*, 1971, *177*, 229—262.

Nottebohm, F. Neural lateralization of vocal control in a passerine bird. II. Subsong, calls, and a theory of vocal learning. *Journal of Experimental Zoology*, 1972, *179*, 35—50. (a)

Nottebohm, F. The origins of vocal learning. *American Naturalist*, 1972, *106*, 116—140. (b)

Nottebohm, F. Vocal behavior in birds. In D. S. Farner & J. R. King (Eds.), *Avian biology*. Vol. 5. New York: Academic Press, 1975. Chap. 5.

Nottebohm, F. Continental patterns of song variability in *Zonotrichia capensis*: some possible ecological correlates. *American Naturalist*, in press.

Nottebohm, F., & Nottebohm, M. E. Vocalizations and breeding behavior of surgically deafened ring doves, *Streptopelia risoria. Animal Behavior*, 1971, *19*, 313—327.

Nottebohm, F., & Nottebohm, M. E. Ecological correlates of vocal variability in *Zonotrichia capensis hypolenca. Condor*, in press.

Paget, R. *Human speech*. New York: Harcourt, 1930.

Payne, R., & McVay, S. Songs of humpback whales. *Science*, 1971, *173*, 585—597.

Peek, F. W., & Phillips, R. E. Repetitive vocalizations evoked by local electrical stimulation of avian brains. *Brain Behavior and Evolution*, 1971, *4*, 417—438.

Pfeiffer, J. E. *The emergence of man.* New York: Harper, 1969.

Penfield, W., & Roberts, L. *Speech and brain-mechanisms.* Princeton, N.J.: Princeton Press, 1959.

Penfield, W., & Welch, K. The supplementary motor area of the cerebral cortex. *AMA Archives of Neurology and Psychiatry,* 1951, *66,* 289–317.

Ploog, D., & Melnechuck, T. (Eds.) Are apes capable of language? A report based on an NRP conference. *Neurosciences Research Program, Bulletin,* 1971, *9,* 600–700.

Popa, G. T., & Popa, F. G. Certain functions of the midbrain in pigeons. *Proceedings of the Royal Society, Series B,* 1933, *113,* 191–195.

Potash, L. M. Neuroanatomical regions relevant to production and analysis of vocalization within the avian *Torus semicircularis. Experientia,* 1970, *26,* 1104–1105. (a)

Potash, L. M. Vocalizations elicited by electrical brain stimulation in *Coturnix coturnix japonica. Behaviour,* 1970, *36,* 149–167. (b)

Poulsen, H. Inheritance and learning in the song of the chaffinch (*Fringilla coelebs* L.). *Behaviour,* 1951, *3,* 216–227.

Poulsen, H. Song learning in the Domestic Canary. *Zeitschrift für Tierpsychologie,* 1959, *16,* 173–178.

Premack, D. Language in chimpanzee? *Science,* 1971, *172,* 808–822. (a)

Premack, D. On the assessment of language competence in the chimpanzee. In A. M. Schrier & F. Stollnitz (Eds.), *Behavior of nonhuman primates.* Vol. 4. New York: Academic Press, 1971. Pp. 186–228. (b)

Putkonen, P. T. S. Electrical stimulation of the avian brain. *Annales Academiae Scientiarum Fennicae, Series A5,* 1967, *130,* 1–95.

Ridgway, S. H. *Mammals of the sea. Biology and medicine.* Springfield, Ill.: Thomas, 1972.

Robinson, B. W. Vocalization evoked from forebrain in *Macaca mulatta. Physiology and Behavior,* 1967, *2,* 345–354.

Rowell, T. E., & Hinde, R. A. Vocal communication by the rhesus monkey (*Macaca mulatta*). *Proceedings of the Zoological Society of London,* 1962, *138,* 279–294.

Rozin, P., Poritsky, S., & Sotsky, R. American children with reading problems can easily learn to read English represented by Chinese characters. *Science,* 1971, *171,* 1264–1267.

Ruch, T. C. Neurophysiology of emotion and motivation. In T. C. Ruch & J. F. Fulton (Eds.), *Medical physiology and biophysics.* Philadelphia: Saunders, 1960. Pp. 483–499.

Sapir, E. A study in phonetic symbolism. *Journal of Experimental Psychology,* 1929, *12,* 225–239.

Savin, H. B., & Bever, T. G. The nonperceptual reality of the phoneme. *Journal of Verbal Learning and Verbal Behavior,* 1970, *9,* 295–302.

Schaltenbrand, G., Spuler, H., Wahren, W., & Rümler, B. Electroanatomy of the thalamic ventro-oral nucleus based on stereotaxic stimulation in man. *Zeitschrift für Neurologie,* 1971, *199,* 259–276.

Schleidt, W. M. Über die Spontaneität von Erbkoordinationen. *Zeitschrift für Tierpsychologie,* 1964, *21,* 235–256.

Showers, M. J. C., & Crosby, E. C. Somatic and visceral responses from the cingulate gyrus. *Neurology,* 1958, *8,* 561–565.

Skultety, F. M. Experimental mutism following electrolytic lesions of the periaqueductal gray matter in dogs. *Transactions of the American Neurological Association,* 1961, *86,* 245–246.

Smith, W. K. The functional significance of the rostral cingular cortex as revealed by its responses to electrical excitation. *Journal of Neurophysiology,* 1945, *8,* 241–255.

Snow, D. W. The singing assemblies of Little Hermits. *Living Bird,* 1968, *3,* 47–55.

Spock, B. *Baby and child care.* New York: Hawthorn, 1968.

Stevens, S. S., & Davis, H. *Hearing, its psychology and physiology.* New York: Wiley, 1938.

Struhsaker, T. T. Auditory communication among Vervet monkeys (*Cercopithecus aethiops*). In S. A. Altmann (Ed.), *Social communication among primates,* Chicago: Univ. of Chicago Press, 1967. Pp. 281–324.

Struhsaker, T. T. & Hunkeler, P. Evidence of tool-using by chimpanzees in the Ivory Coast. *Folia Primatologica,* 1971, *15,* 212–219.

Taylor, I. K., & Taylor, M. M. Phonetic symbolism in four unrelated languages. *Canadian Journal of Psychology,* 1962, *16,* 344–356.

Thorpe, W. H. The learning of song patterns by birds, with special reference to the song of the chaffinch (*Fringilla coelebs*). *Ibis*, 1958, *100*, 535—570.

Thorpe, W. H. Animal vocalization and communication. In C. H. Millikan & F. L. Darley (Eds.), *Brain mechanisms underlying speech and language.* New York: Grune & Stratton, 1967. Pp. 2—12.

Thorpe, W. H. Duetting and antiphonal song in birds: its extent and significance. *Behaviour*, 1972, Suppl. 18, 196 pp.

Thorpe, W. H., & North, M. E. W. Origin and significance of the power of vocal imitation: with special reference to the antiphonal singing of birds. *Nature (London)*, 1965, *208*, 219—222.

Tschanz, B. Trottellummen. Die Entstehung der persönlichen Beziehungen zwischen Jungvogel und Eltern. *Zeitschrift für Tierpsychologie*, 1968, Monogr. No. 4.

von der Gabelentz, G. *Die Sprachwissenschaft.* Leipzig: Tauchnitz, 1901.

von Frisch, K. *The dance language and orientation of bees.* Cambridge, Mass.: Harvard Univ. Press, 1967.

Wagner, H. O. Notes on the life history of the emerald toucanet. *Wilson Bulletin*, 1944, *56*, 65—76.

Washburn, S. L. The evolution of human behavior. In J. D. Roslansky (Ed.), *The Uniqueness of man.* Amsterdam: North-Holland Publ., 1969. Pp. 165—189.

Wasz-Höckert, O., Lind, J., Vuorenkoski, U., Partanen, T., & Valanne, E. *The infant cry: A spectrographic and auditory analysis.* London: Spastics Int. Med. Publ. & Heinemann, 1968.

Webster, R. L. Selective suppression of infant's vocal responses by classes of phonemic stimulation. *Developmental Psychology*, 1969, *1*, 410—414.

White, S. J. Selective responsiveness by the gannet (*Sula basana*) to played-back calls. *Animal Behavior*, 1971, *19*, 125—131.

Whitman, C . O. The behavior of pigeons, In H. A. Carr (Ed.), *Posthumous works of Charles O. Whitman*, Vol. 3. Washington, D.C.: Carnegie Institution, 1919.

Wiley, R. H. Song groups in a singing assembly of Little Hermits. *Condor*, 1971, *73*, 28—35.

Winter, P. Dialects in squirrel monkeys: vocalization of the Roman arch type. *Folia Primatologica*, 1969, *10*, 216—229.

Winter, P., Ploog, D., & Latta, J. Vocal repertoire of the squirrel monkey (*Saimiri sciureus*), its analysis and significance. *Experimental Brain Research*, 1966, *1*, 359—384.

Zigmond, R. E., Nottebohm, F., & Pfaff, D. W. Androgen-concentrating cells in the midbrain of a songbird. *Science*, 1973, *179*, 1005—1007.

Zipf, G. *Human behavior and the principle of least effort.* Reading, Mass.: Addison-Wesley, 1949. Reprinted: New York: Hafner, 1965.

6. Brain Development in Relation to Language

Marcus Jacobson

An attempt is made to view the development of language within the frame of developmental biology. Language development is correlated with the increase in connections in the cerebral cortex and especially with the growth and connectivity of stellate and granule cells (Type II neurons). The neuronal circuits subserving language have not been identified. The concept is proposed of "specification" of neurons subserving language: the specification consisting of progressive, irreversible restriction of their possible functional roles. Regulation or reorganization of language functions after brain injury may occur in a variety of ways: (1) by respecification, resulting in changes in nerve cells' properties and functional operations; (2) by redeployment of nerve cells by selective death, selective replacement, or migration and relocation; (3) by redeployment of nerve connections. All these mechanisms are more active and efficient in young than in old neurons, and this appears to be the reason for greater recovery after brain damage in infancy than at later ages. Some derangements of language following brain damage appear to be malconnection syndromes due to the recovery of inappropriate synaptic connections.

Shortcomings of Linguistic Analysis

The task of finding causal relations between neurobiology and language has met with serious difficulties. Cerebral localization of language function, although a necessary preliminary step, falls far short of a neurophysiological explication of language. If our expectations include such an explication, we have to admit that little progress has been made toward its realization. Indeed, it is not yet possible to describe any complex type of behavior in terms of a program of neural events, and many decades will pass before the neurophysiological mechanisms of cognitive processes in man are understood. With these limitations in mind, we should be free to choose any method that brings us closer to a solution of the problem of the neural substrates of language. I shall attempt to do so by adopting a developmental approach. First, however, I wish to draw attention to the limitations of certain other approaches to this problem, in particular the approach via linguistic analysis.

I have been reading some of the literature of formal linguistic analysis, and while the didactic and rhetorical validity of these procedures—generative and trans-formational grammars—cannot be denied, it is very doubtful whether they have any meaning in relationship to brain mechanisms subserving language. It is hardly an exaggeration to say that, in so far as the propositions of linguistic analysis refer to the nervous system, they are uncertain, and in so far as they are certain they do not refer to the nervous system. In principle it may be possible to establish links between linguistic analysis and neurobiology by searching for causal relationships between neuronal activities and the regularities that are evidently possible to find within any natural language. We may then ask what neuronal activities lie behind such regularities or logical relationships, and are accountable for them. A criticism of this formal or logicomathematical analysis of the relationships between language and the brain is that it remains purely phenomenological (in the etymological not the philosophical meaning) and therefore not explanatory. However rigorous the logical analysis of language may be, it cannot satisfy the requirement of a neurophysiological explanation. Such an analysis can only show relations within the phenomenological system; it cannot show how that system is generated by neurophysiological pro-cesses. Formal linguistic analysis, divorced from its biological substrates, is un-likely to be a profitable approach to the problem of how the brain generates language. Purely psychological approaches to that problem are equally unlikely to succeed. The work of Jean Piaget may serve as an example of an excellent psychological analysis of perception and cognition that constitutes a closed system of relation-ships between psychological phenomena that remain disconnected from their neural substrates. This is most clearly evident in the most important and original aspects of Piaget's analysis, namely his genetic or developmental method. This consists of analyzing the changes in the child's perceptions and corresponding notions and in the child's behavior at different stages of development. Despite the brilliance of Piaget's theory of cognitive development, it remains unrelatable to the development of the brain. In general it fails to show how cognitive develop-ment can be framed in terms of developmental biology, or to show how psycho-logical ontogeny relates to neural ontogeny.

By the term "developmental approach," I mean an approach that employs any techniques for studying development of the neural biological mechanisms that subserve language. Both neural and language functions are less complex at early stages than at later stages of development or in the fully developed organism. Thus it may be easier to establish causal relationships between developing neural functions and developing language functions than to establish such relationships between the final products of neural and linguistic development. There are also advantages in placing the problem of language ontogenesis within the realm of developmental biology. For example, it may be possible to deal with the morphogenesis of language, or the development of patterns in language, in the same way as we deal with these aspects of the ontogenesis of other functional systems. We may expect to find genetic preconditions for the development of language and mechanisms that regulate language ontogeny, just as there are these genetic and regulatory mechanisms in the development of the structural components of the developing organism.

From Neurogenotype to Neurophenotype

The translation of genetic information into the program of development that gives rise to the organism constitutes the transformation of genotype to phenotype. There are no simple isomorphisms between the neurogenotype and the neurophenotype, but they form many-to-many relationships. One expects to find that almost all forms of complex behavior are determined by many genes. This seems to be true even for the relatively simple, species-specific types of behavior that have been termed "fixed actions patterns." For example, in crickets quite simple patterns of stridulation are generated by a few hundred neurons, but these species-specific vocalizations are determined by several genes located on at least two chromosomes (Bentley, 1971). The genetic basis of the relatively simple, species-specific, and invariant patterns of vocalization of certain insects and birds is likely to be extremely complex. Even greater complexity may be met with in the relationship between the genes and human languages. Interest has been focused on the problem of the genetic basis of language by Chomsky's hypothesis that natural languages share certain universal structures that may be derived from innately determined functions of the human brain. There seems to be no means of experimentally testing the validity of Chomsky's formulation. The links between the genes and language are indirect and complex, and it is not yet possible to give any kind of causal analysis of the relationship between the genotype and the neurophenotype. Only the most general notion of this relationship can be obtained at present.

Genes control molecular synthesis and do not contain instructions for the assembly of molecules into cells or of cells into organisms. The genome does not contain instructions specifying the vast number of different neuronal phenotypes. The great diversity of neuronal phenotypes, and the complexity of their interconnections is undoubtedly a precondition for the development of language and of other cognitive functions. Thus it is necessary to give a brief consideration to the problem of neuronal diversity.

It is now generally accepted that although neurons may have considerable diversity they fall into two quite distinct classes, which have been called Class I and Class II neurons (Altman, 1969; Globus & Scheibel, 1967; M. Jacobson, 1970, 1972). Class I neurons are large neurons with long axons. They form the primary afferent and efferent pathways of the nervous system. Their structures and functions are invariant, and they develop under tight genetic and epigenetic constraints. They constitute what may be termed the hard wiring of the brain.

In contradistinction, Class II neurons are small interneurons with short axons. They perform integrative functions between the primary afferent and efferent systems. Class II neurons exhibit great morphological variability. One of the most distinctive differences between these two classes of neurons is shown by the timetable of their ontogeny. In each part of the nervous system, Class I neurons are generated and differentiate before Class II neurons. Class I neurons form a framework that is rather invariant in each species, and the Class II neurons are connected into this framework at a later stage of ontogeny. The neurons that are first in the field are less variable and appear to be less modifiable than those that appear later, and the latter are more susceptible to changes resulting directly from nervous activity or indirectly from endocrine stimulation.

According to this view, neurons develop in two complementary modes that together permit a great variety of neuronal functions to be represented; functions that are innately predetermined are performed largely by the Class I neurons, whereas those that develop as a result of individual experience are subserved largely by Class II neurons. It should be emphasized once again that these two classes of neurons are interdependent and always function as an integrated ensemble. To state that language or any other cognitive function is primarily a function of Class II neurons would be a gross oversimplification, because the Class II neurons, being interneurons, can only function within the framework of the input and output provided for them by Class I neurons.

It is not yet possible to assign specific functional roles, related to language or to any other cognitive functions, to any particular group of neurons. Nor have any clues been found to the functional properties of any neuron in the cerebral cortex that might relate neuronal function or ontogeny to the development of language function. However, there are certain temporospatial regularities in the pattern of development of the cerebral cortex that can roughly be correlated with the development of cognition and behavior.

ONTOGENY OF CEREBRAL NEOCORTEX

All the neurons of the neocortex of man are probably generated before the second half of intrauterine development (Dobbing & Sands, 1970). They develop according to a remarkably invariant timetable (Angevine, 1970), in regular temporospatial order. The first neurons to be generated in the cerebral cortex are the large pyramidal neurons of Layer V, which form the primary efferent projection system of the cortex, linking it to the subcortical centers. The main afferent projection system from the thalamus grows into the cortex at an early stage of development. Thus the reflex circuits through the cerebral cortex, which are mediated by the thalamocortical axons projecting onto the large pyramidal cells of Layer V, are well developed at birth. The pyramidal neurons at successively more superficial levels of the neocortex are formed at progressively later times in the first half of fetal development. The axons of later-forming pyramidal neurons terminate within the cortex. These intracortical, so-called associative, connections, which link different zones of the cortex, are already present at birth in man but become greatly elaborated postnatally. Elaboration of intracortical neuronal connections is related to the development of synaptic connections on the dendrites of cortical neurons (Molliver & Van der Loos, 1970; Purpura, Shofer, Housepian, & Noback, 1964). One may safely infer that the development of behavior of newborn mammals is related to the explosive increase in the number of synapses in the cerebral cortex that occurs during the neonatal period. It is obvious that the functional capacities of the brain develop at the same time as the structural complexity increases, but lack of information prevents one from understanding the development of any form of behavior in terms of development of neuronal circuits.

The stellate cells, which are Class II neurons, are the last to develop in each region of the neocortex. Although they are all formed before birth, they differentiate postnatally. They then undergo extensive growth of their dendrites and elaborate branching of their short axons, which become connected to the dendrites of the pyramidal cells. The differentiation and maturation of the stellate and pyramidal neurons occurs earlier in the deeper than in the superficial layers of the neocortex in all mammals, including man (Angevine & Sidman, 1961; Berry & Rogers, 1966; Poliakov, 1961). Thus the generation as well as the morphological differentiation of cortical neurons progresses in an inside-out gradient. The neurons in the outer or superficial layers of the cortex, which mature last during ontogenesis, are also those which appear to have been added to the cerebral cortex most recently in its phylogeny. Therefore, the superficial regions of the neocortex, expecially the development of connections of the stellate neurons, may hold important clues to the neurobiological correlates of cognitive functions. Poliakov (1961) has reviewed the evidence that different regions of the neocortex developed in a fixed order. The central zones of the primary somatosensory, visual, and auditory cortical projection areas develop first; the periphery of these primary areas develops later; and the regions of overlap of cortical projection areas are the last to mature. Parts of the cerebral cortex that subserve language evidently belong to this third, late developing, component of the cortex.

Studies of cortical ontogenesis show that the major functional zones (visual, auditory, and somatosensory) each develop independently and only overlap during the later stages of their ontogeny (Poliakov, 1961). It is reasonable to suspect that each of these zones arises from a small group of neuroepithelial germinal cells and that the latter are themselves derived from a single stem cell. If this were to be demonstrated, cell lineage in the cerebral cortex would be shown to be related to its functional properties.

As is well known, various regions within the neural plate are committed to develop into restricted regions of the brain: that is, the neural plate is a mosaic of distinct cell groups with different developmental fates (C. O. Jacobson, 1960). We may therefore ask whether there are not some neuroepitheleal germinal cells in the neural plate, or in the germinal zones of the neural tube, which are committed to give rise to "language neurons." Asked in another way: When and to what extent is the prospective fate of "language neurons" determined in the developing nervous system? This question presupposes that there are neurons whose primary function is to generate language, and that the functions of these neurons are predetermined in the developing brain.

This question implies that neurons subserving language undergo a specification process similar to that which has been demonstrated in some other types of neurons such as spinal motoneurons (Székely, 1963) and retinal ganglion cells (M. Jacobson, 1968). The specification consists of a progressive restriction of the neuron's functional capacities, from an initial multipotential state to a final state of unique functional potential. The rate of this process of functional specification is different in different types of neurons. In some types the restriction of functional potential occurs within hours; in others the restrictive process may be prolonged for days or years, but, as far as we know, the process is not reversible (M. Jacobson, 1969).

There are two methods of studying the functional specification of neurons. The first method consists of transplanting neurons to new locations in the nervous system in order to study their capacity to form connections and to recover and modify their functions. Second, neurons may be destroyed in order to determine whether their connections and functions can be taken over by other neurons. Such operations have shown that young neurons are better able to modify their functions than old neurons and that the earlier in development the operations are performed the less the eventual functional derangement. These experimental strategies provide a means for studying the functional development of various types of neurons, including those subserving linguistic functions. The succeeding sections will show to what extent the experimental strategies for studying functional regulation of neuronal systems may have a bearing on the problem of the development of neuronal mechanisms subserving language.

Functional Regulation in the Developing Cerebral Cortex

Complete recovery of function may occur after removal of part of the developing cerebral cortex (Goldman, Rosvold, & Mishkin, 1970; Tucker & Kling, 1967). Functional recovery may also follow serial ablation of the cortex of adult rats and monkeys, although removal of the same volume of cortex in one operation results in serious functional deficits (Rosen, Stein, & Butters, 1971; Stein, Rosen, Graziadei, Mishkin, & Brink, 1969). Removal of one cerebral hemisphere in the adult human results in much less functional loss if the removed hemisphere has been damaged since childhood than if the hemisphere has been removed because of an acute lesion of the mature brain (Ueki, 1966). Recovery in these cases is not due to regeneration of the lost parts of the cerebral cortex. Rather, an entire miniature system that functions harmoniously is reconstituted out of the parts of the developing cerebral cortex that remain after injury or surgical removal. The capacity for functional regulation is maximal during early stages of development of the cerebral cortex and diminishes progressively during later stages of ontogeny. That is, during development there is a progressive loss of the ability of part of the cortex to assume the functions of the whole.

Many examples may be cited to show that brain damage results in greater permanent functional derangement in old than in young mammals. For example, failure of development of the entire left half of the cerebellum may produce negligible symptoms, whereas severe disturbances follow removal of the same part of the brain in the adult. Congenital absence of the corpus callosum in man produces very subtle impairment in coordinating the functions of the left and right side of the brain (Saul & Sperry, 1968), whereas surgical section of the corpus callosum in the adult results in marked disturbances of interhemispheric coordination. In general, functional compensation for brain lesions sustained in infancy may be as great as the compensation that occurs as a result of congenital absence of the same part of the brain, but the later in development the loss of brain tissue occurs the greater the residual loss of function (Obrador, 1964; Ueki, 1966).

This generalization also applies to the case of linguistic impairment that follows brain damage. Lenneberg (1967) has summarized the observations that show that the neural organization of language undergoes a progressive loss of modifiability and of reparative capacity from the age of normal onset of language to the mid-teens. The gradual reduction of the capacity to recover from damage to parts of the brain concerned with linguistic function is correlated with the morphological and functional maturation of the cerebral cortex. At birth the cerebral hemispheres are equipotential as regards language localization. Progressive cerebral lateralization occurs after about 36 months of age, leading finally to the restriction of language function to the dominant cerebral hemisphere at about 14 years of age. As the cerebral cortex matures postnatally, certain linguistic functions become increasingly restricted to the left cerebral hemisphere. Lesions of this hemisphere result in linguistic impairment whose severity is correlated with the maturity of the developing cerebral cortex.

These phenomena, of progressive restriction of the functional potential of parts of the brain subserving language and the progressive reduction of the capacity of the linguistic centers to recover from trauma, are also well known in the development of other functional systems. Such systems exhibit what Morgan (1927) termed *morphallaxis*, meaning that the developmental fates of its parts are not rigidly predetermined, but any isolated part of the developing system will form into a small but normally proportioned and functionally intact system. These systems have the properties of gradient fields in which each cell differentiates according to its position relative to the boundaries of the whole cell population. In such systems each part must have the capacity to differentiate into any other part and to assume the functions of any parts. That is, the prospective fate of the part and its developmental functional potential are not irreversibly determined.

The immature mammalian cerebral cortex, including the part subserving language in man, has many of the characteristics of morphallactic systems. An essential first stage of the process of morphallaxis is that the cells acquire positional information as a result of cellular interactions and communication, and as a second stage the cells interpret this information and differentiate according to it (Hunt & Jacobson, 1972; Wolpert, 1969). It is proposed that after ablation of part of the cerebral cortex the cells in the residual part reacquire positional information relative to the new boundaries of the cortex. The response of the neurons to the positional information must consist of a reallocation of their functional capacities within the residual population of nerve cells. This may involve a redistribution of synaptic connections within the residual cell population, with the result that the original pattern of connections is restored on a smaller scale, and the functional integrity of the system may be restored, albeit only partially.

There are two mechanisms that may account for the recovery of function that has been observed after injuries to the cerebral cortex in the newborn. First, neonatal cortical lesions do not disrupt as many connections as lesions sustained in the adult. It may thus be possible for connections to develop *ab initio* in the correct temporo-spatial order, even after fairly severe injury to the neonatal cortex. Secondly, many neurons in the cerebral cortex of the newborn may be functionally uncommitted or unspecified, and delayed specification of functions may occur in the residual population of neurons. Such respecification will restore the function of the whole cortex but on a diminished scale in a smaller population of neurons. Both of these mechanisms—delayed synaptogenesis and delayed functional specifications— confer some potential plasticity on the developing cerebral cortex. These mechanisms endow the brain with some capacity for functional recovery after trauma, which is maximal in the newborn and diminishes progressively with age. The mechanism of such synaptic rearrangement forms the subject of the next section.

Synaptic Stabilty and Lability

There are various alternative mechanisms that may account for recovery of function after brain damage: There may be multiple choice of available systems subserving the same functions; Recruitment of noncommitted neurons may occur from a population of reserve neurons or of reserve neuronal structures; Reallocation or transfer of connections within the residual population may occur; No anatomical but only functional synaptic changes may be responsible for the recovery of function.

A phenomenon that probably accounts in some part for recovery of function after brain damage is the remarkable redistribution of synaptic terminals that has been found after various types of surgical operations on the brain. It is very likely that similar changes in the distribution of synaptic terminals occur during the normal development of the brain. In all cases the mechanism of redistribution of synapses involves an early phase of sprouting of new axonal presynaptic terminals. Sprouting of presynaptic axonal terminals is always found during the development of synaptic connections (M. Jacobson, 1970). During the normal outgrowth of the axons an excess number of branches is formed. Many axonal terminals that fail to form synaptic connections atrophy and eventually disappear, whereas those that make connections will survive and grow. The initial connections appear to be made at random and in excess and later to become reduced in number as a result of a selective process. The excess number of presynaptic terminals may compete for connection with a limited number of postsynaptic sites.

The factors that may determine specificity of connections during synaptogenesis are cytoaffinity, proper timing of connections, and functional efficiency. Axons may have a selective advantage if they arrive at the postsynaptic site first, or during a specific period of development, or if the pre- and postsynaptic cells have a physicochemical compatibility. Additional advantages may be conferred on nerve terminals that convey impulse traffic that is qualitatively or quantitatively adequate to stimulate the postsynaptic cells. On the basis of these functional criteria, certain interneuronal contacts form stable synaptic connections, whereas other contacts, which lack adequate functional properties, form unstable and temporary connections.

As a result of competition between the presynaptic terminals for a limited number of postsynaptic sites the initial random distribution of presynaptic terminals on postsynaptic sites becomes converted into a stable equilibrium arrangement of synapses. In the equilibrium condition those synapses that are best fitted to survive persist at the expense of those less fit to function. The criteria of best fit may be an inherent physicochemical label of the pre- and postsynaptic membranes such that a certain degree of physicochemical matching is necessary for the stability of the nexus. Presynaptic terminals with a greater chemoaffinity for the postsynaptic site will displace the presynaptic terminals with less chemo-affinity.

Competition between presynaptic sites is thus not based upon the absolute qualities of the pre- and the postsynaptic terminals, but depends upon the relative matching between a set of presynaptic terminals and a set of postsynaptic sites. If the number of postsynaptic sites increases, as it does during normal growth of dendrites, for example in the cerebral cortex, the new synaptic sites will be occupied by collateral sprouting of presynaptic terminals. On the other hand, if the number of postsynaptic sites is depleted or reduced, for example as a result of removal of part of the cerebral cortex, there is an orderly redistribution of the presynaptic terminals in the residual part. As I have already suggested, this redistribution of synaptic connections is the response of neurons to the positional information that they acquire within the residual part of the brain. It is thus an example of Morgan's morphallaxis: the pattern of synaptic connection is re-established on a compressed or expanded scale, and the system shows an elasticity in that the topological invariants are preserved although the metrics are altered.

Synaptic connections may also be formed and reformed on the basis of functional matching between the pre- and postsynaptic neurons. For example, when presynaptic terminals make contact with postsynaptic neurons, the resulting connections may persist if the pattern of impulses in the presynaptic terminals has specific trigger features that fire the postsynaptic neurons. The synaptic connections may break down if there is a mis-match between the functional characteristics of pre- and postsynaptic neurons, or if the quality of impulse traffic in the presynaptic terminals is inadequate.

A combination of physicochemical and functional matching between pre- and postsynaptic components of the synapse is probably necessary for its stability. The immature connectivity is initially profuse and becomes progressively pruned by selective elimination of mismatched connections. The effect is to reduce the initial redundancy of connections and selectively promote the development of neuronal structures that can coexist because they are not mutually contradictory or mutually exclusive.

So far only the changes in the presynaptic terminals have been considered. That is because they have been most fully documented. The response of the post-synaptic cells has not been studied but probably involves a redistribution of synaptic sites during normal development as well as an increase of synaptic sites during the expansion of the dendrites that is the major feature of the postnatal ontogeny of the neuron. The role of neuroglia in these processes is not known.

These preliminary considerations and the examples that will be given later lead to the concept of a dynamic equilibrium of neuronal connections. The connections between any set of presynaptic terminals and the matching set of postsynaptic elements is not invariant but involves a continual readjustment of the pattern of connections. Such plasticity is undoubtedly a feature of the developing nervous system. However, it is most clearly demonstrated experimentally by surgically altering the ratio of pre- to postsynaptic elements. The following examples will show how the redistribution of presynaptic terminals within a population of postsynaptic neurons may occur after various types of surgical operations.

Synaptic Disconnection, Reconnection, and Malconnection

Synaptic disconnection is one of the most common results of injury to the central nervous system. The immediate functional result of the injury may be a disconnection syndrome. However, this acute syndrome is likely to be of temporary duration in the developing brain because synaptic rearrangements may occur that convert the disconnection either into reconnection or malconnection. This occurs because disconnection of one set of presynaptic terminals leaves synaptic sites vacant that may be occupied by other presynaptic terminals. Such rearrangements of synaptic connections may occur at a distance from the site of injury when they occur in the projection zone of the injured neurons. Several kinds of synaptic rearrangements may occur, depending on whether the disconnection is partial or complete and depending on the neighboring sources of presynaptic terminals that are capable of occupying the vacant synaptic sites.

If neurons are only partially disconnected, the residual presynaptic terminals may give rise to collateral branches that reoccupy the disconnected synaptic sites. Totally disconnected neurons may be reconnected by branches of presynaptic terminals supplying neighboring neurons. In either case, the type of functional recovery depends on the efficiency of synaptic reconnection, and particularly on whether the newly formed synapses are functionally appropriate or inappropriate. Examples of these types will be given below, where it will become apparent that these may at best give rise to partial recovery and more frequently may result in malconnection and malfunction.

Sprouting of presynaptic terminals into a zone of disconnected synapses, resulting in functionally inadequate or incorrect connections, has been found in many parts of the mammalian central nervous system. This mechanism has been suggested as an explanation of the spasticity that follows lesions of the spinal cord (Liu & Chambers, 1958; McCouch, Austin, Liu, & Liu, 1958). It is also conceivable that similar malconnections may be responsible for some derangements of language that result from brain injury. These might be termed malconnection syndromes. A variety of such malconnections has been found after lesions in the septum (Moore, Björklund, & Stenevi, 1971; Raisman, 1969), brain stem (Goodman & Horel, 1966), superior colliculus (Schneider, 1970; Schneider & Nauta, 1969), thalamus (Wall & Egger, 1971), and spinal cord (Björklund, Katzman, Stenevi, & West, 1971; Katzman, Björklund, Owman, Stenevi, & West, 1971; Liu & Chambers, 1958).

The example of the formation of new connections in the thalamus of the rat will serve as a paradigm of malconnection syndromes. Wall and Egger (1971) found that some days after destruction of the nucleus gracilis, the cells of the ventral posterior lateral nucleus of the thalamus that normally respond to leg stimulation began to respond to arm stimulation. The nucleus gracilis receives cutaneous sensory afferent nerve fibers from the hind limbs. From the nucleus gracilis, the nerve fibers decussate and project to the ventral posterior lateral nucleus of the thalamus (VPL). Similar projections pass from the forelimb by way of the cuneate nucleus and from the face via the trigeminal nucleus. The entire contralateral surface of the body is represented as a somatotopic map in the thalamus: each individual neuron receives inputs from a small discrete area of the body surface.

Immediately after destruction of the nucleus gracilis, there was almost complete abolition of thalamic responses to stimulation of the hindlimb, and the area of VPL responding to forelimb stimulation remained unchanged. However, three weeks later there was an expansion of the arm area into the regions of VPL that normally respond only to leg stimuli. This expansion started at three days after destruction of the nucleus gracilis and was completed within one to three weeks. The expansion occurred only at the margin of the disconnected region of thalamus, resulting in a lateral expansion of the area subserving lower arm and wrist into the area normally subserving leg. The newly connected thalamic cells had small receptive fields, as in the normal animals, but their connections had switched from leg to arm. One explanation is that sprouts had grown from the terminals of axons from the cuneate nucleus and had occupied the synaptic sites left vacant after destruction of the nucleus gracilis. The new connections do not produce recovery from the lesion because the malconnections result in false referral of arm stimuli to the leg. One can conceive of an analogous situation in the parts of the brain subserving language resulting in a form of aphasia.

Functional adaptation after brain lesions may result from a number of alternative mechanisms. A form of functional recovery may occur, even after destruction of a large proportion of the neurons within a functional group, if there is an adaptive rearrangement of synaptic connections within the residual group of neurons. If the destruction of neurons occurs after the development of synaptic connections, the residual connections may redistribute themselves to restore the original pattern of connections on a reduced scale. If the injury occurs before the development of connections, the latter may form a normal pattern *ab initio*. This type of rearrangement of neuronal connections, before and after their initial development, appears to occur in the visual system of amphibians and fishes (Gaze, Jacobson, & Székely, 1963; Straznicky, Gaze, & Keating, 1971; Yoon, 1971).

In the adult goldfish, removal of the posterior part of the optic tectum results in the elimination of the fiber projection to the tectum from the temporal half of the contralateral retina. However, after a few weeks, this defect disappears and it is then found that the residual terminals of optic nerve fibers in the tectum redistribute themselves in retinotopic order in the residual part of the tectum (Yoon, 1971). The whole retina now projects to the remaining half of the tectum and this involves a complete redistribution of all the optic nerve terminals in the tectum such that the internal relations between the nerve terminals are preserved. Such a change in the metrics of the system without a change in its topological invariants is characteristic of the regulation that occurs in all harmonious equipotential systems. The characteristic of such systems is that, when part of the system is removed, the remainder will develop into a normally proportioned whole of diminished size.

The developing cerebral cortex shows many of the characteristics of a harmonious equipotential system. In the case of the optic tectum and probably also in the cerebral cortex, there seems to be a relative rather than an absolute matching of the presynaptic terminals with postsynaptic sites. For any ratio of pre- to postsynaptic elements there is an equilibrium configuration. This equilibrium is apparently attained by a competition between the presynaptic terminals for the available postsynaptic sites so that all postsynaptic sites are occupied by the presynaptic terminals that match them best. The physicochemical matching between pre- and postsynaptic neurons is not absolute, one-to-one, but relative or graded. It is most likely that the physicochemical differences between neurons develop an axial gradients within the populations of pre- and postsynaptic cells, for example, in the retina and optic tectum. In this way, the physicochemical factors that subserve the formation of synaptic connections are not developed in mosaic fashion, qualitatively different from one neuron to its neighbours, but are graded quantitatively and vectorially in relation to the axes of symmetry of the whole population of neurons. The order of connections between pre- and postsynaptic neurons is specified by the polarity of these axial gradients, namely by quantitative gradation of a specific physiochemical parameter. This gradation will be preserved regardless of the metrics, that is, regardless of the ratio of pre- to postsynaptic elements.

Conclusion

It has been said that the structure of language and its development are predicated by brain structure and development and that the operational and organizational principles underlying the brain have their linguistic parallels. Some piquant parallels between natural languages and communications systems found in living organisms have been remarked upon by Roman Jakobson (1971). An additional parallel may be drawn between the historical development of linguistics and that of biology, and especially neurobiology: both have recently extended and enlarged their mechanistic constructs to include topological and relativistic elements. The cardinal significance of relational and contextual operations in verbal communication and the distinction between context-free and context-sensitive linguistic systems (Chomsky, 1963, 1967) are now the common coinage of linguistics. Such relativistic constructs are quite recent developments in neurobiology and have not yet exerted an influence to counterbalance the concept of the primacy of the individual nerve cell. Our thinking in laboratory practice and in theory is often dominated by single unit analysis, which deals with the properties and operations of individual nerve cells and does not map those functional units into a larger contextual framework. The discipline of neuroanatomy has been even more constrained by the notion that only the invariant features of nerve cells have any significance, and the stability of neuronal structures has been studied to the neglect of the variable and plastic features. Yet it has for decades been well known that the *developing* brain goes through a period of very considerable variability, or, as the greatest neuroanatomist of the past century has put it, "Every ramification, dendritic or axonic, in the course of formation, passes through a chaotic period, so to speak, a period of trials, during which there are sent out at random experimental conductors most of which are destined to disappear [Ramón y Cajal, 1917]." In the past few years the importance of both the variable and invariant properties and operations of nerve cells has been apprehended more fully (M. Jacobson, 1970). We now recognize that the stable and invariant features are most clearly expressed by large nerve cells with long axons (Golgi Type I neurons), which comprise the hard wiring of the brain. On the other hand, we also recognize the structural and functional variability of small, short axoned neurons (Golgi Type II neurons), which may be equated with the plastic component of the brain.

However, when we consider any complex function of the whole brain, and not merely of the single neural units, we see that stability and variability reside in the same context, and we ask whether the morphological dichotomy (invariant versus variable units) subserves the functional dichotomy (stability versus plasticity) that is seen in natural languages as well as in the brain. These parallels between language and the brain invite further speculations from which I shall refrain, merely concluding with a reiteration of Charles Darwin's belief that "Whoever achieves understanding of the baboon's brain will do more for metaphysics than Locke did, which is to say he will do more for philosophy in general, including the problem of knowledge [Notebooks on Evolution, 1837—1839]."

References

Altman, J. Postnatal growth and differentiation of the mammalian brain, with implications for a morphological theory of memory. In G. Quarton, T. Melnechuck, & F. O. Schmitt (eds.), *The neurosciences: A study program*. New York: Rockfeller Univ. Press, 1969. Pp. 723—743.

Angevine, J. B., Jr. Critical cellular events in the shaping of neural centers. In F. O. Schmitt (Ed.-in-chief), *The neurosciences: Second study program*. New York: Rockfeller Univ. Press, 1970. Pp. 62—72.

Angevine, J. B., Jr. & Sidman, R. L. Autoradiographic study of cell migration during histogenesis of cerebral cortex in the mouse. *Nature (London)*, 1961, *192*, 766—768.

Bentley, D. R. Genetic control of an insect neuronal network. *Science*, 1971, *174*, 1139—1141.

Berry, M., & Rogers, A. W. Histogenesis of mammalian neocortex. In R. Hassler & H. Stephan (Eds.), *Evolution of the forebrain*. New York: Plenum, 1966. Pp. 197—205.

Björklund, A., Katzman, R., Stenevi, U., & West, K. A. Development and growth of axonal sprouts from noradrenaline and 5-hydroxytryptamine neurons in the rat spinal cord. *Brain Research*, 1971, *31*, 21—33.

Chomsky, N. Formal properties of grammars. In R. D. Luce, R. R. Bush, & E. Galanter (Eds.), *Handbook of mathematical psychology*. Vol. II. New York: Wiley, 1963. Pp. 323—418.

Chomsky, N. The formal nature of language. Appendix to E. H. Lenneberg, *Biological foundations of language*. New York: Wiley, 1967.

Darwin, C. *Notebooks on evolution, 1837—1839*.

Dobbing, J., & Sands, J. Timing of neuroblast multiplication in developing human brain. *Nature (London)*, 1970, *226*, 639—640.

Gaze, R. M., Jacobson M., & Székely, G. The retinotectal projection in *Xenopus* with compound eyes. *Journal of Physiology (London)*, 1963, *165*, 484—499.

Globus, A., & Scheibel, A. B. Pattern and field in cortical structure: the rabbit. *Journal of Comparative Neurology*, 1967, *131*, 155—172.

Goldman, P. S., Rosvold, H. E. & Mishkin, M. Evidence for behavioral impairment following pre-frontal lobotomy in the infant monkey. *Journal of Comparative Physiological Psychology*, 1970, *70*, 454—463.

Goodman, D. C., & Horel, J. A. Sprouting of optic tract projections in the brain stem of the rat. *Journal of Comparative Neurology*, 1966, *127*, 71—88.

Hunt, R. K., & Jacobson, M. Development and stability of positional information in *Xenopus* retinal ganglion cells. *Proceedings of the National Academy of Sciences, U.S.*, 1972, *69*, 780—783.

Jacobson, C.-O. The localization of the presumptive cerebral regions in the neural plate of the axolotl larva. *Journal of Embryology and Experimental Morphology*, 1959, *7*, 1—21.

Jacobson, M. Development of neuronal specificity in retinal ganglion cells of *Xenopus. Developmental Biology*, 1968, *17*, 202—218.

Jacobson, M. Development of specific neuronal connections. *Science*, 1969, *163*, 543—547.

Jacobson, M. *Developmental neurobiology*. New York: Holt, 1970.

Jacobson, M. A plenitude of neurons. In G. Gottlieb (Ed.), *Studies on the development of behavior and the nervous system*. Chicago: Univ. of Chicago Press, 1973.

Jakobson, R. Linguistics in relation to other sciences. *Selected writings*. Vol. II. The Hague: Mouton, 1971. Pp. 655–696.

Katzman, R., Björklund, A., Owman, C., Stenevi, U., & West, K. A. Evidence for regenerative axon sprouting of central catecholamine neurons in the rat mesencephalon. *Brain Research*, 1971, *25*, 579–596.

Lenneberg, E. H. *Biological foundations of language*. New York: Wiley, 1967.

Liu, C. N., & Chambers, W. W. Intraspinal sprouting of dorsal root axons. *AMA Archives of Neurology and Psychiatry*, 1958, *79*, 46–61.

McCouch, G. P., Austin, G. M., Liu, C. N., & Liu, C. Y. Sprouting as a cause of spasticity. *Journal of Neurophysiology*, 1958, *21*, 205–216.

Molliver, M. E., & Van der Loos, H. The ontogenesis of cortical circuitry: The spatial distribution of synapses in somesthetic cortex of newborn dog. *Ergebnisse der Anatomie Entwicklungsgeschichte*, 1970, *42*, 1–53.

Moore, R. Y., Björklund, A., & Stenevi, U. Plastic changes in the adrenergic innervation of the rat septal area in response to denervation. *Brain Research*, 1971, *33*, 13–35.

Morgan, T. H. *Experimental embryology*. New York: Columbia Univ. Press, 1927.

Obrador, S. Nervous coordination after hemispherectomy in man. In G. Schaltenbrand & C. H. Woolsey (Eds.), *Cerebral localization and organization*. Madison: Univ. of Wisconsin Press, 1964.

Poliakov, G. I. Some results of research into the development of the neuronal structure of the cortical ends of the analyzers in man. *Journal of Comparative Neurology*, 1961, *117*, 197–212.

Purpura, D. P., Shofer, R. J., Housepian, E. M., & Noback, C. R. Comparative ontogenesis of structure-function relations in cerebral and cerebellar cortex. *Progress in Brain Research*, 1964, *4*, 187–221.

Raisman, G. Neuronal plasticity in the septal nuclei of the adult rat. *Brain Research*, 1969, *14*, 25–48.

Ramón y Cajal, S. *Recollections of my life*. Engl. transl. by H. Craigie, 1917. (*Memoirs of the American Philosophical Society*, 1937, *8*.)

Rosen, J., Stein, D., & Butters, N. Recovery of function after serial ablation of prefrontal cortex in the Rhesus monkey. *Science*, 1971, *173*, 353–356.

Saul, R., & Sperry, R. W. Absence of commissurotomy symptoms with agenesis of the corpus callosum. *Neurology*, 1968, *18*, 307.

Schneider, G. E. Mechanisms of functional recovery following lesions of visual cortex or superior colliculus in neonatal and adult hamsters. *Brain Behavior and Evolution*, 1970, *3*, 295–323.

Schneider, G. E., & Nauta, W. J. H. Formation of anomalous retinal projections after removal of the optic tectum in the neonate hamster. *Anatomical Record*, 1969, *163*, 258.

Stein, D. G., Rosen, J. J., Graziadei, J., Mishkin, D., & Brink, J. J. Central nervous system: recovery of function. *Science*, 1969, *166*, 528–530.

Straznicky, K., Gaze, R. M., & Keating, M. H. The retinotectal projections after uncrossing the optic chiasma in *Xenopus* with one compound eye. *Journal of Embryology and Experimental Morphology*, 1971, *26*, 523–542.

Székely, G. Functional specificity of spinal cord segments in the control of limb movements. *Journal of Embryology and Experimental Morphology*, 1963, *11*, 431–444.

Tucker, T. J., & Kling, A. Differential effects of early and late lesions of frontal granular cortex in the monkey. *Brain Research*, 1967, *5*, 377–389.

Ueki, K. Hemispherectomy in the human with special reference to the preservation of function. *Progress in Brain Research*, 1966, *21B*, 285–338.

Wall, P. D., & Egger, M. D. Formation of new connexions in adult rat brains after partial deafferentation. *Nature (London)*, 1971, *232*, 542–545.

Wolpert, L. Positional information and the spatial pattern of cellular differentiation. *Journal of Theoretical Biology*, 1969, *25*, 1–47.

Yoon, M. Reorganization of retinotectal projection following surgical operations on the optic tectum in goldfish. *Experimental Neurology*, 1971, *33*, 395–411.

7. Myelogenetic Correlates of the Development of Speech and Language[1]

André Roch Lecours

The concept of myelogenetic cycle (Yakovlev & Lecours, 1967) is illustrated through a description of myelogenesis in the optic versus the acoustic pathway. It is proposed that a significant parallel can be drawn between behavioral maturation and anatomical maturation as expressed in the myelogenetic cycles of different fiber systems and regions of the brainstem and forebrain. Possible myelogenetic correlates of some of the stages of speech and language acquisition in man are suggested.

Introduction

The process of brain maturation is expressed by numerous chemical and histoanatomical changes, some of which are accessible to observation by simple means. Among the latter, myelogenesis—which is heralded by the regional appearance of an easy to visualize isomorphic oligodendrogliosis (de Robertis, Gerschenfeld & Wald, 1958), and the progression of which can be followed in hematoxylin preparations—has long been the object of rewarding research. The early works of Flechsig (1901, 1920, 1927), together with those of Kaes (1907) and of Vogt and Vogt (1900, 1902, 1904) and, later, the studies of Langworthy (1933), showed that myelogenesis follows an orderly time table in the different components of man's central nervous system. More recently, Yakovlev and Lecours (1967) have reported the results of research on the chronology of myelination in different fiber systems and regions

[1]The author's research activity is supported by the Medical Research Council of Canada.

of the brainstem and forebrain in more than 250 fetal and postnatal human cerebra cut in whole-brain gapless serial sections at a constant thickness (35 micra) and stained following the Loyez method (Bertrand, 1930). These authors have empirically defined the concept of the *myelogenetic cycle* of a given fiber system or region as the period extending from the time of the first appearance of stainable myelin sheaths in that system or region to the age when the tinctorial intensity shows no further visually discernible gain when compared with the same system or region in the (normal) brain of a 28-year-old adult, processed by the same method and arbitrarily taken as a standard of reference. This study has confirmed the fact that myelogenesis of certain systems and regions begins early, whereas that of others begins much later; it has also shown that, whether the cycle begins early or late, it can be relatively short in some cases, completed before the term of gestation or soon thereafter, whereas it is relatively long in other cases, protracted for months or even years after birth.

It is reasonable to assume that the cycles of myelination, among other manifestations of anatomical maturation, reflect the functional maturation of the brain and therefore can be related to the emergence and gradual differentiation in man of behavioral patterns such as locomotion, manipulation of instruments, articulated speech, and language (Yakovlev, 1962). In other words, the development of myelin in the sheaths of a fiber system may be taken as an indication that the impulse conduction in this system has become space-committed in an invariable path; correspondingly, the fiber system that has completed its myelogenetic cycle may be assumed to have reached functional maturity. In the first part of this chapter, we shall illustrate the notion of the myelogenetic cycle in a comparison, with reference to functional considerations, of the myelination of the visual versus the acoustic pathways; we shall then discuss the cycles of some of the fiber systems and regions known to be involved in the production of speech and language in relation to the chronology of some of the behavioral events observed in the human infant and child during the processes of speech and language acquisition. The approximate timetable followed by both the anatomical and the behavioral stages of maturation is diagrammatically represented in Fig. 7–1 and, for each item, a brief comment is given in the accompanying legend. Most of the data on myelogenesis have been abstracted from a previous report by Yakovlev and Lecours (1967), and Graphs 1–10 of Fig. 7–1 have been redrawn and modified from this publication; depending on the degree of stimulation from the environment, the onset of some of the behavioral stages may occur, in a certain percentage of normal children, a few weeks or even months later than indicated in the diagram.

Myelogenesis of the Visual and Acoustic Pathways

The interest of the concept of the myelogenetic cycle as a parameter of functional maturation of the brain is well exemplified by a description of the chronology of myelination in the pre- and postthalamic components of the visual pathway as

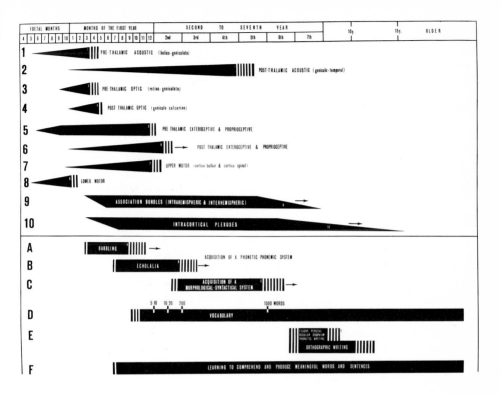

Figure 7–1. Myelogenetic cycles of some of the systems and pathways subserving speech and language production in man (modified and redrawn from Yakovlev & Lecours, 1967) and approximate time schedule of some of the behavioral events observed in the human infant and child during the development of speech and language. In Graphs 1–8, the progressively increasing width of the horizontal black stripes represents the rate of progression in tinctorial intensity and in density of myelinated fibers (Loyez preparations). In Graphs 9 and 10, the shape of the horizontal black stripes indicates that the cycles of several fiber bundles (Graph 9) or cortical areas (Graph 10) are collectively represented. Narrow vertical stripes indicate that the given age of beginning or termination of a represented cycle or event is approximate or variable. Arrows indicate the possibility that the corresponding cycles or events last longer than represented in the diagram.

Graph 1. Prethalamic acoustic pathway. Myelinated fibers are seen in the roots of the eighth cranial pair as early as the twentieth fetal week, and myelogenesis of the acoustic nerves, trapezoid body and lateral lemnisci progresses rapidly until the cycle is completed up to collicular level about 1 month before the term of normal gestation (Fig. 7–2); in the bracchia of the inferior colliculi, where myelogenesis begins during the seventh month of gestation, an increase in tinctorial intensity will be observed during the first 3 or 4 months of postnatal life. On the whole, the myelogenetic cycle of the prethalamic acoustic pathway is thus remarkably brief.

Graph 2. Postthalamic acoustic pathway. By comparison with that of the lateral lemnisci and bracchia of the inferior colliculi, the myelogenetic cycle of the acoustic radiations is strikingly long. A few stainable myelin sheaths appear at or around the time of birth, and a definite increase in tinctorial intensity is still to be observed in the 4-year-old specimen (Fig. 7–3).

Figure 7-1 (continued)

Graph 3. Prethalamic optic pathway. Like that of their acoustic counterparts, the myelogenetic cycle of the optic nerves, chiasma, and tracts is very brief. It begins during the ninth fetal month and is completed by the end of the third or during the fourth postnatal month.

Graph 4. Postthalamic optic pathway. In sharp contrast with that of the acoustic radiations, the myelogenetic cycle of the optic radiations is very brief. It begins approximately 2 weeks before birth at term and is completed by the end of the fourth or early during the fifth postnatal month.

Graph 5. Prethalamic exteroceptive and proprioceptive pathway. Myelinated fibers begin to be seen in the dorsal roots of the spinal nerves and in the posterior columns around the end of the fifth fetal month and, a little later, in the sensory components of cranial nerves. The myelogenetic cycle of the medial lemnisci also begins early during the sixth fetal month, and it progresses rapidly until the tenth month; a slow increase in bulk and tinctorial intensity is thereafter observed in this pathway for a period of approximately 1 year.

Graph 6. Postthalamic exteroceptive and proprioceptive pathway. Myelinated thalamocortical projections from the ventral posterolateral nuclei (dorsal thalamic radiations) appear in the corona radiata and in the core of the postcentral gyrus during the tenth fetal month; their cycle appears to be completed soon after the end of the first postnatal year. It is possible that the cycle of thalamocortical projections to the precentral gyrus (mostly proprioceptive) lasts longer than represented.

Graph 7. Corticobulbar and corticospinal tracts. The first stainable fibers of the pyramidal tracts are seen in sections of the pons at the beginning of the tenth month of gestation. The process of myelination can thereafter be followed, in progressively older specimens, as it spreads cephalad and caudad from the pontine level. Stained sheaths of long efferent axons appear in the core of the precentral gyrus around the time of birth at term, that is, with a lag of several weeks behind afferent axons in the core of the postcentral gyrus. The cycle of the pyramidal pathway as a whole is completed 12–15 months after birth.

Graph 8. Motor components of spinal and cranial nerves. Myelinated fibers are first seen in the motor roots of the spinal nerves around the sixteenth fetal week, in those of the trigeminal nerves around the twentieth week (Fig. 7–2), and, a little later, in the intramedullary roots of the seventh, ninth, and twelfth cranial pairs. The tinctorial intensity in these structures becomes comparable to that in the adult specimen during the first trimester of postnatal life.

Graph 9. Association bundles. Before the age of four to eight postnatal weeks, the only association systems showing hematoxylin stainable myelin sheaths are the cingulum and the U-fibers between primary cortices and their immediately adjacent secondary cortices. Fibers linking specific association areas (secondary cortices) to one another begin their myelogenetic cycles before fibers to and from nonspecific association areas; the long axons of the fasciculus arcuatus that establish linkage between Wernicke's and Broca's areas (Geschwind, 1965) belong with the former group, whereas the afferents to and the efferents from the angular region belong with the latter. In Flechsig's maps (Flechsig, 1920), the central lobule of Ecker, the calcarine area, and Heschl's gyrus are classified as *primordial myelogenetic fields*; the feet of the third and second frontal convolutions, the posterior half of the first temporal convolution, and the portions of the occipital cortex that are concentric with the calcarine area are classified as *intermediate myelogenetic fields*; and the angular and supramarginal gyri are classified as *terminal myelogenetic fields*. The axial fibers of the latter two structures are indeed among

Figure 7—1 (continued)

the very latest to initiate and complete their myelogenetic maturation; their cycle is probably not completed before six or seven years of life, if not more, have passed.

Graph 10. Intracortical plexuses. Between the fourth and the eighth postnatal week, faintly stained myelinated fibers begin to appear in the intracortical neuropil of primary projection centers (central lobule of Ecker, calcarine area, and Heschl's gyrus); only later will myelinated fibers be seen in the neuropil of specific association cortices, for example, in Broca's area and in Wernicke's area proper, and, last of all, in the neuropil of the nonspecific association cortices, for example, in the angular region. As pointed out by Bailey and Von Bonin (1951), this sequence of events, described by Vogt and Vogt (1902, 1904), is strikingly parallel to that described by Flechsig concerning subcortical white matter (see comment to Graph 9). The myelogenetic cycle of the intracortical plexuses progresses for several years and, in nonspecific association areas, for instance in the angular region, the number of stainable myelinated fibers keeps slowly increasing for at least 15 years (Fig. 7—4); according to Kaes (1907), myelogenesis of the tangential fibers running within the supragranular layers of these areas is protracted well beyond the end of the fourth decade of life.

Graph A. Babbling. Babbling behavior, a phase of "spontaneous" production of sounds, is usually observable in the 2- to 3-month-old baby (Brain & Walton, 1969). As a rule, its importance decreases toward the end of the first year of life as that of echolalia increases; it is not exceptional, however, to observe babbling in children aged twelve to fifteen months or even older.

Graph B. Echolalia. Echolalic behavior, a phase of imitation of the sounds made by others, usually begins in the 4- to 6- or 7-month-old infant. Prosody is imitated long before attempts are made at reproduction of articulated speech segments. Echolalia is a dominant linguistic activity through the second year of life and, although with decreasing importance except in learning new words, probably keeps playing a role up to at least the age of 30—36 months.

Graph C. Acquisition of a morphological—syntactical system. Up to the age of 18—24 months, and some-times later, most of the child's utterances are unitary, that is, they are used as single nonassociated linguistic units (Freburg Berry, 1969; Osterrieth, 1966). The complex and multistaged process of acquiring mastery of a morphological—syntactical system will thereafter last 5—6 years if not more.

Graph D. Vocabulary. A 12-month-old child may have acquired 5—10 words and use twice as many 6 months later; by the age of 24 months, he may have a vocabulary of some 200 words (Ey *et al.*, 1963; Osterrieth, 1966). The normal 5-year-old may use up to 1500 words (Freburg Berry, 1969).

Graph E. Reading and Writing. Providing he has a certain familiarity with the lexical components of the texts to be read, the average, finishing, first-grader, aged 7 or so, will have acquired a relatively slow but fluent reading ability; his handwriting will also be slow but his graphism will have become well differentiated and regular, and a competence for "phonetic" writing will have been achieved. In certain linguistic communities, for example, the French and the English, mastering of the orthographic system will take several years longer.

Graph F. Semantics. The process of learning the symbolic significance of speech sounds, which enables one to comprehend and produce meaningful words and sentences, is long and very progressive. A maximal capacity is probably not reached in most individuals before the middle of the second decade of life or later.

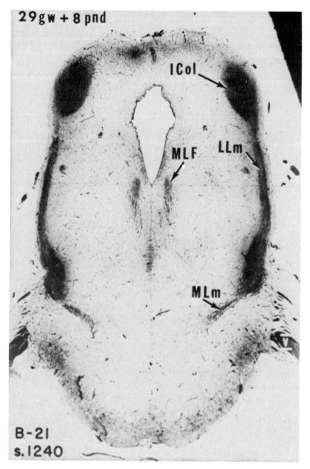

Figure 7–2. Advanced myelination of the prethalamic component of the acoustic pathway at 29 weeks of gestation + 8 days of postnatal life. Frontal section; Loyez method. The myelogenetic cycle is nearly completed up to collicular level. ICol: inferior colliculus. LLm: lateral lemniscus. MLm: medial lemniscus. MLF: medial longitudinal fasciculus. V: trigeminal nerve; there are very few myelinated fibers in the sensory root, whereas myelination of the motor root is quite advanced. [Elmer E. Southard Research Laboratory, Harvard Medical School, case B-21, s.1240 (from Yakovlev & Lecours, 1967).]

compared to that in the pre- and postthalamic components of the acoustic pathway. Both components of the visual system, the retinogeniculate (Graph 3)[2] and the geniculocalcarine (Graph 4), have short cycles of myelination, completed in one rapid spurt between the eighth fetal and the fourth or fifth postnatal month. The sequence of events is strikingly different in the acoustic pathway. In the helico-geniculate component (Graph 1), on the one hand, myelinated fibers are seen in the trapezoid body and lateral lemniscus around the twenty-first week of gestation;

[2]References to graphs refer to Fig. 7–1.

the cycle is completed up to collicular level as early as the thirty-fourth fetal week and up to thalamic level around the third or fourth postnatal month, the former part of the prethalamic component of the acoustic analyzer being the system of the brainstem tegmentum with the most precocious and the shortest myelogenetic cycle (Fig. 7—2). In the geniculotemporal component (Graph 2), on the other hand, faintly myelinated fibers are first seen (in the acoustic radiations) only at or around birth at term and, in sharp contrast to the cycles of both components of the visual pathway and to that of the prethalamic component of the acoustic pathway, the cycle of the post-thalamic component of the acoustic pathway will not be completed before the child is $3\frac{1}{2}$ or 4 years of age (Fig. 7—3).

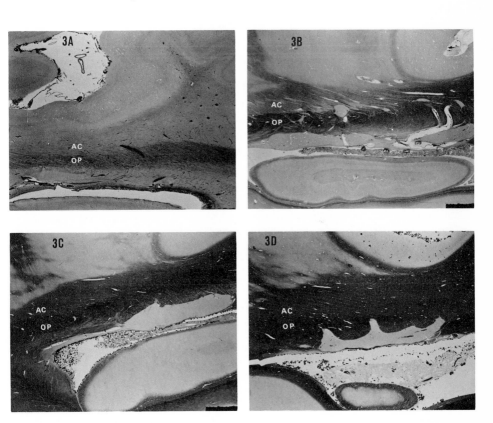

Figure 7—3. Sublenticular sector of the internal capsule, in the normal, at 6 postnatal weeks (3A), 11 months (3B), 4 years (3C), and sixteen years (3D). Sagittal sections; Loyez method. AC: acoustic radiations. OP: optic radiations. Note the contrast in the rapid increase of tinctorial intensity in the geniculocalcarine radiations (short myelogenetic cycle of the postthalamic component of the optic pathway) as compared to the slow increase of tinctorial intensity in the geniculotemporal radiations (long myelogenetic cycle of the postthalamic component of the acoustic pathway). (Elmer E. Southard Research Laboratory, Harvard Medical School, cases B-152, s.700R (3A-6x), B-132, s.700L (3B-5x), MU-108, s.610L (3C-5x), and MU-87, s.570L (3D-5x).

The myelogenetic cycle of the acoustic pathway is thus biphasic: short and largely prenatal in the helicogeniculate component; long and largely postnatal in the geniculotemporal component. The myelogenetic cycle of the visual pathway, on the other hand, is monophasic: short and perinatal in both the retinogeniculate and the geniculocalcarine components. This sequence of events in anatomical maturation closely parallels the timetable following which different modalities of sensory information enter into play as factors of behavioral development in the fetus and infant. Early during gestational life, the fetus is submitted to gravitational (vestibular) and acoustic stimuli (movements of its own body, external sounds, and sounds of maternal life—cardiac beats, respiratory and intestinal noises, and so on—transmitted through the amniotic sac and the maternal body wall, which are impermeable to photic stimuli); one might assume, and this is substantiated by the precocity and shortness of the myelogenetic cycle of the prethalamic component of the acoustic pathway, that the central apparatus for the integration of such stimuli is laid down in the tegmentum of the brainstem. Dramatic changes occur from the time of birth as to the types of inputs that besiege the newborn baby's central nervous system. On the one hand, the relative importance of the stato-acoustic stimuli decreases greatly as the now all-important visual inputs enter into play as factors of behavioral development, and, if the short perinatal myelogenetic cycle of both the pre- and the postthalamic components of the optic pathway is to be taken as a reliable indication, rapidly assume a role which will remain (physiologically) unchanged from childhood to maturity. Acoustic stimuli, on the other hand, assume a radically different role, soon to be largely oriented toward the development of articulated speech and language; the existence of a chronological correlation between the long period during which this apprenticeship takes place and the long protracted myelogenetic cycles of the postthalamic component of the acoustic pathway (Graph 2; Fig. 7—3) and of other intrahemispheric structures (Graphs 9 and 10) is thus to be taken into consideration.

Myelogenetic Correlates of the Development of Speech and Language

In babbling behavior, sounds are produced as unspecific acoustic responses to unspecific stimuli, visceral and somatic as well as visual and acoustic. These sounds are mostly vocalic at first, including both vowels resembling those in the speech of adults and intermediary forms, but more or less clearly articulated consonantal sounds are soon to be heard in the baby's babbling (Freburg Berry, 1969). A certain role should no doubt be attributed to unspecific feedbacks in the production of babbling, but, whatever the stimuli triggering or maintaining this type of production, it appears to be, with regard to the development of speech, an essentially motor exercise giving the infant an initial practice with phonetics, that is, with the use of the various muscles of his bucco-glosso-pharyngo-laryngeal apparatus as a tool for sound production. Relatively few structures have achieved an advanced degree of myelogenetic maturity at the time babbling begins to appear (Graph A). On the one hand, the motor roots of the cranial nerves related to the production of sounds have completed their cycles (Graph 8) and myelogenesis of several brain-stem structures, including the prethalamic pathways for all sensory modalities, is not far from completion (Graphs 1, 3, and 5; Fig. 7–2); on the other hand, the corticobulbar pathway (Graph 7), the association bundles (Graph 9), and, with the exception of the visual radiations, the thalamocortical projections (Graphs 2 and 6), are only beginning their myelogenetic cycles. Thus, if babbling is entirely or partially governed from cortical levels, this is done through still very immature connections between cortical and subcortical levels; or else, babbling might be essentially governed from subcortical levels, where a certain degree of anatomical maturation has already been achieved.

In echolalic behavior, sounds are produced as specific imitative responses to specific acoustic stimuli. Prosodic components of speech may for several months be the only ones the baby endeavors to imitate; as a rule, it is during the last months of his first year of life that he begins to engage in progressively more successful attempts at reproduction of articulated speech segments. Imitative repetition of speech sounds supposes the presence of an already functional if not necessarily fully mature sensorimotor anatomo-physiological substratum; sounds are heard and then mimicked, which, in turn, generates a proprioceptive feedback. At the time when echolalia (Graph B) becomes a dominant form of the child's linguistic activity, that is, during the second year of life, the pathways presumably involved in its production have all reached a certain degree of myelogenetic maturation, but not all of them have completed their cycle. Although going on since birth, myelogenesis of the postthalamic component of the acoustic pathway (Graph 2), through which the specific inputs for echolalic imitation presumably reach the primary acoustic cortex, is not yet complete (Fig. 7–3). Myelination of U-fibers between primary cortices and their immediately concentric specific association cortices is probably nearly complete; the cycles of longer association bundles between specific association cortices (Graph 9), including the fasciculus arcuatus through which auditory information is presumably transmitted to motor areas in order to permit echolalic repetition (Geschwind, 1965), are quite advanced yet still incomplete; and, finally, myelogenesis is terminated or nearly terminated in the pyramidal (Graph 7) and extrapyramidal systems, which govern and modulate the production of speech sounds in repetition as well as in other types of speech activities, and in the pathways that bring proprioceptive feedbacks to the Rolandic cortex (Graphs 5 and 6). Thus, if this circuit is indeed the one sub-serving echolalia in the young child, this type of linguistic activity begins when maturation of its anatomical substratum is not quite complete, and the imitation of speech sounds becomes progressively more perfect as anatomical maturation gets closer to its term.

A limited role could possibly be attributed to babbling, and certainly a primordial one to echolalia, in the learning of the motor patterns of speech production, that is, in the constitution of links between specific sounds and the different movements of the buccophonatory apparatus corresponding to each of them (Malmberg, 1966). In other words, echolalia is an essential factor in leading the child to delineate and master the phonemic[3] stock of his linguistic community. In the course of this process, the child becomes able first to recognize individual phonemes (in context), then, following a scale of lesser to greater difficulty in articulatory realization, to utter them appropriately (in context). In early phases, the phonemic utterances are only approximate, but they progressively improve and finally abide by local convention. Certain pairs of similar phonemes are at first produced one for the other, either with or without preferential use of one of them, but, with successive trials, errors, and corrections, such confusions become less frequent, and the child learns to discriminate the units and groups of units of the phonemic stock he is in the process of acquiring. During the same period, he progressively acquires an operative if not a conscious knowledge of the rules of linear association between phonemic units. In learning to utter individual phonemes correctly (in context), the child gains mastery of a community-accepted phonetic convention; in learning to choose and interoppose them, and to arrange them in proper linear sequence, he gains mastery of a community-accepted phonemic or phonological convention. With perhaps a certain lag of the latter, these two intermingled processes are usually well advanced by the age of 24–36 months, even though occasional phonetic deformations, such as substitutions between well-formed phonemes or metatheses, will still occur in the speech productions of a normal 4- to 5-year-old child (and later).

Acquiring operative knowledge of the rules of linear association between linguistic units of a higher order of complexity (Buyssens, 1967; Lecours, Dordain, & Lhermitte, 1970; Martinet, 1967), that is, gaining mastery of a community-accepted morphological and syntactical convention, does not begin before the child is about 18–24 months of age and sometimes later. At an earlier age, most of his utterances are unitary, that is they are used as single, nonassociated linguistic units whether or not they can be described as including several (adult) words (Osterrieth, 1966). For approximately a year after the child has begun to experiment with syntax, a (decreasing) majority of the strings of words he produces will conform to a set of relatively simple rules that are more or less specific to infantile language and will gradually be given up at a later stage (Freburg Berry, 1969; Gruber, 1967). During this period, the child's use of language is largely oriented toward one-sided expression of his needs, desires or complaints. Between his third and fourth year, or a little earlier in some cases, when the child more and more frequently uses articulated language as a tool for conversational exchange with an interlocutor, he will produce a progressively greater number of sentences that are syntactically adequate by adult standards. He becomes more and more competent in construct-

---

[3]Without taking sides in the quarrel concerning the linguistic existence of phonemes as legitimate units, one might suggest that the undoubted existence of aphasic transformations in which individually well-articulated speech segments of the type usually designated under the name "phoneme" are displaced, added, deleted, or replaced (phonemic paraphasias) is evidence enough for the physiological existence of phonemes.

ing, with words he has recently learned, sentences he presumably has never heard. Attaining (almost) perfect mastery of his community's morphological–syntactical system will take the growing child several years (Graph C), and his progress in doing so will reflect a scale of difficulties particular to this system. Occasional "errors" of morphology and syntax are still to be expected in the language production of normal children during the second half of their first decade of life.

The long process of learning the meanings of sounds, that is of words and groups of words, begins early and is protracted beyond the ill-defined limits of adulthood (Graph F); its complete cessation might indeed be a definite sign of disease or senility. Although room should be spared for marked individual variations, the capacity for learning such meanings probably does not reach its peak, when relatively abstract meanings can be adequately apprehended, before ten to fifteen years of life have passed. In early phases, the child recognizes sounds and attributes to them large semantic values that are more or less diffusely related to their conventional meanings several weeks or months before he attempts to utter them himself. From a psychological point of view, to learn the meanings of words is to establish associations between (heard) sounds and (seen, touched, heard) objects perceived as distinct from their environment, between sounds and the qualities of these objects and the relations they have with one another, and also between sounds and actions observed to occur in the environment (Brain & Walton, 1969). Meanings become more and more precise with gradual enrichment of the child's experience in relation to specific speech sounds, that is, with increment in the number of associations to each particular sequence. Since meanings are modified by the linear relationships words bear to one another, this process merges with that of the acquisition of a syntactical system. In other words, the acquisition of more precise semantics parallels that of more elaborate syntax because, by the very nature of syntax, sentences—not isolated words or phrases—are the ultimate meaningful linguistic units the human must learn to comprehend and produce.

A 12-month-old child may have acquired 5–10 words, which he can utter more or less correctly and to which he attributes rather large and indefinite meanings. Six months later he has twice as many. By the age of 2 years, he may have a vocabulary of some 200 words (Ey, Bernard, & Brisset, 1963; Gesell & Amatruda, 1964; Osterrieth, 1966). The normal 5-year-old may use up to 1500 words (Freburg Berry, 1969), the meanings of which he knows quite precisely, and which he can arrange (with occasional confusions between words that are semantically or structurally related) in sentences that meet the rules of a relatively simple but correct syntax (Graph D). The number of adults who manage with a barely more complex syntactical system, a lexical stock of some 2000 words or so, and only a moderately greater capacity for comprehending abstract linguistic sequences is not negligible.

The neuroanatomical apparatus governing the comprehension and production of meaningful language is not precisely known. It is nevertheless logical, mostly from pathological evidence (Geschwind, 1965; Geschwind, Quadfasel & Segarra, 1968; Lhermitte, 1968; Wernicke, 1874), to assume that specific association

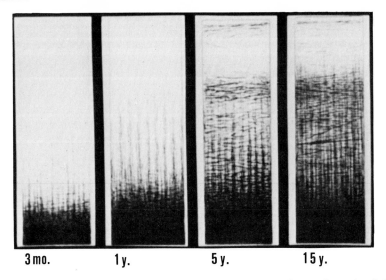

3 mo.   1 y.   5 y.   15 y.

Figure 7—4. Exponential myelination of the intracortical plexuses in the angular region (inferior parietal lobule). From left to right, in specimens aged 3 months (postnatal), 1 year, 5 years, and 15 years. (From Kaes, 1907.)

cortices, nonspecific association cortices, and their connections to and from one another, particularly those to and from the angular region, play a principal role, their function being, on the one hand, the constitution of a complex net of associations as already described, the anatomical substratum of which is laid down in these cortical areas, for learning and stocking the meanings of language segments; and, on the other hand, using the acquired knowledge, that is, producing and comprehending meaningful words and sentences. Therefore, it probably is of great significance that the early-beginning and long-lasting period during which semantics and syntax are progressively and concurrently acquired more or less parallels the protracted myelogenetic cycles not only of the postthalamic component of the acoustic pathway (see previous description and Fig. 7—3), but also of the intra- and interhemispheric association bundles (Graph 9), especially those to and from the nonspecific association cortices (Flechsig, 1901, 1920, 1927), and the still longer cycle observed in the intracortical neuropil (Graph 10; Fig. 7—4), especially in the nonspecific association cortices (Kaes, 1907). The contemporaneity of semantic maturity—that is, the capacity for understanding abstract language and for producing understandable abstract language—and myelogenetic maturity in the neuropil of the angular region (Fig. 7—4) is particularly striking.

For most of the individuals who do learn to read and write,[4] this apprenticeship belongs with schooling, that is, it does not begin before the child is 5—7 years of age. As a rule, learning to read will mean his establishing associations between

---

[4] Comments on written language refer exclusively to the use of nonideographic codes.

visual signs (letters and written words and groups of words) and acoustic signs, the meanings of which he already knows for the major part, that is, which have acquired a definite symbolic value. Seen written words thus become linked with heard spoken sounds and with the corresponding kinaesthetic patterns (buccophonatory apparatus) of these sounds. In learning to write, movements of the hand holding an instrument will permit the reproduction of seen visual signs; this early phase is the counterpart, in the development of written speech, of echolalia in the development of spoken speech. And since one reads as one writes, in the same manner as one hears as one talks, links are also established between visual signs—which, as mentioned earlier, are integrated in an already rich net of associations—and their corresponding kinaesthetic patterns, muscles of the dominant hand (Brain & Walton, 1969).

A first year of school training will give the maturing child a rather extensive experience with the written symbolic code he thus endeavors to superimpose on the oral one. Provided he has a certain familiarity with the lexical components of the texts to be read, the average, finishing, first-grader, aged 7 or so, will have managed to acquire a relatively slow but fluent reading ability; his handwriting will not be very rapid either, but his graphism will have, over a period of a few months, developed into a well-differentiated and regular production; and, but for a few confusions between similar letters or between graphemes standing for similar phonemes (Lecours et al., 1970), a competence for "phonetic" writing will have been achieved (Graph E).[5]

If learning to read and write meant to establish direct associations between seen objects, qualities of objects, relations between objects, and so on, and seen written signs (letters, words, and groups of words), as could no doubt be the case were the visual rather than the acoustic code first acquired,[6] it is likely that this apprenticeship could begin quite early during the first year of life; and the apprenticeship of linguistic expression through a written code could, in such circumstances, take place as soon as a certain control over the movements of the superior limbs had been achieved (Graphs 5—8). But it is a nearly absolute rule that learning to read and write does not mean to associate visual signs directly with objects or events, but to constitute a secondary net of associations, that is, to link a new set of visual signs to a learned set of auditory signs that are already associated with objects and events of which they have become symbols. This fundamental dif-

---

[5] Mastery of the orthographic system of one's community is an altogether different affair; it may be attained much later and the length of training depends, among other factors, on teaching methods and, chiefly, on the greater or lesser lack of one to one parity between phonemic and graphemic signs in the particular language being learned. By the age of 10 or 11, a typical Parisian child—who has had to learn, for instance, the 25 or so written equivalents of the one phoneme $\tilde{a}$ and to acquire some operative knowledge of the rules governing the choice of one rather than of the other—still makes a sizeable number of orthographic "errors," especially since these are compounded by written syntax oddities; one or two years later, these errors are greatly reduced in number.

[6] Since U-fibers myelinate earlier than longer association fibers, one might suggest that the constitution of associations between seen objects and seen signs could begin earlier than the constitution of associations between seen objects and heard signs.

ference between the two apprenticeships probably explains the now widely accepted notion that the degree of brain maturation necessary for optimal learning of the written code is not reached before the second half of the first decade of life has begun (Graph E). It is indeed more than probable that several association bundles, as well as the intracortical plexuses of several cortical areas, which characteristically have protracted myelogenetic cycles (Graphs 9 and 10) and therefore can be said to reach anatomical maturity relatively late in life, are of the utmost importance in the acquisition of a symbolic code used to represent another symbolic code. This is substantiated by the great variety of focal brain lesions resulting in a disorganization of the written mode of linguistic expression (de Ajuriaguerra & Hécaen, 1966).

Acknowledgements

The author of this article would certainly not have been able to write it if he had not had available to him notes, taken over the course of the last few years, of long conversations with his mentor and friend, Professor Paul Ivan Yakovlev. He also would not have been able to add a very striking illustration if he had not had access to Professor Yakovlev's extraordinary neuroanatomical and neuro-pathological collection of serial sections of complete brains, made over a period of more than a quarter of a century, by following a rigorous and invariable standardized method.

Those who are familiar with Professor Yakovlev's writings of the last 25 years will certainly have recognized, in this chapter, the influence of his concepts as to the relations between different spatiotemporal stages of morphological brain maturation, of which myelogenetic cycles are one parameter in man. The concept of dynamic cycles of myelination, as opposed to Flechsig's merely mechanical "schedules," which disregarded the importance of the differential tempo of myelogenesis in the different systems and regions of the central nervous system, is entirely due to Paul Yakovlev's thoughts and experience. In discussions with the author, he oftentimes expressed, for instance, his ideas on the significance of the striking contrast existing between the long biphasic myelogenetic cycle of the acoustic pathway and the short monophasic myelogenetic cycle of the optic pathway.

References

Bailey, P., & Von Bonin, G. *The isocortex of man.* Urbana: Univ. of Illinois Press, 1951.

Bertrand, I. *Techniques histologiques de neuropathologie.* Paris: Masson, 1930.

Brain, R., and Walton, J. N. *Brain's diseases of the nervous system.* London & New York: Oxford Univ. Press, 1969.

Buyssens, E. *La communication et l'articulation linguistique.* Paris: Presses Universitaires de France, 1967.

de Ajuriaguerra, J., & Hécaen, H. *Le cortex cérébral.* Paris: Masson, 1966.

de Robertis, E., Gerschenfeld, H., & Wald, F. Cellular mechanism of myelination in the central nervous system. *Journal of Biophysical and Biochemical Cytology,* 1958, *4,* 651–658.

Ey, H., Bernard, P., & Brisset, C. *Manuel de psychiatrie.* Paris: Masson, 1963.

Flechsig, P. Developmental (myelogenetic) localisation of the cerebral cortex in the human subject. *Lancet,* 1901, *ii,* 1027–1029.

Flechsig, P. *Anatomie des menschlichen Gehirns und Rückenmarks auf myelogenetischer Grundlage.* Leipzig: Thieme, 1920.

Flechsig, P. *Meine myelogenetische Hirnlehre.* Berlin: Springer, 1927.

Freburg Berry, M. *Language disorders of children: The bases and diagnoses.* New York: Appleton, 1969.

Geschwind, N. Disconnexion syndromes in animals and man. *Brain,* 1965, *88,* 237–294, 585–644.

Geschwind, N., Quadfasel, F. A., & Segarra, J. Isolation of the speech area. *Neuropsychologia,* 1968, *6,* 327–340.

Gesell, A., & Amatruda, C. S. *Developmental diagnosis.* New York: Harper, 1964.

Gruber, J. S. Topicalization in child language. *Foundations of Language,* 1967, *3,* 37–65.

Kaes, T. *Die Grosshirnrinde des Meschen in ihrem Massen und in ihrem Fasengehalt.* Jena: Fischer, 1907.

Langworthy, O. Development of behavior patterns and myelination of the nervous system in the human foetus and infant. *Contributions to Embryology,* 1933, *139,* 1–57.

Lecours, A. R., Dordain, G., & Lhermitte, F. Recherches sur le langage des aphasiques: 1. Terminologie neurolinguistique. *L'Encéphale,* 1970, *59,* 520–546.

Lhermitte, F. Bases physiologiques de la mémoire. *Evolution Psychiatrique,* 1968, *4,* 579–603.

Malmberg, B. *La phonétique.* Paris: Presses Universitaires de France, 1966.

Martinet, A. *Eléments de linguistique générale.* Paris: Collin, 1967.

Osterrieth, P. *Introduction à la psychologie de l'enfant.* Paris: Presses Universitaires de France, 1966.

Vogt, C. *Etude sur la Myélinisation des hémisphères cérébraux.* Paris: 1900.

Vogt, C., & Vogt, O. Die Markreifung des Kindergehirns während der ersten vier Lebensmonste und ihre methodologische Bedeutung. In O. Vogt (Ed.), *Neurobiologische Arbeiten.* (Erster Serie, Erster Band), Jena: Fischer, 1902.

Vogt, C., & Vogt, O. Die Markreifung des Kindergehirns während der ersten vier Lebensmonste und ihre methodologische Bedeutung. In O. Vogt (Ed.), *Neurobiologische Arbeiten.* (Erster Serie, Zweiter Band), Jena: Fischer, 1904.

Wernicke, C. *Der aphasische Symptomencomplex—Eine Psychologische Studie und anatomischer Basis.* Breslau: Cohn & Weigert, 1874.

Yakovlev, P. I. Morphological criteria of growth and maturation of the nervous system in man. *Research Publications, Association for Research in Nervous and Mental Disease,* 1962, *39,* 3–46.

Yakovlev, P. I. A proposed definition of the limbic system. In C. Hockman (Ed.), *Limbic system mechanisms and autonomic function.* Springfield, Ill.: Thomas, 1972. Pp. 241–283.

Yakovlev, P. I., & Lecours, A. R. The myelogenetic cycles of regional maturation of the brain. In A. Minkowski (Ed.), *Regional development of the brain in early life.* Oxford: Blackwell, 1967. Pp. 3–70.

8. The Ontogeny of Cerebral Dominance in Man

O. L. Zangwill

This chapter is concerned with handedness and its relation to "brainedness," that is, the hemisphere dominant for language functions. The development of handedness and other aspects of lateral preference is briefly reviewed, and its possible relationship to the "lateralization" of speech is considered. It is pointed out that this relationship is relatively complex—more so in left-handers and in those lacking firm and consistent lateral preferences than in right-handers—and the extent to which the subordinate hemisphere normally participates in the acquisition of language is conjectural. There is some evidence, however, that it plays a more important part in left- and mixed-handers than in right-handers and that it may, in the former, take over language functions more readily in the event of injury to the dominant hemisphere. The possible significance of cerebral dominance in the origin of developmental language disorders is briefly considered.

Introduction

One of the more puzzling differences between man and the subhuman primates lies in man's possession of consistent handedness and articulate speech. While lateral preferences exist in a number of mammalian species, such as rats, cats, and monkeys, they vary a good deal from one situation to another, and, even where they are relatively consistent in the same animal, preference for the right forepaw is no more common than that for the left, that is to say, no species-specific patterns of handedness appear to exist. Furthermore, the effects in animals of lesions of the hemisphere, contralateral to the preferred forepaw are, so far as is known, no different from those of lesions of the ipsilateral hemisphere. It appears, then, that what in man we call *cerebral dominance* is an evolutionary development peculiar to the human species.

It has been known for a little over a century that aphasia and kindred disorders of speech are produced by lesions of one hemisphere alone, as a rule the left but occasionally the right. The temptation to link this odd asymmetry of cerebral function with *handedness* proved irresistible, and it was accepted for many years that the dominant hemisphere, namely, the one that when damaged occasions aphasia, is almost without exception contralateral to the preferred hand. However, we now know that this rule is only approximate (Penfield & Roberts, 1959; Zangwill, 1960, 1967) and that aphasia in left-handed individuals is actually more frequent after left-sided than after right-sided brain injury. Despite this disconcerting finding, though, most neurologists continue to believe that there is a connection of some kind between handedness and hemisphere dominance for speech (cf. Zangwill, 1964), although its nature remains conjectural.

In this chapter, the term "cerebral dominance" will be used to denote the hemisphere most heavily involved in language, irrespective of handedness. This does not, however, imply that handedness is necessarily irrelevant to cerebral dominance, and it is for this reason that a brief account will be given of its development in children. Nor does it imply that the hemisphere dominant for speech is necessarily dominant for all other psychological functions. Indeed there is now a great deal of evidence suggesting that visual and spatial skills, such as those involved in assembly and constructional tasks, are more dependent on the integrity of the subordinate than of the dominant hemisphere (Blakemore, Iversen, & Zangwill, 1972; Zangwill, 1961). It is also noteworthy that recent studies of patients who have undergone operative section of the cerebral commissures ("split brain" patients) indicate that the right hemisphere is pre-eminent not only in the control of spatial judgement but also in the processing of nonverbal information generally (Bogen, 1969; Bogen & Gazzaniga, 1965; Levy, Trevarthen, & Sperry, 1972). Dominance, then, is not a unitary property of one or the other hemisphere but appears to vary appreciably with the functions under consideration.

The aim of this chapter is to outline what is known about the general course of hemispheric specialization and its implications for psychological development. Its relation to some aspects of educational backwardness will also be briefly considered.

The Development of Handedness

Whatever the relation of handedness to cerebral dominance may be, it is not without interest that hand preferences first appear in most children toward the end of the first year of life and during the first months of the second year, which is just the period in which speech is beginning to emerge (McCarthy, 1954). Whereas some children show consistent lateral preference, right or left, from the outset, others go through phases of ambilaterality or fluctuating preference before a firm and consistent pattern of laterality is established (Gesell & Ames, 1947). Although environmental and social factors undoubtedly play some part in the establishment of handedness, it is generally regarded as the outcome of a process of maturation governed by heredity. Indeed, even so convinced a proponent of psychogenesis as Sigmund Freud believed that laterality is genetically determined. At the same time, the genetics of handedness are still very imperfectly understood (Gates, 1952), and we still lack any agreed assessment of the respective parts played by heredity and environment in its determination.

The development of foot, eye, and ear preferences has been less carefully studied. Foot preference, in particular, might repay more careful study in so far as it would appear to be less affected than handedness by custom and convention. In general, foot preference appears to be less consistent than hand preference, although high correlations between the two have been obtained by some investigators (Clark, 1957). Eye preference, on the other hand, is much less highly correlated with handedness, and many doubt whether it bears any essential relation to cerebral dominance. None the less, discordant eye and hand preferences have sometimes been adduced as a factor in educational backwardness (Macmeeken, 1939).

Annett (1970a) has recently pointed out that both the distribution of hand preferences and the relative speed of the two hands on a skilled task remain strikingly constant between the ages of $3\frac{1}{2}$ and 15 and that there is a linear relation between degree of preference and degree of relative manual skill. This would appear to support the maturational hypothesis. At the same time, Annett's findings should not be taken to mean that handedness shifts never occur—indeed they are not uncommon among those who are weakly sinistral—or that the nonpreferred hand is incapable of acquiring a degree of skill equal to that of the preferred hand. Indeed, the work of Provins (1967; Provins & Glencross, 1968) has clearly shown that the two hands (or feet) do not differ in their potential for the acquisition of skill. Although Provins interprets these findings in terms of an environmentalist theory of handedness, it should be borne in mind that those who favor the genetical view have never held that dexterity is necessarily inborn; it is only differential *preference* that is held to be innate, dexterity itself being acquired through training. Further, as Oldfield (1969a) has suggested, the evolution of handedness may well have much more to do with bimanual coordination in the handling of objects than with the speed, agility, and precision of strictly unimanual acts.

In children of school age, lateral preferences are as a rule more consistent among the right-handed than among the left-handed, including those of the latter who have always written with the left hand (Clark, 1957). This is likewise true of young adults (Humphrey, 1951). Whether this inconsistency derives from an inborn ambilaterality or is merely the outcome of social learning is uncertain. Some left-handed children, too, appear to be excessively clumsy with either hand (Burt, 1937; Gillies, MacSweeney, & Zangwill, 1960), and difficulty in establishing firm discrimination between right and left is not uncommon (Benton, 1959). From an educational point of view, no reliable differences seem to exist between left-handed and right-handed schoolchildren, though "shifted sinistrals" (that is, left-handed children who have been taught to write with the right hand) may show somewhat poorer scholastic achievement than the fully lateralized child (Clark, 1957).

It was formerly usual to encourage or even coerce children with left-hand preferences to transfer to the use of the right hand, particularly in regard to the conventional usage of table implements and of course also in writing. Indeed, right-handed writing is still obligatory in some countries. This practice has now been largely discontinued throughout the English-speaking world, despite the fact that it was advocated by so influential a psychologist as Sir Cyril Burt (1937). The main objection to it appears to have been the hazard that children whose handedness has been shifted are liable to develop a stammer (Travis, 1931). Although the evidence upon which this contention is based has been largely discredited (Andrews & Harris, 1964), the incidence of stammering does appear to have fallen in recent years, suggesting that it may not be totally without foundation. It is also interesting that left-handed musicians do not in general experience serious inconvenience in shifting to the use of the nonpreferred hand, except possibly in the case of conductors (Oldfield, 1969b). On general grounds, however, it is doubtful whether the advantage achieved by conformity with the right-handed majority justifies interference with a natural mode of expression if it can possibly be avoided. So far as possible, it seems advisable to allow every child to establish his own particular pattern of laterality.

An interesting model of handedness and its presumed relations with cerebral dominance has been put forward by Annett (1967, 1970b). When handedness is classified in terms of right, left, or mixed, she points out, the percentages of the three groups are in binomial proportions. This she regards as compatible with a genetical model according to which handedness and cerebral dominance are governed by two alleles, one normally dominant and the other recessive. According to this model, heterozygotes may be right, left, or ambilateral, but as a rule, no doubt due to cultural pressures, tend to develop right-handedness and left cerebral dominance. This model accounts for a number of recent findings regarding left-handedness and its relation to cerebral dominance, although it fails to explain "crossed aphasia" (that is, aphasia from right cerebral lesions in dextrals without family history of left-handedness) and must for the present be regarded as speculative.

The Lateralization of Speech

It has long been known that extensive injury to the left hemisphere at or soon after birth does not preclude the development of speech, although it may retard it. More recently, it has been shown that operative removal of the damaged hemisphere at a later stage (hemispherectomy) very seldom occasions aphasia, indicating that speech has been acquired under the exclusive control of the right, normally subordinate, hemisphere (Basser, 1962; Zangwill, 1964). It would therefore appear that, at birth, the two hemispheres are equipotential or almost so and that the right hemisphere can, if need be, function vicariously for the left in the acquisition of language. This reflects the remarkable plasticity of the brain in the earliest years of life.

What are the limits of this plasticity? Although no very definite answer can be given, it is at all events clear that the capacity of the right hemisphere to take over from the left diminishes rapidly with increasing age; it is doubtful whether, after the age of 4 or 5, completely normal acquisition of speech by the right hemisphere alone remains possible, at all events among the fully right-handed. Indeed, restitution of speech appears to become increasingly imperfect with advancing age, indicating that the lateralization of speech to the left hemisphere is associated with diminishing capacity of the right fully to subserve the language functions. In adults, at all events, full restitution of speech following an extensive lesion of the dominant cerebral hemisphere must be regarded as exceptional.

Although shift of speech dominance to the right hemisphere in the event of early injury to the left is usual, it is not invariable. In 27 left-handed or ambilateral patients who had sustained early left-sided brain damage, Milner, Branch, and Rasmussen (1964) report that intracarotid amytal injection indicated right hemisphere dominance in eighteen (67 %) and left hemisphere dominance in six (22 %). In three (11 %) there was evidence of bilateral speech representation, suggesting imperfect transfer of language functions to the right hemisphere. It is difficult to know why in some cases speech continues to be governed by the left hemisphere in spite of severe and extensive damage, whereas in others it transfers readily to the opposite side. Perhaps the age at which the brain injury is sustained and the presence or otherwise of a left-handed familial strain will prove to be relevant factors in determining whether or not transfer will take place.

It was at one time widely believed that the writing hand had a considerable influence upon the establishment of cerebral dominance. Writing with the right hand was thought to reinforce left hemisphere dominance in dextrals and to weaken right hemisphere dominance in sinistrals, though in some cases producing a dissociation between the hemispheric control of speech and writing (Tilney, 1936). Unfortunately the position now appears to be a good deal less straight-forward. In sinistrals, both speech and writing may be equally impaired from a left-sided lesion, irrespective of the writing hand (Hécaen & de Ajuriaguerra, 1963; Hécaen & Sauguet, 1971; Humphrey & Zangwill, 1952). There is, however, considerable evidence that agraphia tends to be more strikingly in evidence if the lesion is contralateral to the preferred writing hand (Gloning & Quatember, 1966; Zangwill, 1954). Whether shift of handedness per se influences speech representation is uncertain. Needles (1942) cited four cases in which the common factors were loss of function of the right hand with consequent enforced left-handedness and the onset of aphasia at a much later date. The lesion giving rise to the aphasia was left-sided in two cases and right-sided in the other two. To explain these findings, Needles assumed that the training of the left hand in writing had produced some transfer of language dominance to the right hemisphere. This may be so, but cases of this kind are very rare and any interpretation is bound to be speculative.

To what extent does the right hemisphere participate in the acquisition of speech in the healthy individual? This is a difficult question. Certainly aphasia associated with right hemisphere lesions appears to be a good deal more common in children than in adults (Basser, 1962; Zangwill, 1964), suggesting that speech is at first imperfectly lateralized to either hemisphere. Even in the adult, moreover, there is evidence that the right hemisphere may possess some latent capacity to subserve speech, although this is as a rule minimal. In the celebrated case of excision of the entire left cerebral hemisphere for glioma in a right-handed man, the patient, aged 47 at the time of his operation, showed tolerable comprehension of spoken speech, and emotional utterance was well preserved. With prompting, he was able to sing and could on occasion generate a short phrase (Smith, 1966). In "split brain" patients (Gazzaniga & Sperry, 1967), comprehension is likewise found to be relatively well preserved, though opinion differs as to whether the right hemisphere is or is not capable of actually generating speech. The observations of Butler and Norsell (1968) and Levy and Sperry (1971) suggest that it does appear to possess a rudimentary capacity for linguistic expression but that the communication channels are normally pre-empted by the dominant hemisphere. All that we can safely conclude at present is that the right hemisphere evidently plays a part (though not necessarily an essential one) in the comprehension of speech and can initiate and control low-level emotional and reactive utterance. In the healthy adult, however, at all events if he is fully right-handed, it seems improbable that the right hemisphere plays any very significant role in linguistic activity, and its removal does not appear in any way to damage speech.

In the left-handed, on the other hand, there is evidence that the right hemisphere may participate to a greater extent in linguistic activity. Indeed Conrad (1949), on the basis of wartime experience with traumatic aphasia resulting from unilateral brain wounds, was led to conclude that left-handedness (complete or partial) implies imperfect lateralization of language to either hemisphere. His views received some support from the observation frequently made by clinicians that aphasia in sinistrals following lesions of either hemisphere is often less severe (Luria, 1970) and more transitory (Subirana, 1958) than in dextrals. It is also supported by the finding of Milner *et al.* (1964) that in 44 left-handed or ambidextrous patients without history of early left-sided brain damage who were investigated with the Wada technique of intracarotid amytal injection, speech was apparently represented in the left hemisphere in 28 (64 %), in the right in 9 (20 %) and in both in 7 (16 %). This certainly suggests a less clear-cut and consistent degree of lateralization than is the rule in fully dextral individuals. Tentatively, therefore, one might conclude that sinistrals differ from dextrals mainly in the rate at which lateralization of cerebral function proceeds and the completeness with which it is established. It is possible, too, that the subordinate hemisphere retains throughout life greater capacity to subserve speech in the sinistral than in the dextral, indicating that cerebral organization in the adult nondextral resembles, in some respects at least, that of the immature brain (Zangwill, 1964).

These considerations may have some bearing on intellectual development in children. Given that the right hemisphere is of special importance in the acquisition of visuospatial skill, it has been argued by Levy (1969) that, in sinistrals, the tendency to bilateral representation of speech might well introduce an incompatibility between the development of linguistic and nonlinguistic skills in the same hemisphere. In consequence, visuospatial aptitude might well be depressed in the nondextral child. This hypothesis gains some support from Levy's finding (Levy, 1969; Levy & Sperry, 1971) of a significant inferiority of performance in relation to verbal IQs on the Wechsler Adult Intelligence Scale in a small group of nondextral undergraduates. A replication of this inquiry using different tests (Miller, 1971) has given a similar result; the differences obtained were relatively small, though significant. Miller (1971) concludes that the results are sufficiently definite for one to say that "real differences in ability between right- and mixed-handers do exist and probably reflect underlying differences in the asymmetrical organization of functions within the brain [p. 112]." Further work is, however, essential before firm conclusions can be drawn.

The possibility of investigating dominance without recourse to pathological conditions has been greatly augmented in recent years by the introduction of techniques of bilateral simultaneous stimulation, especially in the acoustic sphere (cf. Blakemore et al., 1972). The best known of these is the so-called "dichotic digits" test, in which the subject is presented simultaneously with two lists of digits or words, one to each ear, and tested for recall immediately afterwards. In right-handers, the material presented to the right ear is almost always better recalled than that presented to the left, and this ear advantage has been linked with left cerebral dominance for speech (Kimura, 1961). In left-handers, the results are more variable, although reversed (left) ear advantage is not uncommon. If, instead of words or digits, musical sequences or nonverbal sounds are used, left-ear advantage is the rule, greater in amount in dextrals than in sinistrals (Blakemore et al., 1972). Kimura (1963, 1967) has claimed that ear advantage is already apparent by the age of 4 years and that right-ear advantage for verbal material is established earlier in girls than in boys; this may be linked with the well-known sex difference in the growth of verbal ability. On the other hand, boys appear to be superior to girls in identifying nonverbal sounds (left-ear advantage) (Knox & Kimura, 1970). The dichotic stimulation technique might well be developed to trace longitudinally the development of ear advantage and its possible vicissitudes in individual subjects who are either left-handed or who have failed to develop consistent lateral preferences. In this way, valuable light might be thrown on the evolution of cerebral dominance in the nondextral individual.

Specific Educational Backwardness

We owe to Orton (1925, 1937) the view that certain forms of educational backwardness are linked with the faulty establishment of cerebral dominance. In his long-continued studies of schoolchildren with marked and intractable backwardness in reading and spelling, Orton (1937) was impressed, first, by the frequency of left- and mixed-handedness in such children and their families, and, second, by the frequency of reversals of letters or syllables in their reading and spelling which he referred to as "strephosymbolia". He endeavored to explain both these phenomena in terms of a genetically determined failure of one hemisphere to achieve a dominant role. Reversals, he believed, were due to the fact that the "engrams" or memory patterns corresponding to words are laid down bilaterally, those in the subordinate hemisphere being mirror images of those in the dominant hemisphere. Normally, revival of word images in the subordinate hemisphere is suppressed by the activity of the dominant hemisphere, but if cerebral dominance is equivocal, the image generated by the subordinate hemisphere may replace or conflict with that generated by the dominant hemisphere. For the same reason, there may be a correlated tendency toward mirror writing.

Although Orton's theory has generally been viewed as much too simple-minded to be true, it must be admitted that his attempt to link reading and spelling difficulties with cerebral dominance is attractive. The incidence of left-handedness or mixed-hand preference in dyslexic children or in their families seems too high to wholly coincidental (Critchley, 1964; Naidoo, 1972; Zangwill, 1960), although sinistrality is neither a necessary nor a sufficient condition for the incidence of developmental dyslexia. Reversal errors, too, are not peculiar to those with mixed-handedness, and it is in any case improbable that language is represented in the brain in so literal a manner as that proposed by Orton. None the less, there is some indirect evidence in support of his view that speech, reading, and spelling problems may, in some cases at least, be related to the imperfect lateralization of speech (Naidoo, 1972). For example, there is evidence that the electroencephalograms of dyslexic children with mixed-hand preferences show greater asymmetry of alpha rhythm than is usual among otherwise comparable right-handed children without dyslexia (Newton, 1968).

A thorough study of the laterality issue in dyslexic children has recently been presented by Sparrow and Satz (1970). While failing to find significant differences between their dyslexic and control groups in respect to hand preference and manual dexterity—as well, rather surprisingly, as in familial history of left-handedness—they do report significant differences in regard to eye preference, finger differentiation, lateral awareness, and verbal intelligence. They also report that the dyslexic children have a higher frequency of left-ear advantage on a dichotic listening task. This, they point out, may indicate greater participation in speech on the part of the right cerebral hemisphere in the backward than in the normal reader.

The most conservative conclusion seems to be that children with weak or mixed lateral dominance or those with left-handedness in their family histories appear to be at risk in regard to developmental disorders of language. It is not yet clear what additional factors, endogenous or exogenous, are necessary for the appearance of a fully fledged developmental pattern of linguistic backwardness.

Conclusions

1. Cerebral dominance, that is, the predominant role of one cerebral hemisphere in governing the acquisition and use of language, is peculiar to man and may be linked with the evolution of tool use and unilateral manual skill.

2. Handedness begins to appear in most children towards the end of the first and in the early months of the second year of life but may not become firmly established until the age of 4 or 5. Some children go through phases of ambilaterality or fluctuating preferences before definite preference, right or left, is established.

3. Although training and environmental pressure can undoubtedly influence handedness, the basic direction of preference is commonly regarded as innate and as governed by genetic factors.

4. At birth, the two hemispheres of the brain are equipotential, or almost so, in regard to language, and extensive injury to the left hemisphere at birth or soon after does not preclude the acquisition of speech. On the other hand, the capacity of the right hemisphere to subserve speech appears to diminish progressively during childhood and to be virtually negligible in the right-handed adult.

5. Studies of patients who have undergone certain neurosurgical operations (hemispherectomy or commissurotomy) indicate that the right hemisphere in dextrals retains appreciable receptive language capacity but that its expressive powers are quite rudimentary.

6. In left-handed individuals and those with weak- or mixed-hand preferences, there is evidence that the right hemisphere may play a more important and lasting role in the acquisition and control of language. In consequence, some authors have been led to suppose that a degree of bilateral representation of language is the rule in the nondextral individual.

7. Severe and persistent backwardness in learning to speak, read, or spell in children of adequate general intelligence may in some cases be linked with failure to establish clear-cut unilateral hemisphere dominance. At the same time, a sinistral tendency is neither a necessary nor a sufficient condition for the incidence of developmental language disorder.

References

Andrews, G., & Harris, M. *The syndrome of stuttering.* Clinics in Developmental Medicine No. 17. London: Spastics Society & Heinemann, 1964.

Annett, M. The binomial distribution of right, mixed and left-handedness. *Quarterly Journal of Experimental Psychology*, 1967, *29*, 327–333.

Annett, M. The growth of manual preference and speed. *British Journal of Psychology*, 1970, *61*, 545–548. (a)

Annett, M. Handedness, cerebral dominance and the growth of intelligence. In D. J. Bakker & P. Satz (Eds.), *Specific reading disability: Advances in theory and method*. Rotterdam: Rotterdam Univ. Press, 1970. Pp. 61–78. (b)

Basser, L. S. Hemiplegia of early onset and the faculty of speech, with special reference to the effects of hemispherectomy. *Brain*, 1962, *85*, 427–460.

Benton, A. L. *Right-left discrimination and finger localization: Development and pathology*. New York: Harper (Hoeber), 1959.

Blakemore, C., Iversen, S. D., & Zangwill, O. L. Brain functions. *Annual Review of Psychology*, 1972, *23*, 413–456.

Bogen, J. E. The other side of the brain. *Bulletin of the Los Angeles Neurological Society*, 1969, *34*, 135–161.

Bogen, J. E., & Gazzaniga, M. S. Cerebral commissurotomy in man: Minor hemisphere dominance for certain visuo-spatial functions. *Journal of Neurosurgery*, 1965, *23*, 394–399.

Burt, C. *The backward child*. London: Univ. of London Press, 1937.

Butler, S. R., & Norsell, U. Vocalization possibly initiated by the minor hemisphere. *Nature (London)*, 1968, *220*, 793–794.

Clark, M. A. *Left-handedness: Laterality and characteristics and their educational implications*. London: Univ. of London Press, 1957.

Conrad, K. Über aphasische Sprachstörungen bei hirnverletzten Linkshänder. *Nervenarzt*, 1949, *20*, 148–154.

Critchley, M. *Developmental dyslexia*. London: Heinemann, 1964.

Gates, R. R. *Human genetics*. 2 vols. London: Macmillan, 1952.

Gazzaniga, M. S., & Sperry, R. W. Language after section of the cerebral commissures. *Brain*, 1967, *90*, 131–148.

Gesell, A., & Ames, L. B. The development of handedness. *Journal of Genetic Psychology*, 1947, *70*, 155–175.

Gillies, S. M., MacSweeney, D. A., & Zangwill, O. L. A note on some unusual handedness patterns. *Quarterly Journal of Experimental Psychology*, 1960, *12*, 113–116.

Gloning, K., Quatember, R. Statistical evidence of neuropsychological syndromes in left-handed and ambidextrous patients. *Cortex*, 1966, *2*, 484–488.

Hécaen, H., & de Ajuriaguerra, J. *Les gauchers: Prévalence manuelle et dominance cérébral*. Paris: Presses Universitaires de France, 1963.

Hécaen, H., & Sauguet, J. Cerebral dominance in left-handed subjects. *Cortex*, 1971, *7*, 19–48.

Humphrey, M. E. Consistency of hand usage. *British Journal of Educational Psychology*, 1951, *21*, 214–225.

Humphrey, M. E., & Zangwill, O. L. Dysphasia in left-handed patients with unilateral brain wounds. *Journal of Neurology Neurosurgery and Psychiatry*, 1952, *15*, 184–193.

Kimura, D. Cerebral dominance and the perception of verbal stimuli. *Canadian Journal of Psychology*, 1961, *15*, 166–171.

Kimura, D. Speech lateralization in young children as determined by an auditory test. *Journal of Comparative and Physiological Psychology*, 1963, *56*, 899–902.

Kimura, D. Functional asymmetry of the brain in dichotic listening. *Cortex*, 1967, *3*, 163–178.

Knox, C., & Kimura, D. Cerebral processing of non-verbal sounds in boys and girls. *Neuropsychologia*, 1970, *8*, 227–237.

Levy, J. Possible basis for the evolution of lateral specialization of the human brain. *Nature (London)*, 1969, *224*, 614–615.

Levy, J., & Sperry, R. W. Lateral specialization and cerebral dominance in commissurotomy patients. *Proceedings 20th International Congress of Psychology, London*, 1971, p. 244.

Levy, J., Trevarthen, C., & Sperry, R. W. Perception of bilateral chimeric figures following hemisphere deconnexion. *Brain*, 1972, *95*, 61–78.

Luria, A. R. *Traumatic aphasia: Its syndromes, psychology and treatment.* The Hague: Mouton, 1970.

McCarthy, D. Language development in children. In L. Carmichael (Ed.), *Manual of child psychology.* New York: Wiley, 1954. Pp. 492–630.

Macmeeken, A. M. *Ocular dominance in relation to developmental aphasia.* London: Univ. of London Press, 1939.

Miller, E. Handedness and the pattern of human ability. *British Journal of Psychology*, 1971, *62*, 111–112.

Milner, B., Branch, C., & Rasmussen, T. Observations on cerebral dominance. In A. V. S. de Reuck and M. O'Connor (Eds.), *Disorders of language.* London: Churchill, 1964. Pp. 200–222.

Naidoo, S. *Specific dyslexia.* London: Pitman, 1972.

Needles, W. Concerning transfer of cerebral dominance in the function of speech. *Journal of Nervous and Mental Disease*, 1942, *95*, 270–277.

Newton, M. J. *A neuropsychological study of dyslexia.* Applied Psychology Rep. No. 25. Birmingham, Eng.: University of Aston, 1968.

Oldfield, R. C. *Dominance and Hemisphere.* Rep. No. 16/69. Edinburgh: M.R.C. Speech and Communication Unit, 1969. (a)

Oldfield, R. C. Handedness in musicians. *British Journal of Psychology*, 1969, *60*, 91–99. (b)

Orton, S. T. "Word-blindness" in schoolchildren. *Archives of Neurology and Psychiatry*, 1925, *14*, 581–615.

Orton, S. T. *Reading, writing and speech problems in children.* London: Chapman & Hall, 1937.

Penfield, W., & Roberts, L. *Speech and brain mechanisms.* Princeton, N.J.: Princeton Univ. Press, 1959.

Provins, K. A. Motor skill, handedness and behaviour. *Australian Journal of Psychology*, 1967, *19*, 137–150.

Provins, K. A., & Glencross, D. J. Handwriting, typewriting and handedness. *Quarterly Journal of Experimental Psychology*, 1968, *20*, 282–289.

Smith, A. Speech and other functions after left (dominant) hemispherectomy. *Journal of Neurology, Neurosurgery, and Psychiatry*, 1966, *29*, 467–471.

Sparrow, S., & Satz, P. Dyslexia, laterality and neuropsychological development. In D. J. Bakker & P. Satz (Eds.), *Specific reading disability: Advances in theory and method.* Rotterdam: Rotterdam Univ. Press, 1970. Chap. 3, Pp. 41–60.

Subirana, A. The prognosis in aphasia in relation to the factor of cerebral dominance and handedness. *Brain*, 1958, *81*, 415–425.

Tilney, F. Discussion of F. Kennedy and A. Wolf: Relationship of intellect to speech in patients with aphasia, with illustrative cases. *Archives of Neurology and Psychiatry*, 1936, *36*, 897–898.

Travis, L. E. *Speech pathology.* New York: Appleton, 1931.

Zangwill, O. L. Agraphia due to a left parietal glioma in a left-handed man. *Brain*, 1954, 77, 510–520.

Zangwill, O. L. *Cerebral dominance and its relation to psychological function.* Edinburgh: Oliver & Boyd, 1960.

Zangwill, O. L. Asymmetry of cerebral hemisphere function. In H. Garland (Ed.), *Scientific aspects of neurology.* Edinburgh: Livingstone, 1961. Pp. 51–62.

Zangwill, O. L. The current status of cerebral dominance. *Research Publications, Association for Research in Nervous and Mental Disease*, 1964, *42*, 103–118.

Zangwill, O. L. Speech and the right cerebral hemisphere. *Acta Neurological et Psychiatrica Belgica*, 1967, *67*, 1013–1020.

III. Ontogeny

The final section is the "center piece" of this volume. It can hardly be said to cover in detail all of the results of recent investigations into child language, but it does represent well all the current issues in the field. It begins with a critical review of the major theories of developmental phonology (Ferguson and Garnica) and ends with language changes due to senility (de Ajuriaguerra and Tissot). Comparative studies are reported on by Nakazima and by Bowerman; the development of semantics is discussed by Antinucci and Parisi and by Halliday; Schlesinger expounds on problems in the development of syntax. The relationship between language development and cognitive development is dealt with by Sinclair and by O'Connor, and problems of the role of the speech environment are the subject of Slobin's chapter and are also discussed by Cazden and Brown.

The perusal of these contributions—written, as they are, by some of the world's foremost authorities on the subject—should give us pause for humility. How little progress have we made in explaining language and its onset! Even the most elementary questions on the nature of language and its psychobiological mechanisms or its epistemological foundations still elude us. At first, it might appear as if the facts of developmental phonology should be the easiest to ascertain and as if an explanation of their emergence could be accomplished without getting enmeshed in philosophical problems. However, Ferguson's and Garnica's excellent presentation of the existing, competing, but mutually incompatible theories of developmental phonology is eloquent evidence of our actual ignorance on this topic. It is clear that we do not have even simple guidelines of what the rules of the game for theorizing ought to be. Furthermore, it should be clear to linguists that phonology can no longer be treated as a domain unto itself, methodologically dissociable from other levels of language analysis such as language morphology, syntax, or semantics. The reason that computers can still do no better than simulate *approximations* of phonemic processing (there is no program at present that can reliably transform spoken input into graphic—phonemic output) is the interpenetration of the three traditional domains of language (phonology, syntax, and semantics). A language-analyzing instrument, no matter whether of an organic or an artifactual nature, can function accurately only if it has access to information pertaining to all three of these domains. This means that the troublesome issue of language knowledge and, by implication, of knowing on the whole, cannot be kept out of any explanatory theory of any aspect of language.

It is curious to see that even today there is still a deep-seated conviction that all we need to do to understand language and its acquisition is to record and present the facts. However, no matter how detailed our records of facts may be, how much cross-cultured material we manage to gather, it will hardly bring us much closer to understanding the nature of language or the essential mechanism of its acquisition, for facts do not speak for themselves. In the first place, it will be necessary to state more clearly what the questions are that call for answers. Although the behaviorists often disdained theoretical formulations, it was quite clear what questions they were asking by implication and what explanatory mechanisms they were postulating for language. Because they were relatively clear on this score, it was quite simple to test their notions and, alas, it was also simple to show that their assumptions had been wrong. But now that we have triumphantly slain the villain (of mosquito strength), we seem quite helpless in knowing what to do next. Generative grammar is merely promising us a precise, descriptive metalanguage, and it still remains to be seen whether this promise can be made good. Neither Chomsky and his school nor anyone else in linguistics or psychology has given us any indication of how we can approach empirically the problem of language knowledge. What does it mean to "know language"? The problem has been dramatized recently by claims that chimpanzees and computers know language. Such claims seem counter-intuitive, but so far we can neither prove nor disprove them. In fact, we are faced with the same problem day in, day out, when we must assess whether those around us have language knowledge and whether their language knowledge is identical with ours or not. In most instances, we deal with this matter by faith; until we have evidence to the contrary, we simply assume that language knowledge is the same among individuals belonging to the same speech community. When it comes to assessing small children, however, faith is not enough; in recent years it has become amply evident that in fact the epistemological background of their language is not the same as that of adults. However, it is the difference that interests us, and it is precisely in our desire to explore and study this difference that we are at a loss how to proceed.

The present era, with its advances in technology and its penchant for positivism, has an inherent dislike for the raising of philosophical questions on what appear to be scientific matters. It may seem to many that the problem of the epistemological foundations of language is no more vital to empirical research on language than the problem of its epistemological foundations is to mathematics. However, there is an important difference. First, most aspects of mathematics may be completely dissociated from problems of interpretation, meaning, and therefore from knowing the world. One studies formalisms whose "behavior" follows from a set of axioms. Language, on the other hand, particularly language development, cannot be properly separated from meaning and from knowledge of the world. Second, mathematics, being grounded in logic and thus, indirectly, in language itself, is a much more restricted domain than language. The foundations of mathematics are elusive for the same reasons that the foundations of language are elusive; but we may study mathematics without knowing what its foundations are. By the same token, we may practice language or learn a new language without knowing its foundations. However, if we want to find out what the psychobiological mechanisms are that make our practice of language possible (and probably also our practice of mathematics), if we want to discover what it is that the 3-year-old child has that the one-year-old is still lacking, if we want to know what distinguishes man from beast (including the chimpanzee), then the philosophical problem must be faced squarely: What is the nature of knowing, in general, and of knowing a language, in particular? In the present volume the only contributor who approaches this problem is Sinclair; we are certain that she will agree with us that we still have a long way to go.

9. Theories of Phonological Development[1]

Charles A. Ferguson / Olga K. Garnica

A theory of phonological development must account for the development of all the characteristics of an adult phonology as specified by phonological theory, as well as the known facts of child phonology not covered by phonological theory. In addition, it should be consistent with a broader theory of language development, relatable to theories of other aspects of development, and empirically testable. Four major types of theories are examined, using examples from the Leopold diary and other sources: behaviorist theories of several kinds that emphasize the role of reinforcement; structuralist theories based on a universal hierarchy of phonological structure that determines the order of acquisition (Jakobson and others); the natural phonology theory, which assumes a universal, innate hierarchy of phonological processes (Stampe); and the prosodic theory, which emphasizes the importance of input to the child and the development of perception (Waterson). The theories are compared and are seen to be incompatible because of different goals and lack of data on questions of fact. Several major issues are identified for research and theoretical elaboration.

[1] The preparation of this chapter benefited directly from work on the Stanford University Child Phonology Project, which is supported by National Science Foundation grants GS 2320 and GS 30962, for which grateful acknowledgement is made. We also express our appreciation for the work of Linda Kay Brown, who prepared the Bibliography. The Bibliography, in addition to listing those references used in text citations, includes an additional list that endeavors to provide a well-balanced basic bibliography on child phonology. For a more recent (but briefer) annotated bibliography, see Macken, M. L., Child phonology, *Linguistic Reporter*, 1974, 16(10), 9—12.

Introduction

Most children, as a normal part of their development, learn to recognize and pronounce the sounds of the language in their speech community so well that their perception and pronunciation reflect in countless details their competence as "native speakers" of the language, and their speech lacks any trace of the foreign accent of people who learn the language later. Starting from crying and early cooing and babbling, children gradually acquire the complex patterns of the adult phonology of their language. Phonological development is just one aspect of the larger process of acquiring full communicative competence in language structure and the use of language, but it merits special attention as an independent field of investigation.

The acquisition of phonology is, in fact, a particularly promising field for the study of child development, partly due to the state of knowledge in phonetics and the sophistication of phonological theory. Technical descriptions of speech sounds can provide detailed indications of the physiology of speech and hearing and the acoustics of speech phenomena; linguistic theories offer a body of descriptive and explanatory principles derived from the analysis of hundreds of languages. It is possible to specify the child's phonological behavior with great precision and to deal with its development in terms of principles evident elsewhere in language behavior, such as in the processes of language change. This level of precision and theoretical insight is hard to match in other areas of child development. Moreover, the analysis of phonological development, more than other aspects of psycholinguistic research, seems to offer immediate promise for speech therapists and students of speech pathology, since in phonology the abnormalities can often be specified most unequivocally and therapeutic techniques tested most directly.

From another point of view, the study of phonological development is of great interest because of its relation to phonological theory. In the past, most phonological theorists, with a few exceptions such as Roman Jakobson, failed to give much attention to data from children. Recently, however, linguists are increasingly recognizing the importance of child language study, and theories of phonology are beginning to take account of acquisition (Vennemann, 1971). The basic concepts and issues of phonology are often accessible with a special clarity in child language, and phonological development is now recognized as a potential testing ground for empirical studies related to phonological theory.

The research literature on the acquisition of phonology is large, but very varied both in approach (experimental psychology, speech sciences, linguistics, speech pathology) and in degree of sophistication. The most thorough review of this literature, with summaries and interpretive comments, is still McCarthy (1954), but this is largely limited to English, is inadequate in its coverage of linguistic studies, and in any case antedates major shifts in linguistic theory and the whole body of contemporary psycholinguistic research. Menyuk (1971) brings McCarthy up to date in bibliographical coverage and examines the research findings on major issues such as the nature of babbling, the acquisition of intonation, the order of feature acquisition, and the development of phonological rules governing occurrence of sounds, particularly as shown in consonant clusters. Braine's review (1971), which was written earlier and is somewhat less comprehensive, is also useful; he summarizes generalizations that previous authors have noted, and in addition makes several new suggestions, such as his distinction between "low-level" phonological alternations, which are assimilatory in nature, and "high-level" ones, which have a different psychological basis.

The purpose of the present paper is to discuss the requirements of a theory of phonological development and examine major theories advanced in the psycholinguistic literature. The four major types of theory to be discussed are the behaviorist theories of H. O. Mowrer and others, the structuralist theory of Jakobson and its extension, the natural phonology theory of David Stampe, and Natalie Waterson's prosodic theory. In discussion of the theories, examples will be taken, to the extent possible, from Werner Leopold's study of his daughter Hildegard (Leopold, 1947), which is probably still the best report of a single child's phonological development and is often cited by the theorists themselves. Where phonetic transcription is required, the symbols of the International Phonetic Association will be used.[2]

Requirements for a Theory of Phonological Development

A theory of phonological development that is both comprehensive and explanatory must meet at least the following four requirements. It must account for the development of all the characteristics of an adult phonology as specified by a given phonological theory. It must account for known facts of phonological development that are not included in the characterization of adult phonology by existing theories. It must be consistent with a broader theory of language development and be relatable to theories of other aspects of child development. It should make principled predictions that can be empirically verified.

CONCEPTS IN ADULT PHONOLOGY

A full description of the characteristics of adult phonology cannot be attempted here and reference is made to classics in phonological theory (Bloch, 1948; Chomsky & Halle, 1968; Jakobson, Fant, & Halle, 1955; Trubetzkoy, 1969), but it is necessary to explain several basic concepts that appear, in one form or another,

---

[2]The transcription of child speech presents special problems. Suggested solutions include the use of recording devices (Lynip, 1951), restriction of phones to be transcribed and practice for inter-observer reliability (Irwin, 1957), and the training of teams to use special transcription grids (Johnson & Bush, 1972). It is a sobering thought that almost all the classic studies of child phonology, including the Leopold volumes, utilize the transcription of a single observer, without the benefit of recordings.

in all major theories of phonology. The concepts chosen are intended to be illustrative and propaedeutic; they do not constitute a comprehensive set of fundamental notions for phonology.

In every adult phonology, certain sound differences are utilized in making lexical distinctions, and others are not used for this purpose. Thus, in English, the difference between the *k* and *g* sounds is used to signal the difference in *pick* and *pig*. In this case the basic difference is between no vibration of the vocal cords for voiceless *k* and vibration for voiced *g*, the two sounds being articulated about the same way otherwise. On the other hand, the difference between a voiceless *l* and a voiced *l* is not used in English to make lexical distinctions, although many speakers use a voiceless *l* in words like *play* and a voiced *l* in words like *lay*. Languages differ in their use of sound differences: Menomini, an American Indian language, does not use the *k–g* difference lexically, whereas Welsh does make use of the difference between voiceless *l* (spelled *ll* in Welsh) and voiced *l*. This distinguishing role of the sound differences or the individual sounds that exemplify the differences is called the *distinctive* function, the fact of the distinction between two sounds is called *contrast*, and the relationship between two contrasting sounds is called an *opposition*.

Since adult phonologies are characterized by patterns of oppositions, the questions that arise are: At what point does the child's language show the distinctive function of sound differences, and how does the child acquire the full inventory of adult oppositions? These questions, which include the notion of relationship among the speech sounds, have greater significance than the more obvious questions of what sounds the child acquires and in what order.

Every adult phonology has regular patterns ("rules") of adjustment by which particular sounds or classes of sounds take on the value of neighboring sounds, in whole or in part. This process of *assimilation* is seen in English in such phenomena as the adjustment of the prefix *in-* (cf. *inactive, intemperate*) to *im-* in *impossible* when the tongue-tip articulation of the nasal *n* is replaced by a lip articulation *m* like that of the following *p*. The pronunciation of voiceless *l* in *play*, mentioned above, is another example of assimilation, since the normally voiced *l* is voiceless here immediately after the voiceless *p*.

Some patterns of assimilation are very widespread among the world's languages, others are highly language-specific. Some theorists prefer the formulation that all assimilation rules are universal and that language differences reflect the interaction of conflicting rules. In any case, the acquisition questions are apparent: How does the child acquire the assimilation rules of the adult phonology? Does he follow assimilation rules of his own, which he has to unlearn during his development? Can the child use an adult rule even though the sounds to which he applies it differ from the adult sounds?

In analyzing phenomena such as contrast and assimilation, linguists often do not refer to sound segments such as *p* or *n* but use the notion of phonetic *feature*, i.e. a speech sound characteristic such as voicing or nasality which occurs in simultaneous combination with other features to constitute a distinctive segment or *phoneme*. Thus, *pick* and *pig* differ in the absence or presence of voicing in the final segment, which may be indicated [− voice] or [+ voice] respectively. Similarly, in the pronunciation of *play* with voiceless *l*, [+ voice] is replaced by [− voice] after an initial consonant that is [− voice]. Great effort has been expended to identify a minimum universal set of phonetic features that will include all the features that may be distinctive in any language (Chomsky & Halle, 1968; Jakobson *et al.*, 1955; Ladefoged, 1971).

Finally, the concept of *phonological alternation* or *morphophonemic rule* is important in phonological theory. It has been the object of psycholinguistic research and has been considered in some developmental theories. The same word or *morpheme* in a given language may have different forms under different conditions, and this variation is often highly patterned, that is, large classes of words show related alternations that may be stated as rules. For example, many words in English have vowel alternations such as *divine:divinity, serene:serenity, profane:profanity*, where, long, tense diphthongs alternate with short, lax, simple vowels. Adults have many instances of such alternations in their vocabulary and are often able to pronounce new words correctly when they are analogous to these.

There are many kinds of phonological alternations in languages, and they may have very different status. They range from being rare and unproductive (e.g. the vowel change of *woman:women* in English) to being pervasive and central to a phonology (e.g. the high−low vowel alternations in all Bengali simple verb stems). The pertinent developmental questions are when and how does the child acquire mastery of these alternations?

CHILD PHONOLOGY FACTS

One of the facts of child phonology that raises problems for any general theory is the acquisition of the adult use of the many so-called "redundant" or non-distinctive features of the language. For example, the voiceless stops /p t k/ of English have varying amounts of aspiration, i.e. the sound made by the puff of air after the release of the stop. In ordinary conversational American English these stops are heavily aspirated before a stressed vowel, as in *pick* or *report*, but only aspirated lightly or not at all before unstressed vowels, as in *upper* or *happy*. This sound difference is nondistinctive in English (although similar differences may be distinctive in other languages). Adults are in general unaware of the difference and do not overtly correct mispronunciations when they occur. Their behavior towards the child's use of the differences can hardly be understood as reinforcing. Theories of phonological development do not deal with this general question, although some empirical studies bear on it. For example, it seems likely that children of all languages first produce predominantly unaspirated stops and aspirated variants not conditioned by the surrounding sounds, then gradually acquire the pattern of aspiration in the language they are learning (Leopold, 1947, pp. 119−120; Preston, 1971).

In analyzing the phonology of a child at a particular stage of development it is generally possible to find some words that are pronounced with greater exactitude than the majority and seem to be in some sense outside the phonological system of the child. It often happens that the pronunciation of such a word seems to regress for a while, conforming more fully to the child's overall phonology, and only at a much later date achieving the phonetic accuracy it had earlier. An extreme example of this is Hildegard Leopold's word [prIti] *pretty*, which appeared very early and persisted in that form for some time. Only later was it adjusted to [pIti], conforming to her phonology at that stage. The existence of such forms raises the question of how they are perceived, remembered, and produced counter to the constraints that are evident in the child's current phonology. This phenomenon is doubtlessly related to the existence of isolated, marginal items in adult phonologies, but it is more salient in the child, whose entire phonology is in the process of development.

A third fact of child phonology that raises problems for any general theory is what Roger Brown (Berko & Brown, 1960, p. 531) has called the "*fis* phenomenon," a kind of perception–production discrepancy, examples of which have been reported for a number of children in various languages. In the Brown example, the child had difficulty in pronouncing the *sh* sound; he pronounced the word *fish* something like *fis*. However, when an adult, in an effort to be adaptive, tried saying *fis* for *fish*, the child objected, saying something like "Not *fis, fis!*" and was satisfied only when the adult pronounced his normal *fish*.

This phenomenon seems to indicate that a child is able to perceive an adult sound difference and correctly assign the respective sounds to appropriate lexical items, but not make the difference himself and possibly not even perceive the lack of it in his own pronunciation.

Although in some instances it may be that the child actually makes a distinction in pronunciation that the adult does not perceive (cf. the *r* : *w* distinction of older children in Metcalfe, 1963), in most cases the child probably does not make the difference. This phenomenon raises a fundamental question. If the child at a given stage perceives his speech in terms of his own productive phonological system but perceives adult speech on the basis of a more developed phonology, how can one account for the steady improvement in the child's productions without some kind of more sensitive self-monitoring? This question is made even more troublesome by the evidence from Smith (1973) that a child may find difficulty perceiving in terms of the phonological system he was using just a short time previously (as in recordings of his earlier speech).

Similar to the *fis* phenomenon is the widely documented fact that children often produce a certain sound in their speech that they seem unable to replicate from an adult model. Thus, a child may regularly substitute a *g* for a medial *d*, and yet use a *d* as his regular substitute for medial *z* (Smith, 1973). A similar example from Leopold is Hildegard's regular use of [d], for [dʒ], for example, [do·i] *Joey*, [duʃ] *juice*, for a long period during which she pronounced [dʒ] as a substitute for [tʃ], for example, in *church* and *choo-choo* (Leopold, 1947, p. 130). Several theories of phonological development attempt to explain this apparent discrepancy between what the child can pronounce in direct replication and what he can pronounce spontaneously.

Behaviorist Theories

MOWRER

The theory of language development formulated by H. O. Mowrer in the late 1940s is still the best known theory of phonology acquisition to many psychologists and speech therapists. Mowrer presented the theory at a symposium in 1949 and has returned to discussion of it on a number of subsequent occasions; other investigators have also dealt with it. Mowrer (1952) is the most convenient reference; for recent critical reviews of the theory and relevant experimental research see Siegel (1969) and Winitz (1969). Mowrer's rather general theory offers a model for the acquisition of speech sounds and words, although not syntax as such or the acquisition of productive phonological rules. The theory was explicitly intended to fit the general framework of both learning theory and psychoanalysis. The contribution from psychoanalysis lies chiefly in the emphasis on the affective relation between child and mother in the emergence of speech; most of the theory is couched in learning theoretic terms.

Mowrer first adduced evidence in support of the theory from research with "talking birds" (such as parrots or mynas) who learned to produce strings of sounds similar to utterances spoken by their trainer. He seems not to have attempted research with children, although several subsequent investigators have done so.

According to the theory, the first step in development is that the child (or bird) attends to and identifies with the caretaker (i.e., mother or trainer). Next, vocalizations of the caretaker are associated with primary reinforcement such as food or patting. Then vocalizations of the child (bird) also acquire reinforcement value by virtue of their similarity to the caretaker's vocalizations. Finally, there is selective reinforcement of those sounds that are more like the caretaker's sounds, not only by extrinsic reinforcement, but more importantly, by the child's own reinforcement in matching the caretaker's speech. This last notion is the basis of Mowrer's own rather unfortunate name for the theory, the "autism" theory.

Winitz offers the fullest recent account of phonology development in terms of Mowrer's theory (Winitz, 1969, p. 35–48); three early developmental stages are specified in somewhat greater detail. During the first period, the child's vocalizations are said to occur most frequently shortly before feeding because of natural sounds associated with chewing and swallowing and the principle of "fractional anticipatory goal response;" that is, the child, in anticipation, makes the kind of response he will make when he gets the food, and this response includes making sounds with the vocal tract. Following learning theoretic principles, Winitz even holds that the duration of vocalization before feeding will be proportional to the length of the feeding period. During the second developmental period the vocalizations of the mother, and subsequently those of the child by virtue of their similarity to the mother's, acquire secondary reinforcing properties because the mother's vocalizations occur in close proximity with feeding or other primary reinforcement events. The third period begins when several of the child's utterances are identified by the parent as an approximation of a particular word. The parent reinforces these utterances and the child gradually refines this approximation until it matches the adult form.

Although there is virtually no experimental evidence that supports the Mowrer theory on the acquisition of phonology in any specific way, and there is indirect evidence against it, it continues to be cited and given cautious approval by many authors. The theory might be expected to have particular value for the emergence of babbling, but it apparently runs into direct contradiction from empirical data. Mowrer specifically assumes that a normal child does not begin to babble (i.e. move from "reflexive" vocalizations to vocal play) until the secondary reinforcement of his vocalization is established (Mowrer, 1960, p. 84), yet research with deaf children and children of deaf parents shows normal incidence of babbling (Lenneberg, Rebelsky, & Nichols, 1965; Murai, 1961). Winitz maintains that during the second period there is a gradual approximation of babbling sounds to the sounds of the language in certain features of stress, syllabic structure, and the like, but sees no fully satisfactory explanation of this (Winitz, 1969, p. 44). The chief reason for the continued receptivity to the Mowrer theory is probably that it accords with models of learning for other skills, and investigators who tend to accept a behaviorist learning theory of some kind on a quite general basis are prepared to accept it for the acquisition of speech as well. Mowrer himself found his paradigm for language acquisition so attractive that he made it the basis for his more general theory of learning and symbolic processes (Mowrer, 1960). Opponents of the theory generally point out the difference between human language behavior, or the conditions under which it is acquired, and other kinds of behavior that have been investigated by learning theorists (Chomsky, 1959; Milisen, 1966).

EXTENSIONS OF MOWRER

Murai and Olmsted have attempted to extend or modify Mowrer's theory in significant ways (Murai, 1963; Olmsted, 1966, 1971). Murai's empirical studies of babbling and early speech, which draw theoretical insights from other sources as well (Murai, 1963, and references therein), add two notions to the theory: (a) the difference in psychological mechanisms operative in early comprehension and production, and (b) the principle of economy in the origin of symbolic behavior. His factor analytic studies suggest that comprehension tasks are related to an intelligence factor, whereas production tasks are related to a motor factor. He regards early comprehension behavior as essentially identical with the use of signs by animals, while early production is the beginning of the distinctively human use of symbols. In discussing the development of imitative sounds in the babbling period, Murai maintains that the child's vocalization represents an action ("performance") or a physical object, and since the child's sound is not in itself more useful or adaptive than the actual performance or object, some kind of "economy of energy" or adaptiveness to the future must be the explanation of the growth of the symbolic behavior.

Olmsted (1966) presents a theory of phonology acquisition in the form of 21 explicit postulates, and reports a large-scale (100 children) research project designed to test the theory. The form of the postulates and the whole approach to phonology derives from Bernard Bloch's postulate system for adult phonology (Bloch, 1948), which attempted to present the basic principles of phonemic analysis as a deductive system.

In a recent monograph Olmsted reports that his findings offer substantial confirmation of his theory (Olmsted, 1971). Along with greater specification of the phonetic properties of speech, Olmsted adds two elements to Mowrer's theory: frequency of input and ease of perception. Stretches of adult speech uttered in the child's presence gain secondary reinforcing properties in proportion to their frequency (Postulates 5 and 6), and phones whose components are more easily perceived have a higher probability of being learned earlier (Postulates 13 and 18).

Olmsted's theory offers specific predictions about child language behavior and hence is subject to fairly direct (dis)confirmation by empirical studies. For example, his hierarchy of ease of perception in English, which is taken from Miller and Nicely's classic study (G. A. Miller & Nicely, 1955), is quite precise. The features of voicing (vocal cord vibration heard in vowels and such consonants as *b, z, n*) and nasality (nasal resonance as heard in the consonants *m, n, ng*) are more easily perceived than the features of friction and duration, and these more so than features of place of articulation (labial, dental, etc.). Therefore, Olmsted's prediction is that at a given stage of phonological development, before the phones of the language have been "learned to asymptote," the number of errors will be greatest for place of articulation and less for voicing and nasality. This prediction is at odds with the general observation that the distinction between nasals and nonnasals (e.g., *m ≠ b*) is acquired very early in English, whereas the distinction between voiced and unvoiced (e.g., *b ≠ p*) is quite late. Olmsted's theory is, however, not concerned with the development of oppositions. Also, he disregards such phenomena as the child's early preference for voiced initial consonants and unvoiced final consonants. Most phones of English are voiced in most contexts (vowels, semivowels, liquids, nasals; voiced stops and voiced fricatives), and most early child vocalizations are voiced; Olmsted finds confirmation of the Miller–Nicely hierarchy and his own theory in this kind of global low frequency of errors in voicing. Other studies (e.g., Graham & House, 1971) show many problems in the feature analysis of children's perceptual errors, and at least one investigator (Locke, 1970) suggests that relative difficulty of articulation would be a better explanatory factor in this framework.

Olmsted, although a structuralist in linguistic analysis, explicitly rejects

Jakobson's structuralist theory of phonology acquisition, described later, on both theoretical and practical grounds. His theoretical objection is that Jakobson makes too sharp a distinction between babbling and speech, and thereby misses the gradual and systematic approximation of the child's phones to the phonetic characteristics of the adult's phones. His own modified version of the Mowrer theory is intended to account for part of this process.

Olmsted's practical objection, to which he gives considerable emphasis, is the great difficulty of obtaining valid and reliable evidence on the acquisition of oppositions. He points to the difficulty of deciding on a criterion for when an opposition has been acquired, and the fact that evidence cannot be collected on a large scale or by systematic sampling but requires extended observation and analysis of individual children.

Structuralist Theories

JAKOBSON

Perhaps the best-known and most influential theory of phonological development was formulated by the linguist Roman Jakobson in his pioneer work *Kindersprache, Aphasie und allgemeine Lautgesetze* (1941, English translation 1968). Partial revisions and elaborations of the theory appeared in several subsequent works (Jakobson, 1971; Jakobson & Halle, 1956). Jakobson's theory represents the first attempt to explain the acquisition of phonology on the basis of linguistic universals, structural laws that underlie every modification of language, individual or social.

Jakobson distinguishes two discontinuous periods of phonological development: (1) the prelanguage babbling period, during which the sounds composing the child's vocalizations do not exhibit any particular order of development are not related to the productions of the following period; and (2) the acquisition of language proper, during which the child follows a relatively universal and invariant order in gaining intentional control over the sounds of the surrounding adult language. The division of the developmental process into these two periods serves to emphasize the difference between the mere production of sounds and the systematic use of those sounds in a phonological system.

The division into two periods is based on the widely accepted observation that during babbling the vocalizations of most normal children exhibit a great quantity and diversity of sound productions (complex vowels, clicks, palatalized and rounded consonants, etc.), but that as the child begins to acquire words, most of these sounds disappear, and some of them (e.g., sibilants and liquids) reappear only after long effort—often only after several years. "The phonetic richness of the babbling period thus gives way to phonological limitation [Jakobson, 1971, p. 9]."

Jakobson posits that the explanation of this reduction of sounds, which occurs during the transition from the babbling period to language proper (the use of words with meaning), rests solely on the newly acquired function of the sounds as speech sounds possessing distinctive linguistic value. The beginning of the second period ("language proper") is marked by sound utterances that are employed for designation: "To the desire to communicate is added the ability to communicate something [Jakobson, 1968, p. 24]." Just prior to this point, a short period of complete silence on the part of the child may intervene; however, "For the most part one stage [= period] merges unobtrusively into the other, so that the acquisition of vocabulary and the disappearance of the prelanguage inventory occur concurrently [Jakobson, 1968, p. 29]." The criteria suggested for distinguishing speech sounds from babbling sounds during this time of overlap are the persistence of the sound, the intention to express meaning by the formation in which the sound occurs, and the social setting of the utterance. No further elaboration of these criteria is presented.

Once the second period has begun, phonological development consists of the construction of a phonemic system through the selection of sounds. Jakobson posits that, once this has begun, there is a regular and invariant succession of stages of development, although the rate of progression through the stages is individual and variable. The stages are strictly regulated by an inherent universal hierarchy of structural laws, which Jakobson calls "laws of irreversible solidarity." The dissolution of the linguistic sound system as exhibited by aphasics proceeds in stages that provide "an exact mirror-image of the phonological development in child language [Jakobson, 1968, p. 60]."

The sequence of stages is based upon "the principle of maximum contrast" and "development proceeds from the simple and undifferentiated to the stratified and differentiated [Jakobson, 1968, p. 68]." Complexity is measured in terms of the number of oppositions a sound participates in within a system. Oppositions are acquired, not individual sounds. At any given stage of development, the child's phonological system has a structure of its own, and this structure exhibits systematic correspondences (in the form of substitutions) to the adult's system. However, not all of the child's utterances are bound by such limitations; "vocal gestures," such as exclamations and onomatopoeic expressions, form a distinct layer that is marginal to the central, systematic, structural core of speech.

Within Jakobson's theoretical framework, a phonological system is considered to be composed of layers, universal and invariable, superimposed on one another (i.e. a stratified system). The laws governing the hierarchical relationships of these layers are of the following type: The existence of an entity Y in a phonemic system implies the existence of an entity X in that same system (Jakobson, 1971, p. 19). In other words, Y cannot exist in a system without a corresponding X. Furthermore, without the presence of X, Y cannot arise in the system; and without Y, X cannot be eliminated from the system.

Some examples of implications universals of this type are available in Greenberg (1963, 1966) and Ferguson (1966). Let us consider in detail one such universal, dealing with nasal phonemes:

No language has nasal vowels unless it also has one or more primary nasal consonants. [= The existence of nasal vowels in a phonemic system implies the existence of one or more primary nasal consonants;[3] Ferguson, 1966, p. 58].

With respect to *change* in a phonemic system, this universal states that:

1. *for addition of a sound to a phonemic system* (language acquisition and historical change), a nasal vowel cannot appear unless one or more primary nasal consonants already exist in that system, that is, primary nasal consonants are acquired before nasal vowels;

2. *for loss of a sound from a phonemic system* (both in language dissolution through aphasia and in historical change), a primary nasal consonant will not be eliminated as long as a nasal vowel still exists in that system; that is, nasal vowels disappear before primary nasal consonants.

The details of Jakobson's proposed universal order of phonemic development are based on laws of irreversible solidarity (implications) of this type. These are derived from the observation of the phonemic systems of many languages of the world, and on a related factor, namely, the frequency with which a particular phonemic contrast occurs in languages. In regard to the latter factor, the general hypothesis is that oppositions that are comparatively rare are among the last to be acquired by the child and among the first lost by aphasics (Jakobson, 1968, p. 57).

Phonemic development begins, according to Jakobson, with the "labial stage" (Jakobson & Halle, 1956). The acquisition of vowels begins with a wide vowel, usually *a*, while, at the same time, the acquisition of consonants begins with a labial stop, most commonly *p*. This establishes a phonemic distinction of optimal consonant and optimal vowel. The contrast between these two units in succession establishes the universal model of the syllable—CV (consonant + vowel). The earliest meaningful units to appear in child speech are based on this polarity.

So as to distinguish utterances with this opposition from these of the babbling period, the phonemes must be recognizable, distinguishable, and consciously repeated. This repetitiveness is usually expressed by reduplication (e.g., *pa pa pa*), which may serve as "a compulsory process signaling that the uttered sounds do not represent a babble, but a senseful, semantic entity [Jakobson, 1971, p. 25]."

As subsequent oppositions develop as described later, there is a gradual increase in (a) the number of distinctive features in a phoneme and the number of phonemes in the system, (b) the maximum number of phonemes in the word, (c) the number of possibilities for the distribution of phonemes, and (d) the maximum number of phonemic distinctions within a word. For example, in the earlier stages, only one sound functions distinctively within a given word, usually the consonant, with the

---

[3]A nasal vowel is a vowel with nasal resonance, such as French *on, an, in, un*. A primary nasal consonant is a voiced stop with nasal resonance, without any additional articulation, such as English *m, n, ng*

vowel remaining unchanged. Later the child can use two different consonants or two different vowels in the same word, but not both sets at the same time.

The primary contrast manifested in "optimal consonant + optimal vowel" forms the base for all subsequent distinctions. All the inherent distinctive features acquired fall on two axes: the sonority axis, which includes secondary consonantal source features, and the tonality axis, which includes the oral resonance features.

In the next stage the oral stop obtains a counterpart in a nasal consonant. This represents the first distinction on the sonority axis. The opposition, nasal versus oral stop, is one of the earliest acquisitions of the child. However, this opposition may be preceded by oppositions on the tonality axis. The first of these is the opposition grave/acute, which splits the primary consonant to form the "primary triangle" (see a in Fig. 9–1). Further development consists of the splitting of the primary

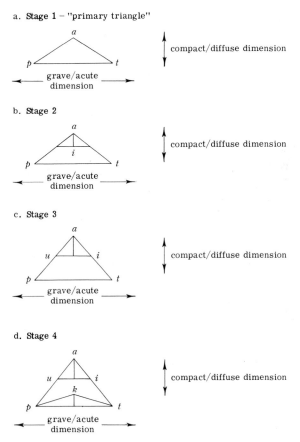

Figure 9–1. Successive developments of the "primary triangle" as proposed by Jakobson's theory of phonological development. (Adapted from McNeill, 1970, p. 1134.)

triangle into two triangles, consonantal and vocalic i.e., into compact (diffuse and grave) acute oppositions (see b—d in Fig. 9—1).

Subsequent development of the oral resonance features (tonality axis) is dependent on the laws of irreversible solidarity. (See Fig. 9—2; also see Jakobson & Halle, 1956, p. 41.) The implicational relationships between various oppositions are indicated by arrows in the figure. For example, the opposition palatal narrow vowel versus velar narrow vowel implies the opposition narrow vowel versus wide vowel, which in turn implies the opposition dental consonant versus labial consonant. Only those distinctions that are present in the language being learned are acquired by the child.

On the sonority axis, Jakobson does not present such a coherent set of implicational statements in relation to the optimal consonant—optimal vowel distinction.

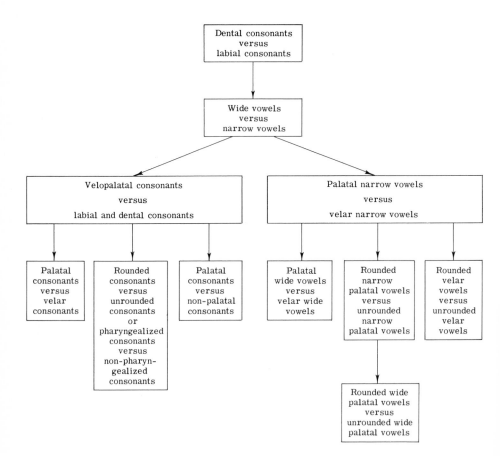

Figure 9—2. Successive developments of the oral resonance features on the tonality axis as suggested by Jakobson's theory. (Based on Jakobson & Halle, 1956.)

He does, however, point out the following specific developments: (a) nasal stops appear early; (b) stops are an earlier acquisition than constrictive phonemes (spirants), for example $p-t$ before $f-s$; (c) at least one liquid is acquired before the opposition strident versus mellow, e.g. r or l before $t\int-t$.

Jakobson gives only the barest outline of his universal order of acquisition. Consider, for example, the stages of development proposed for the tonality axis (see Fig. 9—2). The developments for consonants and for vowels, subsequent to the wide vowel versus narrow vowel distinction, are presented independently with no statement as to their interrelationship. The stages of development proposed for the sonority axis are even less rigorously defined. Statements as to the inter-relationships between the acquisition of oppositions on the sonority axis and those of the tonality axis are almost totally absent. Furthermore, whereas a number of empirical studies (see, e.g., Moskowitz, 1970) have shown that sound distinctions may first appear in one or another position in a word (initial, medial, final), Jakobson does not consider this factor. Finally, Jakobson deals exclusively with the acquisition of the segmental aspects of phonological development and ignores the prosodic features of language, that is, stress and intonation.

Many investigators have found support for the regular and lawful progression of stages of phonological development outlined by Jakobson, both for production (Leopold, 1947, 1953; Nakazima, 1966; Velten, 1943; also see numerous studies discussed in Menyuk, 1971) and for perception (Shvachkin, 1948).[4] However, some points are disputed; for example, Jakobson implies that the glides w and h are acquired late, but empirical evidence (e.g., Leopold, 1947) indicates that these are acquired quite early. Comparison of data from production studies shows that the patterns of acquisition of fricatives in English differ significantly from Jakobson's predictions (Ferguson, 1974).

One major criticism concerning the theory focuses on the issue of strict dis-continuity between the two periods of development, particularly the assertion that there is no order of development during the babbling period. Jakobson's claim that the babbling period is characterized by production of the entire range of human speech sounds, a higher degree of individual variation, and no develop-mental trends has been questioned by recent empirical studies. Blount (1970) presents data from four Luo-speaking children. He reports a convergence to a small number of distinct sounds, predominantly dental and velar stops and labial and velar resonants, toward the end of the babbling period. Cruttenden's (1970) study of a pair of English-speaking twins supports Blount's findings on the more restrictive phonetic range in babbling and the general drift of sounds produced toward those in the mother tongue.

---

[4] Jakobson makes no explicit statement as to whether the proposed order of acquisition applies to perception as well as production, although all the examples he discusses concern the latter. A recent attempt to replicate the results of Shvachkin's study for English-speaking children employing more stringent experimental controls (Garnica, 1973), failed to confirm the findings fully (cf. also Eimas, Sigueland, Jusczyk, & Vigorito, 1971).

Another criticism of Jakobson's theory, less related to phonological development as such, is that the data for aphasia patients, in the opinion of most neurologists, do not substantiate the "mirror-image" dissolution (Lhermitte & Gautier, 1969).

MOSKOWITZ

Breyne Moskowitz modifies and extends Jakobson's theory in a number of directions (Moskowitz, 1970, 1971, 1973). Her theory, presented in fullest form in her unpublished dissertation (Moskowitz, 1971), includes elements of contemporary generative phonology (Chomsky & Halle, 1968) but is still essentially structuralist. She regards phonological development as the acquisition of units and the rules governing the arrangements of those units, and views the child's discovery of successively smaller phonological units as a crucial part of the acquisition process.

The child begins his discoveries during the babbling period, which Moskowitz does not separate so definitely from later speech development as does Jakobson. The child's first step in linguistic analysis is his hypothesis that the stream of adult speech consists of separable strings of sound, and this is reflected in the increased length and structured nature of his babbling. The major achievement of the babbling period is the child's discovery of the sentence unit, characterized by the co-occurrence of an intonation contour with a string of speech sounds.

As a child masters one kind of unit, he can then treat it more automatically and proceed to cope with a smaller unit (cf. also Braine, 1971). Once the child has acquired some control over sentence intonation, he is free to turn to analysis of the segmental material.

The next major unit the child discovers is the syllable, which soon acquires semantic value and becomes the syllable-word. The inventory of syllables that the child acquires and utilizes at this stage constitutes both the phonological and lexical units of his language. Phonetic differences between the syllables become increasingly precise, but the important fact at this time is that the phonetic distinctions are syllable features, not individual speech sounds or phonemes. Thus the difference between *pa* and *ka* is not the distinction between *p* and *k* but a difference in syllable onset (cf. also Ferguson, Peizer, & Weeks, 1973). Moskowitz gives great importance to the role of the syllable in phonological development, referring not only to data from children she has studied, but also to recent theoretical papers on the role of the syllable (e.g., Fudge, 1969).

The first syllable-words that the child acquires are all $\widehat{CV}$ types (Moskowitz uses the tie notation for syllables not analyzed into segment units.) During this period the child acquires many of the articulatory routines he will continue to use throughout his life, even after he has reanalyzed sound sequences into smaller units. He develops the ability to identify "sames" and "differents" in terms of the whole syllable. As the number of syllable-words increases, the syllable structure is also elaborated and $\widehat{CVC}$, $\widehat{VC}$, and V syllables begin to appear.

The next stage is one in which $\widehat{CVCV}$ words occur; word and syllable are now separated and the way is open for contrasting syllables to be analyzed in terms of segments. First the two syllables are identical, for example, *kiki* ("full reduplication"), then come instances in which only the two consonants or only the two vowels are identical, for example, *kiti, babi* ("partial reduplication"). It is at this point that the child discovers the phone or segment as a unit. Moskowitz cites the example of one child (Burling, 1959) who at age 17 months began to use words of two different syllables. Toward the end of that month he acquired a syllable with *l*-onset, *la*, which he used in reduplicated form, *lala*, for the name of his Garo nurse Emula. Although the child already had the syllable *mu* in his inventory, and was beginning to have segment units, the new element (*l*) entered his system at the more primitive level of syllable units and full reduplication.

Once the syllables are analyzed into consonantal and vocalic segments, the child's inventory of segments grows steadily. The order of acquisition of segments varies greatly from one child to another, but Jakobson's order of acquisition of features is followed. At any one time the words used by the child may be at various stages of analysis, some being coded as syllables, others in whole or in part as segments or bundles of features. This is illustrated by "progressive phonological idioms," which have a phonetic accuracy greater than the words typical for the stage of development but have not been analyzed into smaller units. A good example of this is Hildegard Leopold's [pɹIti], discussed earlier (p. 158). The existence of such marginal elements is noted by Jakobson but is given more import in the Moskowitz theory.

Moskowitz also deals explicitly with the acquisition of phonological alternations of the *divine-divinity* type in English (Moskowitz, 1971, 1973). In a series of experiments using nonsense forms, with adults and children as subjects, she explored the nature and extent of speakers' knowledge of these alternations in relation to the set of vowel shift rules that Chomsky and Halle (1968) propose to account for the alternations. She concludes that while some of these are acquired as productive rules fairly early, many of them are acquired late or not at all, and some may be learned as a result of exposure to reading and school experiences. Following Braine's suggestion of different levels of morphophonemic rules, she suggests that they may be acquired at different ages and by different mechanisms but she does not integrate this fully with her general theory.

Natural Phonology Theory

The natural phonology theory of phonological development (Stampe, 1969) assumes a universal, innate system of phonological processes—unlimited and unordered rules—which, in its most language-innocent state, expresses the full set of restrictions of the human speech capacity. It proposes that the phonetic representations of the child's productions are the result of the application of this innate system to an abstract phonological representation. Successive revisions of this innate system occur with the learning of each new phonetic opposition through linguistic experience with the standard (adult) language. The mechanisms hypothesized for this revision are suppression, limitation, and ordering of the given phonological processes.

The utterances produced by children in the post-babbling period, commonly characterized by well-articulated sequences of identical stressed syllables with lax stop or nasal plus low vowel (e.g., [dadada], [mamama]), represent the fullest effect of the innate system. The mature phonological system is the residue of those aspects of the innate system that are left intact by the revisions achieved through mastery plus certain language-specified conditions on processes that are learned.

Since the notion of phonological process is central to this theory, a fuller explanation of what is meant by the term is required. A phonological process is a rule that results in the merger of "a potential phonological opposition into that member of the opposition which least tries the restrictions of the human speech capacity [Stampe, 1969, p. 443]." Characteristically, processes can be classified into contradictory sets that reflect conflicting phonetic restrictions. As an example, consider the following two processes dealing with voicing: (a) obstruents become voiceless; (b) obstruents become voiced in voiced environments.

The primary requirement for the production of voicing is that the air pressure below the vocal bands be sufficiently greater than that of the air above them. The resultant air flow from the lungs passes over the elastic vocal bands and through the open channel above the larynx. The vocal bands repeatedly come together and spread apart, resulting in an alternately releasing and confining action on the airflow. Obstruents are consonants produced by the obstruction of airflow in the cavity above the larynx either totally, as in stops, or in part, as in fricatives or spirants. Because their oral construction impedes the air flow required by voicing, obstruents tend to become voiceless. This process exists irrespective of context.

On the other hand, it is a general phonetic principle that there are adaptive changes that occur in speech sounds due to differences in the contexts in which the speech sounds occur. One such adaptive change, assimilation, occurs when one or both of the two sounds undergoes a change that makes each more like its neighbor. One type of assimilation is that a sound in the environment of two voiced sounds becomes voiced. Assimilation of this type applied to obstruents means that obstruents become voiced in voiced environments.

In contexts where processes (a) and (b) overlap, such as in the sequence vowel—obstruent—vowel, there is a contradiction, since the obstruent cannot be both voiced and voiceless at the same time.

The content of the phonological processes that comprise the innate system is an empirical issue. One possible means of establishing the existence of such a process is first to observe the substitutions made in a child's utterances, and then, by comparing these sounds with the sounds substituted for, to posit the underlying rule(s) that will account for these substitutions. At the present time, the few attempts that have been made to uncover such processes have produced a list that is suggestive rather than definitive. This is due mostly to the necessarily limited scope of the data considered.

Edwards (1971) has proposed some possible processes dealing with a selected set of consonants—liquids and glides. P. Miller (1972) has proposed a preliminary set for monophthong vowels, concentrating on their quality features, and thereby excluding such factors as stress, nasality, tenseness, tone, and so on. Stampe (1969, 1972) suggests still further possibilities, some of which will be discussed later.

The theory claims that such phonological processes are applied to an abstract phonological representation that the child has hypothesized as a result of his observation of the adult phonetic output. Evidence for positing that the child has a phonological representation is based on the observation that when a child revises his innate system, he pronounces the newly acquired segments in precisely the appropriate morphemes without rehearsal, and the old substitutions do not re-appear. The mechanisms by which the child abstracts and stores a phonological representation are not specified by the theory.

Contradictory sets of processes, such as the two dealing with voicing discussed above, must be resolved in some manner. The natural phonology theory proposes that the child employs three mechanisms in the revision of the innate system during phonological development:

1. *Total suppression of a process,* the suppression of one of the processes in a contradictory set. One 2-year-old boy observed by Stampe in successive interviews changed his pronunciation of the word *kitty* from [ki:] to [kḭi] to [kíi] to [kíri] to [kíti] by suppression of the processes of prevocalic tensing of vowels, post-vocalic desyllabification, flap-deletion and flapping. The dialect of the child's parents had an unflapped *t*.

2. *Limitation of processes,* the suppression of some part of a process by means of limiting either the set of segments or the set of contexts to which the process applies. Hildegard Leopold's pronunciation of the word "papa" progressed in two steps that can be characterized as partial suppression of a process through limitation of the contexts to which the process applied. Her pronunciation went from [baba] (obstruents voiced before voiced segments), to [paba] (obstruents voiced only between voiced segments), and finally to the correct adult form [papa], which she finally produced when the process was totally suppressed.

3. *Ordering of processes.* Two processes are said to be "unordered" when there is maximal application so that both processes apply to the phonetic representation. When ordering of these two processes occurs, one of the processes is blocked, resulting in the application of the other process only. Another example from Hildegard's speech serves as an illustration. At 19-months old she pronounced the word *choo-choo* as [dudu], the result of applying to the phonological representation [tʃu tʃu] the two processes: (1) obstruents become voiced before vowels, and (2) despirantization of voiced affricates [dʒ] → [d]. By 20 months these two processes were ordered so that (2) applied before (2), as evidenced by her pronuncia-

tion of the same words as [dʒu dʒu]. Other words in her speech at 20-months old that evidence this ordering has occurred are *June* [du] and *church* [dʒuɪʃ].

An important contribution of the natural phonology theory of phonological development is its attempt to show the role of acquisition in historical change. The main hypothesis is that addition, generalization, and unordering of processes, which characterize historical change, result directly from the failure of the child to exploit fully the mechanisms for resolving contradictory processes. The resultant forms in the child are thereby innovations and differ from the standard form. Such innovations are usually rejected by the standard, which exerts a conservative influence. Those that are not totally lost are optional at first, usually distinguished only in informal speech. The reasons for the persistence of one rather than another innovation have yet to be explained by the theory.

Assuming an innate phonological system composed of processes and the three mechanisms by which contradictions among processes can be resolved, the natural phonology theory of acquisition claims to account for the phonetic representations of the child at every step in his development. It is suggested that "implicational laws," such as those proposed by Jakobson (1968), can be fully explained by the properties of the innate system. Furthermore, given these assumptions it is no longer necessary to posit that the child has a phonemic system of his own, distinct from that of the adult system. Rather, one can assume that the child begins by producing modified versions of the representations in adult speech that he has internalized. By successive modifications of these forms through the various suppressions of processes the "correct" (adult) pronunciation is achieved.

Prosodic Theory

The prosodic theory of phonology acquisition (Waterson, 1970, 1971a, 1971b) represents the Firthian tradition of prosodic analysis (Firth, 1948) and differs from the previous theories in rejecting the importance of phoneme-length segments and in emphasizing both the selective function of perception and the role of the particular input of speech to the given child. The theory differs from structuralist theories in particular by stressing individual differences in patterns of acquisition as opposed to a universal order. Evidence to support the theory is drawn from a detailed study of Waterson's son "P" at about 1½ years of age, as well as from observations from published sources, including the diary of Hildegard Leopold. The theory, which refers especially to the early stages of phonology development in the child, that is, up to about the age of 2, has the following features:

1. The child attends to certain regular, nondeviant, adult forms that recur frequently in the same kinds of situations. The child selectively attends only to particular high-saliency utterances and does not perceive minor variations in the pronunciation of particular words or expressions.

2. The child tends to perceive an utterance as a whole unit, and he perceives certain phonetic features of the utterance without necessarily being aware of their sequential relationships. Thus a child might perceive the nasality of a particular word without locating the nasality at precise points within the word.

3. The child tends to identify some kind of "schema" or "skeleton" consisting of a particular set of features selected from sets of features shared by a number of adult forms. This schema is reflected in a corresponding structural pattern of the child's forms. For P the set of words *finger, window, another,* and *Randall* exemplified a schema characterized by continuance, voicing, stress on the penultimate syllable, and a "strongly articulated" nasal (i.e. a nasal initiating a stressed syllable or followed by a voiced stop). "P's" structural pattern for these words consisted of a partially or fully reduplicated syllable of palatal nasal plus vowel, with stress of the first syllable: $[ɲ\tilde{e}:ɲ\tilde{e}/ɲi:ɲI]$, $[ɲe:ɲe:]$, $[ɲaɲa]$, $[ɲaɲ_wɸ]$.

4. As the child progressively improves his productions he seems, at any particular point, to be perceiving and producing most clearly (a) features already established in his repertoire, or (b) features that are "strongly articulated" or that are either repeated or pervasive in the utterance. The notion of phonetic feature as used by Waterson is very broad, not limited to any presumed universal set of distinctive features. She includes whatever seems relevant to the analysis, for example, prosodic lip-rounding, affrication, sibilance, syllable structure, position of stress. The notion "strongly articulated" is apparently intended to be a noncircular phonetic categorization which correlates highly with perceptual salience (Waterson, 1971b).

5. Although there is a tendency for children to acquire certain sounds earlier than others because their articulation requires less skill in timing and coordination, the phonological patterns of children learning the same language are usually different since every child has a different input from the people around him.

The prosodic theory, at least as presently formulated, does not attempt to generalize or make predictions about (a) the order of acquisition of features or oppositions, or (b) the relation of such an order to the distribution of features and oppositions among the languages of the world. Also, it makes no predictions about the overall nature of errors. Finally, it is based on a very small amount of data. Waterson cites examples from other sources, but most of her discussion depends on the characteristics of only 21 words out of a total lexicon of 155 words of a particular 1½-year-old boy acquiring English.

Despite the limited aims and the very small data base, the prosodic theory has a certain attractiveness. It attempts to answer questions such as why a child uses one substitution in one word and another elsewhere, or why a child omits or replaces some adult sounds he is capable of making, since he uses them in other contexts. It offers explanations for a number of phenomena not accounted for by other theories. For example, Hildegard Leopold's forms [deʃ] *stands* (model: German **steht**), [dɔIʃ] *stone,* and [b·Iʃ] *story* puzzled her linguist father by their irregular substitution patterns, but Waterson shows that the forms are regular in that they share most of the features of the adult models while conforming to one of the patterns of her own system consisting of continuant initial and sibilant final structure (Waterson, 1971a, pp. 203–206). Also, the prosodic theory gives a plausible content to the idea that the child proceeds from grosser distinctions to finer ones in both perception and production, and makes testable predictions about the language behavior of particular individual children (Waterson, 1971c), even though it offers no "universal" predictions. Finally, it suggests contributions to more general theories of linguistic competence, for example, that a child may be born with the capacity to perceive phonetic schemata (Waterson, 1971a, p. 210).

Conclusions

Our examination of competing theories of phonological development has confirmed our original expectation that this is a promising field of investigation, but it has also shown that the present state of theory construction in the field is unsatisfactory. Each of the four kinds of theories discussed makes great claims, and yet the theories are mutually incompatible in major respects; they cannot all be right. The incompatibility among the theories results largely from three factors: differing goals, divergent linguistic theories, and the lack of factual data.

GOALS

A major goal of the behaviorist theories, but not of the others, is the integration of phonological development with more general theories of learning. The behaviorist theories, on the other hand, have not attempted to account for the acquisition of phonological structure as such, which is a major goal of the structuralist theories and leads directly to the question of a universal order of acquisition. In line with their goal of specifying a universal pattern, the structuralist theories regard individual differences as nonsignificant, whereas prosodic theory has as one of its goals the explanation and prediction of individual differences. The goal of natural phonology is to identify the phonological processes that account for both language change through time and child phonological development; other theories are not explicitly concerned with this goal, even though the structuralist principles are held to have diachronic significance. Presumably the goals of individual theorists will continue to differ, depending on such facts as their professional background, allocation of priorities, and preferred research strategies, but we can hope that as their theories are put side by side within a general framework such as that used in their paper, the areas of overlap and disagreement will become clearer and the differing goals will lead to complementary conceptualizations and overall convergence.

LINGUISTIC THEORIES

The four kinds of acquisition theories examined here differ markedly in the kinds of linguistic theory they assume, and to the extent that the linguistic theories themselves diverge or conflict the corresponding theories of phonological development are incompatible. The behaviorist theories seem to assume no linguistic theory at all. In fact, Olmsted as a student of child phonology seems deliberately to put aside the substance of structuralist phonological theory which he holds as a linguist. He uses the postulate form of Bloch's theoretical article, but not its content. The structuralist theories of child phonology assume, as our name for them suggests, the whole body of structuralist phonological theory, and, indeed, Jakobson himself was one of its principal creators; Moskowitz, in addition, incorporates elements of recent generative theory as well. Stampe's natural phonology starts from the assumptions of generative phonology but actually offers an entirely new model of phonological theory for which child development offers one kind of exemplification. Finally, the prosodic theory assumes a Firthian understanding of phonology, in opposition to structuralist and generative models. Unfortunately there is no satisfactory comparison of phonological theories that clarifies their goals and respective merits; the best available treatment is Postal (1968), which is highly partisan and very polemic in tone (cf. Fudge, 1972, for a recent moderate review).

FACTS

The third factor involved in the unsatisfactory nature of present theories of phonological development is the lack of data on certain crucial questions of fact. For example, either babbling does converge in certain regular ways toward the phonology of speech or there really is an essential discontinuity. Different theories assume one or the other of these alternatives to be true and then attempt to account for it. Recent empirical studies (e.g., Blount, 1970; Cruttenden, 1970) indicate that the babbling period is a time of structural development that is neither irrelevant to phonology acquisition nor a gradual approximation. As more data become available the theories will have to be modified accordingly.

The child's early perception is another factual issue on which the absence of data has allowed conflicting theories. Some students of phonological development assume that the child has full perceptual competence very early and has problems with speech production (e.g., Smith, 1973; Stampe, 1969). Evidence of very early sound discrimination by infants (e.g., Eimas et al., 1971; Kaplan, 1970) gives some support to this position. Other studies, including the classic Shvachkin investigation (Shvachkin, 1948) and recent experimental studies (such as Garnica, 1973; Graham & House, 1971) and naturalistic observations (e.g., Waterson, 1971b) suggest that the development of phonological perception, as opposed to simple same—different discrimination, follows a line of development that is related to the development of production. Further investigation of this issue deserves high priority, since the findings will at least enrich existing theories of development and more likely will force drastic modification.

Another crucial question of fact for which data are lacking is the relation between language input to the child and his own phonological grammar. Many recent theorists have taken the position that the nature of the input is unimportant. The line of argument has been, possibly in reaction against simple behaviorist models, that the child seems to acquire competence in his language almost no matter what language input he receives. This position tends to be associated with the view that linguistic structures are largely innate in the child and are merely triggered or drawn forth by the speech input. Typical extremes are the positions that frequency of occurrence in the surrounding language is of critical importance (e.g., Olmsted, Waterson) or that it is of almost no importance (e.g., Stampe, Moskowitz). These positions have been taken without much solid evidence on the actual language interaction between the child and the language speakers— adults and children—in his immediate environment. Early studies (e.g., Ervin, 1964) explored the syntactic consequences of the characteristics of input, and there is considerable current investigation of this, but very little has been done on the phonological side. Ferguson (1964) called attention to the kinds of phono- logical simplification common in the "baby talk" register addressed to the child. Study of this special register has developed, on the one hand, into more elaborate linguistic analyses of it (e.g., Bynon, 1968) and, on the other hand, into increasingly sophisticated studies of its natural use in interaction (e.g., Blount, 1972). Evidence from these lines of research is of obvious value for questions of input, and will bring modifications of the present extreme positions in theories of development.

Clearly, research on child phonology should give high priority to the clarification of goals, the relation of developmental phenomena and phonological theory, and the collection of data on crucial questions of fact. At the present time, the greatest contributions to the development of more satisfying theories of children's acquisition of phonology will come not from elaborate speculation, no matter how sophisticated linguistically, nor from large-scale data collection without reference to particular problems, but from principled investigations focused on specific hypotheses and questions of fact.

Bibliography

Atkinson, K., MacWhinney, B., & Stoel, C. An experiment on the recognition of babbling. Working Paper 15. Language-Behavior Research Laboratory, University of California, Berkeley, 1968.

Atkinson-King, K. Children's perception and identification of stress contrast. *Quarterly Progress Report, Research Laboratory Electronics, MIT*, 1970, *98*, 113—119.

Bar Adon, A., & Leopold, W. F. *Child language: A book of readings.* Englewood Cliffs, N.J.: Prentice-Hall, 1971.

Berko, J. & Brown, R. Psycholinguistic research methods. In P. Mussen (Ed.), *Handbook of research methods in child development.* New York: Wiley, 1960. Pp. 517—557.

Blaisdell, R., & Jensen, P. Stress and word position as determinants of imitation in first-language learners. *Journal of Speech and Hearing Research, 13*, 1970, 193—202.

Blanchard, I. *The genetic development of the articulation of consonant sounds: The Poole dissertation.* LaVerne, Calif.: Preston Printing, 1966.

Bloch, B. A set of postulates for phonemic analysis. *Language*, 1948, *24*, 3—46.

Blount, B. G. The pre-linguistic system of Luo children. *Anthropological Linguistics*, 1970, *12*, 326—342.

Blount, B. G. Parental speech and language acquisition: some Luo and Samoan examples. *Anthropological Linguistics*, 1972, *14*, 119—130.

Bodine, A. M. A phonological analysis of the speech of two mongoloid [Down's Syndrome] children. Unpublished doctoral dissertation, Cornell University, 1971.

Braine, M. D. S. The acquisition of language in infant and child. In C. E. Reed (Ed.), *The learning of language*, New York: Appleton, 1971. Pp. 7—95. (Phonology pp. 20—30).

Burling, R. Language development of a Garo and English-speaking child. *Word* 1959, *15*, 45—68. Reprinted in Ferguson and Slobin (1973).

Bynon, J. Berber nursery language. *Transactions of the Philological Society*, 1968, 107—161.

Chao, Y. R. The Cantian idiolect: an analysis of the Chinese spoken by a 28-month-old child. In W. J. Fischel (Ed.), *Semitic and Oriental studies. University of California Publications in Semitic Philology*, 1951, *11*, 27—44. Reprinted in Ferguson and Slobin (1973).

Chomsky, N. Review of B. F. Skinner, *Verbal behavior. Language*, 1959, *35*, 26—58.

Chomsky. N., & Halle, M. *The sound pattern of English.* New York: Harper, 1968.

Compton, A. J. Generative studies of children's phonological disorders. *Journal of Speech and Hearing Disorder*, 1970, *35*, 315—339.

Crocker, J. R. A phonological model of children's articulation competence. *Journal of Speech and Hearing Disorders*, 1969, *34*, 203—213.

Cruttenden, A. A phonetic study of babbling. *British Journal of Disorders of Communication*, 1970, *5*, 110—117.

Edwards, M. L. The acquisition of liquids. Unpublished master's thesis, Ohio State Univ., 1970.

Edwards, M. L. One child's acquisition of English liquids. *Papers and Reports on Child Language Development, Stanford Univ.*, 1971, *3*, 101—109.

Eimas, P. D., Siqueland, E. R., Jusczyk, P., & Vigorito, J. Speech perception in infants. *Science*, 1971, *171*, 303—306.

Engel, W. von Raffler. The development from sound to phoneme in child language. *Proceedings, International Congress of Phonetic Sciences, 5th*, 1965. (a) Reprinted in Ferguson and Slobin (1973).

Engel, W. von Raffler. An example of "linguistic consciousness" in the child. *Orientamenti Pedagogici*, 1965, *12*, 631—633. (b) Reprinted in Ferguson and Slobin (1973).

Ervin, S. M. Imitation and structural change in children's language. In E. H. Lenneberg (Ed.), *New directions in the study of language.* Cambridge, Mass.: MIT Pres, 1964. Pp. 163—189.

Ervin-Tripp, S. Structure and process in language acquisition. In J. E. Alatis (Ed.), *Report of the twenty-first annual round table meeting on linguistic and language studies.* Washington, D.C.: Georgetown Univ. Press, 1970. Pp. 313—344.

Ferguson, C. A. Baby talk in six languages. In J. Gumperz & D. Hymes (Eds.), *Ethnography of communication.* Suppl. to *American Anthropologist*, 1964, *66*, 103—114.

Ferguson, C. A. Assumptions about nasals: A sample study in phonological universals. In J. H. Greenberg (Ed.), *Universals of language.* Cambridge, Mass.: MIT Press, 1966 Pp. 53—60.

Ferguson, C. A. Some requirements for a general theory of human language behavior. In A. S. Dil (Ed.), *The scientific study of language: Selected LSA presidential addresses.*

Ferguson, C. A. Fricatives in child language acquisition. Paper presented at the 11th International Congress of Linguists, Bologna, 1972. Also in V. Honsa & M. J. Hardman-de-Bautista (Eds.), *Papers on linguistics and child language: Ruth Hirsch Weir memorial volume*, 1974.

Ferguson, C. A., Peizer, D. B., & Weeks, T. E. A model-and-replica phonological grammar of a child's first words. *Lingua*, 1973, *31*, 35—65.

Ferguson, C. A., & Slobin, D. I. *Studies of child language development.* New York: Holt, 1973.

Firth, J. R. Sounds and prosodies. *Transactions of the Philological Society*, 1948, 127—152.

Francescato, G. *Il linguaggio infantile: Strutturazione e apprendimento.* Turin: Einaudi, 1970.

Fudge, E. C. Syllables. *Journal of Linguistics*, 1969, *5*, 253—287.

Fudge, E. C. Review of P. M. Postal, *Aspects of phonological theory. Journal of Linguistics*, 1972, *8*, 136–156.

Garnica, O. K. The development of phonemic speech perception. In T. Moore (Ed.), *Cognitive development and the acquisition of language.* New York: Academic Press, 1973. Pp. 215–222.

Graham, L. W. & House, A. S. Phonological oppositions in children: A perceptual study. *Journal of the Acoustical Society of America*, 1971, *49*, 559–566.

Greenberg, J. H. (Ed.) *Universals of language.* Cambridge, Mass.: MIT Press, 1963.

Greenberg, J. H. *Language universals.* The Hague: Mouton, 1966.

Ingram, D. Phonological rules in young children. *Papers and Reports on Child Language Development, Stanford Univ.*, 1971, *3*, 31–49.

Irwin, O. C. Phonetical description of speech development in childhood. In L. Kaiser (Ed.), *Manual of phonetics.* Amsterdam: North-Holland Publ., 1957. Pp. 403–425.

Jakobson, R. *Child language, aphasia, and phonological universals.* The Hague: Mouton, 1968. (Engl. transl. of *Kindersprache, Aphasie und allgemeine Lautgesetze.* Uppsala: 1941.)

Jakobson, R. 1971. *Studies on child language and aphasia.* The Hague: Mouton, 1971. (Reprints of 3 earlier articles.)

Jakobson, R., Fant, C. G. M., & Halle, M. *Preliminaries to speech analysis.* (3rd printing) Cambridge, Mass.: MIT Acoustics Lab. 1955.

Jakobson R., & Halle, M. Phonemic patterning. In *Fundamentals of language.* The Hague: Mouton, 1956. Pp. 37–44. Also in L. Kaiser (Ed.), *Manual of phonetics.* Amsterdam: North-Holland Publ., 1957; R. Jakobson, *Selected writings.* Vol. I. The Hague: Mouton, 1962; S. Saporta (Ed.), *Psycholinguistics.* New York: Holt, 1966.

Johnson, C., & Bush, C. N. Note on transcribing the speech of young children. *Papers and Reports on Child Language Development, Stanford Univ.*, 1971, *3*, 95–100.

Kaplan, E. L. Intonation and language acquisition. *Papers and Reports on Child Language Development, Stanford Univ.*, 1970, *1*, 1–21.

Kaplan, E. L., & Kaplan, G. A. Is there any such thing as a prelinguistic child? In J. Eliot (Ed.), *Human development and cognitive processes.* New York: Holt, 1970.

Koenigsknecht, R. A. An investigation of the discrimination of certain spectral and temporal acoustic cues for speech sounds in three-year-old children, six-year-old children, and adults. Unpublished doctoral dissertation, Northwestern University, 1968.

Kornfeld, J. R. Theoretical issues in child phonology. *Papers, 7th Regional Meeting, Chicago Linguistics Society*, 1971, 454–468.

Ladefoged, P. *Preliminaries to linguistic phonetics.* Chicago: Univ. of Chicago Press, 1971.

Lenneberg, E. H. *Biological foundations of language.* New York: Wiley, 1967.

Lenneberg, E. H., Rebelsky, F. A., & Nichols, I. A. The vocalizations of infants born to deaf and hearing parents. *Human Development*, 1965, *8*, 23–37.

Leopold, W. F. *Speech development of a bilingual child: A linguist's record.* Vol. II. *Sound learning in the first two years.* Chicago: Northwestern University Press, 1947.

Leopold, W. F. Patterning in children's language learning. *Language Learning*, 1953, *5*, 1–14. Reprinted in Bar Adon and Leopold (1971).

Lewis, M. M. *Infant speech, a study of the beginnings of language.* (2nd rev. ed.) New York: Humanities Press, 1951.

Lhermitte, F., & Gautier, J. C. Aphasia. In P. J. Vinken & G. W. Bruyn (Eds.), *Disorders of speech, perception, and symbolic behavior.* Vol. 4. *Handbook of clinical neurology.* Amsterdam and New York: North-Holland Publ. & Wiley (Interscience), 1969.

Locke, J. L. Children's acquisition of phonology: the learning of acoustic stimuli? Paper presented at the meeting of the Linguistics Society of America, Summer 1970. (Children's Research Center, Univ. of Illinois, Urbana-Champaign.)

Lynip, A. W. The use of magnetic devices in the collection and analysis of the preverbal utterances. *Genetic Psychology Monographs*, 1951, *44*, 211–262.

McCarthy, D. Language development in children. In L. Carmichael *Manual of child psychology.* (2nd ed.) New York: Wiley, 1954. Pp. 492–630.

McNeill, D. Sound development. In *The acquisition of language*. New York: Harper, 1970 Pp. 129–141.

Menn, L. Phonotactic rules in beginning speech: a study in the development of English discourse. *Lingua*, 1971, *26*, 225–251.

Menyuk, P. The role of distinctive features in children's acquisition of phonology. *Journal of Speech and Hearing Research*, 1968, *11*, 138–146.

Menyuk, P. The acquisition and development of phonology. In *The acquisition and development of language*. Englewood Cliffs, N.J.: Prentice-Hall, 1971. Pp. 54–91.

Menyuk,, P., & Anderson, S. Children's identification and reproduction of the speech sound /w/, /r/, and /l/. *Journal of Speech and Hearing Research*, 1969, *12*, 39–52.

Messer, S. Implicit phonology in children. *Journal of Verbal Learning and Verbal Behavior*, 1967, *6*, 609–613.

Metcalfe, J. V. C. An investigation into certain aspects of speech sound discrimination in children. Unpublished doctoral dissertation, Stanford University, 1963.

Milisen, R. Articulatory problems (organic conditions and the disorder of articulation). In R. W. Rieber & R. S. Brubaker (Eds.), *Speech pathology*. Amsterdam: North-Holland Publ., 1966. Pp. 137–149.

Miller, G. A., & Nicely, P. E. An analysis of perceptual confusions among some English consonants. *Journal of the Acoustical Society of America*, 1955, *27*, 338–352. Reprinted in S. Saporta (Ed.), *Psycholinguistics*. New York: Holt, 1966. Pp. 153–175. 1966.

Miller, P. Some context-free processes affecting vowels. Unpublished masters's thesis, Ohio State University, 1972.

Morehead, D. M. Processing of phonological sequences by young children and adults. *Papers and Reports on Child Language Development, Stanford Univ.* 1970, *1*, 56–69.

Moskowitz, A. I. The two-year-old stage in the acquisition of English phonology. *Language*, 1970, *46*, 426–441. Reprinted in Ferguson and Slobin (1973).

Moskowitz, A. I. The acquisition of phonology. Unpublished doctoral dissertation. University California, Berkeley, 1971.

Moskowitz, B. previously A. I. On the status of vowel shift in English phonology. In T. Moore (Ed.), *Cognitive development and the acquisition of language*. New York: Academic Press, 1973. Pp. 223–260.

Mowrer, O. H. Speech development in the young child: the autism theory of speech development and some clinical applications. *Journal of Speech and Hearing Disorder*, 1952, *17*, 263–268.

Mowrer, O. H. *Learning theory and symbolic processes*. New York: Wiley, 1960.

Murai, J. Speech development of an infant suffering from a hearing disorder. *Japanese Journal of Child Psychiatry*, 1961, *2*, 58–69. [In Japanese.]

Murai, J. The sounds of infants, their phonemicization and symbolization. *Studia Phonologica*, 1963, *3*, 18–34.

Naeser, M. A. The American child's acquisition of differential vowel duration. Technical Report No. 144, Research and Development Center for Cognitive Learning, University of Wisconsin, Madison, 1970.

Nakazima, S. A comparative study of the speech development of Japanese and American English in childhood: (1) A comparison of the development of voices at the pre-linguistic period. *Studia Phonologica*, 1962, *2*, 27–46.

Nakazima, S. A comparative study of the speech developments of Japanese and American English in childhood: (2) The acquisition of speech. *Studia Phonologica*, 1966, *4*, 38–55.

Olmsted, D. A theory of the child's learning of phonology. *Language*, 1966, *42*, 531–535. Reprinted in Bar Adon and Leopold (1971).

Olmsted, D. *Out of the mouth of babes*. The Hague: Mouton, 1971.

Postal, P. M. *Aspects of phonological theory*. New York: Harper, 1968.

Preston, M. S. Some comments on the developmental aspects of voicing in stop consonants. In D. L. Horton & J. J. Jenkins (Eds.), *Perception of language*. Columbus, Ohio: Merrill, 1971. Pp. 236–246.

Read, C. A. Pre-school children's knowledge of English phonology. *Harvard Educational Review*, 1971, *41*, 1–34.

Rüķe-Draviņa, V. The process of acquisition of apical /r/ and uvular /R/ in the speech of children. *Linguistics*, 1965, *17*, 58—68. Reprinted in Ferguson and Slobin (1973).

Shvachkin, N. K. The development of phonemic speech perception in early childhood. *Izvestiya Akademii Pedagogicheskikh Nauk RSFSR*, 1948, *13*, 101—132. [In Russian.] [English transl. in Ferguson and Slobin (1973), pp. 91—127.]

Siegel, G. M. Vocal conditioning in infants. *Journal of Speech and Hearing Disorders*, 1969, *34*, 3—19.

Smith, N. V. *The acquisition of phonology*. London & New York: Cambridge University Press, 1973.

Stampe, D. The acquisition of phonetic representation. *Papers, 5th Regional Meeting, Chicago Linguistics Society*, 1969, 443—454.

Stampe, D. A dissertation on natural phonology. Unpublished doctoral dissertation, University of Chicago, 1972.

Stampe, D. On the natural history of diphthongs. *Papers, 8th Regional Meeting Chicago Linguistics Society*, 1972, 578—590.

Templin, M. C. *Certain language skills in children, their development and interrelationships*. Minneapolis: Univ. of Minnesota Press, 1957.

Tischler, H. Schreien, Lallen und erstes Sprechen in der Entwicklung des Säuglings. *Zeitschrift für Psychologie*, 1957, *160*, 210—263.

Trubetzkoy, N. S. *Principles of phonology*. (Engl. transl. from 3rd German ed., 1962) Berkeley & Los Angeles: University of California Press, 1969.

Velten, H. V. The growth of phonemic and lexical patterns in infant language. *Language*, 1943, *19*, 281—292.

Vennemann, T. Language acquisition and phonological theory. *Linguistics*, 1971, *70*, 71—87.

Waterson, N. Some speech forms of an English child—a phonological study. *Transactions of the Philological Society*, 1970, 1—24.

Waterson, N. Child phonology: a prosodic view. *Journal of Linguistics*, 1971, 7, 179—211. (a)

Waterson, N. Some views on speech perception. *Journal of the International Phonetic Association*, 1971, *1*, 81—96. (b)

Waterson, N. Child phonology: comparative studies. *Transactions of the Philological Society*, 1971, 34—50. (c)

Weeks, T. Speech registers in young children. *Papers and Reports on Child Language Development, Stanford Univ.*, 1970, *1*, 22—42.

Weir, R. *Language in the crib*. The Hague: Mouton, 1962.

Weir, R. Some questions on the child's learning of phonology. In F. Smith & G. A. Miller (Eds.), *The genesis of language*. Cambridge, Mass.: MIT Press, 1966. Pp. 153—168.

Winitz, H. *Articulatory acquisition and behavior*. New York: Appleton, 1969.

Winitz, H., & Irwin, O. C. Syllabic and phonetic structure of infants' early words. *Journal of Speech and Hearing Research*, 1958, *1*, 250—6.

Zhurova, L. E. The development of sound analysis of words in pre-school children. *Soviet Psychology and Psychiatry*, 1964, *2*, 17—28.

10. Phonemicization and Symbolization in Language Development

Sei Nakazima

The infant begins to utter sounds other than crying from about the age of 1 month, and at 2 months begins to change his pitch and articulation. Pitch and articulation then become more varied, and between the ages of 6 and 8 months, the child babbles repetitively. Until he is 9-months old, he utters sounds, not as a means of communication, but as if playing with his phonatory—articulatory organs. At about 9 months, he begins to reorganize his babbling phonatory—articulatory—auditory mechanisms and to apply them to language; that is, he begins to develop the ability to call to others and to respond to them with simple sounds. At about 10 months, he begins to be able to imitate and understand adults' speech sounds, and, at about 12 months, begins to use words. From about 17 months, his phonemicization and symbolization develop; that is, there is a rapid increase in the number of phonemes articulated and the number of words used.

Introduction

This chapter will describe the following developmental processes: How in the course of the phonemicization process the infant's sounds are organized into phonemes of the language; How he begins to use his sounds as symbols; What kind of fundamental relationship exists between the phonemicization, symbolization process and the developmental processes of other bodily and mental functions; and What kind of environmental factors influence these processes. These descriptions are based on data from observations of both Japanese and American infants (Nakazima, 1962, 1966, 1969, 1970).

Crying

During the first month, the sound produced by the infant is that of crying. When he is in a state of discomfort and cries, his mother comes to him and takes away the cause of his discomfort. When the mother has satisfied his need, he stops crying.

Expression, evocation, and representation are called the three functions of speech (Bühler, 1958). Crying seems to be the expression of the infant's discomfort and the evocation of his mother; it might, therefore, be considered the origin of speech. As Murai (1964) stated, however, we do not think that crying, a sound directly related to need, is the main origin of speech. It may be the origin of some kind of communication, but not of the symbolic function.

Development of Phonatory— Articulatory—Auditory Mechanisms During the Period of Babbling as One Kind of Circular Reaction

THE BEGINNING OF SPEECH SOUNDS

We would like to define pronunciation as utterance that consists of phonation, which is the production of sounds, mainly by the vocal cords, and articulation, which is the modification of these sounds.

From about the age of 1 month, the infant begins to utter sounds. These un-differentiated sounds are principally ə-like sounds, with relaxed articulation organs. This sound is phonated rhythmically and occurs during the expiration phase of ordinary respiration. During phonation this phase lasts somewhat longer than in silent expiration. When the cavity between the back of the tongue and the soft palate is not open, γ- or χ-like sounds, sometimes k- or g-like sounds are produced, with or without ə-like sounds.

The infant utters these sounds when he is comfortable, that is, after enough sleep and food, and when he is in the arms of his mother or in a similar situation. As Mowrer (1950) stated, both loving care and vocalization are important for the development of speech; the development of these sounds is regulated by the maturation of the phonatory—articulatory organs and is accelerated by the mother's talking to the child. When an infant is in a state of discomfort, he does not utter these calm sounds—he cries. When the baby begins to utter sounds, the mother tends to talk to it more. This talking, in turn, stimulates the baby to utter more.

These sounds are not related to the infant's needs, as crying is, nor are they used for communication. Sometimes the infant responds with sounds when he is called; this kind of response, however, does not develop until the child is about 9 months of age.

The main course of speech development is as follows.

DEVELOPMENT OF PHONATORY–ARTICULATORY–AUDITORY MECHANISMS DURING THE PERIOD OF BABBLING

From about the age of 2 months, the infant begins to change the duration, pitch, and articulatory forms of his sounds. From month to month he increases the variety of his vocalizations, and at about 6–8 months of age he utters repetitive babblings, for example, *babababa, mammammamma*, and so on.

As for the process of articulation of vowel-like sounds, we can observe two developments: (1) starting from *ə*-like sounds, as stated above, to *a*-like sounds, to *æ*-, *ɛ*-, *e*-, *i*-like sounds, that is, from middle vowel-like sounds to front vowel-like sounds; and (2) from *ə*- to *ɔ*-, *o*-, *u*-like sounds, that is, from middle to back vowel-like sounds. The sounds change from being relaxed and undifferentiated to being tense and differentiated. Round vowel-like sounds, for example *u*-like sounds, are articulated from time to time, but not constantly.

As for consonant-like sounds, at first soft palatial sounds appear, as stated above. After the appearance of *h*-, *j*-, and *ç*-like sounds, *p*-, *b*-, and *m*-like sounds appear, accompanied by the movement of the jaw as a whole, especially at the beginning of the repetitive babbling period. As the movement of the tongue differentiates, *t*-, *d*-, and *n*-like sounds, then *k*-, *g*-, and *ŋ*-like sounds appear.

The infant frequently utters clusters consisting of sounds that are vowel-like and consonant-like. He utters these sounds changing both pitch and articulation, sometimes gradually, sometimes rapidly. Therefore we cannot describe these sounds accurately by using a phonetic alphabet.

During the period from about 1 month through 8 months of age, the infant utters sounds not as a means of communication, but rather as if playing with his phonatory–articulatory organs. He tends to utter these sounds more frequently when he is alone than when in the presence of others. He also tends to move his mouth and tongue in various ways without producing sounds. We think that until he is about 8 months old, the infant's utterance can be considered as an example of what Piaget termed a "circular reaction," and repetitive babbling, especially, as an example of "secondary circular reaction [1936, 1945]." Not only his mother's words and the talk of others, but also his own sounds stimulate the child to utter further sounds, just as in other circular reaction schemata.

When an adult talks to an infant, imitating his babbling sounds, the child sometimes responds by uttering almost the same sounds. This might appear to be a kind of imitation of the adult's sounds; we believe, however, that the adult's sounds are, rather, simply a trigger that releases the infant's babbling schemata.

Reorganization of Babbling Phonatory—Articulatory—Auditory Mechanisms and their Application to Language

DEVELOPMENT OF RESPONSE AND EVOCATION WITH SIMPLE SOUNDS

From about 9 months on, the infant tends to decrease his repetitive babbling and to develop evocation of familiar persons and response to their calling him with simple sounds, such as *ə*, *ba*, and so on. We think that he begins to co-ordinate various kinds of phonatory behavior patterns as "secondary circular reaction schemata," and to apply them to a new situation—language. There-fore, we would like to place the turning point at about 9 months of age, which is the beginning of the reorganization of the babbling phonatory—articulatory—auditory mechanisms at the level of language. Until this age, the infant has developed rather complex phonatory—articulatory mechanisms and has uttered various kinds of sounds. But he starts the reorganization process from the begin-ning, that is, with simple sounds.

DEVELOPMENT OF IMITATION AND COGNITION OF ADULT SPEECH SOUNDS

From about the age of 10 months, the infant begins to imitate the speech sounds of adults, especially those of his parents. As Yatabe (1949) stated, at the beginning of infancy, parents' speech sounds are undifferentiated for children. Through the period of babbling, the infant utters sounds in various phonatory—articulatory forms and hears his own varied sounds. By the end of the babbling stage, that is, about the age of 8 months, this kind of experience gradually makes him able to hear external sounds as differentiated stimuli. The differentiation of external sounds as stimuli by phonatory—articulatory—auditory practice under-lies the development of the imitation of adult speech sounds. At this age level, however, the infant cannot imitate adults' articulation correctly, though he imitates their intonation fairly well.

From the time the child is about 10-months old, we also observe his developing cognizance of external voice stimuli. For example, a Japanese female at 10 months waved *Bye-bye* when she heard her mother's *Bye-bye*. At first, she did it only in her mother's arms and at the entrance hall, not in any other situation. She was very fond of being taken out for a morning walk, and this situation had become for her the sign of going out. The second step of the reorganization process is thus the development of imitation and understanding of adult speech sounds.

After the beginning of the reorganization process, the infant's articulatory mechanisms still develop. Both Japanese and American infants, by the time they begin to use words at about 11 months, have articulated almost every sound in both the Japanese and the English phoneme systems, except most of the round vowels and most of the fricatives. Therefore, we think that although the parents' talking stimulates and accelerates the infant's articulatory activity, the parents' phoneme system does not influence the child's articulatory mechanisms.

BEGINNING OF THE USE OF WORDS

From about the age of 11 or 12 months, the infant begins to use a few words. This we classify as the third step of the reorganization process. Let us take, for example, the case of a Japanese female. When at 1 year of age she tried to imitate her mother's saying *Papa*, she could not articulate *p* or any other bilabial, although she had uttered bilabial plosives very frequently during the period of repetitive babbling. After one week's trial, she articulated *pa* sounds. Then she uttered *Papa* with various articulatory forms. As for the consonant /p/, she articulated not only *p*, but also other bilabials, *b* and *m*. She also articulated other plosives, *t* and *k*, and even fricatives like *h*. Most of the vowel sounds she uttered were *a*, *ə*, and *æ*. *Papa* is a two-syllable word. But she uttered one, two, three, and more syllable sounds. She uttered *Papa* in various situations, too. She uttered it not only for her father, but also for any male adult, for her mother, for her maid, and even used the term when she was playing alone. After these attempts, when she was 17 months of age, she uttered *Papa* with the correct articulatory form and in correct situations. An American male, who said *Papa* at the same age, also showed almost the same tendency. Other infants, also, uttered a few words with various articulatory forms and in various situations. The words used were different from infant to infant, for example *Mamma* (food), *Wan wan* (bow wow), *Bu:* (vehicle), and so on by Japanese children and *Bow wow*, *Light*, *Tata* (thank you), and so on, by Americans. We think that such utterances, with their various articulatory forms and the various situations in which they are used, are examples of what Piaget called "tertiary circular reaction."

The words used by the Japanese children and by the Americans were, of course, different. But we did not find significant differences in articulation, between, for example, the sounds of *Wan wan* articulated by the Japanese and those of *Bow wow* by the Americans. (There were a few exceptions, for example, *l* of *Light*, which was articulated by an American child, though only sometimes correctly.)

From the beginning of the first year, the infant expresses his own emotions, though undifferentiated, in whole body action with or without crying. During the babbling period, with the maturation and practice of speech and hearing, the infant's sounds become gradually, though not completely, differentiated from bodily emotional expression. From about the age of 11 or 12 months, he picks up a few of his parents' sounds, both meaningful and meaningless, and tries to use them as a means of expressing his wants. He uses not only these learned sounds, but also articulates sounds at random. The infant's positive emotional connection with his parents underlies and accelerates the development of his verbal communication with them.

During the first several months of the second year, the infant shows strongly this kind of expression in sounds. When he uses words correctly, even when not perfectly, he can communicate with adults; when incorrectly, he cannot. We think that through these efforts at expression, he begins to notice some kind of symbolic relationship between words and the world.

Development of Phonemicization and Symbolization

From about the middle of his second year, the number of phonemes the child articulates and the number of words he uses increase. Of course, there are great individual differences. In some cases, only the number of phonemes and words that the child tries to articulate in imitation increases, and even at the end of his second year the child articulates only a few phonemes spontaneously. On the other hand, one of the Japanese females studied, when she was 17-months old, uttered a few words in almost the same accent as that of her parents' dialect, though not with completely correct articulation.

At the beginning of phonemicization, American and Japanese infants do not show significant differences in articulation. For example, although in English /u/ and /U/ should be articulated with round lips and /ʃ/ with protruding lips, the Americans studied uttered /u/ and /U/ without round lips, in the same way as the Japanese uttered /u/ɯ/, and /ʃ/ without protruding lips, as Japanese ɕ, an allophone of /s/. Some of the Americans articulated these phonemes fairly well from the middle of the second year, but others were not able to do so even by the end of the second year.

Phonemicization and symbolization are not independent. For instance, one of our Japanese subjects showed the differentiation process of bilabial plosive articulatory forms, /p/ in *Papa* (father) and /m/ in *Mama* (mother). She learned *Papa* at 12 months of age, and *Mama* at 13 months. She confused them not only in articulatory form, that is, uttering *mapa, mapapa*, and so on, but also in use. When she met one parent, she uttered *Papa* or *Mama* at random. If she was neglected by one parent, she called the other. This kind of confusion continued for several months. When she began to say *Papa* and *Mama* correctly, she articulated /p/ and /m/ with better differentiation.

As for the symbolization process, Okamoto (1962) reported one interesting case of a Japanese female. Although she had been taught by her mother to call dogs *Wan wan* (bow wow), at the age of 9 months she began to say *Njan njan* (kitty) spontaneously, in reference to a white spitz. Then from the age of 10 to 12 months, her expression *Njan njan* went in two directions: one based on the physiognomic perception of animals, towards, for example, dogs or cats, and the other based on the fur property of the spitz, towards, for example, white rag or white wool. She called all of them *Njan njan*. From the age of 18 months, she began to use *Njan njan* both as an upper and a lower concept, for example, *O : ki njan njan* (big kitty), and *Njan njan kukku* (shoes covered with white fur). From the age of 11 months, when her mother showed her pictures of animals and asked which was a *Wan wan*, she pointed at dogs correctly, but when her mother pointed at a dog picture and asked what it was, she answered *Njan njan*. However, from 21 months of age, the word *Wan wan* became stabilized as a symbol for dogs both in recognition and in utterance. Thus, we think, words' symbolic function in recognition and in spontaneous use becomes operative by the end of the second year.

As for the phonemicization process, the author has data only on Japanese cases (Nakazima, Okamoto, Murai, Tanaka, Okuno, Maeda & Shimizu, 1962; Yasuda, 1970). The quality of articulation always improved after the middle of the second year; by the end of the third year, more than 75% of the children articulated vowels /i/, /e/, /a/, /o/, /u/; semi-vowels /w/, /j/; bilabial plosives and nasal, /p/, /b/, /m/; and by the middle of the fourth year, dental plosives and nasal, /t/, /d/, /n/, and soft palatal plosives /k/ and /g/. As for phonemes difficult to articulate, more than 75% of the children articulated one of the fricatives, /h/, only by the middle of the fifth year, the africates /č/ and /z/ only by the middle of the sixth year, flap /r/ and one of the fricatives, /s/, only by the end of the sixth year.

References

Bühler, K. *Abriss der geistigen Entwicklung des Kindes.* (8 erweiterte Aufl.) Heidelberg: Quelle & Meyer, 1958.

Mowrer, O. H. *Learning theory and personality dynamics.* New York: Ronald Press, 1950.

Murai, J. The sounds of infants. *Studia Phonologica,* 1964, *3,* 17—34.

Nakazima, S. A comparative study of the speech developments of Japanese and American English in childhood (1)—A comparison of the developments of voices at the prelinguistic period. *Studia Phonologica,* 1962, *2,* 27—46.

Nakazima, S. A comparative study of the speech developments of Japanese and American English in childhood (2)—The acquisition of speech. *Studia Phonologica,* 1966, *4,* 38—55.

Nakazima, S. The beginning of the formation of a local dialect in childhood. In Kyotodaigaku-Kinkikensogokenkyukai (Ed.), *Kinkiken.* Tokyo: Kashima-Shuppankai, 1969. [In Japanese.]

Nakazima, S. A comparative study of the speech developments of Japanese and American English in childhood (3)—The re-organization process of babbling articulation mechanisms. *Studia Phonologica,* 1970, *5,* 20—35.

Nakazima, S., Okamoto, N., Murai, J., Tanaka, M., Okuno, S., Maeda, T. & Shimizu, M. The phoneme-systematization and the verbalization process in childhood. *Shinrigakuhyoron,* 1962, *6,* 1—48.

Okamoto, N. Verbalization process in infancy. *Psychologia,* 1962, *5,* 32—40.

Piaget, J. *La naissance de l'intelligence chez l'enfant.* Neuchâtel: Delachaux & Niestlé, 1936.

Piaget, J. *La formation du symbole chez l'enfant.* Neuchâtel: Delachaux & Niestlé, 1945.

Yasuda, A. Articulatory skills in three-year-old children. *Studia Phonologica,* 1970, *5,* 52—71.

Yatabe, T. *Language of children.* Kyoto: Hiei-Shobo, 1949. [In Japanese.]

11. Early Semantic Development in Child Language

Francesco Antinucci / Domenico Parisi

The development of the structural properties of children's utterances in the second year of life is described by means of a model that assumes that the meaning of a sentence is basically a configuration of recursively occurring semantic predicates. Within the overall configuration the following subconfigurations should be distinguished: a performative and a nucleus (necessary elements); adverbials; noun modifiers, and embedded sentences (optional elements). The semantic representation of children's utterances up to about one and a half years of age contains both (and only) the necessary elements, even if limitation in utterance length allows only some of the semantic material to be realized into sounds. The optional elements all make their appearance between $1\frac{1}{2}$ and 2 years. Around two, the ability to express an explicit sentence as part of another such sentence is acquired. This ability relates to the growth of the mechanism that maps meanings onto sounds, more specifically the submechanism that brings the structural properties of the semantic representation to the surface (syntax). The other submechanism is the lexicon, which maps the content properties of this representation onto sounds. Since the content properties are part of the general cognitive capacity of the child, whereas the structural properties could be specific to language, this could explain some differences in the development of lexicon and syntax.

Introduction

Any attempt to characterize child language development in terms other than the enumeration of words and utterances at different ages, depends crucially on what kind of general model of linguistic competence is adopted. Furthermore, an account of the child's speech will be all the more valuable if it shows that the independently motivated mechanisms of linguistic competence play a central role in our understanding of its structure and development. Therefore, in this paper we shall describe the major aspects of the general model and will show how each of them may be applied to the description of children's speech.[1]

Language is a device that pairs meanings to sounds. In accordance with the most recent linguistic theories, meanings are basically represented in our model as configurations of semantic units. Each semantic unit is a predicate having a fixed number of arguments. Predicates combine into configurations by substituting one as argument of another. This type of combination provides the basic recursive mechanism by which semantic representations of any complexity are built up.

In additon, the model has to provide a means to map these semantic representations onto surface strings of words. This is achieved by two projection mechanisms: the lexicon and the syntax. The lexicon is a set of entries associating subparts of semantic configurations with words. Syntax is a set of mapping rules that bring to the surface the structural part of the configurational information.

When we apply this model to a child's speech, we are thus confronted with two tasks. First, we must try to determine what the semantic structure underlying the child's speech is, that is, the meaning of each of his utterances. Second, we have to study what the projection mechanisms are that lead from the semantic representation to the surface form of the child's utterances.

Context and Meaning of Early Utterances

Let us examine data from one of our children to show how this can be done. During the first six or seven months of language development the child produces increasingly longer utterances, which start with one word and later reach a length of three or even four words. During this period we found the following, series of utterances:

(1) **da**   (Claudia gives a pencil to her mother.)
     give

(2) **iacca**   (Claudia wants her mother to give her water.)
     water

---

[1] All the data used are drawn from observational and longitudinal research (Antinucci & Parisi, 1973; Parisi & Antinucci, 1974) conducted on two Italian children (a boy and a girl). Data collection started when both children were approximately 16 months old, and our analysis stops when both were 28 months; The standard methodology in this kind of research was used, that is, periodic recordings (2-hr sessions every 2 weeks) of the spontaneous linguistic production of the children.

(3) **tata da**   (Claudia gives a doll to Francesco.)
     doll give

(4) **da mamma**   (Claudia wants her mother to give her a ball.)
     give mommy

(5) **mamma iacca**   (Claudia wants her mother to give her water.)
     mommy water

(6) **da a nonna bototto** (Grandma gives Claudia a cookie.)
     give grandma cookie

(7) **Acesco, dai a palla** (Francesco gives Claudia a ball.)
     Francesco give ball

As pointed out above, we must first of all try to ascertain what were the semantic intentions of the child when she produced each of these utterances. The first and most important clue to this is a careful and detailed observation of the contexts in which the utterances occurred, of the intentions manifested by the child, and of her actions. (The relevant part of this information is reported on the right side of the utterance.) The meanings of all seven utterances quoted involve basically a person whose action is such that a certain object "comes to be with" another person. On this basis, we assigned to the child's utterances the following semantic representations:[2]

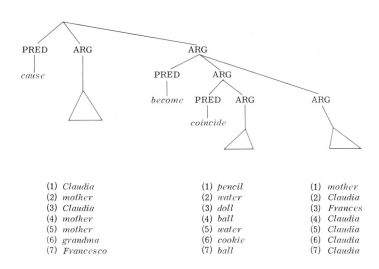

	ARG		ARG		ARG
(1)	Claudia	(1)	pencil	(1)	mother
(2)	mother	(2)	water	(2)	Claudia
(3)	Claudia	(3)	doll	(3)	Frances
(4)	mother	(4)	ball	(4)	Claudia
(5)	mother	(5)	water	(5)	Claudia
(6)	grandma	(6)	cookie	(6)	Claudia
(7)	Francesco	(7)	ball	(7)	Claudia

[2]In all diagrams. Triangles stand for unanalyzed semantic material corresponding to each indicated noun phrase. PRED = predicate; ARG = argument.

What are the main characteristics of semantic representations (1–7)? They are all constituted by a subconfiguration corresponding to a verb (**da** *give*), which has the following lexical entry:

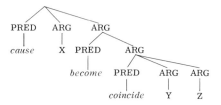

and by the semantic configurations corresponding to its three arguments, the noun-phrases: *Claudia, mother, doll, water,* and so on.

A very interesting observation, which can be made by looking at these representations, is that the semantic structures underlying the child's utterances do not undergo any substantial change during the period we are considering. Semantic representations like (1) or (2), which underlie the one-word utterances of the beginning stage, are of the same type as (6) and (7), which underlie the much later three-word utterances. Still, the surface manifestations of these semantic structures are very different. To account for this, we have to consider the projection mechanism. As we said, the lexicon is a set of entries pairing subparts of semantic representations with words. Each of these pairs may be considered as a mapping operation the child must perform in order to convert a semantic representation into its surface form. Thus, to give full expression to any of the seven representations she would have to perform four of these operations: one to lexicalize the verb and three to lexicalize its three arguments. Suppose now that the child is restricted in the number of times she may perform this mapping operation (lexicalization) to convert a semantic representation into the corresponding sentence. Suppose furthermore that, at the beginning, this restriction allows one operations only. Then, given a semantic representation like (1) or (2) she may lexicalize either the verb (*da*) or one of its arguments and nothing else. This would account for utterances (1) and (2) (lexicalization of the verb in (1) and of its second argument in (2)). But while the semantic capacity of the child remains essentially the same during this period, the span of its projection mechanism gradually increases. Thus, later on she will be able to perform two lexicalizations to manifest its semantic representations. At this point she will produce utterances like 3–5, manifesting verb and second argument, verb and first argument, first and second argument, respectively. A further increase will finally produce utterances like (6–7).

We said earlier that the observation of the context of occurrence is the most important factor in assessing the meaning of the children's utterances. What other evidence do we have for assigning such rich semantic representations to the child's one-, two-, or three-word sentences? First of all, it is difficult to think that when the child pronounces an utterance like (2), *iacca*, or (4), *da mamma*, she does not know who must give, what must be given, and who must receive. If, for example, after the child's uttering (2), her mother gives the water to someone else, the child will insist, thus showing that she is the intended receiver. A second type of evidence is that during the same period the child, on different occasions, produces the verb *da* accompanied by all the three noun phrases we postulate in its semantic representation, even if, owing to limitation in her lexicalization span, only one noun-phrase is present in each sentence. A third piece of evidence comes from the dialogues between the child and adults. In these dialogues we often find that all the hypothesized elements in the semantic representation come to the surface with the help of the interlocutor's promptings (see examples in Antinucci and Parisi, 1973).

What we have just offered was only one paradigmatic example to illustrate the application of our model to the first period of language development. We may apply the same analysis to the whole range of speech produced by the two children during these first 6 or 7 months. We find that all the children's sentences (with some exceptions to be considered immediately hereafter) show the same characteristics as those given above; namely, the semantic configuration corresponds to only one predication and its required arguments (which may be one, two, or as in the case shown above, three), and is successively manifested by one, two, or three elements according to the lexicalization span. A further characteristic of the speech of this period is that the arguments of the predication are all simple; that is, they are constituted by either a common noun, or a proper noun, or a pronoun, and nothing else.

Performative Structures

However, our account of the children's utterances during this first period is still inadequate in one respect. For instance, in terms of our analysis, we would assign to the following two utterances:

(8) **mamma da**   (mother gives something to Claudia.)
     mommy give

(9) **mamma da**   (Claudia asks her mother to give her something.)
     mommy give

an identical semantic representation, on the basis that both the meanings involve the same agent giving an object to the same receiver. Notwithstanding this, the two utterances have quite different functions. In (8) the child is describing the fact that her mother gives her something, whereas in (9) the child is asking her mother to give her something. If we look back at utterances 1–7, we find both of these functions; utterances (1), (3), (6), and (7) are "descriptive," whereas utterances (2), (4), and (5) are "requestive." A full description of the children's speech requires us to account for this difference.

In order to do this, we must illustrate another basic aspect of the general model of linguistic competence. Consider the following sentences:

(10)   *John comes*

(11)   *Does John come?*

(12)   *Come, John!*

According to our model, we would give to all the above sentences a semantic representation composed of the semantic material corresponding to the predicate and its argument, *John*:

(13)

However, sentence (10) tells us that this content is to be taken as an assertion of the speaker, (11) that it is to be taken as a question, and (12) as a command. Following Ross (1970) and others, we represent these differences by means of a semantic structure (called performative structure) superimposed on (13):

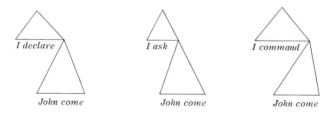

These structures, too, will of course be represented in terms of configurations of semantic predicates. It should be noticed that a performative structure is present in the representation of every sentence of language. Since an actual utterance always has a given function, the performative structure is an obligatory component of the semantic representation of a sentence. Therefore, such a representation will always be made up of at least two parts: the proposition, which represents the semantic content of the sentence, and the performative, which represents how this content is to be taken.

Coming back to the children's speech, the general model will force us to assume that each of the children's utterances has, from the very beginning, a performative and a proposition, these being the obligatory characteristics of the representation of any sentence. This enables us to account for the difference between sentences (8) and (9). Their semantic representation is composed of the same proposition but two different performatives. The first will have a "descriptive" performative, the second a "requestive" performative. Therefore the two semantic representations will look roughly as follows:

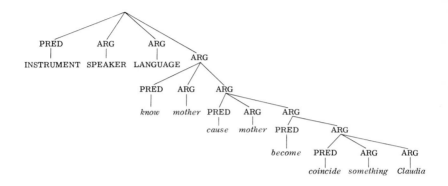

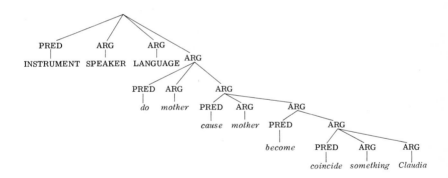

It is interesting to notice that there are at least two other pieces of evidence, besides the observation of the context, that support the assignment of a performative structure to the children's sentences. One is the presence of the often noticed but otherwise unexplained vocatives in the child's utterances. For example:

(14) **Mamma, ianne**   (Claudia tells her mother that the spinning-
      mommy spinning-top   top is turning.)

(15) **Papà, a tati**   (Claudia tells her father that the researchers
      daddy people   are present.)

Vocatives denote the addressee of the speech act. They can, therefore, be interpreted as a lexicalization of the semantic material corresponding to the first argument of $KNOW_{XY}$ in sentences with a descriptive performative, and to the first argument of DO_{XY} in sentences with a requestive performative.

The second piece of evidence is the presence of embedding structures in some of the child's utterances. Thus we have:

(16) **oio pipì**   (Claudia wants to do wee-wee.)
      want wee-wee

(17) **itto pipì**   (Claudia tells her mother that the doll has
      see wee-wee   done wee-wee.)

where both words are verbs. Owing to this characteristic, these sentences seem to deviate from all others, which are composed, as we said, only of a verb and its arguments. In fact, the two verbs *oio* and *itto* may be considered the lexical manifestation of the performative structure corresponding to the requestive and descriptive functions, respectively. (Gruber, 1973, argues in favor of a similar hypothesis for the two verbs *see* and *want*, used by English children.) Therefore, the semantic representation of these sentences does not differ at all from that of the other sentences. The only difference is that the performative in these cases is lexicalized.

Thus, in both (14–15) and (16–17), we find lexicalization of material corresponding to the performative structure, rather than to the proposition. The characterization of the lexical projection mechanism we gave earlier still holds. In fact, the child will lexicalize one, two, or three elements of the semantic representation according to his lexicalization span. But to cover all the data (including sentences where a vocative or a verb like *itto* or *oio* occur), this characterization has to be taken as referring to both the performative and the proposition.

Optional Semantic Mechanisms

As we saw in the previous section, all the early utterances in children's speech can be interpreted as mapping a configuration of semantic predicates onto surface form, with severe limitations as to utterance length. Such a configuration is divided into two subparts, the performative and the proposition, the former specifying the kind of linguistic act the child is performing with the utterance and the latter indicating the content of the utterance. These are the necessary properties of any utterance that can count as a sentence of human language, and we saw that they are present in the child's speech from its inception.

Adults, of course, produce sentences that are much more complex than these early utterances. Basically, this greater complexity can be traced back to the operation of three optional mechanisms added to the necessary schema described earlier. We shall now examine these three mechanisms and their appearance in child language.

ADVERBIALS

Consider the sentences:

(18)   *Bill is eating an apple.*

(19)   *Bill is eating an apple in the kitchen.*

(20)   *Bill is avidly eating an apple.*

(21)   *Bill is eating an apple because he is hungry.*

The proposition within (18) has a predicate, *is eating*, its two necessary arguments, *Bill* and *an apple*, and nothing else. This is not the case with (19–21), where to this necessary nucleus something optional has been added: *in the kitchen* (19), *avidly* (20), *because he is hungry* (21).

We shall call such an optional structure that can be added to the nucleus of a proposition an "adverbial." An adverbial can be represented as a predicate that takes the nucleus as one of its arguments. Thus, 19–21 are represented as:

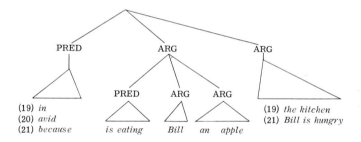

Adverbials do not appear in children's earliest utterances. In the two children we studied, the first adverbials were found at 17 and 20, when the two children had already been producing meaningful utterances for a number of months. This cannot be ascribed to limitations in utterance length, since at this time the child produces two-, three-, and even four-word utterances with no adverbials, whereas adverbials are first found in one- or two-word utterances. The appearance of adverbials seems to mark a real increment in the child's semantic capacity and a new stage in his linguistic development.

NOUN MODIFIERS

In adult language, nouns are often modified by adjectives, prepositional phrases, and relative clauses. These noun modifiers may have one of two functions: they may identify for the hearer the referent of the noun (restrictive modifiers) or they may add new information relative to the noun (nonrestrictive modifiers). In both cases they can be represented as additional sentential configurations associated with the main configuration. The difference lies in the performative of such additional sentences: A restrictive noun modifier is a sentence presupposed by the main sentence; a nonrestrictive noun modifier is a sentence coordinated with the main sentence.

Thus, the sentence

(22)   *The dog which John saw was running.*

has the following representation if the relative clause is of the restrictive type

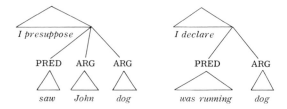

and this representation if the relative clause is not restrictive

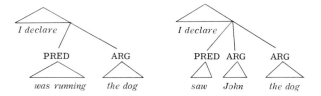

In the children's earliest utterances we find no noun modifiers. The arguments of the nucleus are either simple nouns or pronouns. At about the same time that adverbials make their first appearance (around 18 months) we find that the nouns begin to be modified by these additional structures. The first noun modifiers are restricted in type (mainly genitive constructions and adjectives), but the child seems to be able to use them both in their restrictive and nonrestrictive functions. It must be borne in mind that presupposing and coordinating are very primitive mechanisms of discourse. At 18 months the child has already been identifying noun referents for some months by deictic means, expressed (*this, that, here,* etc.) or not expressed. When nonrestrictive noun modifiers first appear, other surface forms also appear, which we may apparently trace back to coordination structures (juxtaposed noun phrases, use of *and,* plurals).

EMBEDDED SENTENCES

In adult sentences the arguments of both the nucleus and the adverbial may be filled in by nouns or by embedded sentences. If we look at child language, we find surface manifestations of sentence embedding among the earliest utterances. But in such cases the matrix sentence is the performative (as we have seen), so that no more than the two necessary structure of all sentences are present in these utterances. When a sentence is embedded as an argument of the nucleus, we have an expanded configuration with three structures: the performative, the nucleus, and the embedded sentence. For such cases of true embedding, we have to wait 3 or 4 months after the appearance of adverbials and noun modifiers. It is around 21 months that we find the first instances of sentences embedded as arguments of aspectual, modal, and causative verbs.

By way of conclusion, we may state the following hypothesis. There is a first stage in language development in which the child's utterances are surface mappings of semantic structures containing both and only the necessary properties of all sentences of human language: a performative and a nucleus. This stage begins when the child starts producing meaningful utterances and ends when he is about 18-months old. At that time a second stage begins, which is marked by the expansion of the child's semantic structures to include two optional elements: adverbials and noun modifiers. Before the end of the second year a third optional structure appears to have been added: sentence embedding. It must be remarked that, aside from nominalizations, all the basic structural mechanisms of human language appear to have thus been acquired by the 2-year-old child. Language development after this age seems to be restricted to the growth of the ability to use such mechanisms simultaneously in a single sentence, in addition, of course, to lexical and discourse development.

MAPPING OF OPTIONAL MECHANISMS

We have seen that in the second half of his second year the child begins to produce utterances mapping semantic configurations that include the three optional structures: adverbials, noun modifiers, and embedded sentences. Although noun modifiers and embedded sentences are both sentential configurations in the semantic structure, in this period the child never produces utterances in which an explicit sentence, that is, a sentence with a finite verb, is contained in another such sentence. A sentential configuration presupposed by or coordinated with the main configuration, that is, a noun modifier, is always mapped onto surface form as an adjective or a prepositional phrase, never as a relative clause. A sentential structure embedded as an argument of the nucleus always appears in surface form as an implicit embedded sentence, that is, with the verb in the infinitive. As for the adverbials, no adverbials with a sentential argument appear in this period. It is only at the beginning of his third year that the child appears to be able to produce utterances containing an explicit sentence embedded in another sentence.

It is noteworthy that at this age the child almost simultaneously produces noun modifiers that are relative clauses, nuclear arguments that are explicit sentences, and adverbial arguments that are explicit sentences. It is as if until the age of 2 the child is unable to start an explicit sentence mapping routine as part of another such routine. As soon as this ability is acquired, at 2 years, it is almost simultaneously applied to all three optional semantic structures.

It is important to underline that the appearance of adverbials, noun modifiers, and embedded sentences between $1\frac{1}{2}$ and 2 years of age amounts to an expansion of the underlying semantic configuration, whereas the increase in number of words per sentence before age $1\frac{1}{2}$ and the appearance of explicit embedded sentences at age 2 are to be interpreted properly as part of the development of the mechanism that maps semantic configurations onto their surface forms.

Conclusion

We have seen that the meaning of a sentence can be *basically* represented as a configuration of semantic predicates. But we have also seen that a semantic representation must contain more information than that provided by a predicate-argument tree. This additional information includes the distinctions between performative and proposition and between nucleus and adverbial, and the setting up of presuppositional trees associated with the main configuration, of which the tree corresponding to restrictive noun modifiers is just an example. It can be contended that the information corresponding to the predicate-argument tree is, both in form and content, part of the general cognitive information of the speaker, whereas the additional information contained in the semantic representation of sentences is specific to the linguistic or communicative function. The general form of a predicate-argument tree and the actual elementary mental operations that are predicates or arguments of such a tree could be the common ground of language and nonlinguistic abilities like perception, memory, and thinking. On the other hand, the articulation of the predicate-argument tree into performative and proposition, nucleus and adverbials, main configuration and associated configurations, would specifically belong to man as a language user.

If we accept this view of the relationship between cognition and language, language development (or, better, semantic development, since we are not considering here the development of the projection mechanism or of the sound structure) will have to be seen as consisting of two parts; on the one hand, we have the development of the predicate-argument structure itself; on the other hand, we have the development of the specifically linguistic articulation of this structure. The growth of predicate-argument trees relates both to size and to the specific semantic material that is appended to the tree's branches. Both these aspects are closely dependent on the child's general cognitive development. The growth in size of semantic trees can be seen as the result of a progressively wider application of a basic recursive mechanism, which is likely to be innate even if not species-specific. The development of the particular content of semantic trees should be seen as part of general cognitive development. Since the lexicon is a subpart of the projection mechanism that is charged with bringing to the surface the purely cognitive information contained in the semantic representation, it should cause no surprise that lexical development accompanies cognitive development up to adolescence and beyond and that it may appear to be as dependent on experience as cognition itself.

If we now consider the development of the specifically linguistic information contained in the semantic representations of sentences, we get the impression that we are dealing with the development of a mechanism largely independent of general cognition. The acquisition of the basic structural mechanisms is very rapid (as contrasted with the growth of the ability to use them simultaneously and abundantly) and is likely to be much less sensitive to environmental variations. It could well be that such development is more dependent on the unfolding of a very specific genetic program, part of the species-specific endowment of man.

References

Antinucci, F., & Parisi, D. Early language development: a model and some data. In C. Ferguson & D. Slobin (Eds.), *Studies of child language development*. New York: Holt, 1973.

Gruber, J. Correlations between the syntactic constructions of the child and the adult. In C. Ferguson & D. Slobin (Eds.), *Studies of child language development*. New York: Holt, 1973. Pp. 440–445.

Parisi, D., & Antinucci, F. Early language development: a second state. In *Current problems in psycholinguistics*. Paris: CNRS, 1974. Pp. 607–619.

Ross, J. R. On declarative sentences. In R. A. Jacobs & P. S. Rosenbaum (Eds.), *Readings in English transformational grammar*. Waltham, Mass.: Ginn, 1970. Pp. 222–272.

12. Grammatical Development— The First Steps[1]

I. M. Schlesinger

This chapter deals with the first stages of the child's acquisition of the grammar of his language. The first section describes several characteristics of his early utterances. In the next sections, some recent theories regarding the nature of the grammatical rules internalized by the child are discussed. The final section deals with various views concerning the mechanisms responsible for the learning of these rules.

The Nature of the Child's Early Utterances

THE BEGINNINGS

In the first stages of his linguistic development, each of the child's utterances consists of one word. At about 18 months, he begins to string together two, and occasionally more, words. At first the intonation pattern of these utterances often differs from that of short adult sentences: the child pauses after each word, stresses each of the words equally, and the typical terminal intonation is lacking. The impression we get is of one-word sentences following each other; for example (Bloom, 1970, p. 11):

[1]This chapter was written in connection with research supported by a grant from the Human Development Center of the Hebrew University, Jerusalem. The writer is indebted to Drs. C. Greenbaum, H. Grimm, G. Höpp, W. Kaper, and W. Raffler-Engel for their valuable comments and to Mrs. Lila Namir for her helpful suggestions concerning style and presentation.

> *car.   ride.*
>
> *car.   see.*

Presumably, one word is no longer enough to get the child's meaning across, and he therefore adds words to make himself understood. The sequence of words is probably determined by momentary factors, with the word that happens to be most salient for the child appearing first in the utterance.

However, very soon after the appearance of many-word utterances, the child begins to use a natural intonation contour. Moreover, a striking regularity of word order becomes apparent. This shows that the child begins to learn the grammar of the language. The phrase "learn a grammar," which will often be used in the following, should, of course, not be taken to imply that the child is aware of any regularity in the way he talks; it merely expresses the fact that his utterances are structured in conformity with the rules laid down by the grammar of the language. In the present chapter, we shall see how the child gradually acquires adult grammar, starting from the first rudimentary grammatical rules reflected in his utterances. Only the first few steps will be followed. The child's grammatical development continues beyond these for several years, and has been described by a number of researchers (e.g., Brown, 1973; C. S. Chomsky, 1969; Menyuk, 1969).

TELEGRAPHIC SPEECH

The child's earliest utterances have been aptly described as "telegraphic speech" or "telegraphese." Articles, auxiliary verbs, and most of the other function words that serve to hold together the sentence of adult language are usually missing in his utterances. Typical examples, from the speech of some 21 to 22 month-old children (Bloom, 1970, pp. 46, 49, 56), are the following:

> *Mommy busy*
> *Me show Mommy*
> *This baby book*

Telegraphese has been observed in all children studied so far, whether they learn English or any other language as their mother tongue.

Despite the omission of many grammatical words, telegrams are usually intelligible to the receiver. But children in the beginning stages of talking also omit some of the content words that carry the gist of the message. Moreover, inflections are at first almost totally absent. As a result, much of what they say can be understood only within the situation context. A written protocol of child language, therefore, includes many utterances that can be interpreted in more than one way, as for instance:

> *Mommy sock*
> *shopping bag shoe*
> *man sit blocks*

Only the contexts in which these utterances occur make it clear what is meant by them. Taken by itself, *Mommy sock* might be construed as meaning, for example, any one of the following:

> *This is Mommy's sock.*
> *Mommy has a sock.*
> *I will give Mommy the sock.*
> *Mommy puts on my sock.*

In fact, Mommy was putting the child's sock on when *Mommy sock* was uttered, and thus the last interpretation is apparently correct (Bloom, 1970, p. 9). Judging from the situational context, the child's intended meaning in uttering *shopping bag shoe* may probably be paraphrased as *I put the shoe into the shopping bag*, and *man sit block* meant something like *the man sits on the block* (the experimenter was sitting a wire man on the block; Bloom, 1970, pp. 98, 124).[2]

Adults tend to check whether they have understood the child correctly by repeating his utterance in a somewhat fuller form, supplying at least some of the missing words. Examples of such "expansions" (Brown & Bellugi, 1964) are:

Child	Mother
Mommy eggnog.	*Mommy had her eggnog.*
Mommy sandwich.	*Mommy will have a sandwich.*
Sat wall.	*He sat on the wall.*

The first of these utterances is interpreted by the adult as referring to the past, whereas the second utterance, which has a similar structure, is construed as referring to the future. Note also how the adult supplies not only the missing function words (in the first two utterances), but also occasionally content words like *he* in the last utterance. In this way the adult, so to speak, compares notes with the child concerning the meaning of the latter's rudimentary sentences.

Numerous repetitions are found in early child language, for instance (Braine, 1971a):

> *Stevie gun.   Tommy, Stevie gun.   Tommy give gun.*
> *Gun.   Tommy gun.   Tommy give Stevie gun.*

---

[2] Children have been observed to differentiate between otherwise identical utterances by means of stress. Thus *Christy room* would mean *Christy's room* if the first word were stressed, and *Christy is in his room* if the second word were stressed (Miller & Ervin, 1964).

Sequences like these have been called "replacement sequences" by Braine. Here the child seems to be striving to express an idea, but fails to do so at one go. Replacement sequences have also been observed in child soliloquies, as when he is alone in his bed before falling asleep (Weir, 1962). For example:

> *Block.   Yellow block.   Look at all the yellow block.*

Here they do not seem to serve any communicative function. The child seems simply to be playing with words. Perhaps he is practicing how to speak?

Another phenomenon worth noting is that the child often adds a word or two to his utterance, as an afterthought, as it were (Bloom, 1970, pp. 42, 87, 144):

> *This sock.   Dirty.*
> *This under bridge.   Lamb.*
> *Block 'way.   'Way away.*

But let us return to regular telegraphese. Although the skeleton sentences that go by this name are ungrammatical by the standards of adult language, they are evidence that the child is on his way to mastering adult grammar; the order of words uttered by the child tends, in most cases, to conform to the word order in the full adult sentence. Such is the case in pratically all the examples given above. Even in those languages where word order is variable in adult speech, like Finnish and Russian, two children who have been studied adhered to a rigid word order (Slobin, 1970, p. 177). Word order, then, is the first thing the child learns about adult grammar. Only later does he begin to use inflections. With the gradual introduction of function words, his speech comes to resemble that of adults more and more closely.

Of course, deviations from adult word order also occur. The reason for this may be that the child has not yet completely mastered the rules governing word order. Occasionally, he even uses two different sequences one after the other, as in the following (Bloom, 1970, p. 22):

> *my have ə this.   this mys.*
> *this my . . . this ə mine.   my this.*
> *this ə my this.*

A different explanation for deviant word order, which we may apply in some, but not all cases, is that the child's word sequence is influenced by momentary factors that make one word more salient for him than another (Bühler, 1922).

The suggestion has also been made that there is a "natural" word order that reflects the functioning of the child's cognitive system and accounts for some cases in which children consistently place the verb after both subject and object, contrary to adult grammar (Park, 1969).

Finally, a deviant word order may be the result of the child applying a rule in the wrong way (examples of this are given in the following section). Such inappropriate application of rules is at the root of so-called mistakes-by-analogy, where the child over-generalizes a regular form, as in *digged, hisself,* and *sheeps* (Brown & Fraser, 1963). Similarly, children have been observed to pluralize *foot* as *foots* or *feets,* or even (apparently on the model of *box—boxes) footses* (Ervin, 1964). Since it is unlikely that the child has encountered them in adult speech, these mistakes show that he does not merely imitate the adult, but learns the rules of his grammar; in fact, the child's mistakes may often be the best clue to the rules he has acquired. The fact that the child not only imitates certain utterances, but learns the rules underlying them, is of crucial importance, because these rules determine the structure of a great number of utterances made by the child, many of which he has never heard before.

FURTHER DEVELOPMENTS

Gradually, the child's language develops from "telegraphese" to the fully grammatical adult sentence. Function words and inflections begin to appear. The sentence becomes longer and hierarchically organized. Whereas in the first stages of the child's speech we may find utterances like *that flower,* the child may at a later stage be observed to say *that a blue flower* (Brown & Bellugi, 1964). The fact that a noun phrase now occupies the position of the single noun *flower* is an instance of hierarchical organization.

The order of appearance of these features has been the subject of much recent research (see Braine, 1971a; Brown & Hanlon, 1970; Menyuk, 1969), but the picture is far from complete. The emergence of various grammatical forms apparently depends not only on their formal complexity, but also on their cognitive difficulty for the child. For instance, conditional sentences and sentences with certain conjunctions such as *because* and *whether* appear late in child speech in different languages, presumably because of the semantic difficulties of the notions involved (Slobin, 1970). Where a grammatical form has been mastered, it may at first be used inappropriately to signal a distinction that is cognitively simpler than the one the form stands for in adult speech. Thus, children have been observed to use the present form for durative actions like *wash,* while reserving the past form for instantaneous actions like *break* and *drop,* regardless of the time the action took place (Sinclair, 1971, in Huxley & Ingram, Eds., pp. 75–76).

Of special interest are sentence forms in which the word order differs from that of simple declarative sentences. The stages of acquiring the interrogative and negative transformations have been intensively studied by Bellugi (e.g., Bellugi, 1971). Auxiliary verbs like *shall, can, will* begin to appear in questions of English-speaking children at about three years of age, with the order of auxiliary verbs and subject properly inverted in *yes—no* questions as required by adult grammar, for example:

> *Robin will help me.*
> *Will Robin help me?*

During the same period, *wh-* questions (i.e., questions beginning with *where, why, what*, etc.) are produced without this inversion:

> *Why the kitten can't stand up?*

This deviant form is adhered to even after attempts at correction. Bellugi gives the following example:

> ADULT: *Adam, say what I say, "Where can he put them?"*
> ADAM: *Where he can put them?*

It seems that while the child can master the inversion operation, as evidenced by his correct use of *yes–no* questions, he cannot combine it with the additional operation required for formulating *wh-* questions. We see again here that the child does not (as has been claimed) merely imitate adult speech, but rather extracts from it certain rules that he then applies in his own way, so that his speech differs strikingly from that of the adult.

A similar independent system has been noted by Bellugi (1971) for negative sentences with indeterminate forms. At first, the child forms negative sentences with forms appropriate only for affirmative sentences (*some, something,* and *someone*):

> *I don't want some supper.*

Here again, only one of the operations needed for correct negating is carried out. In the next stage, the indeterminate form is replaced by a negative form, resulting in "double negatives":

> *I am not scared of nothing.*
> *I never have none.*

Bellugi argues that this results from the use of a rule spreading "a layer of negative coloring" on all indeterminates, instead of the more complex set of rules required by adult grammar. Other examples resulting from this strategy are:

> *No one's not going to do what I'm doing.*
> *But nobody wasn't gonna know it.*

The foremost question in the acquisition of grammar, then, is that of the nature of rules by which the child operates. In the following sections, we shall concentrate only on (1) rules governing word order and (2) the formation of grammatical categories. The acquisition processes of these two kinds of rules probably go hand-in-hand, but for the purpose of this presentation they are best treated separately.

The Nature of Word Order Rules

It should be kept in mind that when speaking here of rules of grammar, no awareness on the part of the user of language is implied; rather, the term pertains to regularity in his language behavior. The rules of grammatical speech internalized by the child enable him to emit an enormous variety of different sentences, among which there are many that he has never heard. The nature of these grammatical rules is discussed in this and the following section. We deal here with the question of *what* is learned, whereas the question of learning processes will be taken up in the final section.

TRANSFORMATIONAL GRAMMAR

It is one of the main tenets of linguists of the transformational school that a complete description of the grammar of a language comprises, among other things, the *deep structures* of sentences, their *surface structure*, and the *transformational rules* relating the two. Deep structures contain most of the information required for the semantic interpretation of the sentence, whereas it is the surface structure that is realized in speech. (For a concise treatment of these notions, see, e.g., N. Chomsky, 1967.) Any account of how grammar is acquired, then, must show how the child comes to know these two kinds of structures and the transformation rules relating them.

Following this line of thought, there have been a number of studies describing the grammatical development of the child in terms of the concepts of transformational grammar (e.g., McNeill, 1966; Menyuk, 1969). In this section we shall deal only with rules pertaining to word order, and we shall show by example the kind of rules which, according to this school of thought, the child has to master.

Deep structures are generated by a set of so-called *rewrite rules*, and take the form of *underlying phrase-makers*. Some rewrite rules, which may account for a large number of utterances found in children, are the following (adapted from McNeill, 1966, 1971):

> Sentence → Predicate phrase
> Predicate phrase → (Verb) + Noun phrase
> Noun phrase → (Noun) + Noun

(Read: *Sentence* is rewritten as *Predicate phrase*; *Predicate phrase* is rewritten as *Verb* (optional) followed by a *Noun phrase*; and so on. Parentheses indicate optional items.) Among the phrase markers generated by these rules is that in Fig. 12—1 (after insertion of lexical items).

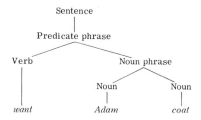

Figure 12—1. The phrase-marker of *want Adam coat* (after McNeill, 1966, 1971).

As far as adult sentences go, complex transformations are often applied to underlying phrase-markers to turn them into surface structures. This is not the case with the phrase marker in Fig. 12—1, which does not differ from surface structure, and the same holds for other early utterances of the child, according to this school of thought.

In addition to *want Adam coat*, these rules permit, of course, formation of other strings, such as *see Mommy coat, want Adam car*, and so on. The same rewrite rules also generate other underlying phrase-markers: those which omit the optional *Noun* in the rewrite rule (e.g. *see coat*) or those which omit the optional *Verb* (e.g. *Adam coat*). As the child matures, the rules become more differentiated, and transformations of increasing complexity are used, which turn the phrase markers into surface structures. Thus the rewrite rules of adult grammar may include, *inter alia*, the following:

> Sentence → Noun phrase + Predicate phrase
> Noun phrase → (Determiner) + Noun
> Predicate phrase → Auxiliary + Verb + Noun phrase

These rules may give rise to the phrase-marker of Fig. 12—2 (simplified from adult grammar).

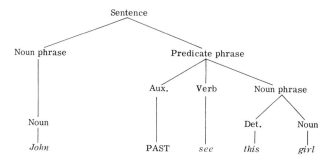

Figure 12—2. Simplified underlying phrase-marker of *John saw this girl*.

The theory that the child acquires rewrite rules meets the requirement of productivity; a small number of rules permit production of a large number of different utterances conforming to them. Further, as the above example shows, the theory accounts for the acquisition of hierarchical structures; the term *Noun phrase*, for instance, may be rewritten either as one term or as two. This approach also comes to grips with semantic relations. According to the transformationalist model, the *semantic component* operates on the deep structures and derives from them the semantic interpretation of the sentence. Of the two noun phrases, in the underlying phrase-markers in Fig. 12—2, that which is dominated by *Predicate phrase* is always the object of the verb in the predicate phrase, whereas the one dominated directly by *Sentence* is the subject of the sentence. On hearing *John saw this girl*, the phrase marker of Fig. 12—2 is inferred, and *John* is therefore correctly understood as the subject and *this girl* as the object of *saw*, instead of vice versa.

Although the problem of semantic interpretation has usually been rather casually dealt with by writers on child language within the transformationalist framework, it has recently received special attention from Bloom (1970), who, in her exemplary analyses of child speech, deals expressly with the semantic relations intended by the child.

There are certain difficulties that arise with the approach outlined here. First, there is the question of how the structures evident in child speech form the groundwork for those that later appear in adult speech. For example, most of the children studied so far used a subject + object construction at the two-word stage, with the subject always preceding the object:

> *Mommy shoe*
> *cat meat*
> *Mommy Roger*

These examples are from Bloom (1970, pp. 49, 61, 93), and the same construction has been observed in other languages (see Schlesinger, 1971a; Slobin, 1970). A rule that rewrites *sentence* as *noun + noun*, in which the first noun is interpreted as subject and the second as object, is not a part of adult grammar, and it does not seem too plausible to credit the child with a rule that he later abrogates in favor of the more mature one. An alternative solution would be to ascribe to the child at this stage a more complete rule system, which generates the full subject—verb—object sequence, but to postulate a reduction transformation, which deletes the verb (Bloom, 1970). The difficulty with this solution is that it assumes, on the one hand, that the child is able to deal with the cognitive complexity of the subject—verb—object construction, and on the other, that he is unable to cope with such a long sentence in speaking, thus requiring a special reduction transformation that is later discarded.

A second problem concerns the ways deep structures are learned. In the case illustrated in Fig. 12—1, there is no difficulty, because here the deep structure presented by the phrase marker does not differ from the surface structure. But mastery of the full adult grammar requires an ability to use deep structures that are related to surface structures via more or less complex transformation rules. The fact that only surface and not deep structures are exhibited directly in adult speech seems to pose a major obstacle in accounting for how the latter can be learned. The opinions of students of child language embracing the transformational position range, therefore, from a cautious admission that the question of *how* grammar is learned remains to be investigated (e.g., Bloom, 1970, p. 233) to the far-reaching conclusion that, since they cannot be learned, deep structures must be part of the innate equipment of the child, requiring only maturation and suitable environmental stimulation to become fully effective (e.g., McNeill, 1966, 1970, 1971). Before commenting on the latter proposition, an approach to the child's grammar will be presented which, although akin to the transformational approach, differs from it in some important respects.

REALIZATION OF SEMANTIC STRUCTURES

Considerations pertaining to a speech production model have led the present writer to postulate that the deep structures learned by the child are semantic in nature (Schlesinger, 1971a, 1971b). While the phrase markers of transformational grammar discussed above need a semantic component to give them their semantic interpretation, the deep structures postulated here represent semantic relations directly.[3] They are formally represented by *input markers*. Suppose the child says

Daddy drinks black coffee.

In making this utterance, the child expresses certain semantic relations between words, namely

1. *black* is an attribute of *coffee*;
2. *black coffee* is the object of drinking;
3. *Daddy* is the agent of the action·of drinking black coffee.

These relations may be formalized by the following input-marker:

AGENT: *Daddy*, (OBJECT: [ATTRIBUTE: *black, coffee*], *drinks*).

Learning the grammar is to learn how input markers are realized in speech. The correct word order of the sentence expressing the preceding input marker is given by the following *realization rules* (there will, of course, be additional realiza-

---

[3] Recently, the notion of the semantic deep structure has been espoused by the generative semantics school of thought. While no claim is made here concerning the superiority of either the generative semantics or the standard, interpretative semantics theory on linguistic grounds, it is proposed that *for a performance model* the notion of a semantic base is indispensable.

tion rules determining the correct inflections, but these are no concern of this section):

ATTRIBUTE: a,b → Noun (Adjective a + Noun b)
OBJECT: a,b → Verb (Verb b + Noun a)
AGENT: a,b → Sentence (Noun a + Verb b)

The first rule states that if *a* is an attribute of *b*, *a* must be expressed by an adjective and followed by *b*, which must be expressed by a noun; the whole expression then functions as a noun (e.g., when it appears as the object of an action—see the second rule).

Gradually the child acquires more and more complex realization rules, permitting him to express longer and more complex input markers. The form of input markers and rules given here should be regarded as tentative and the semantic relations will have to be more precisely defined. (For a formal definition of some semantic relations, see Suppes, 1970.)

As the preceding example shows, input markers are hierarchically organized: the object of a verb may be realized as a single noun (e.g., *coffee*), or else a noun and its attribute (e.g. *black coffee*), which together serve as noun. In both cases, the second of the preceding realization rules will be applicable. This hierarchical organization reflects the semantic relations the child has in mind when speaking or understanding the sentence: it is the *black* coffee—not just any coffee—that is being drunk, and it is the *coffee* that is black, not Daddy.

The important point to note here is that everything that appears in the input marker represents the way the child perceives the environment that he talks about or hears being talked about. In this respect, input markers differ from phrase markers. In the latter, semantic relations can be inferred only indirectly, via such notions as the noun phrase that is dominated by *predicate phrase*; a special semantic component is postulated that interprets the grammatical notions in the phrase marker semantically. Since such phrase markers are not directly exhibited to the child, this raises the problem of how they are learned. With input markers, this problem does not arise. The child learns how the representations of semantic relations perceived in his environment are matched with linguistic expressions, and no specifically linguistic aspects of deep structures must be assumed to be innate.[4] An interesting parallel is provided by the studies of Moeser and Bregman (1972, 1973), who found that subjects learned a miniature artificial language only when exposed to it along with the referents it described.

---

[4] The hypothesis of innate propensities for learning certain grammatical rules has been proposed by N. Chomsky (1968) and has found a vigorous spokesman in McNeill (1966, 1970, 1971). Material concerning the biological basis of language and arguments for a maturational factor have been assembled by Lenneberg (1967) and its implications critically reviewed by Braine (1971a). For various psychological approaches to the problem, see Braine (1971b), Bever (1970), Morton (1971), Sinclair (1971), and Schlesinger (1971a). A philosophers' symposium on this issue is to be found in Hook (1969).

The child, then, learns realization rules that determine how to match sound with meaning, or surface structures of sentences with input markers.

It is possible that as a first step toward learning such realization rules, the child learns a so-called "pivot grammar." The theory that the child learns the position of words in phrases and of phrases in sentences was first proposed by Braine (1963a). Several investigators have observed that at the two-world stage there is a small number of words that recur in many utterances and always in a fixed position. In addition to these *pivots*, there is a large number of words occupying the complementary position in the two-word utterance. An example of a pivot that occurred in first position in one of the children Braine (1963b) studied is *Allgone*: *Allgone shoe, Allgone vitamins, Allgone egg, Allgone watch*. Other first-position pivots were, for example, *this, that, more, other, all*, and *want*. Among second-position pivots reported are *off, on, there, it* (e.g., *Boot off, Shirt off, Water off*.) That such constructions cannot be the result of mere imitation is shown by those cases in which the child produces utterances with a pivot that he is unlikely to have heard from an adult; thus, the pivot word *Allgone* gave rise to *Allgone sticky* (after the child had washed his hands), and the pivot *more* to *more high, more wet*, and *more page* (i.e., *Go on reading*). The child has incorporated rules according to which certain words always come first, and the remaining position is taken up by any other word; certain other words always come second.

Now, when many second-position pivots have the property, in a considerable number of two-word utterances, of expressing the goal or object of an action, the child may generalize that OBJECT is a second-position pivot. Such a *generalized pivot* may perhaps form the basis for the acquisition of a realization rule determining the word order *verb + noun* (Schlesinger, 1971a).

The assumption that the child learns generalized pivots enables us to explain the appearance of agent—object constructions in child speech, which, as shown earlier, present considerable difficulty for an account in terms of phrase markers. If OBJECT is a generalized pivot in second position, any word that goes with the object word in the two-word utterance will occupy first position. Sometimes this will be a word describing the action and sometimes a word referring to the agent of the action. Alternatively, AGENT may be a generalized first-position pivot, which results in any word that accompanies the agent, whether it describes the action or the object, occupying the second position. At a later stage, generalized pivots make way for full-fledged realization rules, and the agent—action—object construction replaces the agent—object construction (Schlesinger, 1971a).

It is suggested, then, that the child learns rules that determine how semantic deep structures are realized in sentences.[5] Deep structures reflect the way we

---

[5] This represents a departure from the standard transformational theory at least as far as a performance model is concerned, and the question has been raised whether a complete grammar can be developed along the lines suggested here. That there is no difficulty in principle can be easily seen. Consider that according to the standard theory there are three kinds of structures: a surface structure, a deep structure, and a semantic interpretation. For each pair of rules that relate (1) a semantic interpretation to a deep structure, and (2) this deep structure to a surface

perceive our environment, and this perception is not learned as part of the grammar of a language (although it may develop in the course of a child's interaction with the environment, as described by Piaget).

Word Classes

The child must not only learn the correct sequence of words in the sentence, but also what kinds of words may appear in a given position. *Good* and *well* stand for very similar, if not identical, ideas, but according to adult grammar, these words cannot be substituted for each other in a given sentence. Likewise, we do not say *This is good eat* for *This is good food* (although the meaning of the former would be quite clear). On the other hand, *eat* can be replaced in any sentence by another transitive verb like *see, throw, give*; the meaning will change (for some verbs the result will be nonsense), but no formal rule will be infringed. Another reason why the child must form word classes is that words of different classes differ in the way they are inflected (verbs add -*s* in present third person singular, but may not add -*er* or -*est*, as some adjectives do).

How does the child form these grammatical categories? The first answer that comes to mind is that the various word classes have semantic correlates: nouns refer to things, verbs to actions and states, and so on. This would be a very shaky basis for acquiring word classes, however, because there are numerous exceptions to this rule. Many nouns do not refer to what one might call "things," unless *thing* is circularly defined as that which is denoted by a noun. *Confusion* is no less a state than *to sleep*, and there is nothing more thing-like in *permission* than in *to permit*. Nevertheless, it seems that in children's speech, the vast majority of nouns refer to objects, almost all verbs refer to actions, states, and processes, and adjectives to properties of objects (Brown, 1957; for parallel considerations from a linguist's point of view, see Lyons, 1968). The semantic correlates of word classes may therefore facilitate their acquisition, but in view of the gradually developing lack of correspondence between meanings of words and their grammatical category, it seems doubtful whether this explanation is sufficient. (For further discussion see Braine, 1971a, Section 2.32.)

Another view regards the acquisition of word classes as on a par with that of word order. In both cases the child learns rules determining how deep structures are realized in speech. Consider the approach according to which deep structures are input markers comprising semantic relations. These relations must be viewed as holding between concepts that are undifferentiated as to word class; that is, there is no distinction between *eat* and *food* in the input marker. What the

---

structure, another rule can be formulated relating the semantic interpretation to the appropriate surface structure directly. In other words, it is possible to map the former directly onto the latter. This is what the present approach postulates, since input markers are defined to contain the same information as the semantic representation.

child learns is that AGENT: *a, b* in the input markers is realized by (1) putting the word expressing the concept *a* before that expressing *b*, and (2) expressing the concept *a* by the word belonging to the class of nouns and the concept *b* by a word belonging to another class. Gradually he learns about more and more words that they are eligible for the second term. Nouns, then, are defined for the child as those words that can express agents, adjectives as those words that express attributes in the ATTRIBUTE: *a, b* relation, and so on.

Note that this account does not assume a one-to-one correspondence between semantic notions like agent and attribute and between grammatical categories. Agents may be either nouns or pronouns, and conversely, a noun may not only be the realization of an agent but also that of an object. Nevertheless, each word class can be uniquely defined by the *whole set* of realization rules in which it figures.

The above explanation leaves open the question of which type of rules is learned first by the child—rules pertaining to word position or those determining by which kinds of words agents, attributes, and so on may be realized. Perhaps position rules and grammatical category rules alternate in the developmental sequence; this is an empirical question awaiting further study.

It is proposed, then, that word classes are acquired primarily through the rules that relate deep structures to speech. This does not preclude the possibility that certain properties of these classes may facilitate such learning. One such property, noted above, is the fact that word classes have semantic correlates, especially in child speech. Another property that may help in learning is that different word classes have different affixes; for example, the plural *-s* of nouns or the *-ly* suffix of adverbs. These affixes may act as cues for the child in sorting words into their appropriate categories.

Learning Mechanisms

We have dealt with the nature of the rules learned by the child; we now turn to the question of what mechanisms are responsible for the learning of these rules. Some proposals made by various theorists will be critically discussed in the following.

REINFORCEMENT

Several learning theorists hold that language behavior, like all behavior, is learned because it is reinforced. Thus Skinner (1957) claims that all verbal behavior is learned by conditioning. According to this view, the child learns to speak according to the rules of grammar because he has been rewarded in some way, for example, by parental approval, for adhering to these rules, and possibly negatively reinforced, by disapproval, for infringing these rules.

Although no one would dispute the importance of reinforcement in shaping the child's behavior, it has been claimed by some writers that as far as the learning of language is concerned, reinforcement does not play a crucial role. Several considerations lead to this conclusion. First, children will talk whether reinforced or not, and they may even engage in soliloquies when there is no one around to listen (Weir, 1962). As for the modeling of the child's grammar by parental approval or disapproval, it should be kept in mind that in many cultures parents are much less concerned with the way their children's speech develops than are middle-class parents in Western culture, and this lack of concern evidently does not keep these children from acquiring the grammar of their language.

Moreover, even the Western middle-class parent does very little to shape his child's behavior into more grammatical molds. To the contrary, one may often observe parents reinforcing by merriment and approval the child's "cute" mistakes, and occasionally even repeating them. If reinforcement were the whole story, it would be hard to understand how the child eventually outgrows these mistakes. In addition to this impressionistic evidence, there is a careful study by Brown and Hanlon (1970) in which no relationship was found between the grammatical correctness of the child's speech and the subsequent approval or disapproval of his (middle-class) parents. Rather, their reaction was based on whether what the child said was true or false and on whether the child performed well phonologically.

Reinforcement of the child's speech is precluded in the rare case of a child with normal hearing who is physiologically unable to speak, yet Lennberg (1962) has reported the case of such a dysarthric boy who attained good understanding of the language without ever having been reinforced for correct speech (for another interesting example, see Chapter 32). The preceding considerations show that explicit reinforcement is not indispensable for learning grammar, but it is still likely that grammar is learned faster and better when parents take an active role in reinforcing the child.

So far, we have considered explicit reinforcement coming from the hearer in response to the child's verbal behavior. There is also the possibility that the child is reinforced by the very fact that someone listens to him without showing lack of understanding. This is so because previously the child would often have been overtly reinforced when he was understood, and as a consequence, another person's listening and understanding per se have become reinforcing. Notice that this would explain the child's motivation for talking, but not his abandoning grammatical mistakes, because he will usually be understood in spite of these. At the most, it may motivate him to attempt longer and more structured sentences that can express his meaning more clearly and precisely.

HYPOTHESIS TESTING

Some linguists and psycholinguists follow N. Chomsky and Miller (1963) in holding that children go about discovering the grammar of their language much the way the scientists discovers laws of nature. They formulate hypotheses (implicitly, of course) about grammatical rules and check these against the sentences heard. Hypotheses that are contrary to evidence are rejected, and of those that stand the test of adult speech, the child retains the simplest. This view of the acquisition of grammar has close links with the theory of strong innate constraints on the possible grammatical rules, since such constraints limit the number of hypotheses the child must generate and test out. The question of innate aspects of language is at present a subject of controversy and, as will have become clear previously, much of the merit of the nativist claim depends on what kinds of rules the child is assumed to learn.

The success of this hypothesis-testing model is accounting for the acquisition of grammar depends on the availability of negative feedback to the child; that is, he must not only get clues as to what is a correct, grammatical sentence, but also as to what is not grammatical (Braine, 1971a, 1971b). Such information must be available to the child if he is to eliminate rules that predict, in addition to grammatical utterances, some utterances that are ungrammatical (e.g., in addition to *Keep this as a present* and *Ask him to be a baby-sitter,* also *Keep this to be a present* and *Ask him as a baby-sitter*). If the child extracts from adult speech only the information as to what *is* a sentence, he will have no reason to reject such an over-inclusive hypothesis, because he will find for it many corroborating instances. Since adults are not wont to expatiate on grammar, nor indulge in the correction of each other's grammatical mistakes, such negative feedback will not occur unless touched off by the child's mistakes. But as noted previously, parents neglect opportunities to correct their children, and moreover, the latter are often quite impervious to corrections when these are offered. Further, Lenneberg's dysarthric boy could not have been corrected, and hence was not supplied with negative information (unless, of course, he had quite extraordinary opportunities to eavesdrop on adults correcting *other* children's mistakes).

PASSIVE LEARNING

A model for learning grammatical rules that is dependent on mere exposure to instances of a rule has been proposed by Braine (1971a, 1971b). The model consists of a scanner and a memory component. The scanner receives the incoming sentence, analyzes it, and finds its pattern properties. The latter are registered in the intermediate memory store. When a pattern property has been registered a sufficient number of times, it moves from the intermediate memory store to the permanent store, and thereby becomes operative as a rule of grammar. As long as the pattern property is in the intermediate store, it may be forgotten after a certain period of time.

This characteristic of the model ensures that unsystematic errors in the speech heard by the child do not lead to the learning of incorrect rules; since these errors are not repeated too often, they are forgotten before they can reach the permanent store. Braine's model thus takes care of the problem of what has been called "degenerate input," that is, the fact that the speech heard in the child's environment is full of false starts, accidental mistakes, and incomplete sentences. To the extent that this is so, it constitutes a problem for a hypothesis-testing theory, whereas Braine's model can deal with this. It has been pointed out, however, that adult speech directed at the young child is relatively free of such imperfections (Brown & Bellugi, 1964; see also Raffler-Engel, 1970). Notice also that, unlike the hypothesis-testing model, Braine's model does not require access to negative information, mere exposure to grammatically correct sentences being sufficient.

The greater the frequency with which a given property is received in the temporary store, the sooner will it reach the permanent store. As a consequence, the child will learn the more general properties first, the more specific ones later, and exceptions and special cases last. This accords with findings on language learning. A further result of this characteristic of the model is that grammar learning is not adversely affected by the fact that some of the adults' sentences exhibit properties contradicting those the child is about to learn. For instance, inversion of word order in negative and interrogative sentences does not disturb his acquisition of word order in the simple declarative sentence, because he is presumably more frequently exposed to the latter, which therefore reaches the permanent store first.

The amount and complexity of spoken utterances that impinge on the child's ears seem to be so large that one might ask how the child could possibly create order out of this chaos and use all this material to extract from it rules appropriate to his particular state of grammatical development. Sentence structures in adult speech are far in advance of the primitive structures used by the child in the beginning stages, and one might wonder what keeps him from being totally frustrated by so much talk that he cannot cope with. However, observation of adult–child interaction shows that speech directed at the child is much simpler in structure, tending to be at a level not far beyond that achieved by him. It is reasonable to suppose that the child filters out speech not directed at him. Possible cues for such a filtering mechanism may be the adult's tone of voice (Kelley, 1967), or an unfamiliar word at the beginning of the utterance (Shipley, Smith & Gleitman, 1969).

According to Braine's theory, the child learns grammar by being exposed to adult speech; no reinforcement is postulated. In an experiment with college students, Braine (1971a, 1971b) has shown that a "language" of nonsense syllables that is structured according to rules like those of a grammar can, in fact, be learned by merely listening to the utterances of many of its "sentences." This suggests that passive learning may be sufficient for the acquisition of grammar, but it remains an open question whether young children learn meaningful material by the same process. Compare also the language-learning experiments of Moeser and Bregman, described above [Moeser & Bregman, 1972, 1973]. Kelley (1967), who has also proposed a model of passive learning, has suggested that the child's understanding of speech may have reinforcing value, because understanding has in the past led to his taking subsequently rewarded action. The child believes he has understood an utterance when his interpretation of it accords with what appears plausible in the light of his knowledge of the world.

IMITATION

At a certain stage of learning to speak, a child tends to imitate everything an adult says to him. It seems reasonable to accord such imitation an important role in the acquisition of language, but before turning to this question, let us see what these imitations are like. As the following examples from Brown and Bellugi (1964) show, imitations resemble spontaneous speech in that they drop inflections, most function words, and sometimes also other words; however, word order of the imitated sentence is usually preserved:

Mother	Child
Fraser will be unhappy.	*Fraser unhappy.*
He's going out.	*He go out.*
No, you can't write on Mr. Cromer's shoe.	*Cromer shoe.*

There are several possible explanations for this reduction of adult utterances to "telegraphese." The words omitted by the child are those that receive less stress in the adult utterance and may have therefore been disregarded by him. Further, the child may tend to retain content words that he has practiced with in one-word utterances. Finally, he may remember better those words heard last in the sentence, as seems to be the case in the third example above. These explanations assume that the reduction of adult utterances in imitation is a function of what the child attends to or remembers (Brown & Bellugi, 1964). Alternatively, it might be argued that in imitating he *reconstructs* the adult utterance and that he does so by employing the grammatical rules at his disposal, which at a given stage permit him to produce only such skeleton sentences. A study by Slobin and Welsh (1971) seems to suggest this. This explanation is also in line with the finding that the child's imitations do not contain more advanced structure than his spontaneous utterances (Ervin, 1964; see also the discussion by Braine, 1971a, of telegraphic speech).

One might hypothesize that by imitating the adult, the child practices new grammatical constructions. The just-mentioned finding that imitations do not tend to be grammatically more advanced than spontaneous speech does not support this hypothesis, though it still seems open to further study (Slobin, 1968). It has also been suggested that repeating the adult's utterance assists the child in comprehending it (Shipley *et al.*, 1969). Much further research is needed to settle this issue.

References

Bellugi, U. Simplification in children's language. In R. Huxley & E. Ingram (Eds.), *Language acquisition: Models and methods.* New York: Academic Press, 1971. pp. 95–117.

Bever, T. G. The cognitive basis of linguistic structures. In J. R. Hayes (Ed.), *Cognition and the development of language.* New York: Wiley, 1970. pp. 279–362.

Bloom, L. M. *Language development: Form and function in emerging grammars.* Cambridge, Mass.: MIT Press, 1970.

Braine, M. D. S. On learning the grammatical order of words. *Psychological Review*, 1963, *70*, 323—348. (a)

Braine, M. D. S. The ontogeny of English phrase structure: The first phase. *Language*, 1963, *39*, 1—13. (b)

Braine, M. D. S. The acquisition of language in infant and child. In C. Reed (Ed.), *The learning of language*. New York: Appleton, 1971. Pp. 153—186. (a)

Braine, M. D. S. On two types of models of the internalization of grammar. In D. Slobin (Ed.), *The ontogenesis of grammar*. New York: Academic Press, 1971. (b)

Brown, R. W. Linguistic determinism and the part of speech. *Journal of Abnormal and Social Psychology*, 1957, *49*, 454—462.

Brown, R. W. *A first language: The early stages*. Cambridge, Mass.: Harvard Univ. Press, 1973.

Brown, R. W., & Bellugi, U. Three processes in the child's acquisition of syntax. *Harvard Educational Review*, 1964, *34*, 133—151.

Brown, R. W., & Fraser, C. The acquisition of syntax. In C. N. Cofer & B. S. Musgrave (Eds.), *Verbal behavior and learning: Problems and processes*. New York: McGraw-Hill, 1963. pp. 158—197.

Brown, R. W., & Hanlon, C. Derivational complexity and order of acquisition in child speech. In J. R. Hayes (Ed.), *Cognition and the development of language*. New York: Wiley, 1970, Pp. 11—53.

Bühler, K. Vom Wesen der Syntax. In *Idealistische Neuphilologie, Festschrift für Karl Vossler*, Heidelberg: Carl Winter, 1922. Pp. 77—83 [Partially reprinted in translation in A. Bar-Adon & W. F. Leopold (Eds.), *Child language*. Englewood Cliffs, N.J.: Prentice Hall, 1971. Pp. 52—56.]

Chomsky, C. S. *The acquisition of language from five to ten*. Cambridge, Mass.: MIT Press, 1969.

Chomsky, N. The formal nature of language. Appendix A in E. H. Lenneberg, *Biological foundations of language*. New York: Wiley, 1967.

Chomsky, N. *Language and mind*. New York: Harcourt, 1968.

Chomsky, N., & Miller, G. A. Introduction to the formal analysis of natural languages. In R. D. Luce, R. R. Bush, & E. Galanter (Eds.) *Handbook of mathematical psychology*. Vol. 2. New York: Wiley, 1963. Pp. 323—418.

Ervin, S. M. Imitation and structural change in children's language. In E. H. Lenneberg (Ed.), *New directions in the study of language*. Cambridge, Mass.: MIT Press, 1964. Pp. 163—189.

Hook, S. (Ed.) *Language and philosophy: A symposium*. New York: N.Y. Univ. Press, 1969.

Huxley, R., & Ingram, E. (Eds.) *Language acquisition: Models and methods*. New York: Academic Press, 1971.

Kelley, K. L. Early syntactic acquisition. P-3719, RAND Corp. Santa Monica, Calif., 1967.

Lenneberg, E. H. Understanding language without ability to speak: A case report, *Journal of Abnormal and Social Psychology*, 1962, *65*, 419—425.

Lenneberg, E. H. *Biological foundations of language*. New York: Wiley, 1967.

Lyons, J. *Introduction to theoretical linguistics*. London & New York: Cambridge Univ. Press, 1968.

McNeill, D. Developmental linguistics. In F. Smith & G. A. Miller (Eds.), *The genesis of language: A psycholinguistic approach*. Cambridge, Mass.: MIT Press, 1966. Pp. 15—87

McNeill, D. *The acquisition of language: The study of developmental psycholinguistics*. New York, Harper, 1970.

McNeill, D. The capacity for the ontogenesis of grammar. In D. Slobin (Ed.), *The ontogenesis of grammar*. New York: Academic Press, 1971.

Menyuk, P. 1969. *Sentences children use*. Cambridge, Mass.: MIT Press, 1969.

Miller, W. R., & Ervin, S. M. The development of grammar in child language. In U. Bellugi & R. Brown (Eds.) *The acquisition of language Monographs of the Society Research in Child Development*, 1964, *29* (1, Serial No. 92), 9—33.

Moeser, S. D. & Bregman, A. S. Imagery and language acquisition, *Journal of Verbal Learning and Verbal Behavior*, 1973, *12*, 91—98.

Moeser, S. D., & Bregman, A. S. The role of reference in the acquisition of a miniature artificial language. *Journal of Verbal Learning and Verbal Behavior*, 1972, *11*, 759—769.

Morton, J. What could possibly be innate? In J. Morton (Ed.), *Biological and social foundations of psycholinguistics*. London: Logos Press, 1971. Pp. 82—97.

Park, T. Z. Language acquisition in a Korean child. Working Paper, Psychologisches Institut, Universtät Münster, 1969.

Raffler-Engel, W. The LAD, our underlying unconscious and more on "felt sets." *Language Science*, 1970, *13*, 15—18.

Schlesinger, I. M. Learning grammar: From pivot to realization rule. In R. Huxley & E. Ingram (Eds.), *Studies in language acquisition: Models and methods*. New York: Academic Press, 1971. Pp. 79—89. (a)

Schlesinger, I. M. Production of utterances and language acquisition. In D. I. Slobin (Ed.), *The ontogenesis of grammar*. New York: Academic Press, 1971. Pp. 63—102.(b)

Shipley, E., Smith, C., & Gleitman, L. A study in the acquisition of language: Free responses to commands. *Language*, 1969, *45*, 322—342.

Sinclair, R. Sensorimotor patterns as a condition for the acquisition of syntax. In R. Huxley & E. Ingram (eds.), *Language acquisition: Models and methods*. New York: Academic Press, 1971. Pp. 75—76.

Skinner, B. F. *Verbal behavior*. New York: Appleton, 1957.

Slobin, D. I. Imitation and grammatical development in children. In N. S. Endler, L. R. Boulter, & H. Osser (Eds.), *Contemporary issues in developmental psychology*. New York: Holt, 1968. Pp. 437—443.

Slobin, D. I. Universals of grammatical development in children. In W. Levelt & G. B. Flores d'Aracais (Eds.), *Advances in psycholinguistic research*. Amsterdam: North-Holland Publ., 1970. Pp. 174—186.

Slobin, D. I., & Welsh, C. A. Elicited imitation as a research tool in developmental psycholinguistics. In C. S. Lavatel (Ed.), *Language training in early childhood education*. Urbana: Univ. of Illinois Press, 1971. Pp. 170—185.

Suppes, P. Semantics of context-free fragments of natural languages. Technical Report No. 171, Institute for Mathematical Studies in the Social Sciences, Stanford University, Stanford, Calif., 1970.

Weir, R. H. *Language in the crib*. The Hague: Mouton, 1962.

13. The Role of Cognitive Structures in Language Acquisition

H. Sinclair

The course of language acquisition is still largely unknown, and speculations about the relationship between linguistic competence and general cognitive competence are bound to reflect the author's adherence to a particular psychological or epistemological theory. In this paper, the role of cognitive structures in the language acquisition process is considered in the light of Piaget's epistemological theory, and language is seen as a specifically human creation, made possible by the more general human cognitive capacity for organizing experience in a way that allows man to produce genuine novelties, far surpassing a copy-type knowledge of his environment.

Introduction: Cognitive and Linguistic Development

To discuss the relationships between language and cognition in the present state of our knowledge of psycholinguistics is a hazardous undertaking. The course of language acquisition is still largely unknown, and any reflections on its relationship to the development of intelligence in general are bound to be speculative and influenced by the author's personal interests or adherence to some epistemological theory. In this paper the possible influence of language on cognition will not be discussed, and the role of cognitive structures in the language acquisition process will be considered in the light of Piaget's theory of cognitive development. Consequently, the term "cognitive structures" will be used in a Piagetian sense—that is, as coherent systems of mental operations, which allow the thinking person to arrive at concepts, to solve problems and come to conclusions (either in logic or about the real world surrounding him) without the person himself being necessarily aware of the operations he performs. These cognitive structures are supposed to be universal in their form, if not in their content, and all human beings, whatever their physical and cultural environment, are supposed to acquire them in the same chronological order and in a very similar manner. In many years of experimental and theoretical work, an impressive amount of evidence has been gathered about the way in which these cognitive structures are built up, as well as about their universality.

It is more difficult to state adherence to a specific theory as far as language, the other term of the relationship, is concerned. Since Chomsky refertilized the field of linguistics, new developments are occurring in rapid succession, and many issues remain controversial. Any model must have properties in common with the real phenomenon it represents; but a choice is made as to what properties are to be kept constant between model and reality—there is more to reality than what is in the model, just as there is more to the model than what is in reality. The choice implies the explicit exclusion of certain properties of the phenomenon, or their relegation to a secondary plane; as against that, the formalized properties of the model permit deductions that can be tested against reality. A model of a phenomenon is not, and is not claimed, to be necessarily a model of the production process, though there have to be compatibilities. Chomsky's essentially syntactic model appears to have more fundamental properties in common with the reality it represents—language in the fluent native speaker—than other models, and it also seems to be more compatible than other proposals with possible process models.

A first question has to be asked: Is it possible to dissociate knowledge of language from other knowledge? In at least one sense, the answer is yes. Although fortunately it is becoming more and more difficult to find deaf children who at the age of primary schooling possess virtually no language at all (neither a natural language in its written form nor any type of conventional sign language), several research workers have conclusively shown that such children solve cognitive problems in the same way as do normal children, and at only slightly later ages, provided the problems are adequately presented in a nonverbal manner (Furth, 1965, 1966). This confirms Piaget's theory that knowledge has its roots in activity, and that its logical organization is not derived from language. Much information, of course, is transmitted verbally, but knowledge in the deeper sense, those operations and concepts that make it possible to absorb information and fit it into a meaningful framework, do not stem from language. This does not mean that such knowledge can be acquired without representation. Representation is what makes it possible to plan future behavior and to recapitulate past actions; these capacities are prerequisites for any kind of thinking process. How deaf children arrive at sufficiently precise and mobile representations is a fascinating problem; but it is clear that they can do so without the help of what to hearing children is the most convenient system of representation, namely, language.

Thought structures can be elaborated in the absence of language. Can language be acquired in the absence of intellectual development? One manifestly does not have to be a mature thinker to be able to talk; two-year-olds talk, and so do mentally backward persons—up to a point. The difficulty lies in the definition of "up to a point." Recently some psycholinguists (C. Chomsky, 1969; Ferreiro, 1971; Sinclair & Ferreiro, 1970) have shown that certain linguistic patterns are not understood in their generality by children until they are six or even older. For example, temporal succession is for young children linked to succession of enunciation, and sentences such as *The girl goes upstairs when the boy has parked the car* are at certain stages of cognitive development interpreted as if the girl goes upstairs first and the boy parks the car afterward (Ferreiro, 1971). It remains to be shown that retarded children in their early teens, with a mental age of, say, below 6, are incapable of understanding and constructing such sentences, although this would seem plausible. From Lenneberg's (1964, 1967) account of language in mongoloid children it appears that retarded children acquire the basic structures of their mother tongue, although they take much more time to do so than normal children, but that they lack the organizational capacities that would permit them to deal with sentences such as the one just mentioned. All these facts point to the conclusion that language and cognition can be clearly separated only in one sense: intellectual development is possible without language, but language acquisition is bound to the elaboration of cognitive structures in general.

In Piaget's theory, language is considered to be one of the manifestations of the human capacity for representing things and events in their absence, other means of doing so being gestures, drawings, mental imagery, and dramatic or symbolic play. As far as these representative activities can be observed in actual behavior, they start more or less at the same time—in, of course, primitive ways. During their second year, children start to "pretend," to act "as if;" they start to imitate activities of adults or older children, such as turning the steering wheel of a car, playing a ball game, and so on, even when no such activities are going on in their presence (imitation in the presence of the model starts, of course, much earlier). Studies of spontaneous drawings (Luquet, 1927) and of mental images in their observable form (Piaget & Inhelder, 1966) have shown that children's representational activities are directed by knowledge of what is represented. For example, at a stage where children's understanding of spatial relationships is limited to relationships within a figure or even part of a figure, and not extended to a figure and its larger framework, children may draw the chimney of a house perpendicular to the sloping roof instead of perpendicular to the base; or they may draw the level of the liquid in a bottle as parallel to its bottom, whatever the position of the bottle in regard to its support. Similarly, children who do not yet have the concept of length and measurement make peculiar drawings of what they think a curved bit of wire will look like if it is pulled straight: just underneath the curved model wire, they draw a straight line that joins the wire's extremities (and is therefore far shorter than the model). Cognitively more advanced children, although of course incapable of drawing a line exactly the right length, announce immediately that the extremities of the wire when pulled straight will go well beyond those of the curved wire.

Representative activities, especially when they require some kind of prevision or anticipation, are clearly under the influence of the subject's knowledge about what has to be represented. Can one generalize and suppose that the same is true for language, and reduce the relationship between language and cognition to a direct one-way dependency of language acquisition on cognitive development?

Cognitive Structures

Looking somewhat more closely at cognitive development, the first remark that must be made is that psychologists have most often been interested in differences between individuals or between groups of individuals. Piaget is one of the rare psychologists who has studied what is common to all normal human beings during their formative years—that is to say, he has studied the acquisition of fundamental, epistemologically important concepts. Roughly speaking, these concepts are of two different kinds: on the one hand, logicomathematical concepts, whose adequacy can be tested only against the logical system as a whole, and, on the other hand, concepts about the physical world, whose validity can be tested against reality. The latter, however, need the logical framework, if only because without it, one would not know how to go about setting up experiments to test an hypothesis, nor how to organize the outcome of the experiment so that it allows new hypotheses. Young children may affirm that "bits of wood float because they're light," and that "boats float because they're strong and heavy," and when they are asked whether a small key will float, or a big block of wood, they may assert that the key will float since it's light, and the big block will sink since it's heavy. Such children have not yet acquired the concept of density, but neither have they elaborated the logical structure that would allow them to set up experiments. In fact, for them there is no reason at all why the floating of boats should have anything to do with the floating of a bit of wood, nor any reason to see a contradiction in the statement that the first floats because it's heavy, and the second because it's light. Although not acquired in exactly the same way, both types of concepts are acquired through interaction with the environment—with people and with things. The interaction principle seems easily acceptable as far as concepts such as weight, gravity, inertia, and so on, are concerned, but may be less so as far as logical concepts go, such as class inclusion and intersection. According to Piaget, these different types of concepts are linked by the fact that they all have their roots in the preverbal sensorimotor period; actions such as putting smaller blocks on top of larger ones, of assembling and separating objects, are the common bases for, on the one hand, logical notions of relations and classes and, on the other hand, physical concepts such as size and weight. Several studies (Bovet, 1968; Dasen, 1970; Opper, 1970) have shown that these concepts are indeed universal, at least up to a certain level of elaboration. The speed of their acquisition and their complete form may differ according to gross cultural differences, but the cognitive operations concerned are essentially the same. The knowledge acquired is built up actively, by generalizing and abstracting from actions; it is not the result of more and more faithful copying of the environment. Obviously, the baby has to be born without grave physical defects, and equally obviously, the quality of the environment may either favor or hinder development. Extreme poverty, emotional neglect, and many other deficiencies may distort, retard, or stop development. Reliable and likeable people have to be around, food and cover have to be provided; but the specific properties of the environment do not seem to change the nature or the mode of acquisition of the basic concepts. To give but one example, the well-known activity of babies who throw all the toys out of their playpen (or who throw behind them the sticks and pebbles with which they were playing) and then scream for the adult to put them back, is no imitation. It is a socially satisfying and exciting game, but it is more than that: it constitutes one of the sources from which number concepts will be built. Every throw increases the pile of objects out of reach, and after a number of throws, the playpen universe of objects is reduced to *none* and the outside universe comprises *all*. The baby quickly learns that this result is repeated every time he goes through the same series of actions; after a few times, he will start to scream even before he has thrown the last object. Much social behavior, and many skills and pieces of information need to be learned by copying—but even such acquisitions often must be inserted into more basic patterns. Almost all need some framework of temporal succession, spatial construction, and hierarchical relationships. On the other hand, these concepts are not innate in the sense of being preprogrammed in the nervous system and only needing activation by an environment that would simply act as a catalyst. The many intermediary stages through which the concepts and mental operations pass and which sometimes seem totally aberrant in adult eyes show that cognitive development is a constructive process. The child generalizes and makes abstractions from his actions; every step forward remodels what was already acquired, and there is just as much interaction with the external environment as there is interaction between action patterns and, later, thought patterns.

Representation

Superficially, the same is not true of language. Every child learns his mother tongue, and languages can be very different one from the other. Moreover, no child learns to talk (some doubtful anecdotes notwithstanding) unless he hears other people talk. In human language, nothing resembling the basic song pattern of certain birds exists. Chaffinches, when reared in a soundproofed room or deafened at birth elaborate what Thorpe (1969, p. 186) calls "the most elementary schema of what is normally regarded as the song of the species." (See also Notlebohm, Chap. 5, this volume.) Though we cannot do any experiments with infants in soundproofed rooms, congenitally deaf babies certainly do not develop anything resembling such a pattern, and there are some examples of hearing children brought up by deaf parents who do not acquire language before they are given special training. Language acquisition seems to depend on a specific exterior model to a much higher degree than cognitive development.

It has often been supposed that the main factor in learning to talk is being able to imitate. In a certain sense this is true; superficially, because the infant has to learn to imitate the adult speech patterns. More profoundly, language learning is also bound to imitation, since in Piaget's theory all representation is considered to stem from imitation. Any specific action of the baby needs to be adapted to whatever particular object he is handling; to quote Furth (1970), "Hand—eye coordination illustrates both the focusing of vision and the motoric imitation vis-à-vis the outline and shape of the particular thing to which the hand-eye coordination is applied." At a later stage, straightforward imitation of an adult's gestures or any other external event becomes possible in the presence of the model; subsequently, it becomes possible in the absence of the model; and later still imitation no longer needs external gestures but becomes internalized—things and events can now be represented by mental images as well as by external behavior. However, for the representing symbol to have a meaning, it is necessary for the child to have acquired knowledge about what is represented; and this knowledge does not come from motoric or sensory accommodation to particular instances of objects and events, but from the coordinations of action patterns that concern the general structure of different actions rather than their particular form in one specific instance. *Meaning* implies *knowing*, which is very different from reacting to signals. Animals can be taught to react to verbal and other signals, but for them these signals do not *mean* the event—they *are* the event, or part of the event.

The capacity for representation, in the sense of the creation, the use, and the understanding of symbols as meaningful entities, depends therefore on the development of knowledge about whatever the symbols represent. This characteristic of symbolic behavior is shared by all forms of representation, language as well as gestures, play, pretend-games, and so on. Observable behavior confirms this tie-in with knowledge: no symbolic activity is present before the baby has reached a final stage of sensorimotor activity, the point where knowing as dissociated from acting starts (some time during the second year of life). As far as the absence of a certain type of behavior can ever be demonstrated, extensive research done by Inhelder, Lezine, Sinclair, and Stambak (1972) on children between the ages of 10 months and 3 years has shown that the beginnings of imitative representation in the absence of the model, some forms of "pretending," and language do not appear in babies before they succeed in Piaget's tasks of object permanency (Piaget, 1937).

All meaningful symbolic behavior is therefore double-faced. It is intimately linked to the subject's knowledge-through-action (which is, even for babies, far more general than just knowledge of one particular action and its outcome, and which for adults can be freed from any particular content as an uninterpreted calculus). At the same time, it is derived from imitation in the broad sense that Piaget gives to this term, that is, the making present of a particular event or object. Beyond the period of sensorimotor intelligence, all behavior comprises components of representation and of knowing. For some activities, the representational component, and therefore the medium chosen for the symbols, may be more important (theatre, painting, poetry), for others the knowledge component may predominate (mathematics, natural sciences); but usually the two aspects cannot be dissociated except in theory.

Inside this complex of representational activities, intimately linked both to cognitive structures and to imitation, language has a place apart. In much symbolic behavior, the subject can invent his own symbols and make his own rules, but to communicate verbally, he has to use the language of his community. Moreover, other symbolic behavior may imply the learning of techniques (drawing) and creative activity within a common framework (dramatic play, games), but no knowledge comparable to that of the complex grammatical systems of human languages (though a special position is occupied by games such as chess—de Saussure's favorite analogy to language). In fact, language is not only a means of communicating and representing what is known; it is also in itself an object to be known—and a highly complex object at that.

On the one hand, language belongs to a class of typically human behaviors that imply meaningful representation and are therefore dependent on cognitive functioning as well as on imitation. On the other hand, language is a productive system that combines meaningful symbols according to rules. These rules must be acquired and applied in talking and understanding; this is in itself a cognitive activity.

Meaning

The link between lexicon and knowing is so obvious that it scarcely needs elaboration. Everyone would agree that children and adults from nonintellectual environments are not likely to talk about *algorithms* and *integrate*—they have no knowledge of such things. However, if they have heard these expressions, and understood that the first is a noun and the second a verb, they can use them in grammatically correct sentences; but then language is not being used as a meaningful means of communication. The question is less trivial if we examine such words as *more, less, all, none, to, unto* (Donaldson & Wales, 1970; Piaget & Inhelder, 1959; Sinclair, 1967). These expressions are frequent in everyday usage, and children will use them in correct sentences, but they may give different meanings to these words according to their level of understanding of the logical principles involved. The same is clearly true of words such as *force, energy, mass, weight*, which have popular meanings as well as scientific meanings; the latter imply much greater knowledge than the former. Even the "everyday" meanings undergo modifications as children develop intellectually (Piaget & Garcia, 1971). The study of the semantic implications of these words at various levels of development tells us something about cognitive development rather than about language acquisition. It is, however, possible that future studies of the semantic content of different expressions may help us to develop some hypotheses about the structure of the lexicon.

The meaningful use of quantifiers and other "logical" expressions occurs early, well before the corresponding concepts have been fully elaborated; the meaning changes with the elaboration of the concepts. In these cases, linguistic complexity is low, and cognitive complexity is higher. The opposite also occurs; as Slobin (1972) remarks, linguistic complexity does not necessarily go together with conceptual complexity. Slobin quotes a study by Margaret Omar on the acquisition of Egyptian Arabic, where noun plurals are difficult to form correctly even for children as old as age 15. The reason for this is to be found in the complexity of Arabic plural formation, not in the difficulty of the concept of plurality.

The intricacy of the psychological relation between the meanings of linguistic elements, which are linked to knowledge and at the same time to imitation, should not cause surprise. It is a direct consequence of what de Saussure called the double-sidedness of the meaning-bearing elements. Signifier (sound complex) and signified (meaning) together form *le signe*, and they organize each other. *Vale* and *bale* have different meanings; *v* and *b* are distinct phonemes in English (although not in Spanish). *Tug* and *gut* have a different order of phonemes; they have different meanings. Meanings change as knowledge (logical, physical, or social) changes; in extreme cases (as in deaf children without any language), there may be knowledge without verbal signifiers; conversely, in pure parroting there may be signifiers without knowledge.

Grammar

The intricate role of cognitive structures in language acquisition becomes even more difficult to define when we consider the acquisition of syntax. Syntax, however, is essential for human language. Whatever can be said about meaning of linguistic elements and knowledge is also true of nonlinguistic signifiers—such as the use of objects-that-stand-for-something-else in play, or gestures. The "meaning" of a pebble used to represent a car changes with the child's knowledge of cars, and this change of meaning can be seen in his use of the pebble. Syntax, by contrast, is specific to language (leaving aside artificial languages, such as mathematical notation). It is also, as Chomsky has argued, independent of meaning in the following sense: "Given the instrument, language, and its formal devices, we can and should investigate their semantic function ... ; but we cannot, apparently, find semantic absolutes, known in advance of grammar, that can be used to determine the objects of grammar in any way [N. Chomsky, 1957, p. 101]." Sentences comprise de Saussure's double-sided elements; but where de Saussure stressed the elements as pairings of sound sequences and meanings, transformational grammar stresses the sentence as such a pairing. The rules of syntax generate abstract structures that permit these pairings. Languages comprise, theoretically, an indefinitely large number of sentences that are grammatically correct. However, it is assumed that there are only a limited number of operations used for the generation (in the mathematical sense) of these sentences. One of the important features of these operations is, therefore, the existence of recursive rules, that is, the possibility that some of the rules are applicable several times in the generation of the same sentence. For example, we can construct a series of relative clauses: *The man saw the car that hit the woman that held a child that carried a kitten that . . . etc.* Another important feature of the linguistic structures generated by the rules is that these structures are not actual sentences, but are more abstract patterns, which have to be rearranged and filled in to produce sentences. An "underlying" structure can be arranged in different ways: *The boy broke the window, The window was broken by the boy,* and *It was the boy who broke the window* are three different arrangements of the same underlying structure. Such secondary operations are called transformations. Generally, these transformations do not change the basic semantic interpretation of the underlying pattern. Finally, it is supposed that however different the sentences of different languages may be, all languages make use of the same types of operations for the construction of grammatical sentences. Notice that although, according to this theory, syntax is independent of lexical meaning, this does not imply that it is ontogenetically prior to meaning. The opposite appears to be true, since meaningful representation by gestures and in symbolic play precedes language, and holophrastic utterances precede two-element utterances.

The fundamental characteristics of transformational grammars reflect the linguistic competence of the fluent, adult speaker; they are also linked to the acquisition of language by the child. Just as Piaget, in contrast with many other psychologists, is interested in the way the universal cognitive structures are developed, Chomsky has revived the interest in linguistic universals, in contrast with other linguists who consider the description of what is particular to one language as their main task.

> *A theory of linguistic structure that aims for explanatory adequacy incorporates an account of linguistic universals, and it attributes tacit knowledge of these universals to the child. It proposes, then, that the child approaches the data with the presumption that they are drawn from a language of a certain antecedently well-defined type, his problem being to determine which of the (humanly) possible languages is that of the community in which he is placed. Language learning would be impossible unless this were the case. The important question is: What are the initial assumptions concerning the nature of language that the child brings to language learning, and how detailed and specific is the innate schema . . . that gradually becomes more explicit and differentiated as the child learns the language? [Chomsky, 1965, p. 27]*

But for the word "innate," Genevan psycholinguists will agree that this is indeed the crucial problem. In our view, however, it is precisely the fact that this initial schema is not innate in the generally accepted sense of the word (although it may be so in the sense of a predisposition) that can provide hypotheses about the child's initial assumptions.

Language Acquisition

Communication takes place as early as during the first year of life, but it is at first a sort of direct, person-to-person communication, by which feelings of pleasure, displeasure, and later surprise, desire, boredom, and so on, are transmitted, without representation of something seen as outside the subject. Children do not talk in the sense of saying something about something before they have the first signs of representational activity by other means—such as feeding a doll with an empty spoon, pushing the spoon several times into the doll's face, or pretending to be asleep, suddenly bursting out laughing when the adult seems to take it seriously. In gesture, posture, and play the first couplings of symbols and meanings are present before the appearance of the "first word."

Holophrases are a step toward conventional language in the sense that the child produces a sound sequence (however approximately) that he has heard from others and in which he has discovered a meaning, that is, a representation of some object or event, and not only a signal that the person producing the sounds is happy, annoyed, tired, and so on. These first words are already double-sided in de Saussure's sense; the meaning face is linked to the sound face, but mainly by the child's own action patterns and his attribution of these patterns to other people. The (for adults) imprecise and shifting character of the meaning of the first words is due to these subjective generalizations: the general, global character of the action on the one hand, and the specific instances of the action on the other. As far as meaning is concerned, these words still resemble the more personal symbols used in play, which can also quickly change (a pebble can be chosen at one moment to represent a car, but at another it can be made to represent the policeman). As far as the sound sequence is concerned, these words are already a reproduction of conventional sequences. And as for communication, they are clearly an effort to say "something about something" rather than just "something." These remarks do not apply to certain words that may have been taught and learned in the same manner as animals learn to obey commands. Such training is probably rare; most children do not go in for copying (even if it brings them rewards) without some active construction.

It is only after these first couplings of meanings and conventional sound complexes that two-element utterances appear. By that time, children have reached a certain level of intelligent activity that shows the structural properties brought to light by Piaget and that certainly cannot be reduced to a list of actions and situations. The organization of this intelligence-in-action is the basis for all later cognitive constructs, which elaborate on different levels this initial type of organization, whose structure resembles, as do the more elaborated structures, a mathematical group. We would like to suggest that this "group" of action patterns also serves as a heuristic model for the acquisition of syntax and that it is precisely what the child (every child!) has learned during his first 18 months or so that provides him with the necessary and sufficient assumptions to start this acquisition. The constraints on the form that human languages can take relate to characteristics of the human mind, to cognitive universals; and these constraints are what makes it possible for children to start talking during their second year and to go about language acquisition in the way they do.

Many studies of child language in different parts of the world have shown the similarity between children and between different languages, from holophrases (e.g., *aplu, alle-alle, allgone*, indicating absence or disappearance) to two- and three-element utterances (*That big truck,* **ça gros camion**, *Want more candy,* **veux encore bonbon**). During this first period, at least, one gets the impression, confirmed by many observations (cf. Slobin, 1970) that all children go about their language-learning task in the same way: paying attention to, and producing, certain features of the speech they hear around them, but not all; creating rules that have something to do with adult sentence patterns, but whose results are far from a parrot-like copy.

Analyses of very early spontaneous utterances are often directed by a theoretical choice regarding which type of fundamental categories appear the most important. Some investigators analyze the first semantic relationships (such as possession, localization) that can be inferred from early child speech (Bloom, 1970) or more generally, in children's lexical competence (Parisi and Antinucci, 1970); others are interested in the prelanguage, babbling period, during which phonological categories are elaborated (Braine, 1971). From many of these accounts of early language behavior, it appears that something very like the progressive integration and differentiation of action- and thought-patterns as described by Piaget takes place in language learning. Ervin (1964), for example, has noticed how irregular plurals such as *feet* appear at first as isolated forms, apparently without any connection to the rest of the plural system that is being elaborated. Subsequently, these forms are absorbed into the system, and appear as *feets, foots,* and even *feetses*. A little later they will reappear in their correct form, but this time, one supposes, they are exceptions to a rule rather than isolated items. Similar phenomena are observed in the account by Klima and Bellugi (1966) of negation formulation: *can't* and *won't* appear as unanalyzed entities before the appearance of *can* and *will;* the auxiliary system takes a long time to construct.

Though such analyses confirm the hypothesis of an active construction, subject to constraints as to what the structure can absorb and what has to be temporarily left aside, they cannot inform us directly about the basic structural strategies themselves.

An Experimental Approach

To devise experimental methods capable of giving us at least some hints about the basic strategies and assumptions, we considered the possibility of presenting very young children with grammatically correct utterances, resembling what one-and-a-half and two-year-old children themselves produce. We hoped that, as N. Chomsky (1961) says, they might "Attempt to impose an interpretation [on them],

exploiting whatever feature of grammatical structure is preserved [p. 303],"
assuming that the basic strategies would be reapplied, even if the subjects were no
longer at the very first beginnings of language acquisition (they were between 2
years, 10 months and 6-years old). We presented these children with utterances
such as *Boy push girl, Girl push boy, Push boy girl,* and so on, in all six possible word
orders, and *Boy box open, Box open boy,* and so on, and we asked them to guess what
was meant, to show with toys the meaning they guessed at (Sinclair & Bronckart,
1972). Notice that these utterances are much more aberrant in French than in
English, where *push* can be both an imperative and a noun, and where nouns,
especially in the plural, often appear without articles.

A succession of strategies emerged from this experiment; the two earliest types
take the following form: either the children make the boy and the girl doll walk on
the table, saying, *they take a walk together,* or they put the two dolls one next to the
other and then proceed to give them a push, remarking, *I push them down, they both
fall.* At this level, word order does not seem to influence solutions. Subsequently,
one of the nouns is taken as acting on the other: that is, the boy pushes the girl or
vice versa. In the case of the word order noun—verb—noun, and especially for
Boy open box, the sequence is interpreted very early on as agent—action—object; but
in the case of two animate nouns either following or preceding the verb, we notice
the following strategies: first, the noun nearest to the very is interpreted as the
agent, whether it precedes or follows the verb; then, the noun nearest to the verb is
interpreted as the object. In a final stage, the proximity link between verb and
noun loses its importance, and the first noun is always taken to be the agent, the
second the object, whatever the position of the verb (for such strategies, cf. Bever,
1970).

From these results, we would like to propose a tentative reconstruction of the
earliest segmentation, functional interpretation, and syntactic construction procedures. A first rule can be formulated as follows: Take each utterance as consisting
of two parts. An utterance is either the description of a state of an object or a person
(examples in spontaneous speech of 2-year olds would be *Truck broke, Birdie there*)
or it is the expression of an action on an object or a person, this action being desired
by the child, or being performed by him in the present (examples in spontaneous
speech: *Hit ball, Coat off*). Notice that it is not necessary that these segments correspond to parts of speech in adult grammar; an action can be represented by what
to us is an adverb, an adjective, or even a noun. At this stage, word order often
follows adult patterns, although perhaps less often than has sometimes been asserted. Order can be modified if part of the event is particularly interesting: **Cassée
poupée** and **Poupée cassée** (*Broke doll* and *Doll broke*) describe the same event,
but with different topicalization. To speculate even further, we can adopt Miller's
idea that recursivity in grammar is mirrored in the human capacity for commenting on a topic, then commenting on the comment, and so on. From this point of
view, topicalization phenomena would acquire a more profound significance. On
the one hand, the early capacity of switching topic and comment may prepare the
later capacity to comment on the topic—comment combination (**Poupée cassée**

parterre *Doll broke on floor*) and announce recursivity; on the other hand, switching topic and comment may prepare rearrangement or transformational operations.

Secondly, a system of rules elaborates the structure of utterances describing actions on objects or persons; at this level, such utterances are considered as consisting of three parts. One rule would be: Look for the action word and for semantic properties. According to the semantic properties of the verb, choose either one of the two following rules: Establish an agent—action proximity link, add whatever is left as the object; or establish an object—action proximaty link, add whatever is left as the agent. Again, ordering can be modified by topicalization.

It is only in a third stage that a new system of rules becomes established: A sentence consists of two parts, a subject and a predicate. Both parts, but especially the predicate, may be composed of subparts; in the case of a "transitive" action, the verb phrase consists of the verb itself and its object. At this stage, reordering for topicalization will leave the verb phrase undivided.

We were especially interested in the first two types of solutions, which seem to recur, at different ages and in different experiments, whenever sentences proposed for interpretation present a difficulty that at the age in question has not yet been mastered.

For example, most children between age $2\frac{1}{2}$ and 3 have no difficulty in correctly acting out sentences such as *The boy plays with the ball*, or *The girl pets the dog* (though a fairly long introductory period is necessary to make them understand the instruction). They can even act out the two sentences if they have to wait until the experimenter has said them both. However, if we join two sentences with a pronoun, the difficulty of finding the word to which the pronoun refers, or perhaps even the general difficulty of understanding that the third person pronouns may refer to words previously said, seems to reactivate the two primitive strategies we described. The sentence *the boy plays with the ball and then he puts the ball into the basket* is acted in the following manner by our youngest subjects: the boy doll is made to kick the ball, and then the child himself puts the ball into the basket; or, alternatively, the boy doll is made to jump into the basket. The second part of the sentence is thus interpreted either as an action to be performed by the child himself, or as an "intransitive" action performed by what grammatically is the object of the verb.

These behavior patterns cannot be explained by manipulatory difficulties, since they occur only in sentences with pronouns and since the same sentence, but with the subject expressed by a noun, is correctly understood. Nor can the action-performed-by-the-child pattern be explained in the sense that boys would take the pronoun *he* to refer to themselves (and girls *she*), since we presented both sentences with *boy-he* and with *girl-she*, and in each case an equal number of boys and girls chose the solution of taking the pronoun to refer to themselves. If we make the sentences more difficult, for example, by using reversible sentences such as *the girl pushes the boy* instead of irreversible ones such as *the boy plays with the ball*, we find that these interpretation patterns (the child performing the action himself or the verb being interpreted as an intransitive verb) occur even beyond the age of three.

We therefore feel justified in considering these patterns not as accidental solutions that may occur from time to time when children are distracted or tired, but as genuine strategies they use when confronted with an utterance they have difficulty in understanding. Some of the first rules for producing and understanding utterances might therefore be the following:

1. An utterance consists of two parts. It expresses the description of a state and names a person or an object and a property thereof.

2. An utterance consists of two parts. It indicates a desired or presently-being-performed action; it names the action and the object thereof.

If we suppose these rules to be part of the basic assumptions young children have about the nature of human language, we can look for the way they may be derived from the heuristic model provided by sensorimotor intelligence. Speaking in general terms, the young baby does not differentiate between action, object, and subject; in the first stages of sensorimotor development, reflex or action patterns constitute unanalyzable wholes. It is only gradually, by performing the same action on a number of different objects (e.g., shaking rattles, spoons, dolls, etc.) and different actions on the same object (e.g., shaking, licking, throwing a rattle) that action and object become differentiated. Similarly, only gradually does the baby understand that not only is he himself an actor, but that other people act too. It would appear that, at a different level, language patterns follow this development. Holophrases form unanalyzable entities. They are followed by two- and three-element utterances that indicate differentiation between agent and action, on the one hand, and between action and object, on the other.

Attempts to link the child's construction of grammar to his previous construction of practical intelligence may seem far fetched. However, they would seem to merit serious examination. Either linguistic structures are innate in a precise sense, or universal cognitive structures, acquired before the onset of language, provide the child with the necessary assumptions about the nature of human languages. Except for possible combinations of these two hypotheses, no other supposition seems tenable. Notice that in either case, neurological bases for human organizational capacities are assumed, and some challenging suggestions have recently been made on this point by McNeill (1971).

Both Piaget's models of cognitive structures at the different levels of development and Chomsky's linguistic model suggest that the thinking and talking person operates with covert rules of a mathematical type. At least one writer has drawn an explicit parallel between arithmetic and linguistic competence (Lenneberg, 1971). However, many objections can be formulated as to the justification for the use of such models for the language acquisition process. First, models never represent all the relationships of the phenomenon represented, and one can doubt whether a particular model represents the fundamental features (cf. Antinucci & Parisi, Chap.

11, this volume). Second, a model of an existing phenomenon does not necessarily reflect the way the phenomenon is produced, nor does it claim to do so. Third, a formal resemblance between two models does not necessarily reflect an actual relationship between the two phenomena they represent. Nonetheless, from the little we know about language acquisition, the prudent conclusion can be drawn that language acquisition is closely linked to cognition in two fundamental ways: first because meaning implies knowing, and second because the linguistic rule system is an example of human organizational abilities that permit not only the construction of grammar but also that of physics and logic.

References

Bever, T. G. The cognitive basis for linguistic structures. In J. R. Hayes (Ed.), *Cognition and the development of language.* New York: Wiley, 1970. Chap. 9, pp. 279—352.

Bloom, L. *Language development: Form and function in emerging grammars.* Cambridge, Mass.: MIT Press, 1970.

Bovet, M. Études interculturelles du développement intellectuel et processus d'apprentissage. *Revue Suisse de Psychologie,* 1968, *27*(3/4), 189—200.

Braine, M. An inquiry into the nature of the morphophoneme in preliterate children. Linguistic Institute Symposium on Psycholinguistics, Buffalo, N.Y., 1971.

Chomsky, C. *The acquisition of syntax in children from 5 to 10.* Cambridge, Mass.: MIT Press, 1969.

Chomsky, N. *Syntactic structures.* The Hague: Mouton, 1957.

Chomsky, N. *Aspects of the theory of syntax.* Cambridge, Mass.: MIT Press, 1965.

Chomsky, N. Some methodological remarks on generative grammar. *Word,* 1961, *17*, 219—239. Reprinted in graham Wilson (Ed.), *A linguistics reader.* New York: Harper & Row, 1967. Pp. 290—308.

Dasen, P. Cognitive development in aborigines of Central Australia. Unpublished doctoral dissertation, Australian National University, Canberra, 1970.

Donaldson, M., & Wales, R. The acquisition of some relational terms. In J. R. Hayes (Ed.), *Cognition and the development of language.* New York: Wiley, 1970. Chap. 7, pp. 109—135.

Ervin, S. Imitation and structural changes in children's language. In E. H. Lenneberg (Ed.), *New directions in the study of language.* Cambridge, Mass.: MIT Press, 1964.

Ferreiro, E. *Les relations temporelles dans le langage de l'enfant.* Geneva: Droz, 1971.

Furth, H. G. The influence of language and experience on the discovery and use of logical symbols. *British Journal of Psychology,* 1965, *56*, 381—390.

Furth, H. G. *Thinking without language.* New York: Free Press, 1966.

Furth, H. G. On language and knowing in Piaget's developmental theory. *Human Development,* 1970, *13*, 241—257.

Inhelder, B., Lezine, I., Sinclair, H., & Stambak, M. Les débuts de la fonction symbolique. *Archives de Psychologie,* 1972, *41*, 187—243.

Klima, E. S., & Bellugi, U. Syntactic regularities in the speech of children. In J. Lyons & R. J. Wales (Eds.), *Psycholinguistics papers, proceedings of the 1966 Edinburgh conference.* Edinburgh: Edinburgh Univ. Press, 1966. Pp. 183—207.

Lenneberg, E. H. Primitive stages of language development in mongolism. *Harvard Educational Review,* 1964, *34*, 152—177.

Lenneberg, E. H. *Biological foundations of language.* New York: Wiley, 1967.

Lenneberg, E. H. Of language knowledge, apes, and brains. *Journal of Psycholinguistic Research,* 1971, *1*, 1—29.

Luquet, G. H. *Le dessin enfantin.* Paris: Presses Universitaires de France, 1927.

McNeill, D. Sentences as biological processes. Paper presented at the C.N.R.S. conference on Psycholinguistics, Paris, 1971.

Opper, S. Intellectual development in Thailand. Unpublished doctoral dissertation, Cornell University, 1970.

Parisi, D., & Antinucci, F. Lexical competence. In G. B. Flores d'Arcais & W. J. Levelt (Eds.), *Advances in psycholinguistics*. Amsterdam: North-Holland Publ., 1970. Pp. 197—210.

Piaget, J. *La construction du réel chez l'enfant*. Neuchâtel: Delachaux & Niestlé, 1937.

Piaget, J., & Garcia, R. Les explications causales. *Études d'Épistémologie Génétique*. 1971, *26*.

Piaget, J., & Inhelder, B. *La genèse des structures logiques élémentaires*. Neuchâtel: Delachaux & Niestlé, 1959.

Piaget, J., & Inhelder, B. *L'image mentale chez l'enfant*. Paris: Presse Universitaires de France, 1966.

Sinclair, H. *Langage et operations. Sous-systemes linguistiques et opérations concrètes*. Paris: Dunod, 1967.

Sinclair, H., & Bronckart, J. P. SVO: A linguistic universal? *Journal of Experimental Child Psychology*, 1972, *14*, 329—348.

Sinclair, H., & Ferreiro, E. Compréhension, production et répétition de phrases au mode passif. *Archives de Psychologie*, 1970, *40*(160), 1—42.

Slobin, D. Universals of grammatical development in children. In G. B. Flores d'Arcais & W. J. Levelt (Eds.), *Advances in psycholinguistics*. Amsterdam: North-Holland Publ., 1970. Pp. 174—184.

Slobin, D. Cognitive prerequisites for the development of grammar. In C. A. Ferguson & D. I. Slobin (Eds.), *Studies of child language development*. New York: Holt, 1972. Pp. 175—209.

Thorpe, W. H. In A. Koestler & J. R. Smythies (Eds.), *Beyond reductionism*. London: Hutchinson, 1969.

14. Learning How to Mean

M. A. K. Halliday

Adult language comprises three interrelated systems, phonological, lexicogrammatical (vocabulary, morphology, syntax), and semantic. Language development studies in the 1960s focused mainly on the lexicogrammatical level; they were also predominantly psycholinguistic in their orientation. More recently, interest has extended into semantics; the present paper is concerned with the learning of meaning, and proposes a complementary approach in sociolinguistic terms.

The paper suggests a socio-semantic interpretation of language development, based on the intensive study of one child, Nigel, from 9 months to 2½ years. Nigel first developed (Phase I) a two-level system, having sounds and meanings but no words or structures, in which the meanings derived from the elementary social functions of interaction with others, satisfaction of needs and the like. This continued to expand for 6–9 months, at which time the child entered the stage of transition to the adult language (Phase II, corresponding to what is generally taken as the starting point). This was characterized by the interpolation of a lexicogrammatical level between meaning and sound, and by the mastery of the principle of dialogue, the adoption and assignment of speech roles. It was also marked by a generalization of the initial set of social functions to form a basic opposition between "language as learning" and "language as doing."

The transition was considered complete when the child had effectively replaced his original two-level system by a three-level one and moved from monologue into dialogue; he then entered the adult system (Phase III). He could now build up the meaning potential of the adult language, and would continue to do so all his life. From a sociolinguistic point of view the major step consisted in once again reinterpreting the concept of "function" so that it became the organizing principle of the adult semantic system, being built into the heart of language in the form of the ideational (representational, referential, cognitive) and the interpersonal (expressive-conative, stylistic, social) components of meaning. All utterances in adult speech contain both these components, which are mapped on to each other by the structure-forming agency of the grammar. The original social functions survive in their concrete sense as types of situation and setting, the social contexts in which language serves in the transmission of culture to the child.

Introduction

Considered in the perspective of language development as a whole, the latest period of intensive study in this field—the last decade and more—has been characterized by what may, in time, come to seem a rather one-sided concentration on grammatical structure. The question that has most frequently been asked is "How does the child acquire structure?"[1] The implication has been that this is really the heart of the language learning process; and also perhaps, in the use of the term *acquisition*, that structure, and therefore language itself, is a commodity of some kind that the child has to gain possession of in the course of maturation.

The dominant standpoint has been a psycholinguistic one, and the dominant issue, at least in the United States where much of the most important work has been carried out, has been between "nativist" and "environmentalist" interpretations (Osser, 1970). There seems, however, to be no necessary connection between these as general philosophical positions and the particular models of the processes involved in the learning of linguistic structure that have been most typically associated with them (cf. Braine, 1971). The nativist view lays more stress on a specific innate language-learning capacity; it does not follow from this that the child necessarily learns by setting up hypothetical rules of grammar and matching them against what he hears, but there has been a widely-held interpretation along these lines. Environmentalist views, by contrast, emphasize the aspect of language learning that relates it to other learning tasks, and stress its dependence on environmental conditions; again, this is often assumed to imply an associationist, stimulus–response model of the learning process, although there is no essential connection between the two.

In the investigation of how the child learns grammatical structure, attention has naturally been focused on the nature of the earliest structures which the child produces for himself, where he combines certain elements—typically, but not necessarily, words—that he also uses in isolation, or in other combinations. There are in principle two ways of looking at these, the one adult-oriented and the other child-oriented. The child's structures may be represented either as approximations

---

[1]For example, Braine (1971) introduces his comprehensive survey of work on "the acquisition of language" with the words "This review is concerned only with the acquisition of linguistic structure. Thus, work on child language where the concern is with social or intellectual development will not be reviewed. Even within the area defined, the subject of lexical development will be reviewed only very sketchily [p. 3]." No mention is made of the development of the semantic system.

to the forms of the adult language or as independent structures *sui generis*. The first approach, which is in a sense presupposed by a nativist view, involves treating many of the child's utterances, perhaps all of them at a certain stage, as ill formed; they are analyzed as the product of distortions of various kinds, particularly the deletion of elements. This brings out their relationship to the adult forms, but it blocks the way to the recognition and interpretation of the child's own system. In the second approach, the child's earliest structures are analyzed as combinations of elements forming a system in their own right, typically based on the contrast between closed and open-ended classes; the best-known example is Braine's (1963) "pivotal" model, with its categories of "pivot" and "open." Such an analysis has been criticized on the grounds that it fails to account for ambiguous forms (e.g., Bloom, 1970: **mommy sock** = (i) *Mummy's sock*, (ii) *Mummy is putting my socks on*); but this is an aspect of a more general limitation, namely that it does not account for the meaning of what the child says. Nor does it easily suggest how, or why, the child moves from his own into the adult system; if language development is primarily the acquisition of structure, why does the child learn one set of structures in order to discard them in favor of another? For an excellent discussion of these and related issues, see Brown (1973).

None of the above objections is very serious, provided it is recognized, first, that structural analysis is a highly abstract exercise, in which both types of representation are valid and each affords its own insight; and second—a related point—that language development is much more than the acquisition of structure. But, by the same token, the form of representation of the grammatical structures of the child's language is then no longer the central issue. The fundamental question is, "How does the child learn language?" In other words, how does he master the adult linguistic system, in which grammar is just one part, and structure is just one part of grammar? How does he build up a multiple coding system consisting of content, form, and expression—of meaning relations, the representation of these as lexicostructural configurations, and the realization of these, in turn, as phonological patterns?

A consideration of this question in its broader context is embodied in what Roger Brown calls a "rich interpretation" of children's language: the approach to language development through the investigation of meaning. This is not, of course, a new idea. But when the psychologists' traditional two-level model of language (as sound and meaning) came to be overtaken by that of structuralist linguistics— which was still in terms of two levels, but this time of sound and form—it rather receded into the background.[2] With the now general recognition of the basically tri-stratal nature of the linguistic system (and Prague theory, glossematics, system-structure theory, tagmemics, stratification theory, and the later versions of transfor-

---

[2] Just how far the latter view prevailed can be seen in the following quotation from Ervin and Miller (1963): "The most important contribution that modern linguistics has brought to child language studies is the conception of what a language is. A language is a system that can be described internally in terms of two primary parts or levels—the phonological (sound system) and the grammatical. A complete description of a language would include an account of all possible phonological sequences and also a set of rules by which we can predict all the possible sentences in that language [p. 108]."

mation theory are all variants on this theme), the semantic perspective has been restored. The "rich interpretation" may still rest on a structural analysis of the utterances of children's speech; but if so, this is an analysis at the semological level in which the elements of structure are functional in character. Most typically, perhaps, they are the transitivity functions of the clause, such as Agent and Process (Schlesinger, 1971); but it is worth commenting here that all functional categories, whether those of transitivity, like Fillmore's (1968) "cases," or those of thematic structure (Gruber, 1967), and including traditional notions like subject and modifier (Kelley, 1967), are semantic in origin (Halliday, 1970), and could therefore figure appropriately in such a description.

The approach to structure through meaning may also be either child-oriented or adult-oriented. For example, the utterance **now room** (see below), which could be glossed as *Now let's go to* (play in) (daddy's) *room*, could be analyzed on the adult model as something like Imperative + Process + Agent + Locative + Temporal, with Imperative, Process and Agent deleted; or, in its own terms, as something like Request for joint action + Arena, with nothing omitted or "understood."

Once again, these are abstract representations, and neither can be said to be wrong. But a child-oriented semantic analysis of the latter kind, which is very suggestive, carries certain further implications. Since the elements of the structure are not being explained as (approximations to) those of the adult language, there is presumably some other source from which they are derived and in terms of which they have any meaning. Why, for example, would we postulate an element such as "Request for joint action"? This is explicable only if one of the functions of language is to call for action on the part of others, to regulate their behavior in some way. No doubt this is true; but to make it explicit implies some specification of the total set of functions of language, some kind of a functional hypothesis that is not just a list of uses of language but a system of developmental functions from each of which a range of meanings, or "meaning potential," is derived.

At this point the attempt to understand the structure of the child's utterances leads directly to questions about the linguistic system as a whole, and specifically about the functions for which that system first develops. There is an important link between the two senses of "function," first as in "functions in structure" and second as in "functions of language;" the former, when interpreted semantically, imply the latter. But whether or not the line of approach is through considerations of structure, once the interest is focused on how the child learns a system of meanings this points to some investigation in functional terms. It becomes necessary to look beyond the language itself, but to do so without presupposing a particular conceptual framework, because this is precisely what the child is using language to construct; and herein lies the value of a functional approach. Early language development may be interpreted as the child's progressive mastery of a functional potential.

There is yet a further implication here, one which takes us into the social foundations of language. If, for example, language is used, from an early stage, to regulate the behavior of others, and it is suggested that the mastery of this function is one of the essential steps in the developmental process, this assumes some general framework of social structure and social processes in terms of which a function such as "regulatory" would make sense. More particularly—since we are concerned with the language of the child—it presupposes a concept of cultural transmission within which the role of language in the transmission process may be highlighted and defined. Here the concept of meaning, and of learning to mean, is in the last analysis interpreted in sociological terms, in the context of some chain of dependence, such as social order—transmission of the social order to the child—role of language in the trasmission process—functions of language in relation to this role—meanings derived from these functions.

In this way the functional interpretation of the child's meanings implies what might be termed a sociolinguistic approach (cf. Osser, 1970), in which the learning of language is seen as a process of interaction between the child and other human beings. From this perspective, which is complementary to the psycholinguistic one (and not in any sense contradictory), the focus of attention is on the linguistic system as a whole, considered as having a (functionally organized) meaning potential, or semantic system, at one end, and a vocal potential, or phonological system, at the other. In this context, structure no longer occupies the center of the stage; it enters in because it is one form of the realization of meanings. This has certain important consequences for the investigation of language development. The analysis does not depend on utterances of more than one element, that is, on combinations of words as structural units. This is significant because, although the word in the sense of a lexical item or lexeme (i.e., vocabulary) soon comes to play an essential part in the development of the linguistic system, the word as a structural unit, which is a different concept, does not do so, or not nearly so prominently; it is merely one type of constituent among others, and the young child has no special awareness of words as constituents (this point is brought out by Braine (1971, p. 87), who for some reason finds it surprising). From the functional point of view, as soon as there are meaningful expressions there is language, and the investigation can begin at a time before words and structures have evolved to take over the burden of realization.

It then emerges that the child has a linguistic system before he has any words or structures at all.[3] He is capable of expressing a range of meanings that at first seem difficult to pin down, because they do not translate easily into adult language, but that become quite transparent when interpreted functionally, in the light of the question "What has the child learnt to do by means of language?" The transition from this first phase into the adult system can also be explained in functional terms, although it is necessary to modify the concept of function very considerably in passing from the developmental origins of the system, where "function" equals "use," to the highly abstract sense in which we can talk of the functional organiza-

---

[3]Cf. Leopold (1939–1949) "Meanings were always developed before sound forms [Vol. I, p. 22]." As it stands this is difficult to interpret; but I take it to mean "before the appearance of sound forms recognizably derived from the adult language."

tion of the adult language. However, this modification in the concept "function of language" is itself one of the major sources of insight into the process whereby the adult system evolves from that of the child.

In what follows we shall suggest a tentative framework for a functional, or sociolinguistic, account of early language development. This will recognize three phases: Phase I, the child's initial functional-linguistic system; Phase II, the transition from this system to that of the adult language; Phase III, the learning of the adult language. The account does not presuppose any one particular psychological model of language acquisition or theory of learning. Linguistically, it assumes some form of a realization model of language; the descriptive techniques used are those of system-structure theory, with the "system" (a set of options with a condition of entry) as the basic concept (Firth, 1957; Halliday, 1973), but such a representation can be readily interpreted in stratificational terms (Lamb, 1970; Reich, 1970). The sociological standpoint is derived from the findings and the theoretical work of Bernstein. But the particular impetus for the detailed study of a developing language system, which provides the observational basis for this sketch, came from working over a number of years with teachers of English as a mother tongue, who were attempting to grapple with the fundamental problem of language in education (for the results of their work, see Doughty, Pearce, & Thornton, 1971; Mackay, Thompson, & Schaub, 1970). Their experience showed that we are still far from understanding the essential patterns of language development in the preschool child, in the deeper sense of being able to answer the question, "How does the child learn how to mean?"

Phase I: Functional Origins

DEVELOPMENTAL FUNCTIONS: A HYPOTHESIS

Seen from a sociolinguistic viewpoint, the learning of the mother tongue appears to comprise three phases of development. The first of these consists of mastering certain basic functions of language, each one having a small range of alternatives, or "meaning potential," associated with it.

A tentative system of developmental (Phase I) functions was suggested (Halliday, 1969) as follows:

Instrumental	*I want*
Regulatory	*Do as I tell you*
Interactional	*Me and you*
Personal	*Here I come*
Heuristic	*Tell me why*
Imaginative	*Let's pretend*
Informative	*I've got something to tell you*

The hypothesis was that these functions would appear, approximately in the order listed, and in any case with the "informative" (originally called "representational") significantly last; that, in Phase I, they would appear as discrete, with each expression (and therefore each utterance) having just one function; and that the mastery of all of them—with the possible exception of the last—would be both a necessary and a sufficient condition for the transition to the adult system. The implication of this is that these functions of language represent universals of human culture, which may in turn have further implications for an understanding of the evolution of language.

The hypothesis was tested, and the pattern of development from Phase I to Phase III followed through in detail, in an intensive study of the language development of one subject, Nigel, from 9 to 24 months of age. This will be the main source of information for the present account.

THE FUNCTIONAL INTERPRETATION OF CHILD LANGUAGE

The criterion adopted for regarding a vocalization by the child as an utterance (i.e. as language) was an observable and constant relation between content and expression, such that, for each content–expression pair, the expression was observed in at least three unambiguous instances and the content was interpretable in functional terms. (In practice the distinction between random vocalizations and systematic forms proved to be obvious, and the latter were observed with far more than minimal frequency.) This means that the content was, in each case, derivable as a possible option in meaning from some point of origin that could reasonably be interpreted as a context for effective verbal action (Firth, 1950), whether or not in the above list. We may compare here Leopold's observation (1939–1949) that his daughter at 8 months showed "the intention of communication, which must be considered the chief criterion of language." [Vol. I, p. 21] Judged by the criterion adopted, Nigel's vocalizations at 9 months were still prelinguistic, or just on the threshold of language. At $10\frac{1}{2}$ months, however, he had a language, consisting of a meaning potential in each of four functions. We shall refer to this as NL 1, meaning "Nigel's Language 1" (Fig. 14–1).

At this stage, there is no grammar. That is to say, there is no level of linguistic "form" (syntax, morphology, vocabulary) intermediate between the content and the expression. In stratificational terms, the child has a semology and a phonology but not yet a lexology. Furthermore, the system owes nothing to the English language (a possible exception being [bɸ] *I want my toy bird*); the sounds are spontaneous and, in general, unexplained, although two or three are attested as imitations of natural sounds the child has heard himself make and then put to systematic use. (Parenthetically, it should be noted that a phonetic alphabet such as the IPA notation is quite inappropriate as a means of representing the child's speech sounds at this stage; it is far too specific. What is wanted is a system of notation showing generalized postures and prosodic values.)

Rather, it might be said that the *expression* owes nothing to the English language.

CONTENT		EXPRESSION		GLOSS
Function	Content systems	Articulation	Tone (falling)	
Instrumental	demand (general)	[nãnãnã]	mid	*give me that*
	demand for bird	[bǿ]	mid	*give me my bird*
Regulatory	normal	[ə̃]	mid	*do that (again)*
	intensified	[mnŋ]	high-wide	*do that right now*
Interactional	initiating — friendliness	[ǿ], [d̥ǿ], [d̥ɔ]	mid-narrow	*nice to see you (shall we look at this together?)*
	impatience	[ənn̩n̩]	mid	*nice to see you—at last*
	response	[ɛ], [ə]	low	*yes it's me*
Personal	withdrawal	[g̊ʷɤy g̊ʷɤy g̊ʷɤy]	low-narrow	*I'm sleepy*
	partici-pation pleasure — general	[a]	low	*that's nice*
	taste	[n̩ŋ]	low	*that tastes nice*
	interest — general	[ǿ]	low	*that's interesting*
	specific	[d̥ɔ], [bǿ], [ǿ]	low	*look it's moving (? dog, bird)*

Figure 14–1.

As far as the content is concerned, the English language probably has played a part, by virtue of the fact that it embodies meanings such as *I want that* somewhere in its semantic system, and the adult hearer therefore recognizes and responds to such meanings. It is of course immaterial, in this regard, whether such meanings are or are not cultural and linguistic universals.

Nigel's language was studied continuously and the description recast every $1\frac{1}{2}$ months, this being the interval that appeared to be optimal: with a longer interval one might fail to note significant steps in the progression; with a shorter one, one would be too much at the mercy of random nonoccurrences in the data. Table 14–1 shows the number of options within each function at each stage from NL 1 ($9-10\frac{1}{2}$ months) to NL 5, the end of Phase I ($15-16\frac{1}{2}$ months). Those for NL 6, which is considered to be the beginning of Phase II, are added for comparison, although it should be stressed that they are not only less reliable but also, as will emerge from what follows, less significant as an index of the system.

CHARACTERISTICS OF PHASE I SYSTEMS

The set of options comprising NL 1 represents what a very small child can do with language—which is quite a lot in relation to his total behavior potential. He can use language to satisfy his own material needs, in terms of goods or services (instrumental); to exert control over the behavior of others (regulatory); to establish and maintain contact with those that matter to him (interactional); and to express his own individuality and self-awareness (personal). Moreover, any

TABLE 14–I NUMBER OF OPTIONS WITHIN EACH FUNCTION AT DIFFERENT LANGUAGE STAGES

	Instru-mental	Regul-atory	Inter-actional	Personal	Heur-istic	Imagin-ative	Inform-ative	Total
Phase I								
NL 1 (9–10½ mo.)	2	2	3	5	—	—	—	12
NL 2 (10½–12 mo.)	3	2	7	9	—	—	—	21
NL 3 (12–13½ mo.)	5	6	7	9	—	2	—	29
NL 4 (13½–15 mo.)	5	6	7	11	(?)	3	—	32
NL 5 (15–16½ mo.)	10	7	15	16	(?)	4	—	52
Phase II								
NL 6 (16½–18 mo.)	31	29	16	61[a]	3	5	—	145

[a] This figure includes all expressions used in observation and recall, reinterpreted in Phase II as "mathetic" (deriving from personal heuristic).

one option may have a very considerable range, not only in the sense that it can be used very frequently (i.e. on numerous occasions, not counting repetitions within one occasion; it is necessary to distinguish "instances" from "tokens" at this stage), but also, and more significantly, in the sense that many of the options are very general in their applicability. There is a tendency, in fact, for each function to include an unmarked option whose meaning is equivalent to the general meaning of the function in question; for example, in the instrumental function there is one option meaning simply *I want that*, where the object of desire is clear from the context—contrasting with one or more specific options such as *I want my bird*. There are various modifications of this pattern; for instance, there may be one unmarked term for an initiating context and another for a response (*Yes I do want that*). But the principle is clearly operative, and perhaps anticipates the "good reason" principle, that of "select this option unless there is a good reason for selecting some other one," that is such a fundamental feature of adult language.

The functions observed in Nigel's Phase I turn out to be those of the initial hypothesis. This will cease to be true in Phase II, but in one important respect the hypothesis fails already: There is no sign of a developmental progression within the first four functions. As a matter of fact, the only two expressions recorded before 9 months that fulfill the criterion for language were in the interactional and personal areas. Furthermore, the imaginative function seems to appear before the heuristic, although a reinterpretation of certain elements (the "problem area" referred to in the next paragraph) in the light of Phase II observations suggests that this may be wrong and that the heuristic function begins to appear at NL4 ($13\frac{1}{2}$–15 months) at the same time as the imaginative. The two are closely related; the heuristic function is language in the exploration of the objective environment—of the "nonself" that has been separated off from the self through the personal function—while the imaginative is language used to create an environment of one's own, which may be one of sound or of meaning and which leads eventually into story, song, and poetry. Finally, the informative function has not appeared at all. What does emerge as some sort of developmental sequence, in Nigel's case, is (1) that the first four functions listed clearly precede the rest, and (2) that all others precede the informative. The informative function does not appear until nearly the end of Phase II, round about NL 9 (21–$22\frac{1}{2}$ months), but this was not entirely unexpected, since the use of language to convey information is clearly a derivative function, one which presupposes various special conditions including, for one thing, the concept of dialogue.

The functions themselves, however, emerge with remarkable clarity. Not only did it prove surprisingly easy to apply the general criterion for identifying a vocal act as language (since the learning of a system cannot be regarded as a function of that system, anything interpreted as linguistic practicing was automatically excluded—Nigel in fact did very little of this); but it was also possible, throughout NL 1–5, to assign utterances to expressions, expressions to meanings, and meanings to functions with relatively little doubt or ambiguity. There was one significant exception to this, a problem area lying at the border of the interactional and the personal functions, which proved extremely difficult to systematize; subsequent interpretation suggests that it was, in fact, the origin of heuristic language, or rather of a more general learning function that is discussed more fully below. Otherwise, although the functions clearly overlap in principle, or at least shade into one another, the value of an element at all levels in the system was usually not difficult to establish.

More important, the fact that the meanings could be derived from functions that were set up on extralinguistic grounds justifies our regarding these early utterances as expressions of language—a step that is necessary if we are to understand the genesis of language as a whole. Phase II, which corresponds to what has usually, in recent years, been taken as the (unexplained) point of origin of the system, is here regarded as being already transitional, and explained as a reinterpretation of the elementary functions in a more generalized form. Ultimately, these evolve into the abstract functional components of the adult grammatical system, and these components then serve as the medium for the encoding, in grammar, of the original functions in their concrete extensions as what we would call simply "uses of language."

Phase II: The Transition

VOCABULARY AND STRUCTURE

The transition to the adult system begins, with Nigel, at NL 6 ($16\frac{1}{2}$—18 months). This phase is characterized by two main features: (1) a shift in the functional orientation, which is described below, and (2) major and very rapid advances in vocabulary, structure, and dialogue.

Vocabulary and structure are in principle the same thing. What emerges at this point is a grammar, in the traditional sense of this term as a level of linguistic "form" (the lexological stratum). This is a system intermediate between the content and the expression, and it is the distinguishing characteristic of human, adult language. The options in the grammatical system are realized as structure and vocabulary, with vocabulary, as a rule, expressing the more specific choices.

VOCABULARY

NL 6 has some 80—100 new meanings, and, for the first time, the majority of the meanings are expressed by means of lexical items—the expressions are English words. In the first instance these are used holophrastically, which in the present context is defined in functional terms: the lexical item forms, by itself, an utterance that is functionally independent and complete. With Nigel, this did not continue very long; he happened to be one of those children who hardly go through a "holophrastic stage," for whom the holophrase is merely the limiting case of a linguistic structure. In any case the holophrase is, in itself, of little importance,

but it serves to signal the very crucial step whereby the child introduces words—
that is, a vocabulary—into his linguistic system.

Why does the child learn words? Do they fit into and enrich the existing functional pattern, or are they demanded by the opening up of new functional possibilities? The answer seems to be, not unexpectedly, both. Many of the words that
are learnt first are called for by existing functions. Of these the majority, in
Nigel's case, are at first restricted to one function only, for example, **cat** means
only *Hullo, cat!* (interactional), **syrup** means only *I want my syrup* (instrumental);
a few begin to appear in more than one function, at different times, for example,
hole means now *Make a hole* (instrumental), now *I want to* (go out for a walk and)
put things in holes (regulatory), and now *Look, there's a hole* (personal-heuristic;
see below); and just once or twice we find a combination of functions in a single
instance, for example, **cake** meaning *Look, there's a cake—and I want some!* This
last is very striking when it first occurs. With the adult, all utterances are plurifunctional; but for a child the ability to mean two things at once marks a great
advance. Thus, as far as the existing functions are concerned, the learning of
vocabulary (1) engenders new meanings within these functions and (2) allows
for functions to be combined. The latter will then impose definite requirements
on the nature of linguistic structure, since the principal role of structure, in the
grammar, is that of mapping one functional meaning on to another.

However, many of the new words—the majority, in Nigel's case—do not fit into
the earlier functional pattern. In the first place, they have clearly not been learnt
for pragmatic contexts. Indeed many of them are not particularly appropriate to
the instrumental or regulatory functions, for example, **bubble, toe, star, hot,
weather-cock**; and even those that are do not appear in these functions until later
on—the words **dog** and **bus**, for example, although perfectly well understood as
also referring to certain toys, are not used to ask for those toys, or in any other pragmatic sense.

It might be surmised, then, that the impetus to the learning of new words would
come from the emergence of the informative function, from the child's desire to use
language for conveying information. But this is not so. At 18 months Nigel has no
conception of language as a means of communicating an experience to someone
who has not shared that experience with him; it is only much later that he inter-
nalizes the fact that language can be used in this way. A further possibility might
be that the child is simply practicing, using new words just in order to learn them.
This also must be rejected, if it implies that the child is learning language in order
to learn language; he cannot seriously be thought to be storing up verbal wealth
for future uses he as yet knows nothing about. But the notion of learning is the relevant one, provided it is interpreted as learning in general, not simply the learning
of language. For Nigel, the main functional impetus behind the move into the
lexical mode is, very distinctly, that of learning about his environment. Most of
the new vocabulary is used, at first, solely in the context of observation and recall:
I see/hear. . . , including *I saw/heard. . . .*

In terms of the developmental functions, this appears to be a blend of the personal and the heuristic, resulting from some such process as the following. First, the self is separated from the "nonself" (the environment). Second, a meaning potential arises in respect of each: personal reactions, for example, *pleasure*, and attention to external phenomena, for example, *Look!* Third, new meanings arise through the combination of the two: involvement with, and reaction to, features of the environment, for example, *Look, that's interesting!* Fourth, the child develops a linguistic semiotic for the interpretation and structuring of the environment in terms of his own experience.

Hence the new words function mainly as a means of categorizing observed phenomena. Many of them represent items having properties that are difficult to assimilate to experience, typically movement (e.g. **dog, bee, train, bubble**) and visual or auditory prominence (e.g. **tower, light, bus, drill**); while others are simply phenomena that are central to the child's personal explorations—in Nigel's case, particularly things in pictures. The child is constructing a heuristic hypothesis about the environment, in the form of an experiential semantic system whose meanings are realized through words and structures, and which is used in contexts of observation and recall—and before long also of prediction.[4]

This "learning" function of language—perhaps we might refer to it as the "mathetic" function—appears to arise as a synthesis of the two principal non-pragmatic Phase I functions: the personal, which is the self-oriented one, and the heuristic, which is other-oriented. Nigel's earliest instances, at the beginning of Phase II, are markedly other-oriented; but this function soon becomes a means of exploring the self as well, and so takes up, on a higher level, the meaning of the original Phase I "personal" function. We can trace the history of this mathetic function of language in Nigel's case from the very beginning; it is of interest because it reveals what was, for one child, the primary mode of entry into grammar.

Prominent in NL 1 is an interactional option in which some pleasurable experience, usually a picture, is used as the channel for contact with another person: ['dɔ̀], etc., glossed as *Nice to see you, and shall we look at this together?* In NI 2, this apparently splits into two meanings, thought still with considerable overlap: one has an interactional emphasis, ['dɔ̀], [ɛ̀ya], etc., *Nice to see you (and look at this!)*; the other is personal, ['dɔ̀], [dɛ̀ə], etc., *That's nice*, reacting to a picture or bright object and not requiring the presence of a second participant. By NL 3, the former has become simply a greeting, and the expression for it is replaced, in NL 4, by **hullo** [a͞lou͞wa], alongside which appear individualized expressions of greeting

---

[4] In a recent article, Ingram (1971) proposes adapting Fillmore's "case" theory of structural function to one-element utterances, with a category of "semantic transitivity," corresponding in general to the concept of "Process" as a structural role (Halliday, 1970); he then suggests that the child identifies objects in terms of their potential "semantic function" (that is, their role in transitivity), such as their ability to move or to operate on other objects, and that this defines for the child concepts such as "Agent" and "animate." This agrees in principle with what is being suggested here, although Ingram's account of transitivity seems to be too simple; but Ingram fails to relate his notions to the language-function perspective of the child—on the one hand, his assumption seems to be that "semantic" can be equated with "ideational," whereas on the other hand, many of his own examples are of utterances having a predominantly pragmatic function.

mummy, daddy, Anna. The latter remains as an expression of personal interest; but meanwhile a third form arises at the intersection of the two, [ādà], [adādādà], etc., which represents the earliest type of *linguistic* interaction, glossed as *Look at this!—now you say its name*—used only where the object is familiar and the name already (receptively) known. In NL 5, this naming request specializes out and becomes the form of demand for a new name, [adȳdà] *What's that?*; and this is used constantly as a heuristic device. Meanwhile, alongside the general expression of personal interest there have appeared a few specific variants, *Look that's a . . .*, which are expressed by English words. At first these occur only in familiar contexts, again typically pictures; but in NL 6 they come to be used in the categorization of new experience, in the form of observation and recall: *I see a . . . , I saw a . . . .* Then, within a very short time (less than one month), and still largely in this same mathetic function, the vocabulary begins to be backed up by structures. We can thus follow through, with Nigel, the process whereby the use of names to record and comment on what is observed, which is a universal feature of child language at a certain stage, arises out of meanings and functions that already existed for the child before any vocabulary had been learnt at all.[5]

STRUCTURE

With Nigel, the structural explosion followed very closely on the lexical one. That it is part of the same general process, the development of a stratum of "grammar" intermediate between the content and the expression, is shown, however, not so much by the shortness of this interval, which with some children is much longer, but by the fact that both vocabulary and structure first appear in the same functional contexts. All that was said, in functional terms, about the learning of vocabulary could apply to structure also.

The origin and early development of structure is dealt with by other contributors to this volume; it will be touched upon here only insofar as it relates to the functional perspective. At the outset of Phase II, Nigel displayed two types of protostructure, or rather two variants of the same type: a specific expression, within a certain function, combined either (1) with a gesture or (2) with a general expression from the same function. Examples: [dà:bi] **Dvořak** + beating time (music gesture), *I want the Dvořak record on* (instrumental function); [ndà] **star** + shaking head (negation gesture), *I can't see the star* (personal); [ɛ̀ lɔu] (command + *hole*),

---

[5]Despite a commonly held belief to the contrary, the speech the child hears around him is, in the typical instance, coherent, well formed, and contextually relevant. In interaction with adults he is not, in general, surrounded by intellectual discourse, with its backtracking, anacolutha, high lexical density and hesitant planning; but by the fluent, smoothly grammatical and richly structured utterances of informal everyday conversation. (Of the first hundred clauses spoken in Nigel's presence on one particular day, only three were in some way "deviant.") He has abundant evidence with which to construct the grammatical system of his language. What he hears from other children, naturally, is different—but in ways that serve as a guide for his own efforts. This is not, of course, an argument *against* the nativist hypothesis; it merely removes one of the arguments that have been used to claim the *necessity* of a nativist interpretation.

Make a hole (regulatory); [ù æyì:] (excitement + **egg**), *Ooh, an egg!* (personal). Shortly after this came word strings; these were of two words only, e.g. [bʌbu nɔumɔ̀] (**bubble, no-more**) *The bubbles have gone away*, except when in lists, when there might be as many as six, for example, **stick, hole, stone, train, ball, bus** *I saw sticks*, etc.; and each word still has its own independent (falling) tone contour. The first "true" structure, in the sense of a string of words on a single tone contour, appeared at 19 months, just 4 weeks after the first major excursion into vocabulary; and within 2 more weeks various types of structure were being produced, as in the following sets of examples:

1. **mummy come, more meat, butter on, squeeze orange, mend train, help juice** (*Help me with the juice*), **come over-there, now room** (*Now let's go to the room*), **star for-you** (*Make a star for me*), **more meat please**
2. **green car, two book** (*two books*), **mummy book** (*Mummy's book*), **bee flower** (*There's a bee on the flower*), **bubble round-round** (*The bubbles are going round and round*), **tiny red light, two fast train**

These structures fall into two distinct groups, on functional criteria. Those under (1) are "pragmatic," corresponding to the instrumental and regulatory functions of Phase I; those of (2) are what we have called "mathetic," deriving from the personal-heuristic functions.[6]

Quite unexpectedly, this binary grouping was made fully explicit by Nigel himself, when within the same two-week period (the end of NL 7, 19−19½ months) he introduced an entirely new distinction into his speech, that between falling and rising tone. From this point on, all pragmatic utterances were spoken on a rising tone and all nonpragmatic (mathetic) ones on a falling tone. The distinction was fully systematic, and was maintained intact for some months; it provided a striking corroboration of the significance of pragmatic/mathetic as a major functional opposition. If Nigel is at all typical, this opposition (though not, of course, Nigel's particular form of realization of it) seems to be fundamental to the transition to Phase III, the adult system; we shall return to it below. Here it is relevant because it enables us to see the development of structure in Phase II as an integral part of the total language-learning process.

What is the relation of linguistic structure to the functions of language? Let us take the examples, from Nigel at the beginning of Phase II (NL 7, 18−19½ months), of **more meat, two book**, and **green car**. All three seem at first sight to display an identical structure, whether this is stated in child-oriented terms, for example; Pivot + Open, or in adult-oriented terms, for example, Modifier + Hear. But **more meat** occurs only in a pragmatic function, whereas the other two occur only in a

---

[6] Cf. the distinction drawn between the "manipulative" and "declarative" functions in Lewis (1936), an important work with which I was unfamiliar at the time of writing. The concept of pragmatic function is very similar to Lewis's manipulative; the mathetic is somewhat different from Lewis's declarative, since Lewis interprets this in terms of self-expression, and the demand for an expressive response, rather than as a mode of learning.

mathetic function. Moreover, this is a general pattern; we find **more omelet, more bread**, and so on, all likewise pragmatic only, and **two train, mummy book** (*mummy's book*), **green peg, red car**, and so on, all mathetic only. It is this functional specialization that relates these structures to the earlier stage of language learning. By a subsequent step, they become functionally derestricted, so that the structure represented by **more meat** becomes compatible with the mathetic sense *Look there's some, . . . ,* and that of **green car** with the pragmatic sense of *I want the. . . .* At first, however, each structure is tied exclusively to just one function or the other.

The structural analysis of **more meat** might be "Request + Object of desire," relating it to the instrumental function from which it derives. The elements of the structure are pragmatic not experiential ones. By contrast, **green car** may be analyzed in experiential terms, as perhaps "Visual property + Object observed." In terms of the introductory discussion, this interpretation of structure is child-oriented semantic: semantic in order to relate it to function, child-oriented to show the part it plays developmentally, which is obscured if we assume from the start a final outcome in the shape of a structure of the adult language. Exactly how a structure such as that represented by **more meat**, initially pragmatic, comes later to take on a nonpragmatic function, first in alternation and then in combination with the pragmatic, is an interesting and difficult question; presumably in this instance the request element **more** comes to be reinterpreted experientially as a comparative quantifier (in Nigel's case, via the aspectual sense of *I want* (you) *to go on, . . . ing,* e.g., **more play rao** *I want us to go on playing lions*); while the request function is generalized and taken over by the modal system in the grammar (in Nigel's case, via the systematic use of the rising tone). We have chosen here what is probably a rather simple example; but the point is a general one. In the beginning, all Nigel's structures, like his vocabulary, are functionally specific; they are either pragmatic (Set 1 on p. 253), or mathetic (Set 2). Only after an interval are they transferred to the other function; and this takes place, not by a shift out of one box into another, but rather by a recasting of the concept of "function" on to a more abstract plane so that all expressions become, in effect, plurifunctional.

Herein lies the essential unity of structure and vocabulary. Words and structures, or rather "words-and-structures," that is, lexicogrammatical units, are the expression of options at a new level appearing in the child's linguistic system intermediate between meaning and sound. This is the stratum of linguistic form, or grammar; and it appears that grammar develops, with the child, as the means of incorporating the functional potential into the heart of the linguistic system. It allows for meanings that derive from different functions to be encoded together, as integrated structures, so that every expression becomes, in principle, functionally complex. Grammar makes it possible to mean more than one thing at a time.

DIALOGUE

The early development of the grammatical system has been fairly thoroughly explored. What has been much less explored, although it is of fundamental importance, is how the child learns dialogue.

Nigel learnt to engage in dialogue at the same time as he started to learn vocabulary, towards the end of NL 6 (just before 18 months), and dialogue could serve as well as vocabulary to mark the beginning of his Phase II. There was some "proto-dialogue" in Phase I: at NL 2, Nigel had three specific responses, to calls, greetings, and gifts, and by NL 5 he could answer questions of the type *Do you want. . . ?*, *Shall I. . . ?*, that is, those where the answers required were instrumental, regulatory, or interactional in function. But he could not initiate dialogue; nor could he give responses of a purely linguistic kind.[7]

Dialogue can be viewed as, essentially, the adoption and assignment of roles. The roles in question are social roles, but of a special kind: they exist only in and through language, as communication roles—speaker, addressee, respondent, questioner, persuader, and the like. But they are of general significance developmentally, since they serve both as a channel and as a model for social interaction. Whenever someone speaks, he normally takes on the role of addresser (*I'm talking to you*), and assigns the role of listener (*Attend!*); but in dialogue these roles have to be made more specific, not merely *I'm talking to you* but, for example, *I am demanding information, and you are to respond by supplying it*. Dialogue involves purely linguistic forms of personal interaction; at the same time, it exemplifies the general principle whereby people adopt roles, assign them, and accept or reject those that are assigned to them.

The mysteries of dialogue were unravelled by Nigel in the 2-week period at the opening of NL 7 (18—18½ months). At the end of this time he could:

1. respond to a *Wh-* question (provided the answer was already known to the questioner); for example:
   What are you eating?
   N<small>IGEL</small>: **Banana**.
2. respond to a command; for example:
   Take the toothpaste to Daddy and go and get your bib.
   N<small>IGEL</small> (does so, saying): **Daddy** . . . **noddy** . . . **train**, that is *Daddy, (give) noddy (toothpaste to him, and go and get your bib with the) train (on it)*.
3. respond to a statement; for example:
   You went on a train yesterday.
   N<small>IGEL</small> (signals attention, by repeating, and continues the conversation):
   Train . . . **byebye**, that is, *Yes, I went on a train, and then (when I got off) the train went away*.
4. respond to a response; for example:
   N<small>IGEL</small>: **Gravel**.
   R<small>ESPONSE</small>: *Yes, you had some gravel in your hand.*
   N<small>IGEL</small>: **Ooh**, (i.e., *It hurt me*).

---

[7] He could not, in other words, respond to utterances where the response would have lain outside his functional potential. He could express the meanings "yes" and "no" in the senses of "Yes I want that" or "No I don't want that" (instrumental), or "Yes do that" or "No don't do that" (regulatory). But he had no general polarity (positive—negative) system; nor could he respond to any question seeking information, such as *Did you see a car?* or *What did you see?*

5. initiate dialogue; for example:
   NIGEL: **What's that?**
   RESPONSE: *That's butter.*
   NIGEL (repeats): **Butter.**

The question *What's that?* is, however, his only option for initiating dialogue at this stage. Apart from this, it is outside his functional potential to demand a linguistic response; he cannot yet assign specific communication roles. But he has gone some way in being able to accept those that are assigned to him.[8] As long as the child's responses are limited to exchanges such as:

(*Nigel!*)
NIGEL: [ǿ] *Yes I'm here*
(*Do you want some cheese?*)
NIGEL: [nò] *No I don't want it*
(*Shall I put the truck in the box for you?*)
NIGEL: [à] *Yes do*

he is simply using language in its original extralinguistic functions; this is not yet true dialogue. The ability to respond to a *Wh-* question, however, is a significant innovation; the child has mastered the principle of the purely communicative functions of language, and is beginning to take on roles that are defined by language itself. This is the first step towards the "informative" use of language, which is late in appearing precisely because it is language in a function that is solely defined by language—a complex and difficult notion.

Once the child can engage in dialogue, new possibilities arise in relation to the functions he has already mastered: the elaboration of existing options, persistence and change in functional "tactics" and so on. Dialogue also plays an essential part in the development of the generalized mathetic function, not only making it possible for the child to ask for new names but also allowing for systematic exploration of the environment and extended patterns of verbal recall. But no less important than this is the role of dialogue in anticipating and leading into Phase III, the mastery of the adult system. Through its embodiment of linguistic role-playing, dialogue opens the way to the options of mood (declarative, interrogative, etc.), and thus to the entire interpersonal component in the language system. This is the component whereby the speaker intrudes or, as it were, builds himself into the linguistic structure, expressing his relations with other participants, his attitudes and judgments, his commitments, desires, and the like (Halliday, 1973). Thus in the course of Phase II, with the help of an increasing amount of imitative, role-playing speech—and also of sheer argument, which plays an essential part—the child learns to participate linguistically, and to intrude his own angle, his individuality, and his personal involvement into the linguistic structure. In this way

---

[8]Nigel cannot at this stage respond explicitly to a yes—no question. But he sometimes does so by implication; for example:
   Are you going shopping?
   NIGEL: **Bread** ... **egg**, that is, *I'm going to buy bread and eggs.*

language becomes for him an effective channel of social learning, a means of participating in and receiving the culture. Meanings are expressed as verbal inter-action in social contexts; this is the essential condition for the transmission of culture, and makes it possible for certain types of context to play a critical part in the socialization process (Bernstein, 1971).

Phase II is thus characterized by two major advances towards the adult linguistic system. On the one hand, the child adds a grammar, a level of linguistic form (syntax and vocabulary) intermediate between content and expression, so develop-ing the basic tri-stratal organization of the adult language. The grammar is a system of potential, a network of options that is capable of "receiving" from the content level and "transmitting" to the expression;[9] in so doing it forms structure, accept-ing options from various functionally distinct content systems and interpreting these into integrated structural patterns. It is a nexus of systems and structures, as defined by Firth (1957). On the other hand, the child learns dialogue; he learns to adopt, accept, and assign linguistic roles, and thus to measure linguistic success in linguistic terms. From now on, success consists no longer simply in obtaining the desired material object or piece of behavior, but rather in playing one's part, in freely accepting the roles that one is assigned, and getting others to accept those that one has assigned to them.

Phase II can be said to end when the child has mastered the principles of gram-mar and of dialogue, and thus effectively completed the transition to the adult language *system*. (He is still, of course, only just beginning his mastery of the adult *language*.) But Phase II is transitional also in the functional sense, in that the child is moving from the original set of discrete developmental functions, where "func-tion" equals "use," through an intermediate stage leading to the more abstract concept of "function" that lies at the heart of the adult language. Naturally the two aspects of the transition, the functional and the systemic, are closely inter-connected; they are the two sides of the developmental process. The development of the functions, however, is significant for interpreting the development of the system—in the sense that language evolves in the way it does because of what it has to do. In the final section, we shall sketch out in tentative fashion the nature of the child's functional progression into the adult language.

Phase III: Into Language

FUNCTIONS OF THE ADULT SYSTEM

Can we relate the "function" of Phase I, where it refers to a set of simple, uninte-grated *uses* of language—instrumental, regulatory, and so on—to "function" in the sense of the highly abstract, integrated networks of relations that make up the adult language system?

---

[9] Or the other way round, in the reception of speech. Our concern here is with productive language, and relatively little is yet known about the processes whereby the child develops his understanding of what is said to and around him. But it is likely that the crucial step here, too, is the develop-ment of this third, intermediate level in his own linguistic coding system.

The answer will depend on our interpretation of "function" in the adult language. Functional theories of language have attempted, as a rule, not so much to explain the nature of language in functional terms, as to explain types of language use; their points of departure have been, for example, ethnographic (Malinowski, 1923), psychological (Bühler, 1934), ethological (Morris, 1967), or educational (Britton, 1970). But although the categories and terminologies differ, all of these incorporate in some form or other a basic distinction between an ideational (representational, referential, cognitive, denotative) and an interpersonal (expressive-conative, orectic, evocative, connotative) function of language.

If we now adapt this functional perspective to a consideration of the nature of language itself, we find that the adult linguistic system is in fact founded on a functional plurality. In particular, it is structured around the two-way distinction of ideational and interpersonal. The grammar of an adult language is a tripartite network of options, deriving from these two basic functions together with a third, that of creating text—the textual or, we could equally well say, "textural" function of language. This last is not treated in most functional theories because it is intrinsic to language; it is an enabling function, providing the conditions whereby the other functions can effectively be served. The textual function arises out of the very nature of language, and we need not therefore look for its independent origin in the developmental process. How, then, does the child progress from the functional pattern of his Phase I linguistic system to the ideational–interpersonal system which is at the foundation of the adult language?

This is the point at which Nigel provided an interesting and unexpected clue. Like all children (cf. Leopold, 1939–1949, Vol. III, pp. 1–30) he had made systematic use of intonation from the start, all his expressions being characterized by particular pitch contours: typically, varieties of falling tone, though with some exceptions; all personal names, for example, were high level. Early in Phase II, Nigel introduced, within one week (NL 7, $19\frac{1}{4}$–$19\frac{1}{2}$ months), a systematic opposition between rising and falling tone; this he maintained throughout the remainder of Phase II with complete consistency. Expressed in Phase I terms, the rising tone was used for all utterances that were instrumental or regulatory in function, the falling tone for all those that were personal or heuristic, while in the interactional function he used both tones but with a contrast between them. We can generalize this distinction by saying that Nigel used the rising tone for utterances demanding a response, and the falling tone for the others. The few exceptions were themselves systematic; for example, demands for music had, as expected, a rising tone unless they were accompanied by the music gesture, in which case the tone was falling, showing that the gesture was an alternative realization of the option "request for music"—and that the falling tone is to be regarded as the unmarked term in the system. The important point to note here is that Nigel is *not* using intonation as it is used in adult English, since the contrasts in meaning that are expressed by intonation in English (Halliday, 1967) are still outside his functional potential. He is adapting the elementary opposition between rising and falling, which he knows to be significant, to a functional system that is within his own limitations and which, as it happens, is perfectly transitional between Phase I and Phase III. This is the distinction that was referred to earlier between the pragmatic function, or language as doing, Nigel's rising tone, and the mathetic function, or language as learning, Nigel's falling tone. The one aspect that lies outside this system is the imaginative or play function of language, which at this stage takes the form of chants and jingles with special intonation patterns of their own.

This distinction between two broad generalized types of language use, the mathetic and the pragmatic, that Nigel expresses by means of the contrast between falling and rising tone, turns out to be the one that leads directly to the abstract functional distinction of ideational and interpersonal that lies at the heart of the adult linguistic system. In order to reach Phase III, the child has to develop two major zones of meaning potential, one ideational, concerned with the representation of experience, the other interpersonal, concerned with the communication process as a form and as a channel of social action. These are clearly marked out in the grammar of the adult language. It seems likely that the ideational component of meaning arises, in general, from the use of language to learn, whereas the interpersonal arises from the use of language to act. The fact that Nigel made the distinction between the mathetic and the pragmatic fully explicit by means of intonation was, of course, merely his own route through Phase II; it is not to be expected that this distinction will be expressed in the same way by all children, or even that it will necessarily be made explicit at all. But for Nigel this was a major step in his development of a grammatical system, as he progressed from the simple duality of content and expression that is characteristic of Phase I.

It is not to be thought that Phase II "mathetic" is *synonymous* with ideational, or "pragmatic" with interpersonal. Pragmatic and mathetic are generalized functional categories of the content, in the developmental system of the child, in which every utterance is, in principle, *either* one *or* the other. Ideational and interpersonal are abstract functional components of the grammar, in the developed, tri-stratal system of the adult; here every utterance is, in principle, *both* one *and* the other at the same time. What changes is the concept of "function"; and from this point of view, Phase II is the developmental process whereby "function" becomes distinct from "use." In other words, the notion "function of language" splits into two distinct notions, that of "use of language" and that of "component of the linguistic system." We shall try to summarize this process, together with other aspects of the entry into Phase III, in the final section that follows (Fig. 14–2).

Summary of Functional Development

1. The origins of language development can be interpreted as the learning of a set of functions, each with its associated "meaning potential." The system is a functional one, in which function is identical with use; each utterance has one function only, and the meanings are such as *Give me that, I'm interested, Let's*

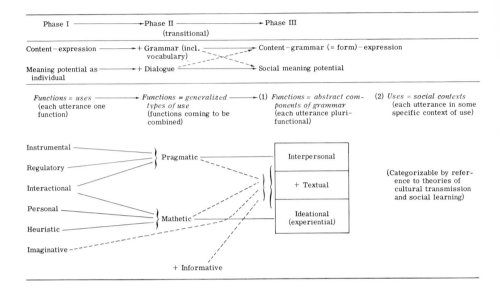

Figure 14—2.

be together. The initial functions are instrumental, regulatory, interactional, and personal; these are then followed by the heuristic and the imaginative. Each item in the language is a simple content-expression pair; there is no level of linguistic "form" (no grammar).

2. At a certain stage, the child begins to use language in a "mathetic" function, for the purpose of learning. This arises as a generalization from the personal and the heuristic; language in the identification of the self and, as a corollary, in the exploration of the nonself. This function is realized through verbal observation and recall (and, later, prediction). It generates a range of new meanings for which the child needs resources of vocabulary (e.g. names of objects and processes) and of structure (e.g. class and property, process and participant).

3. Simultaneously there appears to take place a generalization of the remaining functions under a "pragmatic" rubric, which includes the use of language both to satisfy one's own needs and to control and interact with others (subsuming what is sometimes called "manipulative" language). This also generates new meanings, for which other structures are required (e.g. request plus object of desire), and also other lexical items. With Nigel, however, only a minority of words were first learnt in this function, perhaps because often the specific meaning is recoverable from the situation (e.g. *I want that thing there*).

4. The grouping into mathetic and pragmatic functions appeared, with Nigel, as the dominant characteristic of Phase II, the transitional phase. The distinction is that between language as learning and language as doing; between *separating* the self from the environment, thus identifying the one and interpreting the

other, and *interacting* with the environment so as to intrude on the things and people in it, manipulating them and expressing attitudes towards them. With Nigel, nearly all words and structures were first used to express meanings in either one or the other of these two functions, not in both; after an interval, the resources that had been mastered in the one function were then transferred to the other. But, at the same time, all utterances were becoming plurifunctional (see 10).

5. In its inception, the mathetic–pragmatic distinction corresponds to one of "response required" (pragmatic) versus "response not required" (mathetic). This probably accounts for the remarkably explicit form given to this distinction by Nigel, who used a rising tone to express the pragmatic meaning and a falling tone for the mathetic. The question whether the mathetic–pragmatic distinction represents a general Phase II strategy must be left open at this stage; the use of intonation to express the distinction is, of course, Nigel's own idea.

6. As far as the linguistic system is concerned, Phase II consists of learning grammar; that is, of introducing into the system a level of linguistic form interposed between content and expression and made up of sets of options realized as structure and vocabulary. The need for a grammar arises out of the pragmatic and the mathetic functions; the latter, which is probably of greater significance for cognitive development, seems to provide the main impetus, at least for the learning of vocabulary. The introduction of grammatical structure makes it possible, however, to combine both functions in one utterance.

7. At the same time he is learning grammar, the child also learns dialogue. This is the other major step characterizing Phase II. Here the main impetus probably comes from the pragmatic functions, with their emphasis on involvement. With dialogue, the child acquires a potential for adopting and assigning linguistic roles, which in turn calls for further resources in the grammar (e.g. a set of options in mood—declarative, interrogative, and so on—and the structures used to realize them).[10]

8. Functionally speaking, the grammar of the adult language comprises two major components: (1) ideational, embodying the speaker's experience and interpretation of the world that is around him and inside him, and (2) interpersonal,

---

[10] It is the system of mood that is eventually going to determine the patterns of rising and falling tone. How does Nigel adapt this to his own interpretation of rise and fall? At this stage, he has no system of mood other than that expressed by his own use of the distinction of rise and fall, that is, the pragmatic–mathetic system; the demand for a new name, [adỹdà] *What's that?*, cannot really be regarded as an interrogative—it is true that it always has a falling tone, but this is *not* because it is a *Wh-* question (he has no *Wh-* questions at this stage), but rather because it has a mathetic function. When he does learn the *Wh-* question form, *where* + personal name, this at first has either tone, with (it seems) a difference in meaning between the two; but subsequently this and all other *Wh-* questions take on the rising tone, presumably on the grounds that an answer is a form of response (even though a purely linguistic one), and that demanding an answer is therefore a type of pragmatic function. Later still he learns the yes–no interrogative form, but this is not used for asking questions at all; it is used solely as the realization of the informative function, to communicate experience not shared by the hearer, for example, **Did you fall down** *I want you to know that I fell down—you didn't see the event*, contrasting with **You fell down** *I fell down—as you saw*.

embodying his own involvement in the speech situation—his roles, attitudes, wishes, judgments, and the like. To express this another way, the linguistic system has evolved so as to serve, for the speaker, the "observer" function on the one hand, and the "intruder" function on the other. These two "metafunctions," together with a third, the "textual" function, are incorporated into the system of the adult language as distinct sets of options, each having strong internal but weak external constraints (i.e., a choice within one function affects other choices within the same function but not, in general, those outside it). Each set of options is realized through distinct structures that are mapped on to one another in the production of utterances.

9. It follows that, in Phase III (the adult system), "function" is no longer synonymous with "use." The adult has indefinitely many uses of language; but the typical utterance of the adult language, whatever its use, has both an ideational and an interpersonal component of meaning. For example, every main clause embodies selections—and therefore is structured—simultaneously in transitivity (ideational) and in mood (interpersonal).

10. It appears, then, that the "metafunctions" of the Phase III grammatical system arise, indirectly but unmistakably, out of the primary uses of language that the child develops in Phase I. On the evidence of Nigel, the transition takes place by a process of generalization from these primary functions, which yields the two broad function types of pragmatic and mathetic. The pragmatic is oriented toward meanings such as *I want*, *Will you?*, *May I? Let's*, so it provides the context for the interpersonal systems of the grammar, typically those of mood, modality, person, attitude, and the like. The mathetic is oriented towards experiential meanings, and so provides the context for ideational systems such as those of transitivity (the grammar of processes), time and place, qualifying and quantifying, and so on.

11. Hence the child's Phase I functional system, which is a system of the *content* in a "content, expression" language, evolves along the familiar lines of generalization followed by abstraction into the Phase III (adult) functional system, which is a system of the *form* in a "content, form, expression" language. The concept of function has itself evolved in the process (cf. Fig. 2). In Hjelmslevian terms, the functional basis of language has shifted from the "content substance" (in a system having no level of form) to the "content form." The child, at Phase II, makes the crucial discovery that, with language, he can both observe and interact with the environment at the same time; this is the significance of Nigel's **cake**, meaning *That's cake—and I want some!* By the time he enters Phase III, the child has a great many "uses" of language; but all of them are actualized through the medium of the ideational and the interpersonal "functions;" in other words, through his twofold meaning potential as observer and as intruder.

12. Meanwhile, therefore, the original Phase I functions have not just disappeared. It is these that have become the uses of language—or rather, perhaps, they have become the generalized contexts of language use. In addition to those that seem to have been the key to the transition process, two others had been

postulated, the imaginative and the informative. The imaginative, or play, function of language is present already in Phase I; by the end of Phase II, the child is playing not only with sounds but with forms and meanings as well, reciting, distorting, and inventing rhymes, routines, and stories. Eventually—but not until well into Phase II—he adds the informative function, the use of language to communicate an experience to someone who did not share it with him; this is a highly complex function, since it is one that is solely defined by language itself.[11] At the same time, language still serves, for the child, the uncomplicated functions for which he first learned it. Their scope, however, is now immeasurably enlarged, in breadth and in depth; in other words, in the meaning potential that is associated with each.

Conclusion

By the end of Phase II, the child has entered the adult language. He has built up a system that is multi-stratal (content, form, expression) and multifunctional (ideational, interpersonal, textual). From this point on, he is adding to what he already has. He has learnt *how* to mean; his language development now consists in extending the range of his meaning potential to broader cultural horizons.

In order to follow this process further, we should have to go outside the linguistic system and into the culture. The child's uses of language are interpretable as generalized situation types; the meanings that he can express are referable to specific social contexts, and at least in some instances may be approached through a context-specific semantic analysis such as is exemplified in Turner (1973).

Bernstein (1971) has shown that certain types of social context are critical to the process of cultural transmission; the language of these contexts plays a crucial part in the child's socialization. Now, as we have seen, all language behavior, including that which characterizes these critical contexts, is mediated through the basic functions of language, the observer function and the intruder function; and the meanings that are expressed are linked, in this way, to what Malinowski (1923) called the "context of situation." But because these functions are not simply aspects of the use of language, but are part of—indeed, are the heart of—the linguistic system, the specific meanings expressed are at the same time instances of general semantic categories, and hence are interpreted in the "context of culture" (to use another of Malinowski's concepts).

What is the significance of this for the child? The significance is that, because of the functional basis of language, the particular, concrete meanings that are

---

[11] The imaginative and informative functions call for the narrative mode (within the ideational component) as distinct from simple observation and recall. This, in turn, requires discourse, that is, text that is structured so as to be relevant not only to the situation but also to the verbal context, to what is said before and after. What we referred to as the "textual" component in the linguistic system can be seen developing, with Nigel, in response to the needs of dialogue and of narrative.

expressed in typical everyday situations become, for him, the primary source for *building up* the context of culture. By the time he reaches Phase III, each instance of *I want* or *May I?* or *Let me take part* or *What's going on?* is encoded in words and structures that serve in some measure to categorize the social order and the child's own part in it. So it happens that the child's own early uses of language impose certain requirements on the nature of the linguistic system, determining the functional basis on which it is organized; with the result that, as these early uses evolve into generalized social contexts of language use, the linguistic system is able to act through them as the primary means for the transmission of the culture to the child. In this way language comes to occupy the central role in the processes of social learning.

References

Bernstein, B. (Ed.) *Class, codes and control.* Volume I: *Theoretical studies towards a sociology of language.* Primary Socialization, Language and Education Series. London: Routledge & Kegan Paul, 1971.

Bloom, L. *Language development: Form and function in emerging grammars.* Cambridge, Mass.: MIT Press, 1970.

Braine, M. D. S. The ontogeny of English phrase structure: the first phase. *Language,* 1963, *39,* 1—13.

Braine, M. D. S. The acquisition of language in infant and child. In C. E. Reed (Ed.), *The learning of language.* New York; Appleton, 1971. Pp. 7—95.

Britton, J. N. *Language and learning.* London: Allen Lane (Penguin), 1970.

Brown, R. *A first language: The early stages.* Cambridge, Mass.: Harvard Univ. Press, 1973. (First circulated draft.)

Bühler, K. *Sprachtheorie: die Darstellungsfunktion der Sprache.* Jena: Fischer, 1934.

Doughty, P., Pearce, J., & Thornton, G. *Language in use.* Schools Council Programme in Linguistics and English Teaching. London: Arnold, 1971.

Ervin, S. M., & Miller, W. R. Language development. *Yearbook of the National Society for the Study of Education,* 1963, *62,* 108—143.

Fillmore, C. J. 1968. The case for case. In E. Bach & R. T. Harms (Eds.), *Universals in linguistic theory.* New York: Holt, 1968.

Firth, J. R. Personality and language in society. *Sociological Review,* 1950, *42.* Reprinted in J. R. Firth, *Papers in linguistics 1934—1951.* London & New York: Oxford Univ. Press, 1957.

Firth, J. R. A synopsis of linguistic theory. In *Studies in linguistic analysis.* Special Volume of the Philological Society. Oxford; Blackwell, 1957. Reprinted in F. R. Palmer (Ed.), *Selected papers of J. R. Firth 1952—1959.* London, Longmans, 1968.

Gruber, J. S. Topicalization in child language. *Foundations of Language,* 1967, *3,* 37—65.

Halliday, M. A. K. *Intonation and grammar in British English.* Janua Linguarum Series Practica 48. The Hague: Mouton, 1967.

Halliday, M. A. K. Relevant models of language. In *The state of language. Educational Review* 22.1. Univ. of Birmingham Press, Birmingham, Eng.: 1969. Pp. 26—37. Reprinted in M. A. K. Halliday, *Explorations in the functions of language,* London; Arnold, 1973.

Halliday, M. A. K. Language structure and language function. In J. Lyons (Ed.), *New horizons in linguistics.* Harmondsworth, Eng.: Penguin Books, 1970.

Halliday, M. A. K. *Explorations in the functions of language.* Explorations in Language Study Series. London: Arnold, 1973.

Ingram, D. Transitivity in child language. *Language,* 1971, *47,* 888—910.

Kelley, K. L. Early syntactic acquisition. Rand Corp., Santa Monica, Calif., 1967.

Lamb, S. M. Linguistic and cognitive networks. In P. Garvin (Ed.), *Cognition: A multiple view.* New York: Spartan Books, 1970.

Leopold, W. F. *Speech development of a bilingual child: A linguist's record.* Evanston & Chicago: Northwestern Univ. Press, 1939–1949.

Lewis, M. M. *Infant speech: A study of the beginnings of language.* International Library of Psychology, Philosophy and Scientific Method. London; Routledge & Kegan Paul, 1936. (2nd ed., enlarged, 1951.)

Mackay, D., Thompson, B., & Schaub, P. *Breakthrough to literacy: Teacher's manual.* Schools Council Programme in Linguistics and English Teaching. London: Longmans, 1970.

Malinowski, B. The problem of meaning in primitive languages. Suppl. I to C. K. Ogden & I. A. Richards, *The meaning of meaning.* International Library of Psychology, Philosophy and Scientific Method. London: Kegan Paul, 1923.

Morris, D. *The naked ape.* London: Jonathan Cape, 1967.

Osser, H. Three approaches to the acquisition of language. In F. Williams (Ed.), *Language and poverty: Perspectives on a theme.* Chicago: Markham, 1970.

Reich, P. A. Relational networks. *Canadian Journal of Linguistics,* 1970, *15*, 95–110.

Schlesinger, I. M. Production of utterances and language acquisition. In D. I. Slobin (Ed.), *The ontogenesis of grammar: A theoretical symposium.* New York: Academic Press, 1971.

Turner, G. J. Social class and children's language at age five and age seven. In B. Bernstein (Ed.), *Class, codes and control.* Vol. II: *Applied studies towards a sociology of language.* Primary Socialization, Language and Education Series. London: Routledge & Kegan Paul, 1973.

15. Cross-Linguistic Similarities at Two Stages of Syntactic Development[1]

Melissa F. Bowerman

Do all children, regardless of the language they are acquiring, pass through a similar sequence of developmental stages, each of which is marked by the production of particular kinds of constructions? Samples of early speech from American, Finnish, Samoan, and Luo children are compared in an initial investigation of this question. Extensive similarities are found across languages in the kinds of construction patterns produced at each of two periods of syntactic development, called here "Early Stage I" (mean length of utterance 1.30–1.50 morphemes) and "Late Stage I" (mean length of utterance 1.60–2.00 morphemes). These similarities suggest that there are many commonalities in the developmental order in which children in different linguistic communities learn how to combine words to express various relational concepts.

Introduction

Much recent research on child language has been directed at discovering "universals of language acquisition," or similarities in the way children acquire language regardless of the particular language to which they are exposed. Identifying such universals requires access to language acquisition data from a variety

[1] This research was supported in part by PHS Grant HD-02908 from the National Institute of Child Health and Development; Roger Brown of Harvard University was principal investigator; and by PHS Training Grant NS-05362 from the National Institute of Neurological Disease and Stroke to the Bureau of Child Research, University of Kansas.

of languages, to allow aspects of development that are common to all children to be distinguished from similarities that result from exposure to languages with similar structural features.

Until recently, there has been little adequate comparative material. In the last few years, however, relatively detailed reports on the acquisition of several different languages have become available. In examining these data, investigators have become increasingly aware that children in different linguistic communities begin their syntactic careers in a remarkably similar fashion. For example, Slobin (1970), in comparing the early speech of American, German, Russian, Samoan, Luo, and Finnish children, notes that "if you ignore word order, and read through transcriptions of two-word utterances in the various languages we have studied, the utterances read like direct translations of one another. . . . There is a great similarity of basic vocabulary and basic meanings conveyed by the word combinations [p. 177]."

As yet, cross-linguistic comparisons of early syntactic development have not been fine-grained enough to answer certain questions. For example, we do not know whether the basic meanings to which Slobin refers are expressed in the early speech of all children, or constitute instead a shared pool of possible meanings which different children draw upon in different ways. A related question, also unexplored, is whether all children, regardless of the language they are acquiring, pass through a similar sequence of developmental stages, each of which is marked by the production of particular kinds of constructions. The existence of such stages would suggest that there is a universal order in which the ability to encode certain conceptual meanings linguistically is acquired.

The following is an initial effort to investigate these questions by making comparisons, where possible, of speech samples from *individual* children, and by distinguishing between samples from children at somewhat different developmental points. Data on the acquisition of four languages are used to arrive at a description of cross-linguistic similarities and differences at two stages of development.

Plan of Analysis

The languages represented in this study are English (data collected by Bloom, 1970; Bowerman, 1973a; Brown, 1970, 1973); Finnish (Bowerman, 1973a); Samoan (Kernan, 1969); and Luo (Blount, 1969). The four languages belong to different language families (Indo-European, Finno-Ugric, Austronesian, and Eastern Sudanic, respectively), and have very different structures. Thus, the following description of cross-linguistic similarities at two periods of development provides material for deductively generating hypotheses about the universal characteristics of child speech at these periods, and about the changes that take place between them.

Recent studies of children learning English have used mean length of utterance

(MLU), counted in morphemes, as a method of matching samples from different children for comparison (e.g., Bloom, 1970; Brown, Cazden, & Bellugi, 1968). Whether similar MLUs mark similar developmental stages in children acquiring different languages has not yet been well explored. Therefore, the non-English samples, which are compared to each other and to the English samples in this study, were not originally matched on the basis of MLU but rather by inspection of their internal characteristics. Interestingly, the MLUs of the samples thus matched are, in fact, similar, which suggests that MLU can be used as a nonlanguage-specific measurement of linguistic development.[2]

The matched samples are divided into two groups representing earlier and later periods of development. These periods are marked by MLU boundaries of approximately 1.30 to 1.50 and approximately 1.60 to 2.00. This places them both within the period Brown (1970, 1973) has termed "Stage I" (MLU boundaries of just over 1.00–2.00), so they are called here "Early Stage I" and "Late Stage I" respectively. The children who are compared to each other at each stage, and relevant information about the samples, are presented in Table 15-1.

The following analysis is based on the assumption that the presence or absence of various construction patterns in a sample, and the relative frequencies with which they occur, can provide information about the order in which children acquire knowledge of how to construct sentences of various kinds.[3] It is possible that the particular set of construction patterns present in a sample might be determined primarily by performance factors such as topic of conversation, and therefore not constitute a fair representation of the child's knowledge of sentence construction. However, a major reason for rejecting random performance factors as an explanation for the characteristics of the samples examined here is that, with a few exceptions, the construction patterns that are infrequent or absent in any one child's sample tend to be infrequent or absent in all the samples.

Another way in which determining order of acquisition from the presence, absence, and relative frequencies of constructions in samples of child speech might be misleading is discussed by Brown et al. (1968). These investigators note that if children produced different kinds of constructions with unequal frequencies, the more frequent ones would seem to be acquired earlier even if in fact they were not, because on a probabilistic basis they would be more likely to appear in any particular sample of speech, and would always occur in greater numbers. However,

---

[2]The Luo sample differs from the others, and is less useful for the purposes of this analysis, in that it contains the utterances of several children for whom MLU could not be determined. Blount's earliest sample (9 utterance types from 2 children) and second sample (49 utterance types from 5 children) are here collapsed together and considered with the Early Stage I samples from the other languages because the kinds of constructions involved appear comparable. However, the presence of a greater proportion of three-term strings than in the samples from the other languages suggests that at least some of the children were at a slightly more advanced stage of development.

[3]How this knowledge is related to the development of comprehension or to other behaviors which draw upon underlying knowledge of linguistic structure, or competence, is little understood, and is not investigated in the present study.

TABLE 15–1 THE CHILDREN USED FOR COMPARISON AT TWO STAGES OF DEVELOPMENT

Early Stage I: MLU between approximately 1.30–1.50

Child	Language	MLU	Age	Collection of data	Sample size (total utterance tokens)	Investigator
Seppo	Finnish	1.42	23 months	2 hr, taped over 3 weeks	713	Bowerman (1973a)
Kathryn	English	1.32	21 months	7½ hr, taped in few days	1225	Bloom (1970)
Gia	English	1.34	21 months	7½ hr, taped in few days	1790	Bloom (1970)
Eric	English	1.42	22 months	8½ hr, taped in few days	564	Bloom (1970)
Kendall	English	1.48	23 months	1½ hr, taped in 2 days	713	Bowerman (1973a)
Sipili	Samoan	1.52	30 months	6½ hr, taped over 1 week.	over 850	Kernan (1969)
6 children	Luo	—	19–31 months	Tape recorded	152 (construction tokens only)	Blount (1969)

Late Stage I: MLU between Approximately 1.60 and 2.00

Child	Language	MLU	Age	Collection of data	Sample size (total utterance tokens)	Investigator
Seppo	Finnish	1.81	26 months	1½ hr, taped over 3 weeks	713	Bowerman (1973a)
Rina	Finnish	1.83	25 months	2 hr, taped over 3 weeks	713	Bowerman (1973a)
Eve	English	1.68	18–19 months	3½ hr, taped over 6 weeks	713	Brown (1973)
Sarah	English	1.73	27–28 months	3 hr, taped over 6 weeks	713	Brown (1973)
Adam	English	2.06	27 months	2 hr, taped	713	Brown (1973)
Tofi	Samoan	1.60	26 months	Taped over 1 week	625	Kernan (1969)

systematically unequal frequencies of production and limited sample size are probably not responsible for certain developmental sequences observed in the present study, since several construction patterns which are rare or absent in all the Early Stage I samples are strikingly more frequent in their Late Stage I counterparts, even though sample size is no greater.

Nevertheless, it is often difficult to interpret the significance of differences in the relative frequencies with which utterances representing different construction patterns occur in the samples. It is likely that any pattern that is represented in a sample by many different word combinations was productive (rule-governed) for the child. Patterns represented by few utterances *may* have been productive, but there is also the strong possibility that the utterances were memorized, and do not reflect knowledge of rules for constructing sentences. There is a plausible alternative explanation for those construction patterns that are represented by far more utterances in the samples from Late Stage I than in those from Early Stage I. Utterances of this sort in the early samples may have resulted not from memorization but rather from rules for sentence construction that were in the process of being formulated and were not yet as productive as they would shortly become.

Early Stage I

MAJOR CONSTRUCTION PATTERNS: TWO-TERM STRINGS

In the Early Stage I samples, most utterances are one or two morphemes long. Three-morpheme strings are quite infrequent. The constructions that occur in the various samples are very similar, and most can be classified according to a short listing of structural descriptions (construction patterns), as presented in Table 15—2.[4] The numbers represent frequencies of occurrence.[5]

The following construction patterns occur in every sample:

agent—action. e.g.: *mommy push* (Kathryn); *man dances* (Seppo); *goes Va* (Sipili); *car runs* (Luo).

---

[4] These descriptions are chosen primarily for convenience in data reduction and because the terms are familiar. Since we do not yet know what kinds of structural information children use in producing their utterances, the descriptions may or may not correspond to the form of children's rules (see Bowerman, 1973b; Brown, 1973; for discussion of this problem).

[5] The absolute frequencies in each row are not comparable for several reasons. First, the samples are of different sizes. Second, while the figures for Kendall, Seppo, Sipili, and the Luo children represent utterance *types* only, the figures for Bloom's subjects (Kathryn, Eric, and Gia) represent utterance *tokens*. The absolute frequencies for Bloom's children are thus inflated with respect to those of the other children, but the assumption is that *relative* frequencies are not affected. Finally, the Luo sample is compiled from the constructions of several children (see Footnote 2, page 269). This means that even the relative frequencies in this sample are not comparable to to those in the samples from the individual children, and can only be used as rough indications of what kinds of constructions are common early in the acquisition of Luo.

TABLE 15–2 EARLY STAGE I: MAIN CONSTRUCTION PATTERNS IN FOUR LANGUAGES[a]

Two-term constructions	English Kathryn[b] MLU 1.32	English Gia[b] MLU 1.34	English Eric[b] MLU 1.42	English Kendall MLU 1.48	Finnish Seppo MLU 1.42	Samoan Sipili MLU 1.52	Luo Several Children
Subject–verb:							
agent–action	18	15	(64 I + V[e] and / 3 N + V)	27	25	3	5
person-affected–state[c]				1			3
object-involved–verb[d]				2			1
Verb–direct object:							
action–object[f]	39	38	many V + it / 6 V + N	11	5	6	11
state–object							2
Subject–direct object:							
(mostly agent–object)	31	23		5	3		(1 ?)
Object-located–location[g]	3	3		7	7		
Action or state–location[h]			1	3	1	1	
Demonstrator–object-demonstrated[i]	8	2	4	10	6	28	8
Possessor–Possessed[j]	20	12	1	12	4	23	5
Modifier–noun:							
adjective–noun	many	1	4	6	4	1	2
more or *'nother* noun (or verb, adjective)	26	87	12	1			
attributive noun–noun	5	20		(1)			
Hi–noun	5	several					
Negative constructions	14	5	31	5		5	

Three-term constructions

Subject—verb—direct object:					
agent—action—object	2(4?)		1[e]	7	4
person—affected—state—object	1	1	1	7	4
Subject—verb—locative:					
agent—action—location			1	4	2
person—affected—state—location			1	1	
Demonstrator—modifier—object-demonstrated			1	1–2	2
Other: action—object—location; state—modifier—location; etc.		2	2		1

[a] All word orders of each construction pattern counted.

[b] Bloom (1970) does not give the complete samples for Kathryn, Gia, and Eric. The figures presented here are taken from Bloom where given; otherwise they are drawn from Bloom's tables, examples, and grammars.

[c] Verbs like want, see, receive, be-sick, and know are classified as "states." The semantic role of the sentence subjects associated with these verbs is called "person affected" (cf. Fillmore's [1968] "dative case").

[d] The term "object involved" is given here to the subjects of verbs like fall and break—intransitive (cf. Fillmore [1968] "objective case").

[e] Eric produced many utterances with a preverbal phonological element, which may have been the pronoun "I." This element also occurred in the context ——V + it or N; these strings are classified here as verb—direct object rather than as subject—verb—object strings.

[f] The semantic functions of direct objects are more varied and harder to characterize semantically than those of subjects. Therefore, the term "object" is used here as a cover term for all direct objects. A finer breakdown would reveal that in most samples, most direct objects function semantically as objects physically acted upon.

[g] Strings like there cow, pillow here, sweater chair. Strings like there cow, pillow here, are classified as "demonstrator—object-demonstrated." Strings with locative particles like up, down, off, and away occurred in most of the samples, but these are not counted in this table, since the structural relations intended by them seem variable and are often hard to determine. E.g. should Kendall's shoe off be considered agent—action (Shoe [came] off), action—object [I took] shoe off); or object-located—location (Shoe [is now] off)?

[h] Locatives include both nouns and prolocatives; e.g. sit pool, sit there.

[i] This category corresponds to Brown's (1970, 1973) "nomination" and to Schlesinger's (1971) and Braine's (1971) "ostension." "Words like this, that, here, there, and—in the Samoan sample—the and "sign of nominative" are paired with nouns (and sometimes other words, not counted in this table), with a deictic (pointing out, labeling) semantic function.

[j] The possessor—possessed category primarily includes possessive adjective +N and N + N strings judged to express a possessive relationship. Also included are the few N + N strings which probably derive from adult models like X has Y rather than from those like X's Y; for example, Kendall's doggie hole.

action—object. e.g.: *bite finger* (Kendall); *drives car* (Seppo); *spank me* (Sipili); *eat medicine* (Luo).

possessor—possessed. e.g.: *dolly hat* (Gia); *aunt car* (Seppo); *ball yours* (Sipili); *head mine* (Luo).

demonstrator—object-demonstrated. e.g.: *that candy* (Kendall); *there cow* (both Kendall and Seppo); *ball there, the fan* (Sipili); *she there, it clock* (Luo).

adjective—noun. e.g.: *big bed* (Kendall); *little fish* (Seppo); *children older* (Sipili); *pepper hot* (Luo).

Some of these sentence patterns are more frequent than others, and therefore more surely fully productive. Primary among these are *agent—action* and *action—object*. Subject—verb strings involving nonagentive subjects (with verbs like *want, see, break* [intransitive], and *fall*) do not occur in all the samples and are far rarer where they do occur than are agent—action strings. *Possessor—possessed* strings are frequent in all the samples except Eric's (English). *Demonstrator—object-demonstrated* constructions seem to have been only marginally productive at best for two of the four American children (Eric and Gia), but are frequent in all the other samples.

Adjective—noun combinations (excluding those involving *more* or *'nother*) are present in all the samples, but are infrequent in all except Kathryn's and Kendall's (both English), and therefore may not have been productive yet for most of the children. In contrast, they are much more frequent in all the Late Stage I samples except the Samoan. In all the Finnish and English samples in both Early and Late Stage I, adjectives occur more frequently before the nouns they modify (e.g., *big bed*) than after them in the position of predicate adjectives in adult speech (*hair wet*). This distinction is not relevant for Luo and Samoan, since in those languages adjectives in both syntactic roles occur in postnoun position.

Certain constructions that are very frequent in a few samples do not occur in all the languages nor in all the samples from American children. Thus, they are probably not universal, nor can their presence or absence be related to the particular language being learned. These include:

object-located—location. e.g., *lotion tummy* (Kendall); *car garage* (Seppo); *sweater chair* (Kathryn). Locative utterances like *here cow* and *ball there* occur in every sample except Gia's, but these are classified in the "demonstrator—object demonstrated" category, since their function appears to be identical to that of constructions like *this cow* or *that ball*. What are *not* found in all samples are Noun + Noun constructions expressing a locative relationship.

subject—object (mostly of the subtype *agent—object*), e.g., Kendall's *Kendall spider* ("looked at" implied by context); Seppo's *horsie flower* (*eats* implied by context).

attributive noun modifier—noun. e.g., *animal book* (Gia); *party hat* (Kathryn).

more or *'nother* + N, V, or Adj., and *hi* + N. These two construction patterns are common in samples from many American children, including Bloom's subjects, and have been singled out by Bloom (1970) and Brown (1970, 1973) as expressing the special relations of "recurrence" and "notice" respectively. However, in the sample of another American child, Kendall, there is only one instance of *more* + N and none of *hi* + N. Neither of these patterns occur at all in the Finnish, Samoan, or Luo samples from either Early or Late Stage I, with the single exception of the often-repeated phrase *more cake* in Rina's Late Stage I Finnish sample.

Certain constructions that one might expect children to be able to produce at this time are very rare or absent in all the samples. For example, *action–location* strings (e.g., Kendall's *sit bed*, Sipili's *go home*, Eric's *go here*) occur in only four of the seven samples, and are represented by only one sentence in three of these. In contrast, action–location strings are relatively common in all the Late Stage I samples. Also generally absent are strings involving *indirect objects* (e.g., *give mommy*), *adverbs* (*push hard, sing loud, go soon*), *predicate nominatives* (excluding those beginning with *this* and *that*) (e.g., *mommy* [is a] *lady, ball* [is a] *toy*), and *instruments* used in the execution of actions (*eat spoon, write pencil, cut knife*). While indirect objects do begin to emerge by Late Stage I, constructions with adverbs, predicate nominatives, and instruments remain extremely rare throughout the entire period. Of all the children studied, only Seppo appears to have combined adverbs productively with other lexical items by Late Stage I.

NEGATION

In analyzing the "earliest stage of two-word utterances" in a variety of languages, Slobin (1968) found that "the universality of negative pivot sentences is notable." The data reviewed here do not support the hypothesis that negative constructions are universally among the first set of productive construction patterns. Elementary negative constructions involving words like *no, not,* and *no more* plus a noun or verb occur in the Samoan sample and all the American samples, but are completely absent from the Finnish and Luo samples. Ervin-Tripp (1973) reports that negative constructions were also absent in the early sign-language combinations of a deaf child. Even among the American children investigated here, evidence for productive syntactic negation in Early Stage I is strong only for Kathryn and Eric. Bloom felt that syntactic negation was only marginal at best for Gia, and its productivity in Kendall's speech is also uncertain. In contrast, negative constructions occur in all the Late Stage I samples and are frequent in most. Thus, acquiring a productive means of making negative constructions may, for many children, be an important development between Early and Late Stage I.

INTERROGATION

One striking difference among samples from different languages involves interrogation. Formally marked yes–no questions were asked by all the children except the Finnish boy, Seppo. Even if Seppo sometimes had the *intention* of asking a question, he lacked a formal means of marking it in his speech, and his utterances were virtually never interpreted as questions by his mother. This difference between Seppo and the other children stems from differences in the formal devices for marking questions in the languages involved. English, Samoan, and Luo all offer a question intonation that can be superimposed upon an otherwise undisturbed declarative sentence, and the children learning these languages all took advantage of this device in posing questions. Finnish lacks such an intonation, however. Yes—no questions are primarily formed by the addition of an interrogative suffix, either to a single word (e.g., **kissa-ko**? *cat*?) or—in the stylistically neutral form of a sentence—to the verb. In this case, subject and verb are inverted. Neither of the Finnish children acquired these mechanisms throughout Stage I or for a long time thereafter.

GRAMMATICAL MORPHEMES

Another noteworthy difference among the samples from different languages involves the use of grammatical morphemes (functors). It is well documented that the early speech of children learning English consists primarily of nouns, verbs, and adjectives, and lacks grammatical morphemes (see Cazden and Brown, Chap. 17, this volume). Finnish is a more richly inflected language than English, but the speech of the Finnish children in both Early and Late Stage I was also "telegraphic" in just this way. There are certain exceptions to this description for the Samoan and Luo children, however.

In the Luo sample, inflections are affixed to verbs to mark personal pronouns and "it" in the roles of subject and direct object. Since the expression of subject and object relationships does not involve inflection in the three other languages, the Luo children used inflections only to supply syntactic information which the other children could supply without functors. However, personal pronouns were either absent or very rare and probably not yet productive in the American and Finnish samples. They occurred productively only as direct objects and as possessives in the Samoan sample.

Certain functors were also used productively by the Samoan child, in the construction patterns *the* + Noun, "sign of nominative" + Proper Name or Pronoun, and *and* (*for, with*) + Noun. These patterns do not occur in the Late Stage I sample from another Samoan child, so they may be atypical. Nevertheless, it is interesting to note that two of the patterns, *the* + Noun and "sign of nominative" + Proper Name or Pronoun, correspond in function to the demonstrative constructions of the American, Finnish, and Luo children. The forms such constructions take in child speech seem to be influenced by the way in which parents ask questions about the identity of objects. American parents usually ask *What's this (that)?* and elicit *this (that)* + Noun. Finnish parents more typically ask *What's here (there)?* and receive *here (there)* + Noun in response. The Samoan mother asked *What the thing there?* or *What the name of the thing there?* or "sign of nominative" *Who your father?* and elicited responses like *the* + Noun or "sign of nominative" *So'o* (a name).

The evidence reviewed here on grammatical morphemes suggests that the acquisition of inflections and other functors is not as delayed in the speech of all children as it is in that of typical American and Finnish children. However, it is possible that when children in Stage I do use functors, these functors generally mark only semantic or syntactic meanings that are expressed—more usually without the use of functors—in the early speech of all children. The evidence on this matter is not yet clear, however. Counterevidence for the hypothesis is that Burling's (1959) son, in learning Garo, a Tibeto-Burman language, began to add suffixes to verbs to mark meanings such as "future," "past," "present," and "imperative" at the same time as his first productive two-word combinations appeared. These meanings were not formally marked in the constructions of the children whose speech is analyzed here. Data from other languages are needed before we can come to firm conclusions about the role of grammatical morphemes in early child speech.

THREE-TERM CONSTRUCTIONS

Slobin (1970) has noted that a two-word stage of development appears to be universal, suggesting the "maturation of a language acquisition device with a fairly fixed programming span for utterances at the start." The present data support this view, and indicate that continued maturation results in a relaxation of the two-word constraint at about the same point for all children, when the proportion of two-word to one-word utterances in the child's speech has risen above a certain critical level. Three-term strings occur in all the Early Stage I samples, but are quite infrequent. Most three-term construction patterns are represented by so few utterances in each sample that it is impossible to determine whether they were productive yet. In contrast, three-term strings are frequent in all the Late Stage I samples. This suggests that the ability to combine three morphemes productively may emerge at a mean utterance length of about 1.30 to 1.50.[6] This is not predictable a priori, since it is possible to imagine a child whose mean length of utterance slowly climbs towards two morphemes simply because an increasing proportion of his utterances become exactly two morphemes long.

The sequence in which particular kinds of three-term strings emerge is discussed in the following analysis of Late Stage I speech.

Late Stage I

The analysis of Late Stage I Speech is based on samples from two Finnish, one Samoan, and three American children. No Luo data from this period of development are available.

The structural relations that constitute the common core of the Early Stage I

---

[6] The Luo sample cannot be used for this comparison, since it consists of utterances from several children whose MLUs are unknown.

samples continue to be the basis of most Late Stage I constructions. There are few totally new construction patterns. The primary development that distinguishes the two sets of samples is the increased frequency with which the structural relations, which are initially expressed one at a time in two-word construction patterns like agent—action and action—object, are now combined with each other in strings of three words (e.g., agent—action—object). With the exceptions noted above, the addition of obligatory functors lagged in the languages studied here until past Stage I.

The increased length and variety of construction patterns makes a sample-by-sample breakdown of patterns long and involved, so for considerations of brevity, the general lines along which development takes place will be outlined without this aid.

MAJOR CONSTRUCTION PATTERNS: THREE-TERM STRINGS

Two major kinds of three-term strings occur in all the Late Stage I samples. In one, three major constituents are combined, in strings like agent—action—object (e.g., Seppo's *piggy drives bicycle*, Rina's *Rina eats cake*, Tofi's *got-rid-of baby you*, and Sarah's *I ride horsie*); agent—action—location (Seppo's *bunny walk sand*, Tofi's *goes Usu there*, Adam's *tractor go floor*); action—object—location (Tofi's *bring baby there*, Adam's *put truck window*). A new major constituent that functions as indirect object occurs (infrequently) in samples from every language (although not every child), in two- and three-term strings like action—indirect object and action—object—indirect object (e.g., Rina's *give Rina*, Tofi's *bring candy baby*, and Eve's *show me book*). Not every possible combination of three major constituents occurs in every sample, but omissions are not systematic between languages and may reflect limited sample size rather than real differences in ability.

In the second type of three-term string, two-term relations are elaborated by the use of a modified noun where earlier in development only a single noun had occurred. Both adjectives and possessive nouns or pronouns serve as modifiers. The modified noun usually functions as object of the verb or object demonstrated; the modification of agents (or, more broadly, subjects) was common only in Seppo's speech. Compare typical Early Stage I utterances like Seppo's *baby walks, drives car*, and *there train* with their Late Stage I elaborated counterparts, such as Seppo's *big monkey comes, lifts big stone, there little tractor*; Tofi's *give baby* (object) *toy* (modifier) (baby toy = doll); Adam's *see Daddy car*; Eve's *that Mommy soup*; Rina's *here Rina hand*.

The approximately simultaneous emergence of three-term strings of both kinds (three major constituents versus two major constituents, one of which is a modified noun), has led Brown (1973) and Bowerman (1973a) to conclude that the two types of syntactic elaboration are equivalent in cognitive complexity.

SEMANTIC FUNCTIONS OF SENTENCE SUBJECTS

Another development which distinguishes the Late Stage I samples from the earlier ones is the increased number of sentences with subjects that do not function semantically as *agents*. This change is particularly evident in Seppo's speech. In Seppo's Early Stage I sample, all subjects with main verbs are agents, while by Late Stage I, "persons affected" and "objects involved" (Fillmore's [1968] "dative" and "objective" cases respectively) occasionally function as subjects as well, in utterances like *mouse is-afraid* and *tower falls-down*. There are also a number of nonagentive subjects in the other Finnish child's Late Stage I sample.

No continuous data from one child are available for either English or Samoan, but the existence of the same developmental trend seems likely. The American child Kendall, at MLUs of 1.10 and 1.48, produced none and few nonagentive subjects, respectively. In the Early Stage I samples from Bloom's subjects there are only a few utterances involving nonagentive subjects, with verbs such as *see*, *got*, *want*, and *fit*. In the Late Stage I data from Brown's American subjects, in contrast, nonagentive subjects are relatively common, in utterances like *Adam see that* and *I like jelly*. The Early Stage I Samoan sample contains only three sentence-subjects with main verbs, but these are all agents. The Late Stage I sample from a different Samoan child contains several nonagentive subjects, however.[7]

Elsewhere (Bowerman, 1973a, 1973b), I have proposed that this gradual diversification of the semantic functions performed by sentence subjects may provide a clue to the nature of the structural relationships expressed by children's early constructions. In particular, it suggests that syntactic concepts like "subject" and "predicate"—which some consider to be a part of children's inborn knowledge of language structure (e.g., McNeill, 1970, 1971)—are more abstract and powerful than are needed to account for children's early utterances. Initially, the child may not be seeking the means of expressing relations between subject and predicate, but rather, more concretely, of expressing interactions between semantic concepts like "agent" and "action initiated" or other even less abstract concepts. As the child's experience with various linguistic operations becomes more extensive, and the semantic functions of his subject nouns more varied, he may gradually begin to recognize similarities in the way different semantic concepts are formally dealt with in sentences of different types and to reorganize his knowledge according to more abstract grammatical relations.

WH- QUESTIONS

Wh- questions are very rare in the Early Stage I samples. Those that do occur have the character of memorized routines. In contrast, *Wh-* questions occur in all the Late Stage I samples, although relatively infrequently in most. Simple routines for eliciting labels, such as *that? 'ts'at?*, are present in the three English samples and emerged shortly after Stage I in the Finnish data. They are absent in the Samoan sample. "Where" questions occur in all the samples except Eve's,

[7] See Bowerman (1973b) for frequencies of the various kinds of sentence subjects in the different samples.

in simple utterances like Rina's *where cracker?*, Seppo's *where swims?*, Tofi's *where baby?*, and Adam's *where Daddy go?*

NEGATION

As noted above, negative constructions are much more frequent in the Late Stage I samples than in the earlier ones. Typical examples are Rina's *no wolf*, Seppo's *anymore play*, Tofi's *don't be-headstrong*. Negatives are structurally rudimentary compared to the children's affirmative sentences at this time. This supports Bloom's (1970) proposal that syntactic negation does not initially involve simply placing a negative element before or after an otherwise undisturbed affirmative sentence, as in Bellugi's (1967) account, but rather is an integral part of the sentence and has the effect of reducing its potential complexity.

WORD ORDER

Recent evidence on word order in children's early utterances has been discussed extensively elsewhere (e.g., Slobin, 1970, 1973; Ervin-Tripp, 1973; Bowerman, 1973a), so it will be mentioned only briefly here. The general finding is that in all the samples examined in this study, word order corresponds to the dominant (or only) adult order. Those exceptionally ordered strings that do occur in any one sample are usually few compared to the number of appropriately ordered sentences· of the same sentence pattern. The most common recordering, which occurs in samples from every language, involves the placement of the object noun before the verb rather than in its required or more normal position after the verb.

Finnish is relatively flexible with regard to word order compared to the other languages represented here. By the end of Stage I, and probably earlier, the Finnish children had learned acceptable alternative word orders for many construction patterns and used these with approximately the same rank order frequencies as their mothers did.

Summary

The evidence presented in this study suggests that cross-linguistic similarities in early syntactic development are extensive. There appear to be many commonalities in the developmental order in which children in different language communities learn how to combine words to express various relational concepts linguistically. This is evidenced by the presence of similar construction patterns in matched samples of child speech from different languages.

Certain construction patterns occurred in all the Early Stage I speech samples investigated here, and were highly productive for most of the children. These include agent—action, action—object, demonstrator—object-demonstrated, and possessor—possessed. Other patterns were infrequent or absent in the early samples but became more frequent toward Late Stage I: adjective-noun, action—location, *Wh-* questions, and construction involving indirect objects or nonagentive sentence-subjects.

There was considerable individual variation with respect to still other construction patterns. Subject—object, object-located—location (noun—noun), attributive noun modifier—noun, *hi*—noun, *more* or *'nother*—noun, and negative constructions were used very productively in Early Stage I by some children, but rarely or never by others. These constructions did occur in most of the Late Stage I samples, however. Most differences that occurred among samples from different languages were no greater than those found among samples from the same language. An exception to this was yes—no interrogation. Whether or not children produced questions of this sort was dependent on whether the language being learned provided a questioning intonation that could be superimposed on declarative sentence patterns. The two Finnish children, whose language differs from English, Samoan, and Luo in lacking such an intonation and requiring other formal devices for question marking, were unique among the children studied in not producing yes—no questions until long after Stage I.

The ability to express two structural relations at a time, in three-term strings such as agent—action—object, action—modifier—object, and demonstrator—modifier—object-demonstrated, seems to have emerged at about the same developmental point in all the languages investigated here, and the kinds of three term strings produced were virtually identical across languages.

Construction patterns involving adverbs, instrumentals, and predicate nominatives (excepting those introduced by words like *that*) were absent in all the samples throughout Stage I with only a few exceptions. Unlike the Finnish children's lack of interrogatives, these absences cannot be accounted for purely on grounds of formal complexity, since strings which occurred frequently, such as *eat apple* (action—object), *mommy apple* (agent-object), and *big apple* (modifier—noun) are superficially similar or identical to rare constructions like *cut knife* action—instrument), *mommy lady* (subject—predicate nominative), and *run fast* (verb—adverb).

Although the characteristics of the Early and Late Stage I speech samples from children learning unrelated languages were found in this study to be remarkably similar, it is still too early to conclude that the sequence of development they suggest is universal. Such a conclusion, or its rejection, must await the comparison of these findings with data from children acquiring still other languages.

References

Bellugi, U. The acquisition of negation. Unpublished doctoral dissertation, Harvard University, 1967.

Bloom, L. *Language development: Form and function in emerging grammars.* Cambridge, Mass: MIT Press, 1970.

Blount, B. G. Acquisition of language by Luo children. Unpublished doctoral dissertation, University of California at Berkeley, 1969.

Bowerman, M. *Early syntactic development: A cross-linguistic study with special reference to Finnish.* London & New York: Cambridge Univ. Press, 1973. (a)

Bowerman, M. Structural relationships in children's utterances: syntactic or semantic? in T. E. Moore (ed.), Cognitive development and the acquisition of language. New York: Academic Press, 1973. Pp. 197—213. (b)

Braine, M. D. S. The acquisition of language in infant and child. In C. Reed (Ed.), *The learning of language.* New York: Appleton, 1971. Pp. 7—95.

Brown, R. The first sentences of child and chimpanzee. In *Psycholinguistics: Selected papers by Roger Brown.* New York: Free Press, 1970. Pp. 208—231.

Brown, R. *A first language: The early stages.* Cambridge, Mass.: Harvard Univ. Press, 1973.

Brown, R., Cazden, C., & Bellugi-Klima, U. The child's grammar from I to III. In J. P. Hill (Ed.), *Minnesota symposia on child psychology.* Vol. II. Minneapolis: Univ. of Minnesota Press, 1968. Pp. 28—73.

Burling, R. Language development of a Garo and English speaking child. *Word,* 1959, *15,* 45—68.

Ervin-Tripp, S. Some strategies for the first two years. In T. E. Moore (Ed.), *Cognitive development and the acquisition of language.* New York: Academic Press, 1973. Pp. 261—297.

Fillmore, C. The case for case. In E. Bach & R. T. Harms (Eds.), *Universals in linguistic theory.* New York: Holt, 1968. Pp. 1—88.

Kernan, K. T. The acquisition of language by Samoan children. Unpublished doctoral dissertation, University of California at Berkeley, 1969.

McNeill, D. *The acquisition of language: The study of developmental psycholinguistics.* New York: Harper, 1970.

McNeill D. The capacity for the ontogenesis of grammar. In D. I. Slobin (Ed.), *The ontogenesis of grammar.* New York: Academic Press, 1971. Pp. 17—40.

Schlesinger, I. M. Production of utterances and language acquisition. In D. I. Slobin (Ed.), *The ontogenesis of grammar.* New York: Academic Press, 1971. Pp. 63—101.

Slobin, D. I. Early grammatical development in several languages, with special attention to Soviet research. Working Paper No. 11, Language-Behavior Research Laboratory, Berkeley, California, 1968.

Slobin, D. I. 1970. Universals of grammatical development in children. In W. Levelt & G. B. Flores d'Arcais (Eds.), *Advances in psycholinguistic research.* Amsterdam: North-Holland Publ., 1970. Pp. 174—186.

Slobin, D. I. Cognitive prerequisites for the development of grammar. In C. A. Ferguson & D. I. Slobin, (Eds.), *Studies of child language development.* New York: Holt, 1973. Pp. 175—208.

16. On the Nature of Talk to Children[1]

Dan I. Slobin

This is a review of preliminary findings in regard to differences in syntax, semantics, style, and manner of utterances directed to children as opposed to adults. The author adds further observations of his own and comes to the conclusion that the language-learning child's input is different from the input in verbal communication between adults.

Language cannot really be taught, but can only be awakened in the mind: one can only offer the thread along which language develops on its own [Wilhelm von Humboldt, 1836].[2]

I think that if we contemplate the classical problem of psychology, that of accounting for human knowledge, we cannot avoid being struck by the

---

[1] The research for this chapter was completed in April 1972. Since then the topic of speech to children has received widespread attention. A conference on Language Input and Acquisition was held in Boston in September 1974, and the term "motherese" is beginning to enter the literature. The following references, by no means a comprehensive list of new developments, will bring the chapter somewhat more up-to-date (with thanks to Eve Clark's reading list for a graduate seminar on "Language Input and Register," held at Stanford University in the winter of 1975): Blount (1972); Broen (1972), Farwell (1973), Garnica (1975), Holzman (1974), Moerck (1974), Nelson (1973), Newport (1974), Phillips (1973), Rūķe-Draviņa (1974), Sachs, Brown, & Salerno (1972), Snow (1972, 1974).

[2] "... [Die Sprache] ... lässt sich ... nicht eigentlich lehren, sondern nur im Gemüthe wecken; man kann ihr nur den Faden hingeben, und dem sie sich von selbst entwickelt [von Humboldt, 1836; quoted by Chomsky, 1964, p. 57]."

enormous disparity between knowledge and experience—in the case of language, between the generative grammar that expresses the linguistic competence of the native speaker and the meager and degenerate data on the basis of which he has constructed this grammar for himself [Noam Chomsky, 1968, p. 68].

The disparity between knowledge and experience noted by Chomsky cannot be denied. The complex internal structures of language and cognition are not simple reflections of the data of sense experience. In Chomsky's now classic formulation (1961, 1965):

Primary Linguistic Data → | LAD | → Grammar

That is, the language acquisition device (LAD; or, for little girls, LAS—the language acquisition system) receives primary linguistic data in the form of speech input from other people, and, by the use of complex and little-known intellectual tools, the LAD or LAS constructs the grammar of the particular input language. The grammar is certainly not given in the input; nor can it be easily induced from the input by any means presently conceivable. It is clear that the human child is singularly well endowed to carry out this intellectual task. In order to gain a clearer understanding of this accomplishment, however, we need a thorough description of the primary linguistic data—Humboldt's "thread along which language develops on its own." Are the data indeed "meager and degenerate," or does the thread offer the child something a bit more substantial to hold onto? The study of talk to children has just begun, but already it seems that the characterization of "meager and degenerate" is a bit too severe. Talk to children is not the same as talk to adults. The preliminary findings presented below suggest that the primary linguistic data represent a subcode which may be tuned to the language processing strategies of LAD or LAS. It should be noted at the outset that this suggestion in no way solves the problem of language acquisition posed by Chomsky, but at least it begins to clarify some of the parameters which must govern the work of LAD or LAS.[3]

Structural Characteristics of Input

In a seminar on developmental psycholinguistics at Berkeley, we recently carried out a small introspective exercise on language acquisition and speech input. Our subjective findings will be familiar to anyone who has tried to learn a foreign language *in situ*. We watched an Estonian mother interact with her 2-year-old daughter and listened attentively to the mother's speech. Our only preparation was a 2-hr "course" on the child's lexicon and grammar taught by

---

[3]This chapter deals only with characterizations of speech input; for a detailed discussion of the preliminary operating principles used by the child in scanning input and formulating grammatical rules, see Slobin (1973).

Dr. Marilyn Vihman, who has been studying the girl's linguistic development (cf. Vihman, 1971). What we heard, of course, cannot simulate the child's listening and comprehension, but our subjective impressions are suggestive of processes of linguistic attention and the characteristics of input which help to guide attention. Familiar words and phrases stood out in short-term memory with a peculiar intensity, while the surrounding verbal material reverberated around these anchor points. The mother's utterances were generally short enough for the entire utterance to persist in immediate memory, leaving a blurred impression of segmental phonology, but preserving a fairly good auditory image of such nonsegmental features as rhythm, length, pitch contour, and stress. Our memory was best for stressed syllables and for the ends of utterances. When successive utterances contained the same words, we were frequently able to notice changes in word order or additions of new elements. Such repetitions with slight alteration sometimes made it possible for us to identify new words, and occasionally we could discriminate the meanings of such words from watching what was going on between mother and child. But, lacking the child's many days and months of vocabulary learning, we were poor judges of word boundaries, let alone word meanings. By age two the relations between activities and speech were too complex to reveal new meanings to listeners without a backlog of old meanings. The child, of course, did not share this lack; Dr. Vihman informed us that almost all of the mother's speech contained familiar vocabulary.

In listening to this Estonian mother, participants in our seminar were struck by the extreme differences in her speech when addressing her child and when addressing an adult. Speech to an adult sounded like an endless rapid current, with barely a cue of sentence boundaries—let alone word or morpheme boundaries. By contrast, speech to the child easily fell into clear, short sentences. Thus it was our impression that speech to children may be better suited to primitive strategies of attention and analysis than speech to adults.

In fact, there is some evidence that little children chiefly attend to those aspects of input that they are able to assimilate. Speech not addressed to the child is generally tuned out. An extreme example of this point is the case of a child studied by Todd (1972). The boy—a hearing child of deaf parents—was a fluent user of American Sign Language at age $3\frac{1}{2}$, but neither spoke nor attended to speech, although he had been exposed to a television set in the home. His only source of linguistic interaction was with his signing parents, and it was their language that he had acquired. Similarly, as Ervin-Tripp (1971) has noted, children of immigrant parents do not learn their parents' language unless it is used in parent–child interaction. Apparently a language system will not be attended to unless it plays a role in meaningful interaction in the child's life.

Speech used in meaningful interaction with a child has particular characteristics, as suggested by the Estonian experience related above. At first it is brief, simple, redundant, and fairly closely tied to ongoing events. Pfuderer (1969) found that mothers adjust the complexity of their speech according to the age of the child, increasing in complexity as the child increases in skill. This is probably an intuitive communicative process, reflected also in adults' speech to foreigners and in the speech of older children to younger children. Pfuderer studied the transcripts of adult-to-child speech in the records of the three children studied by Roger Brown and his associates (cf. Brown, 1973), comparing early, middle, and late points in these longitudinal records (unpublished data). Striking changes in the later samples included embeddings and conjoinings of complex sentence structure and greatly increased frequency in the addition of optional verb phrase constituents (modifying prepositional phrases, extra manner adverbials, and so forth). These complex structures were not all present in the children's speech, but seemed to reflect a feeling on the part of the adults that the older children could be engaged in more adult-like conversation. The early adult-to-child samples, on the other hand, were characterized by a predominance of simple, active, affirmative and negative sentences, and simple, active, affirmative questions.[4]

TABLE 16–1 SAMPLE OF ADULT–CHILD SPEECH: BLACK WOMAN SPEAKING TO 26-MONTH-OLD SON[a]

Come play a game wit' me.

Come play a game with me.

Wanna play a game with me?

Come look at Mama's colorin' book.

You wanna see my coloring book?

Look at my coloring book.

Lookit, that's an Indian, huh?

Is that an Indian?

Can you say Indian?

Talk to me.

Watcha been doin' today?

What did you do today?

Look at that.

That's a funny picture, huh?

Oh . . . wheee . . . Look!

What's that?

And that's a church, huh?

[a]*The same speaker is represented in Tables 16–1, 2, 3, and 5. The speech samples were recorded by Claudia Mitchell-Kernan (1971) in Oakland, California. Materials for Tables 16–1 and 2 were prepared by Kerry Drach (1969), and materials for Table 16–3 were prepared by Ben Kobashigawa (1969), in connection with the Berkeley Workshops on the Acquisition of Communicative Competence, Summer 1968.*

[4]Recent observations by Posner (1972) suggest that speech to uncomprehending infants may be of greater complexity, undergoing drastic simplification as the infant develops rudimentary means of linguistic comprehension and expression.

TABLE 16–2 SAMPLE OF ADULT–ADULT SPEECH: BLACK WOMAN SPEAKING TO HER SISTER

An' then well now his father an' I are separated, so he sees me mainly.

An' then I try to do things with him and for him an' all to, kinda make up y'know for this.

But I can't, y'know, 'cause I can't put no man there to be a symbol for him or nothing.

You can take a chil' from basically—what you would call 'em—a bad environment.

No, I really—I really believe that—that church an' the Bible an' all, that's good.

It gives me a certain amount of consolation which allows me to relax my mind and start thinking intelligently an' putting my efforts all in one y'know force goin' in one direction rather than jus' y'know continually feeling sorry for yourself.

It takes a little time.

But they won't keep him at school because he's too sick.

I was on a inhalation series routine.

We wen' aroun' from ward to ward.

People are—y'know, that get all this mucus in their chest.

An' it's very important to breathe properly an' to be able to cough this mucus up and out an' through your chest, y'know as soon as possible.

And we couldn't sterilize the instruments, 'cause they were plastic.

Drach (1969) has systematically compared the speech of a woman when speaking to her 2-year-old child and when speaking to an adult, demonstrating that speech to the child was grammatically simple and free of hesitations, false starts, and errors, as shown in Tables 16–1 and 16–2. The adult–adult sample consisted of sentences that were, on the average, 2.5 times as long as the sentences in the adult–child sample, and was characterized by much greater variability in sentence length. In addition, the rate of speech was significantly faster in the adult-adult sample. On the variety of measures, the adult–adult sample was syntactically more complex.

Juliet Phillips (1970) has carried out the most detailed study to date of the formal characteristics of mother–child speech. In part of her study, 10 mothers of 18-month-old boys and 10 mothers of 28-month-old boys were recorded in converstation with an experimenter and in free play with the child. Mothers' speech to the experimenter, in comparison to their speech to the children, was characterized by longer utterances with more verbs and modifiers per utterance, a greater proportion of function words, a smaller proportion of content words, and a larger number of verb forms. Using these same formal features, Phillips also found that speech addressed to 28-month-old boys was more complex than speech addressed to 18-month-old boys. She summarizes these and other findings in the following terms:

> *From this study we can conclude that there are differences in syntax, vocabulary and intonation between speech addressed to adults and speech addressed to*

children. Furthermore, these differences change with the age of the person ad-
dressed. The language addressed to children during the period in which they
develop basic language skills is specialized and not representative of the language
spoken by adults among themselves [*p. 4*].

Drach (1969), Friedlander (1971; Friedlander, Jacobs, Davis, & Wetstone (1972), and Kobashigawa (1969) have shown that adult-to-child speech is highly repetitive: up to 34% of parental utterances to children under two consists of self-repetitions.

While it seems obvious that speech input of the sort characterized above should facilitate the work of LAD or LAS, it is still not clear how the child actively makes use of such information in forming linguistic generalizations. A finer analysis of parental speech suggests one process that may aid in drawing attention to words as perceptual units. Lyons (1968) gives the following as a special attribute to the word as a unit: "One of the characteristics of the word is that it tends to be internally stable (in terms of the order of the component morphemes), but positionally mobile (permutable with other words in the same sentence) [p. 203]." Another attribute cited by Lyons (1968, p. 204) is "interrruptability"—that is, one can insert elements between words (e.g. *the doll, the big doll,* etc.). Both of these attributes are present in the following sequence of utterances from our Estonian observation. The mother was trying to keep the child from putting something into her mouth, and gave the following sequence of orders:

Ära suhu pane.	*not mouth-into put*
Ära ise suhu pane.	*not your-own mouth-into put*
Ära pane suhu.	*not put mouth-into*

As if from a well-programmed language laboratory, this sequence of utterances left each word reverberating in memory as a separate entity. (Later in the session when *Ära suhu pane* was said again, it leapt out with a familiar clarity.)

Such apparently programmed sequences are commonplace in the speech addressed to little children. Kobashigawa (1969) has shown that most self-repetitions in mother's speech addressed to a 2-year old made slight alterations in form while preserving meaning across a sequence of utterances. He noted changes in word order and intonation, morphophonemic and syntactic alterations, and addition, deletion, and substitution of individual words. Examples are given in Table 16—3. In languages with relatively free word order, such as Estonian, Finnish (Bowerman, 1973), and Turkish (Slobin, unpublished data), word order changes are extremely common in such sequences in parental utterances. In fact, alteration of word order seems to be a natural device when seeking to elicit attention, response, or compliance from a child. (See Table 16—4 for Turkish examples.) And, indeed, it would be surprising if such alterations did not draw children's attention to different utterance segments and the possibilities of manipulating them. At present, however, this is more conjecture than conclusion. These preliminary studies have shown that

TABLE 16–3   EXAMPLES OF REPETITION IN A MOTHER'S SPEECH TO A 2-YEAR-OLD BOY[a]

What's your name?
Tell me what your name is.

Sing me a song.
Sing Mama a song.
Sing me a song.

Oh lookit, that's a funny lookin' thing there, huh?
That's funny lookin', huh?

That was nice. That was very very nice.

An' you got a Popeye ring today, didn't you?
You got a Popeye ring?
Can you say "Popeye"?
"Popeye."
You got a Popeye ring from the doctor, huh?

[a]*See Footnote to Table 16–1, p. 286.*

TABLE 16–4   EXAMPLES OF RE-ORDERED REPETITIONS IN SPEECH OF TURKISH ADULT TO A 2-YEAR-OLD BOY

Is this yours?	**Senin mi bu?** [yours question-particle this]
	Bu senin mi? [this yours question-particle]
Where's the record?	**Nerede plâk?** [where-at record]
	Plâk nerede? [record where-at]
What are you doing?	**Sen ne yapıyorsun?** [you what you-are-doing]
	Ne yapıyorsun sen? [what you-are-doing you]
What's in my hand?	**Benim elimde ne var?** [my in-my-hand what is]
	Ne var elimde? [what is in-my-hand]
	Elimde ne var? [in-my-hand what is]
	Benim elimde ne var? [my in-my-hand what is]
This is my airplane.	**Bu benim uçağım.** [this my my-airplane]
	Benim. [my]
	Bu uçak benim. [this airplane my]
	Bu benim uçak. [this my airplane]
	Bu benimki. [this mine]
	Bu benim uçağım. [this my my-airplane]

adult-to-child speech is systematically structured in ways that differ strikingly from adult-to-adult speech. It remains to be demonstrated, however, to what extent children attend to and utilize such structured input.

Feedback Characteristics of Input

Talk to children is not a one-way process. Adult remarks are often in response to what the child has said. Adult responses may indicate to the child whether he has communicated grammatically or appropriately. What is the evidence in this regard?

The most exhaustive and carefully analyzed data of mother–child interaction and linguistic development are those of Roger Brown and his co-workers at Harvard (Brown, 1973; Brown & Bellugi, 1964; Brown, Cazden, & Bellugi, 1968; Brown & Hanlon, 1970; Cazden, 1968; Klima & Bellugi, 1966; Slobin, 1968). Three children were followed over a number of years, beginning with the earliest period of grammatical development. Weekly or bi-weekly recordings were made in the children's homes. Brown's work allows for examination of possible roles played by mother's speech in the process of language acquisition.

RESPONSES TO GRAMMATICALITY

One possible role of the mother may be to indicate to the child when he has failed to communicate properly. As Brown puts it: "Do ill-formed constructions in child speech give way to well-formed constructions because there is a selection pressure in communication which favors the latter? [Brown & Hanlon, 1970, p. 42]." To answer this question, Brown and Hanlon looked at mothers' responses to "primitive" and to "well-formed" constructions uttered by the child and asked whether the response indicated comprehension or failure to comprehend the child's meaning. Surprisingly, primitive and well-formed utterances were understood equally well by the mothers. There seemed to be no communication pressure for grammatical utterances. A mother is apparently too engaged in interacting with a child to pay attention to the linguistic form of his utterances.

Brown has demonstrated this point in another way as well. He looked at cases in which a child's utterance was followed by an expression of approval or disapproval on the part of the adult, again finding no evidence that parental responses shape the child's sense of grammaticality. Parents pay attention to the content of child speech, approving true utterances and criticizing false ones, without regard to grammaticality.

> *In general, the parents fitted propositions to the child's utterances, however incomplete or distorted the utterances, and then approved or not according to the correspondence between proposition and reality. Thus,* **Her curl my hair** *was approved because the mother was, in fact, curling Eve's hair.*

However, Sarah's grammatically impeccable **There's the animal farm-house** *was disapproved because the building was a lighthouse, and Adam's* **Walt Disney comes on on Tuesday** *was disapproved because Walt Disney came on on some other day* [*Brown, Cazden and Bellugi, 1968, pp. 70–71*].

The infrequency of adult correction of the grammatical form of child speech is also reported in the field notes of the Berkeley cross-cultural studies of child language development (cf. Ervin-Tripp, 1969; Slobin, 1967, 1970). For example, Jan Brukman, working with the Koya in India, notes: "Certainly there is no evidence that children are ever corrected on matters of grammar. . . . I would say that most of the corrections are on matters of etiquette (like swear words) [personal communication]." In similar fashion, Keith Kernan notes: "I never heard anyone correct a child's speech in Samoa with the exception of telling a child not to use words considered to be 'profane' [personal communication]."

EXPANSIONS OF CHILD SPEECH

Another characteristic of adult response to children is to repeat the child's utterance, filling in what has been left out by the child. Brown and Bellugi (1964) have called such responses "expansions." They are a sort of paraphrase, offered to the child as an affirmation (with falling intonation) or comprehension check (with rising intonation). Expansions are frequent in the early stages of development, becoming less frequent as more mature communication becomes possible. At an early stage in Brown's data, as many as 30% of child utterances are followed by expansions (Slobin, 1968). Brown and Bellugi note (1964): "Indeed we found it very difficult to withhold expansions. A reduced or incomplete English sentence seems to constrain the English-speaking adult to expand it into the nearest properly formed complete sentence [p. 144]."

Expansions offer a child an adult paraphrase of an utterance he has just produced. For example, a child says *Oh no raining*, and the mother asks, *Oh no, it's not raining?* Yet there is no evidence that children make use of such feedback in their grammatical development. Cazden (1965), in an explicit training study, did not appreciably accelerate grammatical development by the concentrated use of adult expansions of child speech. Of the three children studied by Brown, Sarah received the lowest rate of parental expansions of her speech, yet was the most advanced in the development of inflections—which are just the items omitted in early child speech and filled in by expansions (Brown, Cazden, and Bellugi, 1968, p. 69).

Thus it seems that although children may use parental speech as a data base for linguistic development, explicit parental responses to child speech may not play a significant role in guiding the child to the discovery of grammatical rules. Children in all cultures learn to speak according to a universal timetable (Slobin, 1970, 1972), yet parental practices differ widely in regard to feedback and expansion. Furthermore, children in many cultures receive their primary speech input from other children. Therefore it seems that the major role of input is to provide examples of meaningful utterances in a communicative context, leaving it to the LAD or LAS to figure out the structure of the language without explicit tuituion or guidance from adult speakers.

Input from Adults versus Input from Children

As noted, the primary linguistic data do not always come from parents. Indeed, in some cultures parental input plays a minimal role during the active period of preschool language acquisition. Examples are offered by the Berkeley cross-cultural studies, especially in societies with extended family households. Keith Kernan notes that in Samoa:

> ... *The effect of the social structure upon the linguistic input to the child is that no one adult female serves as the linguistic model for the very young children as is often the case in American nuclear households. In addition other children serve as important sources of linguistic input for the child from the time of its birth, and after the child has reached age two-and-a-half years other children are more important as sources for linguistic input than are adults [personal communication; cf. Kernan, 1969].*

Ben Blount's comments about the Luo of Kenya present a similar picture:

> *After the age of one, an older sibling, preferably a girl between the ages of four and eleven, will be assigned as a nursemaid for the child, and she gradually will take over responsibility for the child's welfare. The child's mother will begin to return to her regular work in the gardens, which she must do for several hours every day, and by the time a child is two-and-a-half, the major source of speech input has shifted from his mother to his nursemaid. . . . The nursemaid continues to be the major source of speech input until the child is three or three-and-a-half, at which time the peer group becomes the most important source. Peer groups of this type are made up of children in the age range of three to seven. . . . From my observations, the speech input from other adults seems to be quite insignificant during this period [personal communication: cf. Blount, 1969].*

Although the major speech input in such cultures is from other children, rather than parents, the course and rate of linguistic development do not seem to be affected (Blount, 1969; Kernan, 1969). It seems, in addition, that input from older children to preschoolers is structurally similar to input from parents. The data are scanty but suggestive. It has not been possible to compare parent and older child input in Samoan and Luo, but a suggestive comparison is possible between two English-speaking groups.

As part of the Berkeley cross-cultural studies, Claudia Mitchell-Kernan studied language acquisition in the Black ghetto of West Oakland, California (Mitchell-Kernan, 1971). Her description of the contexts of language acquisition is similar to the foreign studies in Kenya and Samoa:

> *In general, with increasing size of family, children spend greater portions of their time in play groups with other children. . . . Most of the conversation that I witnessed between mothers and children took the form of requests by children to mothers for basic needs to be taken care of, or for disputes to be settled. Most of the speech of mothers to children . . . took the form of imperatives or such questions as* **Where are your shoes, Are you hungry***, etc.* [*personal communication*].

Detailed studies of Mitchell-Kernan's acquisition data (Mitchell-Kernan and Slobin, in preparation) show no significant differences from the general course and rate of acquisition in white, middle class, English-speaking children, though the speech input situation seems quite different from the characteristic mother–child interaction of previous studies. Because the language is the same in both settings (with relatively minor dialectal differences on the grammatical level), an explicit comparison is possible between the input from mothers in Brown's Cambridge sample and the input from children in Mitchell-Kernan's sample. It is instructive to compare the samples in terms of frequency of occurrence of various grammatical structures.

Brown has examined frequencies of numerous grammatical forms in the speech of the three mothers in his study. While there is obviously great difference in the frequency of occurrence of various forms in the speech of a given mother, the striking fact is that the *profile* of frequencies is remarkably similar for the three mothers. That is, "There seems to be something like a standard frequency profile for mother-to-child English [Brown, et al., 1968, p. 64]." Furthermore, these frequency profiles tend to be matched by the children, the more frequent forms emerging earlier in the child's language. These investigators report: "We have examined frequencies on many levels, from major sentence types all the way down to the several allomorphs of *be*, and the story is always the same: rank order correlations among the mothers and between each mother and her child ranging from .65 to .90 [p. 64]." The more frequent forms also tend to be less complex in formal linguistic terms, so that the interrelated variables of frequency and complexity cannot be easily sorted out. But, at any rate, it seems clear that the child is making selective use of the input he receives, at least to the extent that he is brought to attend more to some forms than others.

Perhaps in this regard—in respect to the frequency profile of grammatical forms—mothers provide preschoolers with a different sort of input than that provided by older children. Are there any special grammatical characteristics of the data base provided by Brown's "mother-to-child English?" In Claudia Mitchell-Kernan's data there is a recording of spontaneous talk between two little

TABLE 16–5 FREQUENCY OF OCCURRENCE OF GRAMMATICAL FORMS IN THE SPEECH OF TWO OAKLAND BLACK CHILDREN AND AN OAKLAND BLACK MOTHER SPEAKING TO A 26-MONTH-OLD BOY[a]

Grammatical form	Frequency		
	Girl (4½-years old)	Girl (5-years old)	Mother
Sentence types			
Active, affirmative declarative	97	165	79
Negative	31	53	4
Yes/no interrogative	19	13	40
Wh-interrogative	12	14	17
Passive	1	0	0
Impersonal pronoun + *be*	15	26	28
Impersonal pronoun + main verb	4	9	0
Personal pronoun + *be*[b]	7	5	19
Personal pronoun + main verb	132	153	84
Where	3	0	0
Why	0	0	2
How	0	0	1
When	0	0	3
Wanna	3	3	5
Gonna	7	9	9
Ima[c]	3	4	0
Will	1	0	0
Can	10	10	11
May	0	1	0
Must	0	0	0
-ing	13	26	15
-ed	0	7	0
Irregular past	34	52	9

[a]*See Footnote to Table 16–1, p. 286.*
[b]*There were a few cases of personal pronoun with deletion of be: 3 cases for each of the children and 7 for the mother.*
[c]*Ima is a contracted form of* **I'm gonna***, as in* **Ima hit you.**

girls, one 4½ years old and one 5 years old. Presumably this is a limited example of the sort of speech heard by a preschool child in West Oakland. Although the sample is small—328 utterances for the younger child and 461 for the older—the data are highly suggestive of a provocative conclusion. The frequency profiles seem to match those reported by Brown for his Cambridge mothers. The frequencies are given in Table 16—5, along with those for a black mother speaking to her 2 year-old son (the same speaker represented in Tables 1, 2, and 3). Compare these three West Oakland profiles with the following summary of Brown's profiles (Brown et al., 1968):

> *Some of the stable inequalities one might have guessed: active affirmative, declarative sentences are much more common than negatives, yes—no interrogatives or wh-interrogatives, and well-formed passives are almost nonexistent. Others are easy to understand but are not likely to have occurred to anyone who has not counted:the impersonal pronouns* **it, this,** *and* **that** *as sentence subjects almost always have their allomorph of* **be** *(***is***) as verb, whereas the personal pronouns* **I, you, he,** *and so forth as subjects have a main verb much more often than an allomorph of* **be**; **where** *questions are very much more frequent than* **when** *or* **how** *or* **why** *questions; catenative semiauxiliaries like* **wanna** *and* **gonna** *are much more frequent than the modal auxiliaries* **will** *or* **can,** *and* **may** *and* **must** *are seldom heard; the progressive inflection* **-ing** *is much more frequent than the regular past* **-ed,** *and irregular pasts (e.g.,* **ran, saw, did***) are more frequent than regular pasts, and so on* [*p. 64*].

Most of these trends are reflected in Table 5. Of course, the figures given there are only suggestive, and the list of grammatical forms is as yet gross and scanty. Yet these comparisons do suggest that mother-to-child English may not be strikingly different from child-to-child English.

If this suggestion finds further support, it may well be that children, universally, are exposed to a special, simplified version of the language of their community. The simplification may come about either because the speech input comes from other immature speakers, or because adults and older children make a special selection of grammatical forms when speaking to small children. A large amount of work remains to be done, however, before we can adequately describe the input to LAD or LAS, and even more in order to discern the functioning of those marvelous and mysterious devices and systems with which all of us are born. It is clear, however, that the thread thrown out to guide LAD and LAS through the labyrinth of language is substantial enough to give them a start through the maze.

References

Blount, B. G. Acquisition of language by Luo children. Unpublished doctoral dissertation, University of California, Berkeley, 1969. (Working Paper 19, Language-Behavior Research Laboratory, University of California, Berkeley.)

Blount, B. G. Parental speech and language acquisition: Some Luo and Samoan examples. *Anthropological Linguistics*, 1972, *14*, 119–130.

Bowerman, M. F. *Early syntactic development: A cross-linguistic study with special reference to Finnish.* London & New York: Cambridge Univ. Press, 1973. (Based on unpublished doctoral dissertation, Harvard University, 1970.)

Broen, P. The verbal environment of the language-learning child. *Monographs of the American Speech and Hearing Association*, 1972, *17*.

Brown, R. *A first language.* Cambridge, Mass.: Harvard Univ. Press, 1973.

Brown, R., & Bellugi, U. Three processes in the child's acquisition of syntax. *Harvard Educational Review*, 1964, *34*, 133–151.

Brown, R., Cazden, C. B., & Bellugi, U. The child's grammar from I to III. In J. P. Hill (Ed.), *Minnesota symposium on child development.* Vol. 2. Minneapolis: Univ. of Minnesota Press, 1968. Pp. 28–73.

Brown, R., & Hanlon, C. Derivational complexity and order of acquisition in child speech. In J. R. Hayes (Ed.), *Cognition and the development of language.* New York: Wiley, 1970. Pp. 11–53.

Cazden, C. B. Environmental assistance to the child's acquisition of grammar. Unpubl. doctoral dissertation, Harvard University, 1965.

Cazden, C. B. The acquisition of noun and verb inflections. *Child Development*, 1968, *39*, 433–448.

Chomsky, N. Some methodological remarks on generative grammar. *Word*, 1961, *17*, 219–239.

Chomsky, N. 1964. Current issues in linguistic theory. In J. A. Fodor & J. J. Katz (Eds.), *The structure of language: Readings in the philosophy of language.* Englewood Cliffs, N. J.: Prentice-Hall, 1964. Pp. 50–118. (Published separately by Mouton, The Hague, 1964.)

Chomsky, N. 1965. *Aspects of the theory of syntax.* Cambridge, Mass.: MIT Press, 1965.

Chomsky, N. *Language and mind.* New York: Harcourt, 1968.

Drach, K. The language of the parent: A pilot study. In Working Paper 14: The structure of linguistic input to children, Language-Behavior Research Laboratory, University of California, Berkeley, 1969.

Ervin-Tripp, S. M. Summer workshops in sociolinguistics: Research on children's acquisition of communicative competence. *Items*, 1969, *23*, 22–26.

Ervin-Tripp, S. An overview of theories of grammatical development. In D. I. Slobin (Ed.), *The ontogenesis of grammar: A theoretical symposium.* New York: Academic Press, 1971. Pp. 189–212.

Farwell, C. B. The language spoken to children. *Papers and Reports on Child Language Development* (Stanford University), 1973, *5*, 31–62.

Friedlander, B. Z. Listening, language, and the auditory environment: Automated evaluation and intervention. In J. Hellmuth (Ed.), *Exceptional infant.* Vol. 2, New York: Bruner/Mazel, 1971. Pp. 248–275.

Friedlander, B. Z., Jacobs, A. C., Davis, B. B., & Wetstone, H. S. Time-sampling analysis of infants' natural language environments in the home. *Child Development*, 1972, *43*, 730–740.

Garnica, O. K. Some characteristics of prosodic input to young children. Unpublished Ph. D. dissertation, Stanford University, 1975.

Holzman, M. The verbal environment provided by mothers for their very young children. *Merrill-Palmer Quarterly*, 1974, *20*, 31–42.

Kernan, K. The acquisition of language by Samoan children. Unpubl. doctoral dissertation, University of California, Berkeley, 1969. (Working Paper 21, Language-Behavior Research Laboratory, University of California, Berkeley.)

Klima, E. S., & Bellugi, U. 1966. Syntactic regularities in the speech of children. In J. Lyons & R. J. Wales (Eds.), *Psycholinguistics papers: Proceedings of the 1966 Edinburgh conference.* Edinburgh: Edinburgh Univ. Press, 1966. Pp. 183–208.

Kobashigawa, B. Repetitions in a mother's speech to her child. In Working Paper 14: The structure of linguistic input to children, Language-Behavior Research Laboratory, University of California, Berkeley, 1969.

Lyons, J. *Introduction to theoretical linguistics.* London & New York: Cambridge Univ. Press, 1968.

Mitchell-Kernan, C. Language behavior in a Black urban community. Monographs of the Language-Behavior Research Laboratory, No. 2. University of California, Berkeley, 1971.

Moerk, E. L. Changes in verbal child-mother interactions with increasing language skills of the child. *Journal of Psycholinguistic Research*, 1974, *3*, 101—116.

Nelson, K. Structure and strategy in learning to talk. *Monographs of the Society for Research in Child Development*, 1973, *38*, [Serial No. 149].

Newport, E. Motherese and its relation to the child's acquisition of language. Paper presented at Conference on Language Input and Acquisition, Boston, September 1974.

Pfuderer, C. Some suggestions for a syntactic characterization of baby talk style. In Working Paper 14: The structure of linguistic input to children. Language-Behavior Research Laboratory, University of California, Berkeley, 1969.

Phillips, J. R. Syntax and vocabulary of mothers' speech to young children: Age and sex comparisons. *Child Development*, 1973, *44*, 182—185.

Posner, R. Determining the onset of speech. Unpublished senior honors thesis, Department of Psychology, University of California, Berkeley, 1972.

Rūķe-Draviņa, V. Modifications of speech addressed to young children in Latvian. Paper presented at Conference on Language Input and Acquisition, Boston, September 1974.

Sachs, J., Brown, R., & Salerno, R. A. Adults' speech to children. Paper presented at the International Symposium on First Language Acquisition, Florence, September 1972. (To appear in the Proceedings.)

Slobin, D. I. (Ed.) *A field manual for cross-cultural study of the acquisition of communicative competence.* Berkeley: Univ. of California ASUC Bookstore, 1967.

Slobin, D. I. Imitation and grammatical development in children. In N. S. Endler, L. R. Boulter, & H. Osser (Eds.), *Contemporary issues in developmental psychology*, New York: Holt, 1968. Pp. 437—443.

Slobin D. I. Universals of grammatical development in children. In G. B. Flores d'Arcais & W. J. M. Levelt (Eds.), *Advances in psycholinguistic research*, Amsterdam: North-Holland Publ., 1970. Pp. 174—186.

Slobin, D. I. Cognitive prerequisites for the development of grammar. In C. A. Ferguson & D. I. Slobin (Eds.), *Studies of child language development*, New York: Holt, 1973. Pp. 175—208.

Snow, C. E. Mothers' speech to children learning language. *Child Development*, 1972, *43*, 549—565.

Snow, C. E. Mother's speech research: An overview. Paper presented at Conference on Language Input and Acquisition, Boston, September 1974.

Todd, P. H., III. Learning to talk with delayed exposure to speech. Unpublished doctoral dissertation, University of California, Berkeley, 1972.

Vihman, M. M. On the acquisition of Estonian. *Papers and Reports on Child Language Development*, (Stanford University), 1971, No. 3, 51—94.

Von Humboldt, W. *Über die Verschiedenheit des menschlichen Sprachbaues.* Berlin: 1836. (Facsimile ed., Bonn: Dümmlers Verlag, 1960.)

17. The Early Development of The Mother Tongue

Courtney B. Cazden / Roger Brown

Recent research on early stages of the child's acquisition of his first language, or "mother tongue," in many countries is summarized. This chapter presents evidence that the sentence construction process develops through some universal sequences, discusses possible determinants of this order of acquisition, and then turns to speculations about what impels development through these stages and controversies about the nature of environmental influences on developmental rate.

Evidence for Universal Sequences

There is at present evidence for three major progressions in first language acquisition: evolution of the basic operations of reference and semantic relations in the two-word utterances of very young children; the acquisition of 14 English grammatical morphemes and the modulations of meaning they express; and, still later, the acquisition of English tag questions like *doesn't it*? or *can't I*? Since Bowerman (see Chap. 15,) reports in detail the first of these progressions, we start with the acquisition of grammatical morphemes in English.

GRAMMATICAL MORPHEMES

Universally missing from children's earliest utterances are the grammatical morphemes often called "function words"—articles, prepositions, conjunctions, auxiliary words, inflections, and affixes—which do not name places, things, or processes, but rather express subtle modulations of meaning; they generally have

TABLE 17-1 THE ORDER OF ACQUISITION OF 14 GRAMMATICAL MORPHEMES IN 3 CHILDREN[a]

ADAM	SARAH	EVE
I (2;3)[b]	**I (2;3)**[b]	**I (1;6)**[b]
II (2;6) Present progressive, in, on, plural	**II (2;10)** Plural, in, on, Present progressive, past irregular	**II (1;9)** Present progressive, on, in
III (2;11) Uncontractible copula, past irregular	**III (3;1)** Possessive, Uncontractible copula, Articles	**III (1;11)** Plural, possessive
IV (3;2) Articles, Third person irregular, possessive	**IV (3;8)** Third person regular	**IV (2;2)** Past regular
V (3;6) Third person regular, Past regular, Uncontractible auxiliary, Contractible copula, Contractible auxiliary	**V (4;0)** Past regular, Uncontractible auxiliary, Contractible copula, Third person irregular, Contractible auxiliary	**V (2;3)** Uncontractible copula, Past irregular, Articles, Third person regular, Third person irregular, Uncontractible auxiliary, Contractible copula, Contractible auxiliary

[a] From Fig. 3 of Stage II, Brown, 1974.
[b] Stage and chronological age. Stage is defined by mean length of utterance: I = 1.75; II = 2.25; III = 2.75; IV = 3.50; V = 4.00. Age is given in years and months

minimal perceptual salience and very considerable grammatical complexity. Unfortunately, our account of the acquisition of grammatical morphemes is limited to English, and largely to data on the three children we have studied: Adam, Eve, and Sarah.

We are interested in the acquisition of knowledge, both grammatical and semantic. Yet the principal data we have are samples of spontaneous speech. There are many difficulties in defining a criterion of knowledge acquisition from performance data. With grammatical morphemes, we are in a relatively stronger position, because they are obligatory in certain contexts (such as the plural morpheme after a number greater than one), and an acquisition criterion can be set in terms of "produced-where-required." We arbitrarily set that point at the first speech sample of three, such that in all three the inflection is supplied in at least 90% of the contexts in which it is clearly required.

The acquisition of 14 English grammatical morphemes was tracked through the speech samples of Adam, Eve, and Sarah (Brown, 1974; Cazden, 1968). Table 17–1 shows the order of acquisition for all three children from Stage I, which is defined by a mean utterance length of 1.75 morphemes, to Stage V, defined by a mean utterance length of 4.00; Table 17–2 gives examples of each morpheme and the average order of acquisition across the three children (both from Brown, 1974). Spearman rank order correlations, corrected for ties, for the order of development of these morphemes are as follows: Adam and Sarah, .88; Adam and Eve, .86; Sarah and Eve, .87.

To our knowledge, no other research on the acquisition of English has coded

TABLE 17–2   MEAN ORDER OF ACQUISITION OF 14 MORPHEMES ACROSS 3 CHILDREN[a]

Morpheme	Average Rank
1. Present Progressive: *riding*	2.33
2–3. *in; on*	2.50
4. Plural: *Two dogs.*	3.00
5. Past, Irregular: *saw; went*	6.00
6. Possessive: *Mommy's hat*	6.33
7. Uncontractible copula: *Here I am* in response to *Where are you?*	6.50
8. Articles: *a, the*	7.00
9. Past, regular: *walked, wanted*	9.00
10. Third person, regular: *goes*	9.66
11. Third person, irregular; *has, does*	10.83
12. Uncontractible auxiliary: *I am* in response to *Who's coming?*	11.66
13. Contractible copula: *He's sick.*	12.66
14. Contractible auxiliary: *He's running.*	14.00

[a]From Table 3 of Stage II, Brown, 1974.

data as we have done for the presence or absence over time of particular morphemes in obligatory contexts. Other studies do report data on one or another of these 14 morphemes (Brown & Fraser, 1963; Leopold, 1949; Menyuk, 1969; Miller & Ervin, 1964; and the well-known experimental study by Berko, 1958). For the most part, their results support the ranking given in Table 2 for Adam, Eve, and Sarah.

Three important questions are raised by these data: Why are grammatical morphemes, as a class, acquired later than the basic operations of reference and semantic relations? Why are they acquired in such a surprisingly constant order? More generally, how do semantic and grammatical complexity interact to determine this order of acquisition? We shall return to these questions after presenting the third developmental sequence.

TAG QUESTIONS

The complications of structure that follow Stage I almost all add to sentence length. However, it is not the number of words that limits what the child can do at a particular time but rather the complexity of the construction. The clearest evidence of this is the difficulty Adam, Eve, and Sarah had with what are called tag questions. Tag questions are requests for confirmation, communication checks like *N'est-ce pas?* or *Nicht wahr?*, except that the grammar of English tags is more complex. One can add a tag to any statement. Thus:

> *John won't be late, will he?*
> *His wife can drive, can't she?*

And so on. The tag itself is very short, three or four words long, which means that as far as superficial length is concerned, it would even be within the capacity of the child at the end of Stage I. In fact, however, tags are not to be heard until some two or three years later, when some sentences are as long as 15 words or even more. What delays their appearance until this time?

In English, the form of the tag varies with the form of the sentence to which it is added and is always a strict derivative of that sentence. Suppose the basic sentence is *His wife can drive.* The derivation of the tag *Can't she?* is a completely determinate procedure which could, in principle, be done by a machine. But it would have to be a machine that knew a large part of the grammar of English. The machine would have to be able to identify sentence subjects, replace subjects with pronouns while preserving number and gender, construct negatives and interrogatives, and do predicate deletions. Which, of course, is why children seldom produce tags before they are about five years old. Brown and Hanlon (1970) showed that they do not produce them until they are able to carry out all the constituent operations like negation, interrogation, and so on, both singly and in simple combinations.

Determinants of Order of Acquisition

Frequency, perceptual salience, and complexity—both semantic and gram-matical—have been proposed as determinants of the sequences of acquisition described above. Frequency and perceptual salience seem to be minor deter-minants. The possibility that the frequency with which either specific utterances or construction types are modeled for small children affects order of acquisition has been exhaustively probed for the grammatical morphemes (Brown, 1974). The upshot of several kinds of tests made is that, at least for this developmental sequence, there is no evidence whatever that frequency of any sort is a significant determinant of order of acquisition. Some marginal role for frequency is natur-ally guaranteed; children will not learn constructions they never hear. What the minimal essential values may be is unknown, but it is certainly possible that the very low frequency of full passives and perfectives in adult speech to young children is a factor in the late acquisition of these constructions. The possibility also exists that frequency is important for irregular forms that must be memorized as such.

Perceptual salience, broken down into such variables as amount of phonetic substance, stress level, usual serial position in a sentence, and so on, is probably a more important variable. Experiments by Scholes (1968, 1970) and by Blaisdell and Jenson (1970), for instance, suggest that salience may have a role in producing the telegraphic quality of early English speech. In the naturalistic data there are numerous points at which one suspects that salience is a significant factor— for example the acquisition of uncontractible copulas and auxiliaries before their contractible equivalents—though this is never quite provable because of a natural confounding with other variables in the language. As in the case of frequency, some role for salience is guaranteed; the child will not learn what he cannot hear.

The primary determinant of acquisition order seems to be cumulative com-plexity, both semantic and grammatical. Recourse to grammatical complexity as a determining variable requires defense today because of its unhappy recent history in another domain of psycholinguistics: the experimental study of sentence pro-cessing by adults. [See the retrospective analysis of this research by Fodor and Garrett (1966).]

First, our problem is different in that we are not concerned with the efficiency of sentence processing, in the sense of speed of accuracy of recall, but rather with the acquisition of construction types, with their first utilization in what may be considered a productive and comprehending way. Although no generative gram-mar can reasonably be considered a model of the process of sentence production or comprehension, generative grammars have a distinctly psychological goal. They are intended to represent formally the knowledge that the native speaker must somehow utilize in producing and understanding sentences. Insofar as a grammar has correctly characterized this knowledge, it does not seem unreasonable that the relative complexity of constructions, in terms of the number of optional transformations in their derivation, will be a determinant of the order of their acquisition.

Furthermore, our definition of grammatical complexity (semantic complexity, too) is limited in a way that has not been true of all conceptions of complexity utilized in psycholinguistic research. In brief, it is limited to the cumulative sense. We do not, for example, simply count the number of optional transformations in a derivation, or any other feature of a derivation, since this procedure involves the generally unwarranted assumption that any one transformation, or some other feature, involves the same increment to complexity of knowledge as any other. In our cumulative sense of complexity, a construction $x + y$ may be regarded as more complex than either x or y because it involves everything involved in either of the constructions alone plus something more. The construction $x + y$ cannot be ordered with respect to a construction z even though $x + y$ might contain one more of some unit or other than does z. This is because we are not prepared to assume equality of units. So agent-action-object is considered more complex than any pair of relations separately, and a tag question more complex than its components—interrogation, negation, pronominalization, and predicate ellipsis— either singly or in pairs.

In Stage I, word order is, in languages utilizing it, the clearest evidence that the child has the semantic intentions with which we are concerned. In languages not making significant use of word order, one must rely on the weaker evidence of contextual appropriateness as a basis for attributing certain semantic relations. For the investigator who is willing to lean on this evidence, as we and a number of others are, it is cumulative semantic complexity that predicts and, perhaps, determines order of acquisition in Stage I.

The clearest evidence for the importance of grammatical complexity in its own right appears in Brown and Hanlon's (1970) study of English tag questions. The peculiar beauty of the English tag question is that it is semantically rather trifling—a request for confirmation—and it has such simple equivalents as *Huh?* and *Right?* which are produced as early as Stage I. Grammatically, however, well-formed tag questions are at a high level of cumulative complexity. It seems, then, that in this case the long-deferred appearance of well-formed tags must be attributed to grammatical complexity alone.

In the acquisition of the fourteen English grammatical morphemes, analysis of determinants of the order of acquisition is more complex and the results less conclusive. Brown (1974) presents detailed arguments. All one can say in summary is that semantic or grammatical complexity does a good job of predicting order of acquisition.

What Impels Development?

We do not know what impels the child to progress through the sequences described above and gradually make his speech patterns converge on the patterns of mature speakers in his community. It is surprising that there should be any mystery about the forces impelling development, since it is just this aspect of the process that most people imagine that they understand. Surely the progress is a response to selection pressures of various kinds; ill-formed or incomplete utterances must be less effective than well-formed and complete utterances in accomplishing the child's intent; parents probably approve of well-formed utterances and disapprove or correct the ill-formed. These ideas sound sensible and may be correct, but the still-scant evidence available does not support them.

In Stage I, the child's constructions are characterized by optional omission of every sort of major constituent, including subjects, objects, verbs, locatives, and so on. Yet that omission seldom seems to impede communication. The other person, usually the mother, being in the same situation and familiar with the child's stock of knowledge, understands correctly so far as one can tell. In other words, if we accept parental glosses as veridical readings of the child's intended meaning, as Slobin (1971) suggests, the child is correctly understood even though his utterances are incomplete.

Later, when all of the fourteen grammatical morphemes are at first missing, then occasionally present in obligatory contexts, it is again surprisingly difficult to find cases in which omission results in incomprehension or misunderstanding. Two examples are particularly striking. With respect to the definite and nondefinite articles, it looks as if listeners almost never really need them, and yet child speakers learn to operate with the exceedingly intricate rules governing their production. In contrast, adult speakers of Japanese, a language not utilizing definite and indefinite articles, do not seem to learn how to operate with English articles as we might expect they would if listeners needed them. And why should the child learn the complex apparatus of tag questions when *Right*? or *Huh*? seem to do just the same job? Again one notes that adults learning English often do not learn tag questions, and the possibility comes to mind that children operate on language in a way that adults do not.

To these observations of the seeming efficacy of the child's incomplete utterances, at least at home with the family, we can add the results of two studies reported by Brown and Hanlon (1970). Here it was not primarily a question of the ommission of obligatory forms but of the contrast between ill-formed primitive constructions and well-formed mature versions at a time in each child's development when both were being produced. Brown and Hanlon found no evidence whatever of a difference in communicative efficacy, and therefore no selection pressure, nor any evidence that adult approval was selectively governed by more mature syntax. In general, the parents seemed to pay no attention to immature syntax, nor did they even seem to be aware of it. They approved or disapproved an utterance usually on the grounds of the truth value of the proposition that they supposed the child intended to assert. This is a surprising outcome to many parents, since they are generally under the impression that they correct their child's speech. From inquiry and observation we find that what parents generally correct is pronunciation, "naughty" words, regularized irregular allomorphs such as *digged* or *goed*, and matters of usage we might call speech etiquette, such as reminders to say *please*. These facts of the child's speech seem to penetrate parental awareness. But syntax—the child saying, for instance, *Why the dog won't eat?* instead of *Why won't the dog eat?*—seems to be automatically set right in the parent's mind, with the mistake never registering as such.

In sum, then, we do not presently have evidence that there are selection pressures of any kind operating on children to impel them to bring their speech into line with adult models. It is, however, entirely possible that such pressures do operate in situations unlike the situations we have sampled; for instance, away from home or with strangers. It is also possible that one should look more closely at the small number of child utterances spoken within the family where the adult just does not seem to be able to make out what the child means. Perhaps there is the growing edge where the pressures operate.

A radically different possibility is that children work out rules for the speech they hear, passing from levels of lesser to greater complexity, simply because the human species is programmed at a certain period in its life to operate in this fashion on linguistic input. Perhaps language use is to the human species as nut burying is to the squirrel. A squirrel raised in isolation from its kind and given no opportunity to learn how to bury nuts will, nonetheless, when it first encounters a nut or nut-like object, undertake to dig a hole and tap it into the ground. It will attempt to carry out this fixed action pattern even in very unaccommodating circumstances, as on a linoleum floor. Speaking English or Samoan or any particular language is certainly not a fixed action pattern released in the human species by contact with the language. But perhaps there are fixed analytic patterns, processes of information analysis, which are released by any materials having the universal properties of language. And perhaps these processes succeed one another in a relatively fixed order and produce the invariant features of the development of language in children.

Such a period of progressive rule extraction may correspond to Lenneberg's (1967, and elsewhere) proposed "critical period," and may explain the differences between language learning in children and adults. Comparison of the kinds of errors made by child and adult second-language learners of a given language with the kinds of errors made by children learning that language as their mother tongue should be informative and also helpful in designing more effective second-language instruction (see e.g., Dulay, 1972).

Environmental Assistance

Although the order of acquisition of linguistic knowledge seems to be generally invariant across children learning one language and, at a higher level of abstraction, across children learning any language, the rate of progression varies radically among children, as we have already seen among Adam, Eve, and Sarah. What will the determinants of rate prove to be? No one can know at present. No doubt, within some as yet unknown limits of interaction variation, the rate will depend on what the intelligence testers call g or general intelligence. In fact, a reasonable conceptual definition of comparative intelligence is the rate at which individuals build general rule systems or theories comprehending sets of data to which they are exposed. This is a notion that would fit Piaget's approach to intelligence as well as the study of language development. But the phrase "within some as yet unknown limits of interaction variation" begs all the important questions about the nature of that variation and how it makes a difference.

Attempts to isolate aspects of the child's environment that aid his acquisition of syntax have been made both in naturalistic and experimental studies [For extensive discussions, see Brown, Cazden, and Bellugi (1969) and Cazden (1972).] Both research methodologies present problems. In naturalistic settings, such as spontaneous family conversations, variables are inevitably confounded. Parents who talk more in general (thereby giving the child more models of mature language to learn from) also talk more with their children (thereby providing more contexts that provoke the child to construct sentences in response). On a finer level of analysis, confounding also exists within the category of parental responses that are contingent on the child's utterance. Those responses that gloss the child's incomplete utterance we have called expansions (as when the parent responds to *Mommy soup* with *Yes, that's Mommy's soup*); those responses that presuppose a certain gloss and then give a related idea we have called extensions (as when the parent responds, *Yes, and it's hot* to the same child utterance). Expansions and extensions vary together in frequency, and so it is impossible to determine their separate benefits to the child within the naturalistic setting.

Experimental treatments present problems too. For instance, Cazden (1965) carried out an experiment to test the effect on the development of 3 years olds' syntax of deliberately providing expansions versus extensions during a daily conversation period for three months. The expansion treatment had no effect; the extension treatment had some effect but not enough to be educationally significant. Caution must be exercised in interpreting these results, however, because of the artificial nature of the treatment variables. We know from many current studies of child development that stimuli of a certain degree of novelty—not too familiar and not too strange—command the greatest attention. The acquisition of language should be facilitated by those environmental events that enhance the child's attention to the adult's utterance and to relevant features of the verbal and non-verbal context in which it is spoken. In these particular experimental treatments, a greater degree of novelty may have been attained in the extension treatment. Expansions, when separated from the extensions with which they so frequently and naturally occur, may become uninteresting and so invite inattention. But one cannot conclude that they are necessarily also impotent in their natural environment. [See Moerk (in press) for discussion of this point.]

There have been a few other experimental studies that have attempted over a period of several months to assist preschool children's acquisition of grammar. When Ammon and Ammon (1970) contrasted "vocabulary training" and "sentence training," they achieved gains in vocabulary but no effect on a sentence imitation test, even for constructions previously taught. Moore (1971) contrasted an "extension" treatment adapted from Cazden (1965) with a "patterning" treatment adapted from Bereiter and Englemann (1966). He achieved gains on communication tests but no treatment effects on a sentence imitation test, even though the patterning treatment included a great deal of practice in imitation itself.

One conclusion to be drawn from these few studies is that acquisition of syntax, unlike vocabulary or communication skills, seems remarkably impervious to deliberate assistance. That it is somehow a different kind of learning is also supported by evidence from factor analysis research. In two recent studies (Bruck, 1972; Moore, 1971), measures of the child's grammar (on both imitation and comprehension tests) became factors separate from other aspects of communicative competence.

Two other hypotheses about environmental assistance might be tested. One rests on the notion of readiness as possession of all the components necessary for the next step in a sequence of increasing complexity. Our knowledge of sequences in the development of grammar, limited though it still is, would make it possible to provide a high density of examples (either in adult-initiated utterances or in extensions or expansions of child utterances) of morphemes or syntactic patterns for which the child seemed to be "ready."

A quite different hypothesis rests on the notion that interaction patterns vary in the pressure they exert on the child to engage in the sentence construction (or comprehension) process. We have seen that differential communication effectiveness cannot explain the child's shift from particular incomplete to mature forms. But a more compelling need to express his intentions may affect the functioning of the child's entire language acquisition system. Recall the description of the young child who is understood within his family despite the omission of any obligatory constituents in his speech. Speaking to strangers or speaking about new experiences, he might have to learn to express those constituents if he wanted to get his message across. And that may be the answer: selection pressures to communicate may chiefly operate outside our sampling situation, which is typically the child at home. As more preschool children spend more of their day in child care centers with less familiar persons, it will be important to determine if, and under what conditions, such added communicative challenges can in fact help.

References

Ammon, P. R., & Ammon, M. Effects of training young black children in vocabulary vs. sentence construction. Paper presented at the meeting of the American Educational Research Association, Minneapolis, March 1970.

Bereiter, C., & Englemann, S. *Teaching disadvantaged children in the preschool.* Englewood Cliffs, N.J.: Prentice-Hall, 1966.

Berko, J. The child's learning of English morphology. *Word,* 1958, *14,* 150–177.

Blaisdell, R., & Jenson, P. Stress and word position as determinants of imitation in first-language learners. *Journal of Speech and Hearing Research*, 1970, *13*, 193–202.

Brown, R. *A first language, the early stages*. Cambridge, Mass.: Harvard Univ. Press, 1974.

Brown, R., Cazden, C. B. & Bellugi, U. The child's grammar from I to III. In J. P. Hill (Ed.), *Minnesota symposium on child psychology*, 1967. Minneapolis: Univ. of Minnesota Press, 1969. Pp. 28–73.

Brown, R., & Fraser, C. The acquisition of syntax. In C. N. Cofer & B. S. Musgrave (Eds.), *Verbal behavior and learning: Problems and processes*, New York: McGraw-Hill, 1963. Pp. 158–201.

Brown, R., & Hanlon, C. Derivational complexity and order of acquisition in child speech. In J. R. Hayes (Ed.), *Cognition and the development of language*, New York: Wiley, 1970. Pp. 11–53.

Bruck, M. The influence of kindergarten experience on the language acquisition of children from different socioeconomic backgrounds. Unpublished doctoral dissertation, McGill University, 1972.

Cazden, C. B. Environmental assistance to the child's acquisition of grammar. Unpublished doctoral dissertation, Harvard University, 1965.

Cazden, C. B. The acquisition of noun and verb inflections. *Child Development*, 1968, *39*, 433–448.

Cazden, C. B. *Child language and education*. New York: Holt, 1972.

Dulay, H. C. Children's goofs in second language acquisition. Unpublished qualifying paper, Harvard. Graduate School of Education, 1972.

Fodor, J., & Garrett, M. Some reflections on competence and performance. In J. Lyons & R. J. Wales (Eds.), *Psycholinguistic papers*, Edinburgh: Edinburgh Univ. Press, 1966. Pp. 135–154.

Lenneberg, E. H. *Biological foundations of language*. New York: Wiley, 1967.

Leopold, W. F. *Speech development of a bilingual child: A linguist's record*, Vol. III. *Grammar and general problems in the first two years*. Evanston, Ill.: Northwestern Univ. Press, 1949.

Menyuk, P. *Sentences children use*. Cambridge, Mass.: MIT Press, 1969.

Miller, W., & Ervin, S. The development of grammar in child language. In U. Bellugi & R. Brown (Eds.), *The acquisition of language, Monographs of the Society for Research in Child Development*, 1964, *29*, 9–34.

Moerk, E. Principles of interaction in language learning. *Merrill-Palmer Quarterly*, (in press)

Moore, D. A comparison of two methods of teaching specific language skills to lower-class pre-school children. Unpublished doctoral dissertation, Harvard University, 1971.

Scholes, R. J. The role of grammaticality in the imitation of word strings by children and adults. *Journal of Verbal Learning and Verbal Behavior*, 1968, *8*, 225–228.

Scholes, R. J. On functors and contentives in children's imitations of word strings. *Journal of Verbal Learning and Verbal Behavior*, 1970, *9*, 167–170.

Slobin, D. I. *Cognitive prerequisites for the development of grammar*. Edmonton, Alberta: Linguistic Research, 1971.

18. Cognitive Processes and Language Ability in the Severely Retarded

Neil O'Connor

Binet and Simon first drew attention to the lack of any close correspondence between language and thought in the subnormal. The questions they raised concerning speech and thought in subnormality anticipate the current controversy in psycholinguistics. Contemporary studies suggest that the subnormal, like young children, refer to an independent conceptual reconstruction of the world in building their language. The syntactic rules they generate, like those of normal children, only imperfectly reflect this structure. Some other diagnostic groups, such as autistic children, may lack this infrastructure; their language, such as it is, is syntactically unlike that of the subnormal. Subnormal language may reflect the logic of identity and relationship, but it is undeveloped and shows an additional inertia, which inhibits its use as a coding medium.

Introduction

The study of cognitive processes in the subnormal has had a long history from the early experimental studies of Itard and Seguin. However, some of the most pertinent observations on language ability in relation to the severely retarded were made by Binet and Simon in the early years of this century. One can hardly do better than to quote them at length. They discuss the distinction between thought and the image, saying that "to think cannot be reduced simply to recalling an image." They then give many examples that are intended to show that thought is richer than images and can exist without them.

They consider whether the thought can be a word if not an image, but conclude that the word is no more a complete thought than is an image.

> *Like the image, [they write] the word corresponds only to a fragment of the thought; to translate the thought in its entirety into words would require a long discourse. Thus one asks a person if she has read a certain book, and she replies "No." This negation, to which she limits herself, does not correspond to her complex thought, because that **No** is a general negation, consequently very vague; while the person makes a negation of an extraordinary precision, special-ized to a certain question and regarding a certain book. Thus, evidently, the thought surpasses the word [Binet & Simon, 1916].*

Binet and Simon then consider the question of whether the thought surpasses not only the word uttered, but the words of inner language, which may possibly be fuller and more complex in their structure and implications. They give a number of answers to this query, of which perhaps the most relevant refers to conversation conducted with a severely subnormal patient. Binet discusses a question asked of a patient called Denise:

> *We asked her, "Who gave you that pretty ring?" Without hesitation she replied, "Mama." Let us weigh this word. Let us note that in order for the thought contained in this reply to be completely developed in language, it would be necessary that Denise had replied to us or had simply thought to herself the following sentence, "It was Mama who gave me this ring." But she cannot articulate even mentally this sentence, which is very evident, since her vocabulary is reduced to five or six words and her mental level does not permit her to make sentences. We are therefore very certain that, in this case, her thought has no corresponding series of necessary words; it is indeed a thought without sufficient words and consequently there is in her a thought without words [Binet & Simon, 1916].*

This quotation is given at length because it states the kernel of the controversy which is now widely discussed among those concerned with child development, namely whether thought is aided by speech or in any way made responsible for it, or is either antecedent to or independent of speech. Additionally, Binet considers the problem of the development of syntax and the way in which syntactic rules develop. This he does by implication in considering the answer given by Denise, *Mama*, which he construes as meaning "*It was* **mama** *who gave me this ring*. The example was offered also by de Laguna (1963) in relation to normal child develop-ment, with different implications. She quoted the case of the one-word sentence, noting that a child who pointed to a pair of slippers and said *Daddy* was already uttering a complete sentence, unlike the child who pointed and said *slippers*.

Clearly the problem of the association between cognitive development and language or speech is a complex one, which is not easily reduced to simple questions. The long controversy concerning the relationship between words and things has not yet reached a stage where students can issue a useful communique. Lenneberg (1967) has suggested that meaning cannot be entirely divorced from grammatical structure, and there is some support for such a view if one follows Russell's (1940) belief that language is an empirical phenomenon and that the study of syntax can lead us to knowledge of the structure of the world. Chomsky (1957) might be obliged to demur from this view, because, for him, interpretation of any semantically ambiguous or indeed any statement is made to depend on an underlying and precedent deep structure. In other words, as distinct from Russell, linguists of Chomsky's persuasion must hold that language only mirrors less perfectly our conceptual reconstruction of what Russell called the "structure of the world." Binet might be thought to have anticipated Chomsky's opinions.

The phenomenon of language as manifest in the development of infant speech or the speech of the subnormal makes it clear that underlying language is a structure of relational concepts which reflect the spatial and temporal structure of events as experienced by the human organism. In the past this structure has been seen by some as an inbuilt structure. The most complete philosophical development of this view was, of course, that presented by Kant (1781) in the *Critique of Pure Reason*. It is a view that has been resisted by empiricists, but not always completely. Hume (1738) was at pains to point out that "beasts are endowed with thought and reason as well as men," so both schools can assume the pre-existence of reason, whether or not one takes the view, as Hume did, that reason was derived from custom, or as Kant did, that it was the bringing out of experience what reason had already put into the concept of that experience—a priori. The idea of a sense of structure in the world is therefore no novelty in man's concept of animals. And yet communication in animals is demonstrably underdeveloped. Only one chimpanzee has been shown by Premack (1971) to be capable of learning a primitive form of syntactically organized sign language, and apes, in general the most developed communicators, have such a small repertoire of signals that they are on a level similar to that of Binet's Denise. Both the apes and Denise in their lives make it clear that reason can surpass language.

What must be said, therefore, from these observations is that animals behave as if they understood the properties of objects and their interrelations. Children likewise appear to show a grasp of many aspects of the real world before they are able to understand language—let alone speak. This, at least, is apparent to many who have followed the experiments of Piaget. However, although some degree of comprehension can be conceded as occurring before speech develops, this fact, of course, in no way guarantees the development of speech in an organism, otherwise animals would speak. Nor can we assume that it is a necessary pre-requisite for rational speech, although this seems likely. In science, unlike metaphysics, we can only construct a hypothesis; its verification must await the development of appropriate techniques.

The question of the precedence or dependence of speech on thought or of thought on speech is, therefore, a sterile question if asked in the abstract. The presence of thought in animals and speechlessness in intelligent children shows that there is no necessary connection. Binet's clinical observations were clearly fundamental. Therefore the linguistic development of subnormal children cannot be directly associated with their reasoning ability.

One other question is intertwined with this question of primacy—it is the ancient question of nativism or environmentalism in language learning mentioned above. This question is logically distinct from the question of the primacy of thought or language. The current nativism of such psycholinguists as Chomsky (1957) would have earned them the title of idealists or rationalists in the period of positivist thinking, and both Broadbent (1970) and Hebb, Lambert, and Tucker (1971) have contended against such a view, pointing out that conditions can influence linguistic response. The argument here centers around the capacity of young children to generate in their native tongue sentences they have never heard, but which are grammatically correct. Some psycholinguists have presented the undoubted facts as an argument in favor of something like a preprogrammed ability to construct grammatical forms. Against the assumption of a preprogrammed wiring diagram in the central nervous system, a learning model has been proposed by Broadbent (1970), who notes that learning is not necessarily a mechanical form of conditioning applying strictly to the stimulus–response connection originally taught, but to connections between classes of events. Hull (1943) quite a long time ago developed his principle of stimulus–response generalization. This was based on responses shown by animals to apparently simple stimuli, which were generalized to similar stimuli. Hull states the principle as follows: "Stimuli not involved in the original reinforcement but lying in a zone related to it become connected with reactions not involved in the original reinforcement but lying in a zone related to it; this may be called *stimulus response generalization* [p. 183]." Elsewhere he explains this principle in relation to a conditioned response to a tone: "The reaction is conditioned not only to a tone (Ṡ) but to a whole zone of tones of other pitches and intensities spreading in both directions along each dimension from the point conditioned. All of these stimuli are functionally equivalent in that they have the capacity to evoke the same reaction [p. 197]." The generalization decreases as the difference between stimuli increases, following a simple negative growth function. Skinner (1957) does not mention this principle, but in discussing generalization, makes the comment that responses are made to stimuli similar to those originally conditioned.

This is not the place to discuss the issue of how children learn to utter correctly sentences they may never have heard. However, it should be noted that few psycholinguists accept theories based on the concept of stimulus generalization or contextual generalization as explanations of language learning. The work of Braine (1963) and Jenkins and Palermo (1964) might be taken as characteristic of the contextual generalization school, and the criticism offered of their work by Bever, Fodor, and Weksel (1965) as typical of the attitude of most psycholinguists. The argument is that through appreciating the subdivision of basic units in the structure of kernel sentences by observing stresses and similar signs, children learn the correct syntactic order of such basic parts of simple sentences.

The criticism of this position is that kernel sentences are not the foundation of simple declarative sentences, but that such foundations can be transformed into any sentence type whatever. Among the criticisms of contextual generalization as a theory of language acquisition falls the problem of word position in sentences. Whereas generalization is an acceptable explanation of the way in which children acquire some rules, it will lead to peculiarities in many instances—the passive form of one sentence is no model for the passive form of another, for example, *The doll cost four dollars* cannot be transformed as *Four dollars was cost by the doll,* although *The ball was hit by the boy* is a legitimate form of *The boy hit the ball.* So the ordering of distinguishable elements is not necessarily the best way to learn a language and tends, say its critics, to ignore a basic feature of language learning, that is, the relationship between deep structure and surface structure. Even more basically from some points of view, empirical data suggest that children acquire language not by imitating the language structures used by adults, but by developing their own rules. In this chapter, we are not concerned to offer a solution to this problem. In fact, no solution has yet been offered, and both Braine and his critics are unable to account for more than the most elementary steps in language acquisition. The point to be made here is that some knowledge of an underlying structure to which language refers is a basic requisite for generating an acceptable syntax. It is interesting to note that Skinner's account of genetic extension and metaphysical extension, although not currently in vogue, has a surprisingly close logical similarity to the account given by Lenneberg (1967) of words as labels for categorization processes. What all workers in this field seem to agree upon is the need for some underlying logical structure that is, in part, independent of language. To some degree, the source of this logical structure is irrelevant if one considers its relationship to language. In other words, one need not hold a rationalist or an empiricist view of the growth of this infrastructure, providing one is concerned chiefly with its role in supporting or preventing the growth of language or speech. It is with the interactions of language and the capacity to categorize, or language and the capacity to structure the world of stimuli, language and deep structure, or language and the capacity of genetic extension, that we are chiefly concerned in studying the language and cognitive function of the subnormal. However, this has not always been the preoccupation of workers in this field, and their findings in previous years may in future seem as relevant as contemporary observations. The next section, therefore, gives a brief survey of various approaches to the subject. An important theoretical consideration, namely the problem of cognitive processes in the deaf, must be deferred to the second and third sections of this chapter. It will be easier to consider the questions raised by this specific handicap when the research with the subnormal has been reviewed.

Learning and Language in the Retarded

Investigations of language and thinking in the subnormal could be dated from the early work of Dorothea McCarthy (1930), who described how the development of speech in children followed a pattern of increasing vocabulary and of the relative increase of verbs in relation to nouns as children grew older. She also noted the later increase of pronouns and prepositions. Although a great deal of information was collected at this time, the analysis of language development in children was very often descriptive and nontheoretical. At the same time, however, Vygotsky was concerned with the function of language in children's development and summarized his views in a monograph. A succinct statement of his opinions, insofar as they are relevant to our topic, is given in the 1962 translation:

In brief, we must conclude that:-

1. *In their autogenetic development, thought and speech have different roots.*
2. *In the speech development of the child, we can with certainty establish a pre-intellectual stage, and in his thought development a prelinguistic stage.*
3. *Up to a certain point in time, the two follow different lines independently of each other.*
4. *At a certain point these lines meet, thereupon thought becomes verbal and speech rational [Vygotsky, 1962, p. 44].*

So once again, an early authority on language development shows that he, too, was persuaded that thought precedes connected speech, like Binet and so many more recent students of psycholinguistics (e.g., Cromer, 1968; Sinclair-de Zwart, 1967; Slobin, 1966).

Vygotsky did not work with the subnormal, but one of his students did. Luria (1961) published his views on the relationship between thought and language in the subnormal by reviewing the capacity of language to control motor behavior. Basing his work on the failure of the retarded to form an adequate connection between the primary and secondary signaling systems, Luria tried to show that the subnormal of imbecile level were unable to regulate behavior by general commands. In this sense they had failed to develop to an adequate level and therefore needed the reinforcement of a new command for every event, because for an undetermined reason they could not continue the force of a general self-instruction such as "I must always press the button when the green light appears." Other aspects of Luria's work showed that the internalization of commands was weak in the subnormal and their capacity to inhibit action on self-instruction was undeveloped. O'Connor and Hermelin (1963) were able to show that there was a failure to verbalize on visual inspection among the subnormal. This appeared in the subsequent recognition of visually presented material, and also in the verbalization of principles of solution. Thus severely subnormal children who learned a size discrimination task could not verbally describe their (correct) methodology, although, if aided, they could learn to do so.

In simple tasks, therefore, the principle of a weak connection between the visual (or tactile) and the acoustic-verbal aspects of behavior seemed established.

O'Connor and Hermelin (1959) showed, however, that Luria was probably wrong about elective generalization along a semantic dimension within the known vocabulary of the subnormal. Luria had claimed that the subnormal formed connections between words phonically rather than semantically. By using words that had been shown by Mein and O'Connor (1960) to be equally available and frequent in the vocabulary of the subnormal, we were able to show that semantic generalization occurred normally in this group.

In some respects, therefore, the failure of connection between primary and secondary signal systems is part of the problem of subnormal thinking and language. This may represent a failure of Vygotsky's two processes to become linked. However, it is also apparent from Bryant's (1965) work with transfer of learned behavior that not only do specific verbal instructions fail to aid transfer in the subnormal, but this failure also occurs when nonverbal instructions are given. Normal children of matched mental age transfer more effectively with both verbal and nonverbal instructions. These findings indicate that some failure occurs at a nonverbal level, perhaps in what is usually called capacity to select a dimensional cue, and not solely in the linguistic superstructure or the connections between language and infrastructure or language and logic.

However, that logic can be used by the subnormal in shortening the learning process has been shown in experiments conducted by Hermelin and O'Connor (1958). For example, subnormal children will learn a series of discriminations more quickly if there is a common element in the correct solution on each occasion. In another instance it has been shown that subnormal children with a memory span of three items can perfectly easily recall eight words if the words are arranged in sentence form. Lest this capacity should seem too obvious, it is worth noting that no such increase based on meaning can be achieved by autistic children, who may lack the capacity to refer to a properly organized basic structure or organized category system.

It is reasonable to infer, therefore, that cognition and language are related in a complex fashion in the subnormal. As Luria noted, language is not always developed to the level of universal propositions in terms of self-instruction. This would seem to be partly because generalization at a linguistic level, or at any level, may be poorly developed in the subnormal. There are some suggestions in the literature that language generalization may be less developed in the subnormal than are some other kinds of generalization. In addition, even where cognitive structure would support a particular verbal formulation of principle, the extension to language does not always occur, although connections can be produced in the subnormal by encouragement. Moreover, where a relationship between structure and linguistic reflection of this structure occurs, the relationship seems adequate. There is no evidence that the subnormal lack an appreciation of basic structure— simply that this appreciation is limited, and that their language structure, based on this limited understanding, is itself restricted.

Perhaps the best demonstration of the overall limitation of language according to understanding in this group of children is the small study made by Lackner

(1968). Although based on only five subjects, it shows clearly how the increase of mental age, and presumably also of comprehension of basic structure, is accompanied by an increase in sentence complexity following the pattern of development of normal children. Lackner notes that in such a matter as sentence length, for example, although the pattern of development is similar, normal children examined by McCarthy tend to produce longer sentences than subnormal children of matched mental age. He produced examples comparing his own study of subnormal with gifted children. Up to the age of 4 years, the subnormal of like mental age produced sentences of similar length, but beyond this age they were outstripped by the gifted children. He also makes a comparison of sentence types, showing that questions first occurred in the subnormal at the mental age of 2 years, 3 months, but that negative questions did not occur until nearly 3 years, and the passive not until 3 years, 3 months. Negative passives based on sentence production occurred in the mildly subnormal children only at a mental age of nearly 9 years. As with normal children, sentence repetition tests showed that the subnormal below a requisite mental age could not repeat sentences involving certain complex transformations, but uttered a structurally simple form of such sentences.

The juxtaposition of sentence length and comprehension of the rules of syntactic transformation in Lackner's study raises an interesting question. Graham and Gulliford (1968) in their study of the language deficits of educationally subnormal children draw on a suggestion made by Miller and Chomsky (1963), who point out that language deficiencies might arise from an inadequate program or from a deficient memory storage. As Miller (1956) notes, short-term memory in humans can be measured in terms of chunks, rather than in terms of the amount of information that can be stored. If structure exists, more can be stored. Therefore, Graham and Gulliford suggest, if no increased storage occurs in the presence of structured material, then no appreciation of structure, that is, no chunking, has occurred. However, as has been shown earlier, this does occur in the subnormal, so it may be assumed that their language in general matches their appreciation of structure, and that their programs are to a great degree related to their mental ages. What is, of course, deficient is their short-term storage capacity, a fact that is well authenticated clinically. What is most defective in the subnormal—their structural grasp or their short-term memory—is a matter for investigation. The most likely hypothesis in view of other findings would be that they are most probably equally handicapped in both.

The nature and limitations of the logic underlying the language of the subnormal can be illustrated by considering the language of autistic and receptive aphasic children. The language in autistic children is often distorted in so far as object and indirect object can be reversed in a manner unlikely to occur in the subnormal. So, for example, an autistic child may offer the sentence *Take park to doggy* or *Do you want a sweet?* meaning "I want a sweet," or *Mummy not gone home* meaning "I would like to see Mummy." It remains to be seen from further investigation whether this degree of departure from acceptable syntax represents a more primitive stage of development than that found in subnormal children. But it is seemingly very different. It should be kept in mind that the average memory span for autistic children is much greater than that for subnormal children of matched mental age, although their grasp of basic structure may be worse. Their linguistic deficiencies would seem not to be related to immediate storage capacity therefore, but to a failure to appreciate the syntactic significance of language. Hermelin and O'Connor (1970) discuss these questions at length, and a recent study by Hughes (1971) extended Premack's (1971) work with a chimpanzee to the study of children. In connection with this interesting venture, in which aphasic and deaf children were successfully taught a simple sign language. Hughes notes the problem shown by the aphasic in appreciating the significance of word order. This failure to order signs as well as words in any particular order is known to be characteristic of children with specific language handicaps. However, it can be shown that in other respects, aphasic children, for example, easily outstrip subnormal children in discrimination and ordering tasks. Recent work in our laboratories suggests that deaf children may use iconic recording as an aid to recall, reading off a fixed order of digits, for example, spatially, from an iconic store arranged in a left-to-right order. This phenomenon is rare in the subnormal, although it occurs in some cases.

The examples given from cases of specific deficit suggest that in these instances logic and language are less well matched than they are in subnormal children, and that their deficiencies are more unequal.

However, for the subnormal, these peculiarities and disparities are less obvious and, with the exceptions noted, the subnormal seem to show a verbal or linguistic ability that parallels their cognitive development. Sometimes their linguistic abilities can be shown to match their chronological age as distinct from their mental age. Lenneberg, Nichols, and Rosenberger (1964) have produced evidence that this may be so in children with Down's syndrome, and Dodd (1972) in an ongoing study of children with Down's syndrome and matched normal children, has demonstrated that babbling does not differ between these two groups at about 9—12 months of age.

Further summaries of the massive amount of data collected on speech and language in the subnormal are available in the writings of Spradlin (1963), Schiefelbusch, Copeland, and Smith (1967), and through Peins' (1969) bibliography.

Concluding Observations

If one tries to draw together the rather incomplete evidence surveyed in this chapter, one is left with an impression that the state of knowledge concerning language acquisition in general is too primitive to allow of even a preliminary constructive theory. While this situation holds, it would obviously be premature to advance strong views on language and its relation to thinking in the handicapped.

Some things can be said, however, that summarize the findings so far. The nature of cognition would appear to be such that it exists in some degree before the development of language. I have said nothing in this chapter about the nature or limits of this cognitive function, but it has already been explored in part by Piaget and Inhelder (1969) in many experiments. Obviously, capacity to discriminate, capacity to abstract or categorize, and capacity to code categorized material in memory and to retrieve such coded memories, precedes the active and effective use of language and furthermore precedes its comprehension. However, language would appear to follow this categorizing process, at least expressing the relationships on which more basic categorizing and discrimination are based. One can speculate that the prelinguistic logic mentioned by Vygotsky is iconic, but as Binet pointed out, this cannot be the whole story. Prelogical language, if the psycholinguists are to be believed, is unlikely, although it can occur. Presyntactic language can and does occur, but this language usually has a logic of its own, based on primitive concepts of identity, association, and interaction.

The subnormal show two main distortions of language development, which might be called slowing and arrest on the one hand, and inertia on the other. In the first case, the level of development of language follows that of logic, and this is both slowed and prematurely terminated in many instances. The inertia of language in the subnormal exists over and above its logic-based limitations. This is the apparent difficulty of verbal encoding in this group. If coding is encouraged, normal language—logic relations result. If, however, encoding into language is not encouraged, the subnormal tend to show poorer recall and more flexible or alterable patterns of behavior. At least this would seem to be the indication from some of our findings. Apart from this inertia, the language of the subnormal would seem to follow a developmental pattern in relation to cognition. In this respect it may differ from the language of the autistic child, which we have suggested is less evenly related to logic. The autistic child appears to have less access to a reality-oriented logic than either subnormal or aphasic children. The latter make reasonable use of signs, and can be taught a visual and syntactically organized sign language, as can the deaf. Although the experiment has not been done, it seems unlikely that autistic children could easily acquire a sign language. The position of the subnormal in relation to the deaf is more equivocal. Our own recent findings show very clearly that deaf children do not code visually presented material in words; they therefore have a different memory pattern from normal children. The subnormal seem to fall into two subgroups in relation to the use of iconic, versus verbal-acoustic, short-term memory store. Some use one and some the other. This subgrouping might be based on the relationship between thought and an image, on the one hand, and thought and a word, on the other. If one could find two linguistic levels among the subnormal, perhaps related to intelligence or laterality, one might begin to clarify the issue raised by Binet and Simon more than 60 years ago. Obviously some of the subnormal think at a prelinguistic level, probably iconically; others have a capacity to link their thinking with language. In certain respects, as we have shown in experiments, this can have different consequences. The full effects, however, of the marriage of thought and language, as foreseen by Vygotsky, have never been fully described. What happens in the case of a great many severely subnormal patients is that they barely reach the level of development where an adequate merger can occur. The ground plan of such an association does, however, exist, and its main outlines have been given above. There is little doubt that although a basic understanding or logic must precede an effective language, in the case of many of the subnormal, language is additionally handicapped in assisting cognition because of the verbal acoustic inertia operating in their case to interfere with the effective reception of meaning, and hence to prevent a rich association between surface structure and infrastructure.

References

Bever, T. G., Fodor, J. A., & Weksel, W. Is linguistics empirical? *Psychological Review*, 1965, *72* 493—500.

Binet, A., & Simon, R. The relation between thought and language. In *Intelligence of the feebleminded*. (Engl. transl. by E. S. Kite) Vineland, N.J.: The Training School & Baltimore: Williams & Wilkins, 1916. (First publ., *L'Année Psychologique*, 1908.)

Braine, M. D. S. On learning the grammatical order of words. *Psychological Review*, 1963, *70*, 323—348.

Broadbent, D. E. In defence of empirical psychology. *Bulletin of the British Psychological Society*, 1970, *23*, 87—96.

Bryant, P. E. The transfer of positive and negative learning by normal and severely subnormal children. *British Journal of Psychology*, 1965, *56*, 81—86.

Chomsky, N. *Syntactic structures*. The Hague: Mouton, 1957.

Cromer, R. F. The development of temporal reference during the acquisition of language. Unpublished doctoral dissertation, Harvard University, 1968.

de Laguna, G. A. *Speech, its function and development*. Bloomington: Indiana Univ. Press, 1963. (First publ., 1927.)

Dodd, B. J. Comparison of babbling patterns in normal and Down syndrome infants. *Journal of Mental Deficiency Research*, 1972, *16*, 35—40.

Graham, N. C., & Gulliford, R. A psycholinguistic approach to the language deficiencies of educationally subnormal children. *Educational Review*, 1968, *20*, 136—145.

Hebb, D. O., Lambert, W. E., & Tucker, G. R. Language, thought and experience. *Modern Language Journal*, 1971, *LV*, 212—222.

Hermelin, B., & O'Connor, N. The rote and concept learning of imbeciles. *Journal of Mental Deficiency Research*, 1958, *2*, 21—27.

Hermelin, B., & O'Connor, N. *Psychological experiments with autistic children*. Oxford: Pergamon, 1970.

Hughes, J. 1975. The acquisition of a non-vocal "language" by aphasic children. *Cognition*, 1975, *3*.

Hull, C. L. *Principles of behavior*. New York: Appleton, 1943.

Hume, D. *A treatise of human nature*. 1738. (London: Dent, 1911.)

Jenkins, J., & Palermo, D. S. Mediational processes and the acquisition of linguistic structure. In U. Bellugi & R. Brown (Eds.), *The acquisition of language. Monographs of the Society for Research in Child Development*, 1964, *29*, 141—169.

Kant, I. *Kritik der Reinen Vernunft*. Riga: Hartknoch, 1781. (N. Kemp Smith, transl., London: Macmillan, 1933.)

Lackner, J. R. A developmental study of language behaviour in retarded children. *Neuropsychologia*, 1968, *6*, 301—320.

Lenneberg, E. H. *Biological foundations of language.* New York: Wiley, 1967.

Lenneberg, E. H., Nichols, I. A., & Rosenberger, E. F. Primitive stages of language development in mongolism. In *Disorders of communication. Research Publications, Association for Research in Nervous and Mental Disease,* 1964, *42,* 119—137.

Luria, A. R. In J. Tizard (Ed.), *The role of speech in the regulation of normal and abnormal behaviour.* Oxford: Pergamon, 1961.

McCarthy, D. The language and development of the preschool child. *Institute of Child Welfare Monographs,* 1930, No. 4.

Mein, R., & O'Connor, N. A study of the oral vocabularies of severely subnormal patients. *Journal of Mental Deficiency Research,* 1960, *4,* 130—143.

Miller, G. A. The magical number seven plus or minus two. *Psychological Review,* 1956, *83,* 81—91.

Miller, G. A., & Chomsky, N. Finitary models of language users. In R. D. Luce, R. R. Bush, & E. Galanter (Eds.), *Handbook of mathematical psychology.* Vol. 2. New York: Wiley, 1963. Pp. 419—491.

O'Connor, N., & Hermelin, B. Some effects of word learning in imbeciles. *Language and Speech,* 1959, *2,* 63—71.

O'Connor, N., & Hermelin, B. *Speech and thought in severe subnormality.* Oxford: Pergamon, 1963.

Peins, M. *Bibliography on speech, hearing and language in relation to mental retardation, 1900—1968.* P. H. S. Publ. 2022. Washington, D.C.: U.S. Dep. Health, Education, and Welfare, 1969.

Piaget, J., & Inhelder, B. *The psychology of the child.* London: Routledge & Kegan Paul, 1969.

Premack, D. Language in chimpanzee? *Science,* 1971, *172,* 808—822.

Russell, B. *An inquiry into meaning and truth.* London: Allen & Unwin, 1940.

Schiefelbusch, R. L., Copeland, R. H. & Smith, J. O. *Language and mental retardation.* New York, Holt, 1967.

Sinclair-de Zwart, H. *Acquisition du langage et développement de la pensée.* Paris: Dunod, 1967.

Skinner, B. F. *Verbal behavior.* New York: Appleton, 1957.

Slobin, D. I. The acquisition of Russian as a native language. In F. Smith & G. A. Miller (Eds.), *The genesis of language.* Cambridge, Mass.: MIT Press, 1966. Pp. 129—148.

Spradlin, J. E. Language and communication of mental defectives. In N. R. Ellis (Ed.), *Handbook of mental deficiency.* New York: McGraw-Hill, 1963. Ch. 16, Pp. 512—555.

Vygotsky, L. S. *Thought and language.* Cambridge, Mass.: MIT Press & New York: Wiley, 1962.

19. Some Aspects of Language in Various Forms of Senile Dementia (Comparisons with Language in Childhood)

J. de Ajuriaguerra / R. Tissot

A comparison of child language with deteriorated language in senile dementia shows the two to be very dissimilar. The principal language symptoms in dementia are impoverished vocabulary, word groping, repetitiveness, disorders of syntax, semantics, and phonology resembling the paraphasic phenomena in aphasia due to sudden focal lesions. It is proposed that the language disorganization is due to a combination of breakdowns in various functions and processes. The authors reject the notion that aphasias due to localized lesions are simply disturbances in performance (in Chomsky's sense) while the language disturbances in the demented are a simple consequence of underlying thought disorders.

Introduction

Why should a chapter on the disintegration of language in forms of senile dementia be included in a book dealing with language development? There would be obvious justification for it if we were in a position to make an item-by-item comparison of the genesis of language in infancy with its disintegration in dementia. Many studies have, of course, been made on the development of language, but they are on the lines of the Binet–Simon study on the development of intelligence; they describe levels of language development in children rather than actual ontogenetic stages. As Richelle (1971) has observed in a recent, well-informed book, the gaps in our knowledge on this subject bulk far larger than what we know for certain. The same may be said of our knowledge of language in dementia. We shall find we have to compare the pieces of two jigsaw puzzles, many of which are still missing, while we are not certain that a particular piece in one puzzle corresponds to another particular piece in the other. The results of such comparisons cannot therefore be regarded as anything more than heuristic hypotheses.

The disintegration of language in dementia is a consequence of the combined disorganization of many functions of the central nervous system. Two pitfalls are to be avoided in studying it: reducing all language disturbances in dementia to instrumental disorders by seeking to group them with those found in aphasia due to circumscribed lesions or, on the contrary, neglecting their instrumental aspect and reducing the truly aphasic semiology of language in dementia to a weakening of the intellect and the memory. This warning is not sounded simply as a matter of form. A comparison with apraxia will demonstrate the fact. According to Piaget's conception, which we endorse, there is no sharp break, in the development of the intellect, between the first sensorimotor circular reactions linking up with the outside world and the operations of thought. Piaget's developmental explanation of the sensorimotor period right through to the higher stages of infralogical operations amounts to no more than an ontogeny of praxes taken in the widest sense. The study of the degeneration of these praxes in various forms of dementia can therefore be based on an unambiguous and above all well-integrated body of knowledge. In this field, the instrumental aspect of behavior is scarcely to be dissociated from its global structure. The latter is practically coterminal with the sensorimotor instrument whose organization it expresses. Grasping the permanence of an object means mastering Poincaré's (1902) and Piaget's grouping of time—space movements, which is itself only the result of the mutual assimilation and accommodation of the sensorimotor schemas.

In the case of language, the problem is quite different and much more complex. It arises not only from the organization of action on the outside world, from which—with all due deference to the linguists—the greater part of the system of significata is derived, but also from the symbolic or semiotic function. Viewed thus as a symbolic function, language becomes the optional mediator in infralogical operations and the indispensable mediator in logical operations. In this respect, it can already be seen as an instrument of the intellect, for which it mediates in its most sophisticated forms, but which it also helps to fashion. Furthermore, language is built up and produced through sensorimotor auditive—phonatory schemata borrowed and fashioned for its use, although there is no reason for saying that this was their primary purpose. From this point of view, it is, so to speak, a secondary instrument. It is therefore not surprising that the study of the ontogeny of language is far less advanced than the study of the onto-geny of operations in Piaget's sense. If it is to be taken further, much more extensive research will be needed, and far more difficult obstacles in the way of interdisciplinary systematization will have to be overcome.

Despite these limitations, on the basis of the few research results on which we can draw—and which are very far from constituting a systematic study of language in dementia—it seems possible, both from the semiological standpoint and from that of the context in which the disorders develop, to distinguish provisionally, in cases of dementia, between

1. speech disturbances that it is hard not to ascribe to memory deficiencies;
2. disturbances in the use and function of language that seem to result from the simultaneous disorganization of the subject's cognitive and affective faculties;
3. semantic and syntactic disturbances that correlate closely with the operational disintegration of the subjects and thus produce a symptomatology that is reminiscent of disturbances of the cognitive functions;
4. disturbances in the first and second articulation (classically termed semantic paraphasia and phonemic paraphasia, respectively), presenting symptoms that resemble those found in forms of aphasia following circumscribed lesions (the interpretation of which is still conjectural);
5. repetition and stereotypy of speech, which are found in conjunction with other forms of stereotypy of movement in cases of neurological disorganization.

Language Disturbances Due to Memory Failure

We are not referring here to the confabulation and repetition that may be features of language in dementia; an effect of memory disturbances on language, they do not involve any change in its formal structure. A more difficult, and also more interesting problem is that of failure to find the desired word, an isolated phenomenon observed in certain cases of sensile dementia in which cognitive activity is not affected. Inability to recall words is, of course, an integral part of the semiology of all forms of aphasia due to circumscribed lesions. The attitude of the patient may, however, be instructive. When inability to recall a word is due to loss of memory, the patient appears embarrassed, as a normal person does when unable to recall a proper name. When the inability to recall a word is due to aphasia, the patient gives the impression rather of trying out in succession different courses of action.

What is probably of more significance than the patient's attitude, however, is the practice—common in simple forms of senile dementia (where the symptoms are practically reduced to fixation amnesia)—of replacing the missing word with adequate explanatory paraphrases and satisfactory (or nearly satisfactory) synonyms. In more advanced cases, it becomes impossible to decide whether the inability to recall words is due to amnesia or to aphasia. In the last resort, it is necessary to infer the nature of the inability from the presence or absence of other language disturbances.

Quite revealing is what happens to patients with progressive dementia when their search for a word is facilitated by being given a selection of words from which to choose: Until they reach the middle of Piaget's stage of concrete operations, the number of correctly chosen words increases with the degree of their word-finding difficulty. Thereafter there is a progressive collapse, which shows clearly that the mechanisms of word recall are not the only ones involved at the preoperational stage. This breakdown is inevitable; these patients can no longer avail themselves of anything but intensive classes that do not overlap semantically.

Disturbances in the Use and Function of Language

Ombredane (1951) listed five uses of language: (1) affective, (2) ludic, (3) practical, (4) representative, and (5) dialectical. These traditional distinctions, as well as their succession and hierarchization in the development of language, are still generally accepted. Their correlation with the level of structural language development, however, is much less certain; moreover, their significance for communication and relations with other people is highly controversial.

It is generally believed that only the affective and ludic uses are involved in the prelinguistic or presemantic stage of language acquisition. These two aspects, however, already foreshadow a dichotomy to be found in all subsequent uses of language: that of "language for others" and "language for oneself." The affective language, at first inarticulate and made up of stereotypes that cannot be analyzed, resembling the interjections of the adult (Alarchos Llorach, 1968), stems directly from the cries by means of which an infant expresses his needs. But, in the first place, the child quickly discovers the effects that the sounds he makes produce on adults. From then on, he uses them to attract attention and secure satisfaction. Again, while the child is acting on someone else, he is stimulating himself. In this way, auditive–phonatory and probably somesthetic–phonatory circular reactions are set up and self-sustained on the basis of motivations connected with exercise and play. During the semantic period, when first the practical, then the representative, and finally the dialectical usages of language develop, these two aspects—"for others and for oneself"—still subsist, even if in varying proportions.

According to Alarchos Llorach (1968), as soon as the first signs are learned, there is a choice of three ways in which they can be used: for calling, for willing, and for designating, that is, *I call X, I want X, This is X.* The first two uses are clearly interrelated. The third, as Piaget rightly appreciated, remains predominantly egocentric for a long time. It is an extension of the word play of the presemantic period and a source of pleasure, like all circular reactions, while being also an exercise in the acquisition of the phonological system and syntax. The following sing-song of a little girl of age 3 was noted, for example, by Ombredane (1951):

> *le papo de papa, le papo de maman, le papo du couteau, le papo du papo, le tuco du tapo, le capo du capo.*

As the practical usage of language develops, this third use enters into the regulating of action; as Vugotsky (1962) puts it, egocentric language begins by marking the end of an activity, or a turning point, then moves gradually toward the middle, then the beginning of the activity, bringing to light a function in the directing or planning of the child's activity, and raising it to the level of purposive acts.

Once it has become representative, language is used by the child to make statements about the world and to describe present, past, or future events; it enables him to characterize, fix, and conceptualize them.

In all three cases, the use of language is egocentric. It does not matter to whom the child is speaking or whether or not he is listened to; he is speaking for himself or in order to associate someone with his immediate action. While not necessarily talking about himself, he does not put himself in the place of the person with whom he is speaking; he feels no need to act on the other person or to tell him anything (Piaget).

Although between the ages of 3 and 7 most language is language for oneself, at least in our societies, language for others is developing just the same, and it is during this fundamental period and through it that the appetitive function is strengthened. The latter depends directly on the possibility of talking with another person and is so important that it conditions the whole development of language. Without language for others between the ages of 3 and 7, language does not develop, does not go beyond the stage of *I call—I want—This is,* as observation of infantile psychoses has shown. But this language for others, so fraught with meaning on the affective plane, is still poor when it comes to transmitting information, from the standpoints of variety and of semantics alike. It is enough for this practical language to cover affirmation, negation, the expression of needs, pleasure, displeasure, a few practical orders, and a few signs, the precision of which is lessened and the comprehension of which is more closely dependent on extra-linguistic factors, because the significata are only preconcepts, in Piaget's terminology.

Naturally, it is only when the stage of concrete operations is reached that representative language can be socialized and become a vehicle for cognitive information, and then for socialized logical speech.

What do we find in regard to the uses and function of language when it is disintegrating in dementia? Here opinions are divergent in the extreme. According to one psycholinguist, Irigaray (no date), the patient is, strictly speaking, no longer actively producing utterances, no longer generating speech; he is simply the passive reciter of previously produced utterances. If we understand Irigary correctly, the dementia patient would thus be simply a talking machine, which would go into action automatically or whenever the examiner manages to switch on the robot mechanism. We are thus not very far removed from Goldstein's "soulless" patients (Goldstein, 1933).

The real situation seems in our view to be quite different. At the amnesic stage, when there is no operational failing, the speech function in senile dementia is normal. Only its content is affected by the patient's handicaps. We have recorded many examples of patients faced with psychological tests beyond their ability (de Ajuriaguerra, Gainotti, & Tissot, 1969). Reactions range from pure confabulation (*We have a lot of work on Saturdays with the customers, you know, and now I am tired*) through indignation (*I am not in school. Do that with your children if it amuses you*) and anxiety (*What will happen if I don't manage to reply?*) to admission of helplessness (*I just can't grasp it. My brain's not working properly today*).

At the stage of gradual disintegration of infralogical operations, before or after structural disturbances of language have appeared, the proportion of egocentric speech becomes much greater. Conversation with others is still possible, but only in connection with practical tasks. It may still be representative and explanatory. This is indeed what makes it possible, in a number of cases, clearly to recognize Piaget's operational ontogenetic levels. A case in point is a patient who explained—thereby showing that she was unable to dissociate time from space—that if the blue doll had walked longer than the red doll, it would of course have passed it. In quite a short time, however, the only communication possible is through an elliptical practical language, the meaning of which is closely dependent upon extralinguistic information. During a weight-conservation test the following conversation took place (the examiner had shaped a ball of plasticine into a roll):

EXAMINER: *Will that weigh the same?*
PATIENT: *Yes.*
EXAMINER: *Why?*
PATIENT: *It's the same thing.*
EXAMINER: *Yesterday someone told me that the sausage weighed more because it was longer.*
PATIENT: *Well I never! It is much longer. It is thin!*
(Or again)
EXAMINER: *The same thing?*
PATIENT: *No, like that it weighs more.*
EXAMINER: *Why?*
PATIENT: *It is long. It sticks out.*
(The plasticine roll in fact sticks out beyond the pan of the scales.)

As with children, this practical language is no longer a vehicle for explicit thought, but serves as an auxiliary to action. When not connected with action, language often becomes declaratory, as it is in children, and the speaker takes little account of any other person present. Pseudoconversations may, however, still take place, in which the utterances of one speaker serve only as a stimulus to those of the other. At table, while waiting for breakfast,

FIRST SPEAKER: *I'm having trouble with my "mounin."*
SECOND SPEAKER: *I wonder where it is.*
FIRST SPEAKER (bending down as if he were hunting for something):   *Can't find it.*

At the lowest levels, speech is reduced practically to the occasional appeal to be extricated from a difficult situation. Even the expression of wants and needs becomes increasingly rare. It is not certain, moreover, that speech is directly involved here. In a current study of nutritional behavior, we observed that, in the most advanced stages of dementia, patients who had been made to miss the midday meal showed overall changes in behavior that afternoon in the form of anxiety and slight psychomotor agitation, but did not say they were hungry, even when their language ability would still have permitted it. Finally, in many respects, the verbal stereotypy of the most seriously affected patients is reminiscent of the circular reactions of the infant at play. It obviously does not have the same function, however. Much more iterative and monotonous, it never gives the impression of exercise, as it does so strongly in infants, and does not seem to produce the same satisfaction, although it is often accompanied by smiles. Set off apparently by chance, or following other stereotyped movements—for instance, of the arms—it sometimes appears still to be motivated. An instance of this may be seen in the film we took of a woman patient, not even aware of the permanence of objects, smiling at a doll she had in her arms and repeating in stereotyped fashion *papapapapa.*

All in all, in the course of the disintegration of language in dementia, we find the uses described in connection with childhood—although they do not have the same meaning—and even more or less the same hierarchical succession, but in reverse.

Semantic and Syntactic Language Disturbances Closely Correlated with the Subject's Operational Level

In dementia, language rapidly becomes both elliptical and redundant. Terms implicit in the situation are omitted, whereas more and more predicates are added. Asked to compare two pencils of different lengths, patients respond with something like: *That is the maximum, just a little longer.* Or, when asked to define a washbasin: *It is where there is water. . . . You turn and then it comes, with hot water and cold water taps. . . . You wash yourself.* These prosaic statements in themselves give rise to a host of questions. The omission of all the terms implicit in the extralinguistic situation may perhaps be explained to some extent by the use of language in its practical form, as an auxiliary in action, as mentioned earlier. In this latter use, even with normal people, any term implicit in the situation is understood and predicates are added even if they are redundant. However, it cannot be forgotten that, in the opinion of the older authorities and of Wepman, Bock, Jones, and Van Pelt (1956), the language of so-called amnesic aphasics, affected by circumscribed lesions, has similar characteristics: decrease in nouns and, to a lesser degree, verbs, and a marked increase in adjectives and adverbs, or "descriptive modifiers," to use Wepman's term. However, it would be dangerous to conclude, on the basis of this symptomatological parallel, that the physical pathogeny is identical in both cases.

Redundancy, in the language of the demented, is also evident in other respects, for instance in the naming of things, as observed by Haag and Brabant (1963). A pencil becomes "a drawing pencil," a cup becomes "a tea cup," a duck becomes "a wild duck." This need to qualify lexemes arises almost simultaneously with difficulties in the expression of asymmetrical relations. As mentioned by Sinclair (1967), a longer pencil is described by the same patients as "a tiny bit longer" or "much longer," as if "longer" could not adequately describe all the pencils longer than the one taken as the basis for comparison. These patients seem to have become incapable of making extensive classifications and are reduced to intensive qualifications.

At an equivalent level of development, children use preconcepts. As they are not able to form a hierarchy of classes and subclasses, their lexemes do not yet have all the attributes of a sign as understood by Saussure. To take a well-known example quoted by Piaget, the wind that drives the clouds is the white wind (*amein blanc*), whereas the wind that makes the trees tremble is the blue wind (*amein bleu*). The characteristic feature of preconcepts, according to Piaget, is that they remain half way between the generality of concepts and the individuality of the elements of which the latter are composed.

The use of the terms *drawing pencil* and *tea cup* by our patients clearly suggests an identical process. It would appear that the word "pencil" could no longer represent all the individual objects in the pencil category.

The disorganization of semantic fields rapidly becomes much more obvious, however. In naming tests *inter alia* it appears in the form of the classic verbal paraphasia, which we prefer to describe as semantic or first articulation paraphasia. In this, symptomatology, which is entirely comparable with that of certain forms of Wernicke's aphasia, it seems to us very difficult to ascertain to what extent cognitive disturbances are involved, and to what extent instrumental disturbances. In the naming of things, replies extend from adequate lexemes down to words without any evident semantic relationship with the object, passing through all manner of semantic deviations. Some of the latter very clearly indicate a cognitive disturbance, or even a semantic dedifferentiation akin to the "indifferentiation" of semantic fields in childhood. For instance, "trumpet" is regularly employed to name all wind instruments. Recourse to a generic class (as "animal" for a slug), semantic shift to neighbouring terms in the same category (as "cup" instead of bowl, or "penknife" instead of knife), or slipping into an adjoining subfield (as "stew" instead of stew pot), are difficult to interpret. Sometimes it is probably a case of cognitive disturbance, sometimes of not being able to find the word or of substituting one word for another. A woman patient who could not recall the word "funnel" gave an apt definition of it: *What you put on a bottle and you pour*. When she was asked to choose the word from among "watering-can," "funnel," and "filter," she laughed and said, *It can be all three*. A better analysis of the logical relations between *significata* and *significans*, as proposed by Prieto (1966), might perhaps make it possible to obtain a clearer idea of the nature of the disturbances leading to these semantic deviations.

Be that as it may, the semantic distance is very soon much greater in the paraphasia of the demented than it is in aphasia due to circumscribed lesions. In a word-classification test administered to 50 aphasics, for example, Lhermitte, Desrovenes, and Lecours (1971) observed only negligible number of mistakes that would indicate a total loss of the delimiting influences of semantic fields. In demented patients, on the other hand, inappropriate words without any identifiable semantic relationship with the key word are frequent. Whereas first articulation paraphasia with limited semantic deviations occurs constantly as soon as words cannot be recalled, cases of paraphasia where there is no semantic relationship with the appropriate word are only occasional at the level of infralogical operations; they are numerous and preponderant at the preoperational level. At the same time, when words cannot be recalled, the number of adequate substitute definitions is practically nil. These facts definitely suggests that dedifferentiation of semantic fields is in direct correlation with the regression of the patient's operational level. Not only do they tend to confirm Piaget's (1923, 1936, 1937, 1946) conception, developed in relation to symbol formation in children, but they also justify the approach of those linguists who have abandoned the search for semantic distinctive features and reverted to the logic of classes (Mounin, 1973, Prieto, 1966).

In this connection, Irigaray's conclusions seem to coincide with our own. She says that, in extreme cases, words do not appear to be coded units but elements determined by an idiolect. She immediately adds, however, that vocabulary is therefore definitely affected in dementia, but that one must be careful not to ascribe this too hastily to the language model. Does it really involve, she asks, a dysfunction of the language model, or rather the subject's inability to make use of that model?

So far we have considered only language disturbances in dementia situated in the lexical or paradigmatic axis of language. Those affecting discourse, or the syntagmatic axis of language, are no less evident. With H. Sinclair and M. Boehme (Sinclair, Boehme, Tissot, & de Ajuriaguerra, 1966) we tested the comprehension of a sequence of events or acts in sentences that the subjects read with the examiner. The succession was expressed solely by means of morphosyntax (verb tenses and word order). All autonomous monemes such as "yesterday," "already," "afterwards," whose semantic value might supply the deficiencies of morphosyntax, were avoided. In three of the sentences, the simultaneity of two acts was expressed in three different ways. In the rest of the sentences, one of the acts preceded the other.

The results obtained were quite coherent. Besides an increase in failures going hand in hand with operational disintegration, we observed a close correlation between the arguments used by the subject to justify his replies and the subject's operational level. With few exceptions, at the level of the transition to formal operations, the patients understood the sequence of acts and reasoned only about the morphosyntax, even if they did not manage to explain the verb tenses adequately (future, perfect, imperfect, etc.). At the level of concrete operations, there were mistakes and the reasoning involved both morphosyntax and semantics. For instance, with the sentence, *We shall invite the gardener who did our garden*, we obtained answers such as, *Of course you don't invite him before he has done the work.* In this particular case, semantics is brought in to back up a correct reply based on an understanding of the morphosyntax, which the subject is unable to express in words. At the preoperational level, most of the answers were wrong, and the reasoning constantly brought in either semantics or the order of the words in the clause. The sentence quoted above was not understood; we received answers such as *I can keep up a garden* or *They invite him first. You see, that's what they say*, with the subject pointing to the words *shall invite*, which come before the words *did our garden* in the sentence.

The apprehension of a time sequence through the morphosyntax of the language thus closely parallels the subject's operational level. However, by comparison with the inmates of an old people's home, not affected by degenerative dementia but in some cases with low operational levels, the test results of those suffering from dementia come low on the scale in relation to their operational levels (as measured by tests on conservation). Their understanding of morphosyntax seems to follow their ability to deal with the representation of space and physical time. This is not the place to put forward hypotheses that might explain this phenomenon. Suffice it to say that, in cases of dementia, mobilization by operations of symbols—whether figurative, analogical, or merely conventional signs—is rendered difficult by disturbances in the programmed anticipation of behavioral strategy.

It should be noted, however, that though the results of this morphosyntactical test are coherent, and though they clearly show that the intellectual decline of our subjects has some effect on their language, their interpretation is neither easy nor unambiguous. For although, in the artificial, purely linguistic situation in which we placed them, our demented patients at the preoperational level could no longer apprehend a sequence of events or acts through purely morphosyntactical data, and although, in operational physical-time tests, they were no longer capable of dissociating time from space (Ajuriaguerra *et al.*, 1967) it seems likely that in a more natural, practical linguistic and extralinguistic situation they would understand similar sentences. This impression is borne out by the fact that, in conversation, almost all of them are capable of constructing sentences of equivalent structure correctly. We noted many examples of the type: *When I have had dinner, I shall go for a walk.*

These distinctions are confirmed by the results of a very ordinary sentence-correction test, which we administered with F. Duval (1966), Tissot, Richard, Duval, and de Ajuriaguerra, (1967). These sentences contained essentially two types of mistakes: Some were clearly morphosyntactical in character, as in the following example *Peter and John has left*; whereas others involved relations of cause and effect or logic, indicated either by conjunctions such as "why" and "for" or by autonomous monemes such as "yesterday," e.g., *It is raining for I cannot go out* or *Yesterday he is sick.* Sentences with purely morphosyntactical mistakes quite out of keeping with the syntactical schemes of the language were generally corrected, even at the preoperational level. Illogicalities, on the contrary, were either overlooked or inadequately corrected; *It is raining for I cannot go out* was corrected to *It is raining because I cannot go out* or *It is raining for I am going to leave.* Another sentence *I am eating why I am hungry* was corrected to *I am eating. Why am I hungry?* Mistakes due to the incompatibility of an autonomous moneme and the morphosyntax, such as *Yesterday he is sick*, occupy an intermediate position. Although not picked up so readily as mistakes involving morphosyntax alone, they are recognized better than illogicalities. Here again we find a phenomenon familiar in children.

In Alarchos Llorach's opinion (1968), the morphological elements first acquired by children are those reinforced by the redundancy of agreements. For a long time functional monemes proper, such as prepositions, for instance, are used only as grammatical expedients. In other words, although they already serve to introduce expansions of the sentence, their logical value as indicating the nature of the relation between the predicate nucleus and the expansions is still very vague. Children, like the demented, accept and can say *It is raining for I am going to leave.*

All in all, the language disturbances of patients with degenerative dementia that appear to result from their intellectual decline chiefly affect the semantic values of the language. As with children, who have only transductive reasoning at their disposal and who use intensive classifications only, the significata of the signs still used by the demented seem to be more than preconcepts in Piaget's sense of the term. Very soon thereafter, the semantic value of the lexemes deteriorates still further. Finally, although in a purely linguistic context, comparable with that of the classic syllogisms, the morphosyntactical values of the language seem indeed to suffer the same fate as the conceptions based on intellectual operations; they are fairly well preserved for a long while in more or less automatic verbal utterances, but often serve only as grammatical expedients, as they do in children. Consequently, we cannot agree with Irigaray that, in dementia patients, the syntagmatic model and the transformational model seem to remain intact.

Language Disturbances Clinically Resembling Those of Aphasia Due to Circumscribed Lesions

We have already noted that even at the operational level of transition from concrete to formal operations, instances of semantic first-articulation paraphasia make their appearance. It seems clear to us that the semantic distance between the substituted word and the appropriate word is partly dependent on the subject's operational level. This, however, cannot be taken as settling the question of the mechanisms that underlie the production of semantic paraphasia, especially when it is consciously experienced or is accompanied by verbal behavior or gestures showing that the subject is aware that he is not using quite the right word. In this case, which is by no means unusual in dementia, mechanisms similar to those involved in Wernicke's aphasia must come into play (Alajouanine, Lhermitte, Ledoux, & Vignolo, 1964). Here as elsewhere it is not easy to set boundaries. Instrumental disturbance seems beyond doubt when a patient calls a slug *a grasshopper*, but then immediately adds *No, it crawls along*. Then again, these patients, like those suffering from Wernicke's aphasia, coin words, although this is rather exceptional. For instance, a **pinceau** (*paintbrush*) is first called a **plumeau** (*feather duster*), but then an *époussoir* (**épousseter**—*to dust*). Although physiopathological identity cannot be inferred from these clinical similarities without further evidence, we cannot exclude the possibility—particularly since the corresponding forms of aphasia, although connected with circumscribed lesions, are those in which the semantic disturbances are not merely verbal, as was noted by Goldstein (1933). They are also to be found in nonverbal classification tests. It is thus probably not accidental that language disturbances in dementia are so reminiscent of the symptomatology of certain forms of aphasia. Lhermitte and his colleagues, when administering a classification test, had to exclude from the group several patients suffering from Wernicke's aphasia with semantic predominance because their PM 38 results were inadequate.

While second-articulation paraphasia in senile dementia is much rarer, according to our observations, it has no symptomatological characteristic that might differentiate it from the classic forms of phonemic paraphasia in Wernicke's aphasia: *pailler, carmaillon*, instead of *pinceau*; *gramont* instead of *canif*; *poupi* instead of *serrure*; *séran* instead of *salière*. The most that could be said is that distorted lexemes in which some elements of the appropriate word are still to be recognized are less frequent than they are in Wernicke's aphasia. As in the latter, the neologisms produced by the patient are sometimes accepted and sometimes rejected when they are reproduced by the examiner.

Alongside these classic forms of phonemic paraphasia, however, others are found in degenerative dementia; these comprise commutations of isolated phonemes, although they do not appear to be of a phonetic or articulatory nature, as understood by Pierre Marie and subsequently by Alajouanine, Ombredane, and Durand (1939). On the one hand, they are very seldom encountered in spontaneous speech or in the repetition of lexemes before the third clinical stage of disintegration. On the other hand, they are very common in the repetition of nonsense syllables, even in mild cases, which would make them appear rather akin to the similar errors observed in dysphasic children. Lastly, the very nature of the commutations observed in dementia seems to us to differ in certain respects from that of the phonetic disintegration symptoms due to anarthria or Broca's aphasia.

The main characteristics of the latter, as described by Alajouanine *et al.* (1964), are as follows:

oral vowels are better preserved than consonants;
nasal vowels are replaced by oral vowels;

fricative consonants are replaced by plosives with the same or a neighboring point of articulation;

articulation-initial vowels are replaced by articulation-initial consonants; elisions;

assimilations, which are more likely to occur when the phoneme replaced is weak (fricative, voiced, or nasal) or is in a weak position (consonant group); metatheses.

The question has been reconsidered of late by Cohen, Dubois, Gauthier, Hécaen, and Angelergues (1963). Their analysis confirms and fills out the picture given above. Not only are vowels more resistant than consonants, but they seem to serve as guides for articulation. The French *u* [y] is the oral vowel most frequently affected. Of the consonants, it is the liquid oral ones (*l* and *r*), the apicodental ones (*s* and *z*), and *g* that present most difficulty. The authors lay special stress on the contextual determination of the distortions. Here the vowels play a vital part, clearly marked by the extent of the articulatory shift they may impose on adjacent consonants in the syllable. The prepalatal, dental, and in many cases even labial consonants are turned into [k] in front of [o] or following [a]. Similarly [k] and [g] come forward as far as [t] and [d] under the influence of [i] and from time to time under the influence of other front vowels.

Elements of the phonetic disintegration syndrome are certainly to be found among the phonetic transformations of our patients. Lhermitte and his colleagues, however, observed the same phenomenon in definite cases of Wernicke's aphasia. As in the phonetic disintegration syndrome, vowels are more firmly established than consonants. Many elisions, metatheses, assimilations between consonants, and consonant shifts occur under the influence of a contiguous vowel. Here, too, the same phonemes are found to be weak. But, whereas in the phonetic disintegration syndrome many of these transformations show a one-to-one correspondence, the same is not true in dementia. Although buccalization of nasal vowels is the phenomenon most often observed, nasalization of oral vowels is not uncommon. With consonants, although the fricatives are most frequently modified, they commute with each other by changes in the point of articulation, but keep the same degree of aperture and often of voicing: [f] becomes [s] and vice versa, [v] becomes [z] and vice versa. Changes into plosives are not observed, or only very seldom. Similarly, commutations of plosive consonants are very frequent by forward or backward shifting of the point of articulation, depending on the neighbouring influences, but the distinctive features of the series—voicelessness, voicing, nasalization—are usually unchanged. Finally, although there is a shift from one series to another, it is not one way. Voicing is noted more often than devoicing, and although buccalization predominates, nasalization is not uncommon.

Comparison with children is particularly enlightening here. The commutations observed clearly point to dedifferentiation between the third articulation distinctive features rather than between the phonemes themselves. This would therefore entirely bear out the views of the linguists, from Jakobson to Alarchos Llorach, who have described in children not the acquisition of individual phonemes, but the gradual differentiation of the phonological system as a whole, with the more or less symmetrical appearance of corresponding distinctive features.

The following table is most instructive, although the relative frequency of phonemes is not taken into account. In children, as we know, after the first vowel—consonant opposition is established, the whole set of bilabial (labial feature) plosives, *p, b, m,* though still confused with one another, are differentiated from the whole set of (lingual feature) plosives, pronounced further back, which are subsequently differentiated into apicodental and velar features:

$$
\begin{array}{c|c}
t & \\
d & k \\
n & g
\end{array}
$$

Our findings show that commutations are frequent between *p, t,* and *k,* the *p* being stronger than the *t* and *k,* which are frequently interchanged.

To sum up, speech disturbances in degenerative dementia that are symptomatologically close to those of aphasia due to circumscribed lesions affect the two articulations of language. Semantic paraphasia is the more frequent and appears first. The classic phonemic paraphasia is much rarer, but it undoubtedly occurs. Commutations of phonemes are also observed; these are akin in certain respects to those found in the phonetic disintegration syndrome, but differ in others, to the point of seeming on a first approximation closer to phonemic than to phonetic disturbances.

Here too we are in direct disagreement with Irigaray, who goes so far as to say that the phonological code appears to remain intact in dementia; that even mistakes such as a change in the point of articulation of a phoneme, phonemic or syllabic permutation, or reduction of syllabic groups, seem too unsystematic to be interpreted as incapacity in phonemic realization; and that they come, rather, under the heading of fluctuations in the functioning of the reception and transmission of messages. Here again we have the rather sterile dichotomy of competence and performance. For our part, we prefer the old distinction between *langue* and *parole* and are convinced that in dementia there are phonological disturbances that are language phenomena (*faits de langue*), in Saussure's sense.

Verbal Stereotypy and Iteration Appearing in Cases of Neurological Disorganization

The term verbal stereotypy may be taken in a broad sense. Without going too far, it could be made to include endless repetition and substitution perseveration in Guiraud's (1936) sense of the term. Such is not our intention. Endless repetition results from a combination of amnesia and intellectual decline. If the distinction is worth retaining, it is a question of thought rather than of language. As for the substitution perseverations, or "word intoxication," these appear to us to be identical, both in their form and in the circumstances in which they develop, to those found in aphasia due to circumscribed lesions.

What we have in mind is phonemic iteration proper. The iteration seldom consists of a word. Sometimes it consists of a series of phonemes—more often than not, two or three phonemes making up a syllable. This is the syllabic palilalia of Guiraud (1936), the logoclonia of the earlier authorities. It acts exactly like the interference with the subject's language due to the "atmosphere effect." With certain patients, it interrupts what are still fairly wellstructured utterances. With most, it occurs on the occasion of any intentional tensing of the buccophonatory organs, or even spontaneously when the patient is alone. It has often been said that this is the final stage of the instrumental disorganization of language. That contention seems to us difficult to maintain. For, as we have just pointed out, the iteration, in some subjects, produces "atmosphere interference" in what are still fairly well-structured utterances. Furthermore, as a rule, it is never isolated. It also encroaches on writing in the form of endless repetitions of the same syllable or the same letter. This graphic palilalia is not, of course, an argument against the aphasic origin of the iteration. But these forms of oral and graphic iteration are accompanied by other forms of motor iteration: kneading or plucking at the bedclothes, pseudotrembling, fidgeting with the feet, crossing and uncrossing the legs, facial and oral (nonvocal) stereotypy, and so on. In some cases, pseudotrembling and verbal iteration are synchronous and seem to set each other off. Either the trembling or the verbal iteration may start first. We have verified some cases of the synchronization of the two phenomena by means of simultaneous electromyograms and voice recordings.

All these instances of stereotypy occur in the context of muscle tonus disorders and primitive reflexes or behavior components. The subjects show a forced prehension, of tactile and proprioceptive origin, often accompanied by what is called the instinctive grasping reflex, a visual and tactile oral reflex, a fixed gaze, an oppositional hypertonicity, with an increase in the postural reflexes, a tendency to conserve attitudes and to repeat motions.

All in all, the forms of verbal iteration observed in degenerative dementia in the narrower sense adopted here seem, like the other forms of stereotypy of motion shown by these subjects, to be bound up with their neurological dystonic syndrome. They appear in advanced cases of dementia—usually, therefore, at a stage when language is profoundly disorganized. This disorganization of language does not, however, seem to us to be a sufficient or necessary cause of them. Can they be grouped with the forms of stereotypy observed in children? This seems to us to be difficult. The stereotypy observed in children is not of the same strictly iterative nature. It puts one in mind of the circular reaction of play and exercise, which is never suggested by the stereotypy found in dementia. If the two phenomena involve similar mechanisms—and above all similar anatomical and functional structures, which is not impossible—they do not in any case have the same function.

Summary and Conclusions

The disintegration of language in degenerative dementia is the result of various types of disturbances. The initial impoverishment of the vocabulary, the endless repetition, the inability to recall words, the disordered syntax, the semantic paraphasia, the phonemic paraphasia, the phonemic or phonetic disturbances, and the verbal iteration that occur with the aggravation of the dementia cannot all be reduced to a common denominator. Nor can these defects be attributed to a general, or mnesic, intellectual decline alone or to instrumental disturbances alone. They result from the combined disorganization of different functions.

In the study of apraxia in dementia, a similar view is, in practice, generally accepted. So far as language disturbances are concerned, a number of authors do not agree with this view, or do so with great reluctance. Those who persist in regarding aphasia due to circumscribed lesions in adults as simply a disturbance of performance in Chomsky's sense of the term, consider that only disturbances of thought can exist in dementia, though admitting that they have repercussions on language. Such a position is not borne out by the facts. In degenerative dementia, the following phenomena are observed:

1. structural failings probably connected with fixation amnesia;
2. disintegration of the function and uses of language probably resulting from simultaneous disintegration of the subject's cognitive and affective functions;
3. semantic and syntactical disturbances that correlate closely with the subject's operational disintegration;
4. disturbances in the first and the second articulations resembling those of aphasia due to circumscribed lesions;
5. verbal stereotypy and iteration appearing against a background of neurological disorganization.

Some of the behavior components mentioned under 2, 3, and 4 may usefully be compared with those of the child learning to speak.

References

Alajouanine, T., Lhermitte, F., Ledoux, R. O., & Vignolo, L. A. Les composantes phonémiques et sémantiques de la jargonaphasie. *Revue Neurologique*, 1964, *110*, 5—20.

Alajouanine, T., Ombredane, A., & Durand, M. *Le syndrome de désintégration phonétique dans l'aphasie.* Paris: Masson, 1939.

Alarchos Llorach, E. L'acquisition du langage par l'enfant. In *Le langage.* Encyclopédie la pléiade. Paris: Gallimard, 1968.

Cohen, D., Dubois, J., Gauthier, M., Hécaen, H., & Angelergues, R. Aspects du fonctionnement du code linguistique chez les aphasiques moteurs. *Neuropsychologia*, 1963, *1*, 165—177.

de Ajuriaguerra, J., Boehme, M., Richard, J., Sinclair, H., & Tissot, R. Désintégration des notions de temps dans les démences dégénératives du grand âge. *Encéphale*, 1967, *5*, 385—438.

de Ajuriaguerra, J., Gainotti, J., & Tissot, R. Le comportement des déments du grand âge face à l'échec ou au risque d'échec. *Journal de Psychologie Normale et Pathologique*, 1969, *3*, 319—346.

Duval, F. Désintégration du langage au cours des démences séniles dégénératives. Thèse, Université de Paris, 1966.

Goldstein, K. L'analyse de l'aphasie et d'étude de l'essence du langage. *Journal de Psychologie Normale et Pathologique*, 1933, *30*, 430—496.

Guiraud, P. Analyse du symptôme stéréotypie. *Encéphale*, 1936, *31*, 229—270.

Haag, M., & Brabant, G. P. Le vocabulaire de 15 déments séniles dans la perspective de leur perte de l'attitude catégorielle de K. Goldstein. In *Préfecture de la Seine, Direction de l'Hygiène Sociale Recherches sur les maladies mentales*. Vol. II. Paris: Imprimerie municipale Hôtel de Ville, 1963. Pp. 111—129.

Irigaray, L. Approche psycholinguistique du langage des déments. Unpublished thèse, Université de Paris (doctorat 3e cycle), 1967.

Lhermitte, F., Desrouenes, J., & Lecours, A. R. Contribution à l'étude des troubles sémantiques dans l'aphasie. *Revue Neurologique*, 1971, *125*, 6—101.

Mounin, G. *Clefs pour la sémantique*. Paris: Seghers, 1972.

Ombredane, A. *L'aphasie et l'élaboration de la pensée explicite*. Paris: Presses Universitaires de France, 1951.

Piaget, J. *Le langage et la pensée chez l'enfant*. Neuchâtel: Delachaux & Niestlé, 1923.

Piaget, J. *La construction de réel chez l'enfant*. Neuchâtel: Delachaux & Niestlé, 1937.

Piaget, J. *La naissance de l'intelligence*. Neuchâtel: Delachaux et Niestlé, 1936.

Piaget, J. *La formation du symbole chez l'enfant*. Neuchâtel: Delachaux & Niestlé, 1946.

Poincaré, H. *La science et l'hypothèse*. Paris: Flammarion, 1902.

Prieto, L. J. *Messages et signaux*. Paris: Presses Universitaires de France, 1966.

Richelle, M. *L'acquisition du langage*. Brussels: Dessart, 1971.

Sinclair, H. Conduites verbales et déficits opératoires. *Acta Neurologica et Psychiatrica Belgica*, 1967, *67*, 852—860.

Sinclair, H., Boehme, M., Tissot, R., & de Ajuriaguerra, J. Quelques aspects de la désintégration des notions de temps à travers des épreuves morphosyntaxiques de langage et à travers des épreuves opératoires chez des vieillards atteints de démence dégénérative. *Bulletin de Psychologie*, 1966, *19*, 745—751.

Tissot, R., Richard, J., Duval, F., & de Ajuriaguerra, J. Quelques aspects du langage des démences dégénératives du grand âge. *Acta Neurologica et Psychiatrica Belgica*, 67, 911—923.

Vygotsky, L. S. *Thought and language*. Cambridge, Mass.: MIT Press & New York: Wiley, 1962.

Wepman, J. M., Bock, R. D., Jones, L., & Van Pelt, D. Psycholinguistic study of aphasia: a revision of the concept of anomia. *Journal of Speech and Hearing Disorders*, 1956, *21*, 468—477.

Subject Index

A

Acoustic pathway, myelination of, 126–128

Acquisition process, in grammatical structure, 240–241

Activity, speech as, 50–51

Adult-to-child speech, 283–295
  feedback characteristics of input in, 290–292
  grammatical forms in, 292–294
  input from, 292–295
  repetition in, 288–289
  samples of, 286–287

Adult language, compared with child's, 255–259

Agelaius phoeniceus, 91

Agraphia, 141

Alalia, 9

Algorithm, in speech behavior, 45

American Sign Language, 83

Anas platyrrhynchos, 81, 92

Animal calls, language and, 4–6

Animal noises, 4

Animals
  acoustic location of prey by, 63
  communication in, 4–5
  vocal learning in, 61–98

Aotus trivirgatus, 64

Aphasia
  agraphia and, 141

bilingual or polyglot, 15
  cerebral lesion and, 138
  concept of, 10
  and language disturbance due to lesions, 333–336
  phonological development and, 162
  repertoire in, 13

Aphasiology, science of, 15

Aphemia, 9–10

Aphrasia, 10

Artificial languages, 13

Association bundles, 124

Auditory feedback, in vocal learning, 66–71

Autistic child, language of, 318–319

B

Babbling, 125, 129–130
  application of to language, 184–186
  phonatory-articulatory-auditory development in, 182–183
  phonemicization and, 181
  in phonological development, 167

Backwardness, cerebral dominance in, 144–145

Barking, in dogs, 88

Bats, vocal development in, 66

Behaviorist theories, in phonological development, 159–162